Landscapes of Power

Landscapes of Power:
From Detroit to Disney World

Sharon Zukin

UNIVERSITY OF CALIFORNIA PRESS
Berkeley   Los Angeles   Oxford

University of California Press
Berkeley and Los Angeles, California

University of California Press, Ltd.
Oxford, England

© 1991 by
The Regents of the University of California

First Paperback Printing 1993

Library of Congress Cataloging-in-Publication Data

Zukin, Sharon.
    Landscapes of power : from Detroit to Disney World / Sharon Zukin.
        p.   cm.
    Includes bibliographical references and index.
    ISBN 0-520-07221-9
    ISBN 0-520-08288-5 (ppb.)
        1. United States—Social conditions—1980–   2. United States—
    Economic conditions—1981–   —Regional disparities.   3. Cities and
    towns—United States.   4. United States—Industries—Location.
    5. Regional planning—United States.   I. Title.
    HN59.2.Z85   1991
    307.1′2′0973—dc20   90-11167
                                                                         CIP

Printed in the United States of America
9 8 7 6 5 4 3 2

The paper used in this publication meets the minimum requirements of
American National Standard for Information Sciences—Permanence of Paper
for Printed Library Materials, ANSI Z39.48-1984. ⊗

For Richard, *toujours*

Contents

Illustrations

Acknowledgments

During the writing of this book, I have relied on many sources of support: personal, social, and financial. In the early 1980s I started research on old industrial regions in Europe and the United States. I sought interviews with a wide variety of men and women in business, government, labor unions, and local planning organizations, who took the time to answer detailed questions about their work. I also collected suggestions and examples from all my colleagues who learned I was writing a book about the culture of the contemporary market economy. Because of its complexity, this book came to focus on the United States.

My early research and travel were financed by grants from the German Marshall Fund of the United States, the National Science Foundation, and a BHE-PSC faculty research award from the City University of New York. Although all funding organizations find themselves in ever more dire financial straits, their willingness to sponsor unusual research like mine that crosses disciplinary bounds is an essential support to independent scholarship. This project would not have got off the ground without these organizations' substantial help.

The men and women whom I interviewed deserve equal thanks. Because I have tried to preserve their anonymity, I cannot signal individual appreciation. But they all did their best to make me understand their work from their point of view. While these views do not necessarily conform to mine, I have tried to portray them honestly. I was also able to call upon three interview subjects—from Lazard Frères, IBM, and the U.S. Economic Development Agency—to read those parts of the manuscript that reflect their contributions and correct them for accuracy.

Other chapters were read by colleagues who offered helpful suggestions. Thanks to Richard Child Hill, Harvey Molotch, and Louis Asekoff, who commented on the first drafts of the chapters on Detroit, gentrification, and Disney World, respectively.

My deepest debt is owed to my friends Paul DiMaggio and Neil Smith, who read the entire manuscript and presented me with subtle but gentle requests for clear writing and firm control over the material. If I have satisfied even a small portion of their demands, I shall have achieved much more than I began with and much less than they deserve. I, of course, bear full responsibility for the result.

The material production of this book also reflects the kindness of others. Some materials were gathered or checked by research assistants Philip Kasinitz (now a professor himself), David Radick, and Bruce Haynes. Steve Yoman of the Computer Center at the City University Graduate Center saved the chapter on Westchester County from eternal perdition in the computer. Jennifer Parker at the Russell Sage Foundation, where I completed final revisions of the manuscript, handled many chores of manuscript and index preparation with good cheer and helpful criticism. My editor, Naomi Schneider, encouraged me from the moment she read the first draft of the first two chapters; this encouragement extended from all matters concerning publication to personal friendship.

For institutional encouragement, I am grateful to the Wolfe Institute for the Humanities at Brooklyn College and my colleagues there from 1985 to 1989: executive director Robert Viscusi, Lou Asekoff, Bruce Hoffacker, Geri DeLuca, and Paulo Spedicato. They humored me during many a long discussion and always believed that a sociologist could write tolerably about culture. The Russell Sage Foundation, where I spent 1989–90 as a visiting fellow, provided a warm berth and intellectual stimuli. Although final revisions on this book took up only a small portion of my stay there, I thank President Eric Wanner and the staff for easing this final passage.

Finally and always, I have drawn both material and spiritual support from Richard Rosen. Many of his ideas have been welded to mine and gone into the book in the usual, uncredited, spousal way. He has helped me to keep faith in the project without losing his critical distance from either my intentions or my conclusions.

Introduction

Janet K. Ruttenberg, *After Leonardo* (1990).

1 Market, Place, and Landscape

"The other ambassadors warn me of famines, extortions, conspiracies, or else they inform me of newly discovered turquoise mines, advantageous prices in marten furs, suggestions for supplying damascened blades. And you?" the Great Khan asked Polo, "you return from lands equally distant and you can tell me only the thoughts that come to a man who sits on his doorstep at evening to enjoy the cool air. What is the use, then, of all your traveling?"

ITALO CALVINO, *Invisible Cities*

Great social transformations mark both an end and a beginning. In the structural changes of the past twenty years, Americans have struggled to define which elements of their lives have been destroyed forever and which are in the process of being created. Swiftly fading from mind are the industrial prosperity that was guaranteed by U.S. dominance in the world economy and a shared middle-class way of life that was accessible by work and skill. In their place rise alternate images of great wealth, insecurity, and fragmentation.

Few towns write to Pope John Paul II, as Waverly, New York, did, to bless their application for designation as an economic development zone. And only a small number of cities—Chicago, New Bedford, Yonkers—have tried to use the legal system to force companies to keep plants open. More often assembly-line workers at GM in Detroit and Apple computer assemblers in the Silicon Valley lose their jobs in shutdowns, relocations, or overseas investment by the parent firm. More

3

commonly, too, large numbers of white-collar employees are cut loose from industrial giants like DuPont and Eastman Kodak, pushed into early retirement or unemployment.

When Joseph Schumpeter wrote forty years ago about capitalism's creative destruction, he was not thinking about local communities that mortgage their survival to economic growth. Instead, the "essential fact" that he stressed about capitalism is recurrent innovation. He meant the new product, the new organization, the new link between desire and demand "that incessantly revolutionizes the economic structure *from within,* incessantly destroying the old one, incessantly creating a new one."[1] Schumpeter admitted that the "perennial gale" of capitalist innovation imposes costs on those who are unable to compete. But the "process of decline, of loss of caste, of elimination" that kills "old businesses" compensates by clearing ground for new men and women to rise. The balanced "circular flow" of economic life that he described has its counterpart in constant upward (and downward) social mobility. Choosing the very image that had earlier struck Henry James as typical of America's consumer society, Schumpeter depicts the upper classes as "hotels which are indeed always full of people, but people who are forever changing."[2]

This image of progress has been hard to sustain in the post-postwar period of economic growth. We know that U.S. businesses must compete with cheaper or smarter competitors, that organizations have to be global to survive, and that automated technology has replaced much human labor. But attempts to reorganize production for greater profits have imposed painful social costs. Fewer Americans can count on the high income, good skills, and steady work that traditional industry fostered. Regional cleavages—between Sunbelt and Frostbelt, city and suburbs, "bicoastal economy" and heartland—are common. Moreover, the cultural understandings and social structures that constitute economic institutions are in disarray. These days, workers are important because they consume, not because they produce anything the culture values. Public arenas of work and community foster private pursuits. Like the "great transformation" that occurred in England in the eighteenth and nineteenth centuries, abstract market forces that detach people from social institutions have overpowered specific forces of attachment identified with place.[3]

Creative destruction along these lines creates a dramatically different landscape of economic power. Banks are independent of the industries they finance; corporate headquarters are isolated from plants under their control. The wealth of cities seeps out to border regions, and within the city, the center acquires a new, aggressive-seductive lure. Place, moreover, is sharply divided between landscapes of consumption and devastation. Those places that remain part of a production economy, where men and women produce a physical product for a living, are losers. To the extent they do survive in a service economy, they lack income and prestige, and owe their soul to bankers and politicians. By contrast, those places that thrive are connected to real estate development, financial exchanges, entertainment—the business of moving money and people—where consumer pleasures hide the reins of concentrated economic control. Some people identify these shifts as part of a process of decline and decentralization called deindustrialization. Others accept them as evidence of a high-technology, postindustrial society. But neither of these terms captures the simultaneous advance and decline of economic forms, or the sense that as the ground shifts under our feet, taller buildings continue to rise.

The late-twentieth-century landscape of economy and culture is both varied and changing. Following Schumpeter, who suggested that economic factors were not enough to explain institutional change, I look at this landscape as a social, cultural, and political product of creative destruction. Influenced by the economic historian Karl Polanyi, I define it as a fragile compromise between market and place. Tracing a critical social geography in landscapes of power challenges an ingrained belief in markets. Markets represent free movement and impersonal judgment, hallmarks of the American way of life from de Tocqueville to Reagan. By emphasizing earning over either giving or taking, markets satisfy Americans' moral yearning for a peculiar sort of social equality.[4] Yet ironically, just as a market culture has finally been exported from America around the world, it poses most danger to the cultural values of place.

THE SEPARATION OF MARKET AND PLACE

The opposition between *market* and *place* really dates from the beginning of modern market society. Exploring debate over the Enclosure movement in seventeenth-century England, Karl Polanyi finds the Tudor aristocracy aware of a contradiction between the "gentleman" 's desire for "Improvement" and the "poor man" 's goal of "Habitation."

Polanyi points out that English aristocrats already expected "to achieve improvement at the price of social dislocation" whose costs would mostly be borne by poor peasants and their households. But in his view, the contrast between habitation and improvement drawn in 1607 "also hints at the tragic necessity" of protecting the places where people put down roots from the leveling forces of market production.[5]

Historically, of course, market and place are tightly interwoven. At its origins, a market was both a literal place and a symbolic threshold, a "socially constructed space" and "a culturally inscribed limit" that nonetheless involved a crossing of boundaries by long-distance trade and socially marginal traders.[6] But markets were also inextricably bound up with local communities. In feudal times and beyond, local markets occupied a specific place and time, usually in front of the church on festival days. The denseness of interactions and the goods that were exchanged offered local communities the material and cultural means for their social reproduction—that is, their survival as communities. At least until the seventeenth century, the market in England "was an is-land in space and time, a threshold at which the antagonisms, reciproc-ities, and solidarities of a particular locality could be periodically con-fined and tempered into the social and cultural matrix of simple or small commodity production."[7] Evidently, the social institutions of markets and places supported each other.

Nowhere is this shown more clearly than in the spatial and tem-poral effects of market practices on a "sense of place." In the great towns of Europe in the eighteenth century, markets defined streets and quarters as well as the rhythm of daily life. "A whole book could be written on the Halles in Paris and the smaller market for game, on the Quai de la Vallée," Fernand Braudel says; "on the regular dawn inva-sion of the town by bakers from Gonesse; on the five to six thousand peasants who came in the middle of every night half-asleep on their carts 'bringing vegetables, fruit, flowers.' . . . The ears of the servants on the upper floors were well accustomed to interpreting the babble, so as not to go down at the wrong moment."[8]

Yet prior to the nineteenth century, market transactions did not create a culture divorced from that of specific places. When this sepa-ration first emerged, it did so in the labor market. In the decades follow-ing the French Revolution, a conception gradually arose of a distinct entrepreneurial role. Entrepreneurialism was identified with employers, whose priority of cutting production costs included transforming production from home work or shop work to piece work, and shifting this work back and forth among different groups of workers. Each of these practices stoked the workers' resistance. Working at home, in familiar surroundings, often with their own tools and materials, the workers were used to acting as their own bosses. To a degree, they were both entrepreneurial and exploited. They thought in terms of product rather than production. But slowly, between 1815 and 1900, both employers' claims and workers' counterclaims began to echo the distinctly quantitative rhetoric and symbolic language of market forces.[9]

From that point, market no longer internalized place. Instead, in a long and painful process that lasted through most of the nineteenth century, place began to internalize market culture. Newly built factory towns from Pullman, Illinois (1880), and Gary, Indiana (1905–8), to Le Creusot and Décazeville represented the extreme case of socio-spatial structuring by market norms. They created a social regime that responded to industrial capitalists' needs by housing a labor reserve and attaching workers to their employers on a permanent basis. The employers were concerned with utilizing fixed capital in their factories, satisfying increased demand for their products in domestic and world markets, and securing a labor supply with sufficient skills to work complex new machines. Planners of these towns reflected labor market conditions by recruiting workers before building schools, stores, and hospitals. They also stratified workers' housing according to skill level, and imposed conditions of sobriety and morally satisfactory family life on worker-residents. To live in this space was to be subjected to factory control: unlike the freer labor market in cities, the factory town provided employers with a captive labor market.

To this end, employers called for theories of moral education, schemes of sanitation, and strategies of urban design that would permit them to build an agglomeration of labor without reproducing the social promiscuity—involving both sexual license and unsupervised social contacts—of big-city environments. Employers believed that resistance to market norms was endemic in urban working-class communities. But by providing both the public buildings and private housing, all utilities, and rules of order for both the factory and the town, the paternalistic company that owned a factory town attempted to create a "tempered, pacified mass. This domesticated people was a swarm of bees and the mining town, their hive."[10]

Throughout the nineteenth century, two contradictory processes juxtaposed market to place. On the one hand, employers organized production to take advantage of both temporary workers—migrants to industrial towns and seasonal labor who "camped out" or boarded in the town in "nomadic" conditions—and a permanent work force of more highly skilled craftsmen who were firmly attached to the factory. On the other hand, workers entered into community life with every desire to socialize, organize, and institutionalize their own cultural patterns. When employers tried to change the customary basis of wages or simply lower them, often playing one group of workers against another, their manipulation of the labor market threatened to fragment the cohesion of specific places.[11]

Over the years, the closely related issue of whether workers should be attached to—or free to float from—their place of employment divided professional economists. For more than two centuries, shifts of opinion joined practical, theoretical, and moral concerns. Adam Smith stated the classical position by asserting that only the free movement of workers from job to job would permit labor to find its "best" price. During the nineteenth century, however, the discourse of factory-town planners reversed this approach by maximizing workers' attachment to their jobs for maximum employers' control. Yet the frequent use of migrant and immigrant workers recognized a de facto labor mobility.

At the beginning of the twentieth century, economic opinion shifted again. Reflecting employers' concern about the costs of labor turnover, economists recommended reattaching the work force to the factory. But after World War II, as capital investment flowed to new regions, their judgment shifted back in favor of labor mobility. That climate of opinion lasted until the 1970s, when economists again advocated attaching workers to the firm. This time, employers would develop internal labor markets that would move workers from job to job within a company throughout their entire careers. This shift of opinion was part of a larger consensus on authority relations and social as well as economic costs. The professional judgment against labor mobility in the 1970s accompanied a renewed interest in strengthening institutions based on property rights and a growing tolerance of unemployment.[12]

By the 1980s, a neoclassical consensus again endorsed labor mobility. Employers' interest in downsizing firms, reducing excess production capacity, and transferring work from one geographical region to another required that workers be detached from the company. Business literature extolled worker "flexibility," and institutional means were devised for facilitating both voluntary and involuntary separations.

By changing retirement conditions and pension benefits, establishing job-placement services for outbound workers, and contributing to community programs for retraining unemployable workers, employers shed large portions of their work force. At most, employers like IBM offered highly trained employees the opportunity to move to a plant or office in another region, generally changing jobs in the process. Yet all employees were never offered this option. When Westinghouse closed the robotics operations of a high-technology company in Connecticut it had bought several years before, and moved some of the jobs to Pittsburgh, it invited only 50 of 210 workers to move with it.

Faced with employers' changing interests, economists sharply divided between neoclassical and neoliberal positions. Some professional economists and government officials favored "portable pensions" and giving tax advantages to workers who saved for their own retraining and eventual geographical move. Others supported more active government intervention in trade policy and a minimal advance notice to workers and employees before business closings. The problem is not a small one. From January 1981 to January 1986, more than five million American workers lost their jobs because of plant closings, slack work, or elimination of their positions, and these workers had "significant attachment," as researchers put it, to their employers.[13]

An interesting aspect of these changes is that they have a different impact on executives, who get golden parachutes to take early retirement or otherwise move from their firms, and displaced workers who depend on short-term unemployment benefits. There is a similar difference in the way these detachments affect different sorts of communities. Executives, like all white-collar employees, tend to live in areas that mix people from different industries. Workers, however, live in areas where individual firms and industries are concentrated. Therefore, when plants, companies, or networks of customers and suppliers in related businesses lay off workers, the communities where they live and shop are devastated. Executives' communities are buffered by the diversification of their economic base—including residents' stock ownership as well as employment. Another difference concerns the tendency for more or less geographical mobility among different groups in the work force. In all industrial societies, professional and managerial employees tend to be more mobile than manual workers. For these reasons, market changes affect communities where workers' residences are concentrated more than most upper-middle-class and upper-class communities. The major exceptions occur in areas like Detroit, Houston, or Rochester, New York, where the historical predominance of a single industry or firm—the Big Three auto makers in Motown, the oil industry throughout the Southwest, and Eastman Kodak in Rochester—imposes its product and profit cycles on the life cycle of all surrounding communities.[14]

Although the opposition between market and place has every structural reason to persist in a capitalist world economy, it can be altered by elites and buffered by the organization of consumption.

Local businesses and local governments play an increasingly important role in the survival of local social institutions. State governors and their commerce departments have actively moved into business restructuring, especially in the Middle West. They have pursued nonlocal business investment to the extent of studying Japanese etiquette in the new car-assembly regions of Ohio, Tennessee, and Kentucky. On a regional level within states, local government officials have transformed community protests against plant closings into economic development commissions with new revenue-raising powers. The church-sponsored ecumenical coalitions that opposed steel shutdowns in the Monongahela Valley near Pittsburgh, Pennsylvania, have grown into a regional development commission that issues industrial development bonds.

Among economic elites, major businesses in Boston have organized a program that will guarantee financial aid to all graduates of the city's high schools who get into college, and then provide jobs for them when they finish their education. Under the Boston Compact, an earlier and a more modest plan, graduates of fourteen public high schools were matched with entry-level jobs in local businesses. With the sponsorship of the National Alliance of Business and funding from the U.S. Department of Health and Human Services and private industry, similar programs have recently been established in Albuquerque, Cincinnati, Louisville, Memphis, Indianapolis, San Diego, and Seattle. Although such efforts have little effect on structural changes, they cushion the impact on places of market forces.[15]

The organization of consumption can also mitigate the opposition between market and place. Unemployed workers often exchange services instead of paying cash. Sharing with relatives also relieves economic strain. In an expanding economy, however, men and women may forget their insecure market position because consumer goods are "affordable." Cheap prices, credit, and an ideology that legitimized individual purchases made mass consumption a pillar of the "Fordist" production system (with assembly lines, unionized workers, and government welfare guarantees) that stretched through the middle of the twentieth century. During that period, cars, houses, and televisions were bought in such quantities that they introduced a new consumer society.

Owning or renting a home is probably the most important means of consumption, and certainly the most important expenditure in most people's lives. But homeownership is surrounded by a contradictory aura of both autonomy and dependence. On the one hand, owning the roof over one's head, and a little plot of land around it, means liberation from the landlord or landlady and from boarding with relatives. On the other hand, eviction is just as likely at the hands of the bank or mortgage-holder, whose payment at regular intervals compels job stability, saving, and, most important, staying in place. Homeownership also indicates a relationship between investment and consumption. Over the past forty years, buying a home has become a ticket in the great sweepstakes of rising land values, as well as a traditional means of securing shelter. Yet owning a home may be "a costly asset," the authors of a historical study of homeownership in the Boston area tell us. The social mobility it implies may in the long run bring only "the accumulation of devaluing assets." In the short run, moreover, because of the costs of buying and maintaining a home, a person's place in the housing market shapes his or her entry into the labor market.[16]

Homeownership is one of those institutions that tie economic production to social and cultural life. It also bridges the means of production and means of consumption. When mortgage rates rise or the housing market gets tight, the change affects an individual's position in the housing, labor, and capital markets. Depending on these interrelated effects, homeownership may emphasize either stability or lack of mobility. In this sense, it represents a cultural compromise between market and place.

PLACE

In contrast to the preeminence of markets, most modern cultures either trivialize or ignore the idea of place. The language of modernism expresses a universal experience of movement *away* from place, and as-pires to submerge or incorporate it into a "larger" whole. Until the Iranian revolution, localism—a concept related to place—had no role in theories of social and economic modernization. It was assumed that traditional status systems and parochial loyalties would wither away in the course of economic growth. Recent efforts at decentralization or separatism around the world indicate how much place was repressed—like ethnicity or religion—in this notion of modern life.[17]

Technology reinforces the idea that local communities are archaic, even while making their image more available. In the nineteenth century, the railroad and photograph lost the immediacy and depth of a foreground view of place, although they made distant places more accessible. Today, simultaneous exchanges by electronic media tie together even the smallest places, but they destroy the social distance that made experiencing them so distinctive.[18] In brief, as markets have been globalized, place has been diminished.

We are used to thinking of place as a geographical location, a point on a well-bounded map. Place on that level indeed refers to territory—a territory with its own flora and fauna and local allegiances. Closely related is the idea of specific places as concentrations of people and economic activity. Place in this sense is a form of local society rendered so special by economy and demography that it instantly conjures up an image: Detroit, Chicago, Manhattan, Miami. Place in a third, broader sense is a cultural artifact of social conflict and cohesion. The layers of experience that are created by capital investment and labor organization make factory towns and downtowns special types of places that have a predictable response to change. A "deindustrializing" region, a "gentrifying" urban neighborhood, a suburb transformed from an enclave of the rich into a corporate headquarters location: these should be understood as both specific places and representations of a more general notion of place. A useful concept in social theory, place expresses how a spatially connected group of people mediate the demands of cultural identity, state power, and capital accumulation.[19]

One of the most fascinating aspects of place in recent years is that it has become more homogeneous in some ways and more heterogeneous in others. The spread of national and even global cultures (especially those that emanate from Hollywood and Disney World) tends to weaken local distinctiveness. So do cheaper transportation costs, which encourage the long-distance diffusion and consumption of industrial products. The use of new technologies, moreover, equalizes conditions of *producing* goods in different regions of the world. The same standardized motors or jeans can be produced anywhere from Oshkosh to Singapore. And the job of manufacturing them can be shifted from North Americans to Mexicans and Chinese, or from middle-aged men to young women. As more women have entered the labor force, and more jobs have been shifted outside the advanced industrial economies, traditional wage differences have been reduced. This equalizing tendency has in turn eroded labor militance and bargaining strategies based on the historic acquisition of skills and gains by specific groups. All in all, the net effect of these technological and organizational changes is to make places "more equal." [20]

At the same time places have also become more differentiated. New patterns of regional specialization reflect the selective location of highly skilled and highly valued economic activities—finance, corporate leadership, and research and development—in zones that offer amenities. These concentrations enable places to capitalize on their initial advantage. By the same token, areas that begin to lose business investment become even less attractive. They utterly fail to develop high-status production and consumption. The same country, and the same region, can easily be divided between these two paths of development. [21]

We often think that these processes originate in decisions made by the largest corporations. Yet there is a tension between corporate power to remake geography and labor-force potential to resist change. The organizational ability to split parts of the production process among different places often confronts forceful opposition by local residents, workers, and employees. Business organizations also respond to the image of place: an image of docility or autonomy, homogeneity or social mixing, central power or decline.

In traditional coal-mining areas of Britain and France, for instance, the decline of old industries and the partial entry of new ones have reduced the number of jobs for highly paid skilled men. With the ebb and flow of industries and male employment, many untrained women, often the wives of unemployed miners, have been recruited into the labor force. Meanwhile, in seaside regions, where agriculture and tourism have been more important than mining, both men who work in industry and women who earn money by self-employment lack the militant history of high wages and unionization for which miners are well known. These areas become a more attractive site for new capital investment. [22]

Other factors also account for increasing regional specialization. Like the services in southeast England, high-tech firms in the United States are attracted to such amenities as educational opportunities and climate. This seems especially to be the case for the most dynamic activities, such as electronics, computers, and communications equipment. The availability of business services is also important, particularly for mature sectors like receivers, transmitters, plastics, and paints. In the fastest-growing sectors, however—those associated with military spending—labor-force characteristics, including the percentage of black workers, influence firms against certain locations.[23]

But the process of capital accumulation can create surprising divergence within the same locality. A city or a metropolitan area may experience growth in some areas and decline in others. The central business district may grow while the rest of the city sleeps. In the past few years, moreover, old industrial regions have gained new jobs that fail to generate long-term prospects for development. Subcontracting generates those jobs, as do part-time and temporary employment. The divergence between well-paid, highly skilled jobs and jobs that offer few chances of upward social mobility is responsible for a persistent new kind of regional dualism.

Most worrisome of all are the problem regions that no longer create highly skilled, highly paid jobs. Every country has its own negative examples: Britain's south Wales, Tyneside, and Clydeside, the Nord and the Lorraine in France, and the Middle West in the United States show the same pattern of decline relative to growing areas of the country. During the first half of the 1980s, for example, the Middle West lost the greatest proportion of high-wage jobs in the United States and had the greatest increase in low-wage employment. At the same time, interregional economic differences in the country as a whole widened. Between 1979 and 1986, a 50-year trend toward regional parity in per capita income was reversed.[24]

Regional disparities have in fact become so pervasive that people now speak of a "bicoastal economy." The sixteen states on the country's East and West coasts practically monopolize the highly differentiated benefits of economic growth. During the 1980s they had three times as much real economic growth as, and experienced 90 percent more job growth per capita than, the rest of the country. A small proportion of residents of these states also benefited from the lion's share of real growth in wages and ownership income in the entire United States.[25]

This social and spatial restructuring contrasts with the desires expressed by existing populations and many local governments. The basic problem derives from a simple imbalance between investment and employment: capital moves, the community doesn't. For many people who are enthusiastic about the next economic transformation, imbalance and dislocation are a painful but necessary part of the transition. But for those who worry about the present, and find the future still uncertain, dichotomous landscapes pose a major problem. Not only do they embody alternative economic and political strategies; these strategies also carry a burden of existential choice.

Some people find the source of dichotomy is an opposition between capital mobility and labor mobility, or capital and community. Alternatively, they contrast "life space" with "economic space." Still others juxtapose restructuring "for capital," in which return on investment takes priority over people and place, to restructuring "for labor," in which investment provides an existing work force with a means of survival. A related issue concerns whether men and women can be considered separate from place. Should economic growth primarily benefit people or the places where people live?[26]

The same disputes mark debate over the "deindustrialization" of America. In terms of aggregates—the manufacturing sector's contribution to GNP, total employment, value of exports—U.S. industry has not completely failed. Moreover, the continued profitability of many U.S. businesses, especially the overseas operations of American-based transnational corporations, suggests that some Americans still know how to manage industry—although they may be doing it outside the country. The same goes for patterns of increased overseas investment in research and development.[27]

Business considerations maintain the illusion that response to *market* forces is the only factor on which the survival of America's industrial society—or the creation of its postindustrial society—depends. But critics who argue that America is being deindustrialized draw attention to factors associated with *place*. For them, the reduction of high-wage, highly skilled jobs and the cutbacks that have sapped labor unions' strength destroy the culture that underlies the U.S. economy. Shaped by both market and place, this culture is based on a high standard of living, self-generated organizational capacity, and local influence on dominant social institutions. Until recently, these have constituted the American landscape.[28]

LANDSCAPE

Landscape, as I use the term here, stretches the imagination. Not only does it denote the usual geographical meaning of "physical surroundings," but it also refers to an ensemble of material and social practices and their symbolic representation. In a narrow sense, *landscape* represents the architecture of social class, gender, and race relations imposed by powerful institutions. In a broader sense, however, it connotes the entire panorama that we see: both the landscape of the powerful—cathedrals, factories, and skyscrapers—and the subordinate, resistant, or expressive vernacular of the powerless—village chapels, shantytowns, and tenements. A landscape mediates, both symbolically and materially, between the socio-spatial differentiation of capital implied by *market* and the socio-spatial homogeneity of labor suggested by *place.*[29]

The concept *landscape* has recently emerged from a long period of reification to become a potent tool of cultural analysis. It connotes a contentious, compromised product of society. It also embodies a point of view. As the opposition with vernacular implies, powerful institutions have a preeminent capacity to impose their view on the landscape—weakening, reshaping, and displacing the view from the vernacular.

Even in art history, a landscape's inclusion and denial of physical reality have always been highly selective. The term itself refers to both a piece of rural scenery and the conceptual prism through which it is viewed. At the outset of landscape painting in Western Europe in the fourteenth century, landscapes were pictures of symbols rather than fact. These pictures combined elements familiar to the viewer to represent a religious or moral system. Similarly, in eighteenth-century English landscapes, painters' portrayals of the countryside and its inhabitants reflected a way of seeing that was part of the larger social system. Artists generally shared in the upper classes' shift from seeing rural areas as places of leisure and indolence to viewing them as sites of entrepreneurial farming and industrious agricultural laborers. More picturesque landscapes, however, either ignored recent rural improvements or persisted in depicting older practices as if they were unchanged.[30]

Throughout the early modern period in Europe, to make a landscape was also to recreate natural topography in images of power. It was normal for such activities as landscaping the grounds of a country estate and drawing maps of the world to distort, obliterate, and rearrange geography to serve the interests of the viewer. More generally, landscape both imposes and represents a visual order. In the origins of modern art, the concept *landscape* refers to a painting that stimulates the viewer's recognition by both the repetition and singularity of its constituent elements.[31]

Today the concept landscape is almost less likely to refer to a genre of painting than to a sociological image. When we hear people speak about "the urban" or "the suburban landscape," we picture either the density of production and transportation in city life—human society swallowed up by skyscrapers, bridges, and freeways—or small-scale outcroppings in the hinterland of shopping malls, ranch houses, and office parks. Similarly, the smokestacks and red-brick chimneys of an earlier "industrial landscape" evoke a way of life, its rhythms, and— such is the power of this built environment—its abstract social controls. The struggle to impose the factory owners' idea of discipline created *"the familiar landscape* of industrial capitalism, with the time-sheet, the timekeeper, the informers, and the fines."[32] The "postindustrial landscape" in modern Vancouver or Silicon Valley is also evocative. Its image of ecology, leisure, and "liveability" feeds off the consumption preferences of professionals in a service economy, even though those preferences conceal an underbelly of business and personal strain, female minority workers jammed into assembly jobs, and mounting suburban blight.[33]

Increasingly complex and suggesting an inclusive social reality, this concept of landscape has crept into the common vocabulary of our time.* The most interesting thing about the variety of landscapes that I have mentioned is that today we know them all. Although they were constructed sequentially, on different scales, they now coexist in space and time. They make us more aware of the asymmetry of economic power. Certainly, in the course of social change, men and women have always confronted, or been forced to move between, different landscapes. For a runaway serf from a medieval manor, there were vital differences be-

---

* This term is used so extensively that even the president of the Federal Reserve Bank of New York said in a speech to the Overseas Bankers Club in London (February 2, 1987), "Individual firms can choose their position on the *financial landscape*" (emphasis mine).

tween town and country. Before Emancipation, an escaped slave in the United States often found survival by moving from the south to the north. But since the nineteenth century, shifting from one landscape to another has depended less on individual mobility than on a broad-scale, varied remaking of landscape itself.

The urban scale and commercial variety of Haussmann's Paris in the mid nineteenth century led into the aesthetic and technological monumentality and rapid pace of change that helped to define the modern use of space and time in major cities. By contrast, the persistence of older landscapes began to suggest a general economic and social decline. With modernism, "old" was rarely "better." The tortured viability of older landscapes was viewed as an irritant, or a stimulant to an additional and ultimately homogenizing round of structural changes.[34]

For several years, at least since Robert Venturi published *Learning from Las Vegas,* architects have taken on the task of interpreting the development of modern landscapes. Recently, however, geographers have also reclaimed landscape as part of their professional terrain. To do so, geography has to focus on the built rather than the natural environment and to open itself to cultural as well as physical analysis. Taking "ordinary landscape" to be the "continuous surface all around us," cultural geographers "regard all landscapes as symbolic, as expressions of cultural values, social behavior, and individual actions worked upon particular localities over a span of time." In this broad sense, landscape is "at once a panorama, a composition, a palimpsest, a microcosm."[35]

Like early European landscape painting, historical American landscapes often represent panoramas of a moral or philosophical system. In the eighteenth century, newly built churches revolutionized the hierarchical spatiality of organized religion by both the intimacy of their interior design and their geographical distance from established communities. This spatial organization represents in a panorama the influence of Isaac Newton's scientific ideas. Another sort of panorama emerges in the grid pattern by which streets were laid out in midwestern towns in the early nineteenth century. The sense of permanence in this panorama negated earlier patterns of transience and mobility by which Americans had continually extended the western frontier.[36]

In a different sense, landscape also represents a microcosm of social relations. During the centuries before the rise of the modern state, landscape represented a field of impact between authority and resistance.

This concept of landscape contrasts with that of *country*. Landscape is the area where peasants thrive, the cottages and fields that embody their collective and vernacular use of space. By contrast, *country* represents the spatial organization imposed by the powerful on the powerless; country embodies "the aristocratic or political concepts of space" upheld by the bishop, the lord and lady of the manor, or the monarch.* Like our contemporary landscapes, however, the peasants' vernacular and the aristocrats' country coexist in space and time. Then as now, to read landscape is to study the society and technology "underneath . . . symbols of permanent political power," where communities governed by tradition and custom "involuntarily" adapt to mobility and change.[37]

Themes of power, coercion, and collective resistance shape landscape as a social microcosm. Yet the task falls to economic geography to provide a sense of landscape's "structured coherence." For a radical economic geographer, landscape is the tabula rasa of capital accumulation. It reflects the "spatiality" of the capitalist mode of production in each of its historical phases. From this perspective, the underlying cause of repetition and singularity in the landscape is the profit motive, shifting capital between investment in industry and in property, cycling it into new construction or reconstruction, shuttling it between the downtown and the suburban periphery. This idea of landscape also suggests the opposition between market and place that I have described. Relations between social classes determine and are in turn affected by "the tension between free geographical mobility and the organized reproduction processes." This ongoing and conflict-laden structuring of people's lives derives its social coherence from the fact of local political autonomy and the unifying factors of local experience and collective consciousness. But in the struggle for expansion in the built environment, and control over the uses of space, economic power predominates over both the state and vernacular culture. "Capital creates and destroys its own landscape."[38]

---

* At the beginning of the twentieth century, however, in *The Decline of the West*, Oswald Spengler considered *landscape* to be the equivalent of *country*. He contrasted the civilization of cities with "the rustic drawl of the landscape" ("The Soul of the City," in *Classic Essays on the Culture of Cities*, ed. Richard Sennett [New York: Appleton-Century-Crofts, 1969], p. 69). Yet again, the tendency to draw an opposition between aristocratic, official, or political culture—the spatiality of the powerful—and the vernacular landscape or popular culture of the powerless is common to many geographers and all structuralist analysis.

Economic power provides the structured coherence behind America's shifting landscapes. The replicas of smokestack America, their dispersal and eventual abandonment, precede another historical phase, one marked by supermarkets, shopping malls, office towers. This leads in turn to their replication, dispersal, and abandonment. The simultaneous combinations of concentration and dispersal, of growth and decline, make it difficult to grasp the character of American landscape today.

In a cultural sense, no single clear-cut landscape represents the contemporary American community. Nor do we have spatial images of the built environment that would adequately describe the landscape of "metropolitan deconcentration"—neither urban nor suburban—in which most Americans live. As foreshadowed by Martin Heidegger in the early 1950s, American landscape is a series of unbounded spaces where mass production and mass consumption reproduce a standardized, quasi-global culture.[39]

It takes an effort of imagination to distinguish among the "nonplace places" in such a landscape. Yet in the quest for an image of distinction, local business and political leaders continue to build and rebuild as a sign of economic growth. Their blueprint for growth is often limited to constructing a microcosm of the past or a panorama of the future, and presenting this landscape by techniques of historic preservation or futuristic new construction that are completely detached from specific places. Without a specific social and material context, the organizing principle in these landscapes is simply a visual *theme*. Just as Busch Gardens and Disney World decontextualize the future, Inner Harbor, Faneuil Hall, and South Street Seaport decontextualize the past, turning a landscape of devastation in the inner city into a landscape of consumption. At best, when market forces destroy and re-create an existing landscape, its artifacts—like the 110,000-pound cast-iron facade of the Fava Fruit Company in Baltimore—are stored, restored, and even relocated to create an "authentic" sense of place.[40]

MAPPING CULTURE AND ECONOMIC POWER

In writing about contemporary great transformations, there is a tendency to think that every set of economic structures breeds its own cultural forms. Whether we believe we are living through a transition to a postindustrial society or a late capitalist economy influences our acceptance of postmodern culture. Whether we believe that today is the crisis of late capitalism in turn shapes our willingness to see decadence or resistance in new writing, architecture, and art. Yet each set of economic structures coexists with a diversity of aesthetic forms, material practices, and political institutions. The uncertainty surrounding the outcome of current structural changes—related to what Daniel Bell describes as the "sense of living in interstitial time"[41]—echoes the possibility that each area of social life, especially politics and culture, creates its own implicit limits on our understanding of economic power.

Some recent work in sociology and geography signals a way to restore lustre to materialist analysis without dimming the autonomy of culture and politics. Starting with the material basis of the social world, this work aims to explore interrelations of social structure, especially institutions of power and class, and social reproduction, or the forms that represent, transmit, and transform institutionally embedded power relations. The point of these analyses varies. While some theorists, such as Anthony Giddens, David Harvey, and Edward Soja, seek to define general principles that structure social worlds, other researchers (Scott Lash and John Urry, Allen Scott, Michael Storper) seek to delineate specific situations. Their common concerns, however, derive from a fluid application of materialist critique in social history and political economy.

Three of those concerns influence this book's agenda. First, there is a common effort to integrate space and time into the description and explanation of social patterns. Second, there is a focus on the mutual effects of economics, politics, and culture in restructuring processes. And third, changes in the economic system are treated equally with changes in the cultural context of economic behavior. This marks a small contribution to the convergence of two intellectual trends: the resurgence of institutional economics and the reassertion of equity among economic, political, and cultural factors.

Others have already directed considerable research effort toward documenting the socially constructed values and relations that tell us about the local context of global economic changes, especially in labor markets.[42] Such studies tie together macroeconomic and microeconomic strategies—understanding both levels as centered on social processes relating to power—and social institutions like the family or the occupational community. This research falls into three general categories:

Research that connects industrial investment, occupational changes, and restructuring of class, gender, race, and ethnic relations in a local community

Studies of political changes that link national government policies and emergence of a more resourceful or entrepreneurial "local state"

Research that relates international business decisions to adaptation by a flexible (although hardly buoyant) household economy

While I agree that these topics are important, I sought for my own work an overarching concept that conveys a sense of both disruption and integration in the world economy. Such a concept must embrace material practices as well as aesthetic forms, underlining the convergence between economic structure and cultural project, representing the experience of all social classes without mistaking the basic asymmetry of economic power. Finally, then, this became a book about landscape.

The spatial consequences of combined social and economic power suggest that landscape is the major cultural product of our time. Our cognitive maps, aesthetic forms, and ideologies reflect the multiple shifts and contrasting patterns of growth and decline that shape the landscape. A search for individual autonomy is, therefore, a search for landscape's structural rules. On one level, these are the general rules of order of the capitalist economy. On another level, they are the market decisions that shift production from one place to another. On a third level, however, they are the tangible compromises made in specific places between workers and employers, developers and consumers, entrepreneurs and creative personnel.[43]

In the history of painting, a landscape includes both real scenes and the perspective from which we view them. This suggests the sociologist's problem of how to describe the real social world from a convincing point of view. Because no single view can include the variety of changes that are sweeping the American economy, a sociological approach must sample the spectrum and produce a composite picture that respects differences. We begin with two polar experiences of structural change—the inner and the urban landscapes—that both represent and resist the abstraction, internationalization, and consumption bias of the new market economy. From that point, a series of case studies—five twentieth-century landscapes—explores the spectrum of change between deindustrialization and the shift to a postindustrial or service economy. Some readers may argue that culture takes primacy over economics in these views. Indeed, the rules of a market economy are both represented and challenged by market culture.

Paul Strand, "Wall Street, New York, 1915." Copyright © 1971, Aperture Foundation, Inc., Paul Strand Archive. Reproduction courtesy the Philadelphia Museum of Art: The Paul Strand Retrospective Collection, 1915–1975. Gift of the Estate of Paul Strand.

2 "Creative Destruction": The Inner Landscape

[Two characters in the cartoon strip "Doonesbury," an artist in overalls and her husband, gaze at her new work, a collage of broken dishes mounted on a wall.]
SHE: Basically, Mike, the fragmented surfaces speak to the vulgarity of recent image appropriation. They celebrate continuity while deploring the sterility of post-graffiti solidism. A comment on a comment, if you will.
HE: Oh. Isn't that our wedding china?
SHE: The viewer won't know that. To him, it's the shards of the American dream.

G. B. TRUDEAU, *Washington Post*, August 29, 1985

Several years ago, the literary critic Fredric Jameson suggested that we look to postmodern culture for a "cognitive map" of the changing economic landscape. The recommendation was impressive, partly because of the absorbing images that he described: the alienation induced by John Portman's atrium-hotels, the sense of "hyperspace" conveyed by many large, inward-looking architectural projects such as urban/suburban malls. Partly, too, Jameson appealed because he looked for the material basis of cultural symbols. Rightly or not, he identified the style of postmodernism with the triumph of contemporary, multinational capitalism.[1]

Although the urge to "map" economic change is not unique to Jameson, the term *postmodernism* is confusing.* It is a label applied to

---

* I have often been greeted on the way to giving a talk on postmodern landscapes by colleagues who urge me to define postmodernism so that they understand it once and for

many different cultural fields, from cinema to architecture, fiction to design. It has an affinity with visual representations, especially in rock videos, architecture, and advertising. However, among painters, architects, and urban planners who share the label, the visual techniques of postmodernism include both allegory and realism. As an aesthetic opposition to modernism that began in the 1970s, postmodernism claims to create something new, while revering preindustrial design; but it coexists with many different forms of modernism, to which it supplies an alternative rather than an heir. Moreover, as a theory with something to say about society—that the world has many different centers of initiative, knowledge, and power—it is a global theory, "like the Toyota of thought, produced and assembled in several different places and then sold everywhere."[2]

Yet postmodernism has made its mark on the landscape. Postmodern architecture is visible to the point of caricature: postmodernism is a new building with a triangle on top. Although architectural juries have already declared the style dead,[3] it provides a visual rhetoric for an all-pervasive consumer culture. When Arby's, the seventh-largest fast-food chain in the United States, decided to upgrade its image, it commissioned a prototype "new concept" restaurant in postmodern style (with "curving walls of smoothly finished exterior insulation material painted in stripes of mauve, rose, and burgundy; neon banding; and a formal entrance pavilion marked by a tall pole") and placed it in Louisville, Kentucky. Arby's postmodernism is the "individualized" mass product, decorated with a neon palette, that makes an unthreatening, even playful, emblem of economic power. This implies as much about the resonance of postmodernism with the late twentieth-century economy as it says about the commercial pliancy of postmodern styles.[4]

Market competition in a complex economy with a highly differentiated social structure breeds cultural products that strive to be distinctive. While Arby's management may see no contradiction in using postmodern decor to sell a standardized burger, this situation pinpoints two dilemmas at postmodernism's core. How can an oppositional aesthetic movement combat market culture if it is commercially applied? How can postmodernism respect "local" context if it is reproduced on high-

---

all. On the other hand, I once heard one of our graduate students readily describe a piece of clothing to a classmate as "a postmodern sweater." This turned out to refer to a knitted product that looked like "fake patchwork."

ways all over the world? In theory, a postmodern culture suggests the possibility of reconciling landscape and vernacular, and market and place; but the more visible it becomes, the more it takes on the decontextualized, market-oriented look of franchise culture. Postmodern architecture then makes places less distinctive. They become "nonplaces" in global markets.[5]

The opposition between market and place is built into postmodernism. That is why no single landscape can control the difference between "outrageous" and "contextual" postmodern architecture, why one part of postmodern cultural style—that is, fragility, degradation, fragmentation—can refer to deindustrialization while another part—that is, the decentering of pluralism, the preeminence of visual over literal codes, and the freewheeling appropriation of different artistic modes—describes a postindustrial society. Postmodernism inspires two market cultures, each with its own practice, aesthetic, and political implications. Between "a postmodernism of resistance and a postmodernism of reaction" lies the unresolved ambiguity of market and place as loci of creative destruction. Perhaps postmodernism is best understood as the landscape of contemporary economic transformation: as both an uncertain social context and an ironic perspective on it.[6]

This suggests an interior as well as a material landscape. Conveying a sense of rupture and discontinuity, and taking for granted that progress is fragile, the postmodern symbolic landscape represents the same destruction of longevity, of cultural layers, and of vested interests that opposes markets to place. But this is not so different from late-nineteenth-century modernism. Modernism at that time, especially in the visual arts, also represented (and opposed) the "high" capitalism of an advancing industrial age. It also conveyed a sense of speed, of change, of dissolution of limits, that loosened the bounds of traditional authority and transformed social control.[7]

The art historian T. J. Clark suggests that there was a symbiosis, in that period of artistic experimentation, between new forms of modern culture and new forms of social control. Regardless of an artist's individual ideology, the innovative representation of modern art around the time of Manet only contrived "to map one form of control upon another."[8] While the Impressionists commented on markets' disruption of place by painting the city as an anarchic realm of free-floating signs and eminently acquirable badges of distinction, financial and real estate markets more rigidly stigmatized the districts of Paris in terms of social class. Modernism portrayed the city as illegible, argues Clark, but this seeming incoherence really marked a new, more polarized social order.

Despite its ideology of resistance, postmodernism suggests a similar accommodation with the culture of market transactions. It decorates the city with legible, local, "friendly" emblems of economic power while real economic structures are more abstract, more influenced by international flows, and less likely to be understood as they appear in public view. But postmodernism emerges in a different context from modernism, when markets are more volatile and places—especially the occupational community of artists—even less autonomous. A historically new part of the symbolic landscape is a postmodern anxiety over whether cultural authority derives from autonomy from market forces or, conversely, from market power.

It is as difficult to map this ambiguous landscape as to map the dual concept of culture itself. Culture is, after all, both the property of cultivated people and a general way of life. The more culture is confined to the first, high art conception, the more it becomes—despite the artist's conviction—a marketable sign of distinction. The more it is restricted to the latter, general meaning, however, the more it remains an inalienable product of place. Torn between these opposing modes of cultural appropriation, postmodernism's central problem is to discover and restore an "eternal" social meaning to processes of continual differentiation.[9]

The only possible perspective on this process of creative destruction is one of liminality. The anthropologist Victor Turner first used *liminality* to describe rites of passage in which a social group passes from one status or category to another. On such occasions, the usual social norms are suspended, for the group has given up one position while not yet adopting another position that prescribes new behavior. These transitions are not completely fluid situations. As rites, they carry their own cultural scripts, often reversing people's roles in a temporary subversion of social values. Jean-Christophe Agnew's study of English history extends Turner's concept to the *liminal space* of the market. This is a zone that situates buyers and sellers in a brief, socially recognized transition or "transaction." It is also a zone that stands "betwixt and between" major social institutions, as the market square is located between the world of commerce and that of religion, between work days and feasts.[10]

Today, however, economic restructuring makes liminality a pervasive experience. With the creative destruction of an industrial market economy, individuals experience the simultaneous expansion of some, and contraction of other, culturally transmitted economic roles. In crucial ways some economic roles are reversed. With—and despite—the expansion of employment in the services, people experience a qualitative shift in the source of social meaning from the sphere of production to consumption. With—and despite—the contraction of employment in manufacturing, producers who want to save their jobs often become investors in worker buyouts. In the abstract, economic restructuring can be thought of as a process of liminality. It socially reorganizes space and time, reformulates economic roles, and revalues cultures of production and consumption.

What is always new about these processes is their mutual impact with specific social groups. Once it is culturally mediated, the experience of relative gains and losses inflects a general consciousness of change. The feminization of the labor force in declining regions, the deskilling of much manufacturing work, the visible balance among "producers" shifting from hard-hats to artists and investment bankers: these qualitative changes in market positions force a change of perspective in the landscape of economic power.

We begin exploring the inner landscape of creative destruction with individual perceptions of structural displacement as they are represented in literary works, mainly novels, that have a fairly standard narrative line. It may be argued that narrative works should not be considered postmodern in any sense, and that films rather than books are the key postmodern products. Yet if we seek the dislocating, fragmenting experience of a great social transformation, we shall find it in the shifting landscapes of these novels.

SHIFTING LANDSCAPES

Much of the postmodern quality in contemporary fiction reflects the existential anguish of simultaneously living in multiple shifting landscapes. In a few novels, industrial decline of the birthplace deprives the main character of his birthright and forms the backdrop for a preoccupation with time. A character's middle age then becomes a fulcrum, juxtaposing the duration of a social community with the inevitability of an individual death. In John Updike's *Rabbit Is Rich*, Harry ("Rabbit") Angstrom is a moderately successful car dealer in a small town in Pennsylvania, whose strong attachment to dead friends and relatives—his literal preoccupation with his roots—is reflected in the economic landscape.[11] As he drives around the county, Harry notes the abandoned factories. And as he drives through town, he thinks about the declining shops in the center, which have undergone a pallid conversion to a shopping strip.

Angstrom himself used to be a Linotype operator. When typesetting became economically obsolete and he lost any chance of finding a job, his wife's father took him into his car dealership. His new prosperity hinges on two factors that both confirm and deny continuity with the past. On the one hand, although Harry's wife and mother-in-law retain the major share of the agency, selling cars has given him a toehold in the local middle class—including membership at a respectable, though not patrician, country club—and the opportunity to be a boss. On the other hand, the dealership's profits are based on sales of imported Toyotas. In contrast to the American cars the agency sold when Angstrom's father-in-law owned it, the Japanese imports seem flimsy, tiny, an unexpected and tragic consequence of the contemporary fuel crisis, which strikes Harry (and struck Updike when he wrote the novel in 1980) as a permanent existential limitation. Angstrom's son seems flimsy, too. A college dropout who moves back into Harry's home—really Harry's mother-in-law's house—with a pregnant wife, he continually manufactures accidents with Harry's cars. The son confronts Harry's guilt over the unresolved promise of an athletic youth and a series of romantic alliances. Under these conditions, the desolation of Rabbit Angstrom's inner landscape echoes his hometown's.

A similar perspective pervades Don DeLillo's *White Noise,* a novel written in a very different style.[12] Jack Gladney, the narrator of this book, is a college professor at an affluent, Gothic-style campus that is also located—we assume—in western Pennsylvania. The professor is more comfortable with a "postindustrial" social structure than Rabbit Angstrom. He has a lot of leisure time, for which he apparently feels no guilt. By contrast, Rabbit remembers how his father, a manual worker, used to come home from work exhausted; he thinks about his father's dirty fingernails. He also compares his mother's backbreaking life of labor with his mother-in-law's and his own relative ease.

In *White Noise,* however, DeLillo's narrator lives comfortably off useless knowledge. A professor of "Hitler studies" at his university, he pals around with colleagues who study popular culture. Their recall of trivial information about old movies and observation of etiquette in the supermarket drive them to both despair and rapture. Yet the relative prosperity of Professor Gladney's milieu denies the impoverishment of the surrounding landscape. Gladney records the sights driving through "the city's main street, a series of discount stores, check-cashing places, wholesale outlets. A tall old Moorish movie theater, now remarkably a mosque. Blank structures called the Terminal Building, the Packer Building, the Commerce Building. How close this was to a classic photography of regret. 'A gray day in Iron City,' I said" (p. 89).

The notion that his protected enclave of the good life is engulfed by a universal threat—an idea that slowly comes to invade Gladney's life with a series of ecological and medical disasters—creates the tension against which Gladney's midlife crisis plays. Cruising the supermarket aisles with a full cart and his buxom wife, Professor Gladney is seized by the certainty of global disaster and his own death.

Both Rabbit Angstrom and Jack Gladney inhabit dichotomous landscapes, sleeping in the grip of the dead and working among the living, walking on an island of prosperity amid the ruins of the industrial age. But for a displaced industrial worker like the eponymous Baltimore narrator of Robert Ward's novel *Red Baker*, social disaster and the tragedy of individual life are not juxtaposed: they are one.[13] Red Baker simultaneously faces his fortieth birthday and the shutdown of the steel mill where he has spent his entire career. Consequently, losing his livelihood and living out his life are part of the same landscape. The local manufacturing economy is bounded by the same space and time as the rowhouses, parks, and bars of the working-class community where Red grew up and still resides.

In the novel as in life, the place in Red's landscape is juxtaposed with the market-driven urban revitalization to which cities like Baltimore aspire. Looking for a new job one morning, Red sees his life passing in the replacement of a familiar landscape of neighborhood by another that holds no hope.

> For three hours I drove around Highlandtown [he says], past the old boarded-up National Brewery and up and down Broadway, past the Circus Movie Theatre, which was playing a picture called *Behind the Green Door*, where I used to go see my serials like *Gangbusters* . . . and along with them would be two or three Woody Woodpeckers or Looney Tunes, and

then a double feature. Saw my first 3-D movie in that picture house, *Bwana Devil*. Now it's all horny sailors from off the Greek ships down on Pratt Street, with newspapers on their laps.

And in the old days all of those pictures, serials, cartoons, and double features cost thirteen cents. 1948. When I was five years old.

This was Broadway, and on Easter people would march down this street past the Johns Hopkins Hospital, and they'd be dressed in their finest clothes, and the Navy and Marine color guard would lead the parade.

Now it was nothing but bars for artists and lawyers and a bunch of dead-assed stores, and not one of them needed help.   (Pp. 46–47)

If the service economy offers Red Baker any chance of a job, he must be demoted from highly skilled to unskilled work. Red naturally resists this. In the unemployment office, where a crowd of recent layoffs reminds him of a photograph of a soup line in the Depression, he faces a clerk who assigns him to the unskilled line. There he will be condemned, he knows from past experience, to "a new career stuffing newspapers with the Sunday supplements along with junkies and Thunderbird winos from down on Pratt Street."

"Now wait a minute, Miss . . . [he says]. . . , Maybe you don't understand just what it is a rougher does. I turn bars of steel that are hotter than hell. I don't do it right, the steel jumps the track and somebody ends up walking on stumps for the rest of their life. There's plenty of skill in that, you better believe it."   (Pp. 26–27)

The clerk refuses to classify him differently, and when the slow-moving line finally brings him face-to-face with the weary employment counselor for unskilled workers, Red sinks to the nadir of the service economy.* The counselor offers the possibility of a public-works job collecting garbage at Inner Harbor, the shopping and entertainment

* Perhaps a clerk in the unemployment office slips to the nadir when facing his or her own unemployment. In states where unemployment levels decline, usually because of increases in employment in the service sector, federal funding for state unemployment agencies is reduced, resulting in fewer jobs for clerks.

emporium on the Baltimore waterfront where Red's wife has just got back her old job.

> "Yeah, I got the picture [Red says]. . . . My wife is work-
> ing as a waitress in Weaver's Crab House, and she looks out
> the window and sees me, her husband, bagging trash, crab
> claws, and french fries people have thrown out. Picking up
> candy wrappers and ice cream sticks. You think I'm going to
> be able to hack that?"
> Red Baker, Garbage Guy.   (P. 30)

While work in the service economy represents nothing but shame for Red, it's a sham for writers, models, and their friends in New York's *Bright Lights, Big City* and a scam for the Hollywood and university hangers-on in the L.A. of *Less than Zero*. But the new landscape belongs to them, mobile denizens of the two growth centers of the bicoastal economy. Contrary to expectations, however, work in this economy is deadly, unproductive, and hierarchical.

The narrator of *Bright Lights, Big City* wants to be a writer.[14] After college and a brief stint as a newspaper reporter in Kansas City, he spends a couple of years in New York confronting his limitations. By day, he checks manuscripts for accuracy at a magazine modeled on the *New Yorker*—a place of employment, if not a job, that people would kill for.

> The Department of Factual Verification is the largest room in
> the magazine. If chess teams had locker rooms they might look
> like this. There are six desks—one reserved for visiting writ-
> ers—and thousands of reference books on the walls. Gray lin-
> oleum desktops, brown linoleum floors. An absolute hier-
> archy is reflected in the desk assignments . . . but in general
> the department is a clubhouse of democratic fellowship. The
> fanatic loyalty to the magazine which rules elsewhere is com-
> promised here by a sense of departmental loyalty: us against
> them. If an error slips into the magazine, it is one of you, and
> not the writer, who will be crucified. Not fired, but scolded,
> perhaps even demoted to the messenger room or the typing
> pool.   (Pp. 16–17)

Creative talent is everything. To be near it, at the magazine, in New York, is somehow to be part of a new landscape that is intellectual, pleasurable, but also littered with dead hopes for individual expression. To be there is to be stuck there. The only way out is down "to the messenger room or the typing pool."

Except for the bureaucratic difference between employment and self-employment, this is the same landscape inhabited by Tama Janowitz's floating, yet unfree, guilds of New Wave craftsmen in *Slaves of New York*. They are artists, musicians, jewelry designers who live together in the formerly low-rent, still shabby, apartments of the East Village. They stick together because alone they couldn't pay the rent. This sense of spatial and social limitation overpowers the narrator of "The Blue Room," a story published in the *New Yorker*. He and his wife, living in a cramped studio on the Upper East Side, begin reading aloud in the evening the autobiography of a nineteenth-century Englishwoman. They become convinced "that the New York we saw most closely and knew best—the New York of graduate students and aspiring artists and writers, the New York of tiny apartments and part-time jobs at libraries and publishing houses—was in its essential forms Victorian."[15]

They mean this precisely in the sense of living with lowered expectations. On the one hand, office work in the service economy recreates "the condition of clerkship. The new age in New York, as we saw it, looked less like a stockbroker in a Lamborghini and more like a scrivener wrapped in a woolen muffler." On the other hand, the permanent penury of small apartments at high rents imposes a modest lifestyle. They and their friends have little furniture, few noisy parties, no hope of children as the issue of marriage. Making do in these conditions, "we had the pallor of clerks, the wistful intricacy of naturalists, the complicated scruples of vicars."*

On the far side of this landscape is the postmodern ennui of *Less than Zero*'s drugged-out rich kids. For them and seemingly for their parents, work in the service economy is narcissism and prostitution, a contemporary version of the Hollywood landscape depicted in Nathanael West's *The Day of the Locust* except for the youth of the characters. Their Los Angeles stretches along the freeways and canyons of the fragmented metropolis, from the university campus in Westwood where some of them are desultory students to their parents' houses in Beverly

---

* This bohemianism of the garret, an urban limbo for bourgeois *manqués*, is exactly like Eugène Goudeau's novelistic description of Parisian bohemianism in the 1870s and 1880s. See Jerrold Siegel, *Bohemian Paris: Culture, Politics, and the Boundaries of Bourgeois Life, 1830–1930* (New York: Viking Penguin, 1986), pp. 216ff.

Hills and Bel Air, beach houses and country houses in Malibu and Palm Springs, weekend quarters in Aspen or possibly Las Vegas, and frequent, though shadowy, sojourns in Mexico, London, Switzerland.[16] The absence of spatial and social limitation, reflecting the market power of dream merchants (their parents) and drug merchants (often themselves), evokes a boundless, but monolithic place. The existential agony of the narrator's inner landscape is no less a representation of the outer landscape than Rabbit Angstrom's. The book's last images of Los Angeles are of interlopers, rapists, cannibals. To be part of that landscape is to lose one's mind.

Despite fairly obvious differences between the postmodern and the modern city, both *Less than Zero* and *Bright Lights, Big City* define the genre of novel that Bill Sharpe and Leonard Wallock describe as "literary gentrification."[17] In contrast to their interpretation, however, these novels share only two elements of a similar landscape. (Another similarity, not noted by Sharpe and Wallock, is a tendency on the part of many people to take the representation of this landscape as social reality in its entirety.) Both novels deal with a college-educated, quasi-professional and quasi-intellectual group of young people who connect in some way with the arts. Affluent or not, these characters represent the economic motif of growth amid decay that is so typical of the concept *gentrification*. This in turn reflects the social motif of regional dualism, a worrisome aspect of structural change.

The two novels also furnish a Baedeker to the city as a landscape of consumption. Both narrators survive the day to live by night, hopping from restaurant to nightclub to after-hours club in an endless party of alcohol and drugs. The club scene is an integral part of the novels: the characters bored and boring, barely conscious that the anarchy of their lives is an existential limitation. "Your presence here is only a matter of conducting an experiment in limits," says the narrator about nightclubs in *Bright Lights, Big City*, "reminding yourself of what you aren't." In fact, he visualizes the opposite of the nightclub crawler—his inner self—only as a variation on the same pattern of consumption:

> You see yourself as the kind of guy who wakes up early on Sunday morning and steps out to cop the *Times* and croissants. Who might take a cue from the Arts and Leisure section and decide to check out an exhibition—costumes of the Hapsburg Court at the Met, say, or Japanese lacquerware of the

> Muromachi period at the Asia Society. The kind of guy who
> calls up the woman he met at a publishing party Friday night.
> . . . She may have been out late, perhaps at a nightclub. And
> maybe a couple of sets of tennis before the museum.   (P. 4)

The young characters of *Less than Zero* also continually migrate from
diner and fast-food restaurant to ice-cream shop, nightclub, and temple
of nouvelle cuisine. They seem no different from others of their age and
income level except, perhaps, for the utter indifference with which they
consume.

While the narrator's Los Angeles barely comes alive except in visions of his past and future, the narrator of *Bright Lights, Big City*
starts to see New York pleasurably (again) when he can view it as a
tourist. On a date with an attractive woman, he shows her around his
neighborhood, one of the quainter and more exotic areas of Manhattan. Now the food smells are pleasantly ethnic rather than putrid; the
streets and townhouses are small-scale, reminiscent of civil society. Unlike the weirdness in the human landscape, the tourist landscape is not
intimidating.

The narrator of "The Blue Room," living in a small studio apartment that is also in New York, goes to modest evenings at his friends'
apartments. "Our parties involved makeshift arrangements of collapsi-
ble furniture—doors as tables, bathtubs as wine cellars—just like Bob
Sawyer's supper party in 'Pickwick,' and we even had to struggle not to
make too much noise for the landlady." In *Less than Zero*, the narrator
goes to friends' houses, too, but these gatherings are practically unbounded in space and time.

> It's a Saturday night and on some Saturday nights when there's
> not a party to go to and no concerts around town and every-
> one's seen all the movies, most people stay at home and invite
> friends over and talk on the phone. Sometimes someone will
> drop by and talk and have a drink and then get back into his
> car and drive over to somebody else's house. On some Satur-
> day nights there'll be three or four people who drive from one
> house to another. Who drive from about ten on Saturday night
> until just before dawn the next morning.   (P. 77)

Landmarks and pastimes of consumption provide the landscape of
postmodern fiction. Taking place in the south-southwest of the country,

Frederick Barthelme's novel and short stories are filled with fast-food restaurants, diners, seedy bars, and palm-tree-and-brick-wall eateries. One of his stories ends when the narrator discovers that the girl who arrived on his doorstep works in a bakeshop called Pie Country he sometimes goes to. Another begins with the description of a "restaurant [that] used to be a hardware store; now it's all done up in cheesy L.A. late-thirties gear, the hard-boiled version—palms, ratty paintings, neon, ersatz columns, colored lights, pale-salmon walls in bad plaster, black tile floor" (p. 87).[18]

The trailer parks, apartment complexes, and tacky bars and fast-food restaurants in Barthelme's work recapitulate the vernacular culture, the love of mobility, that are typical of American society. Barthelme's restaurants are cheaper than Jay McInerney's and Brett Easton Ellis's, and the food is crass, but this is where his characters spend their time. In *White Noise*, too, the landscape that is described is a landscape of consumption, the supermarket and the shopping mall replacing the restaurant or the club.

What a contrast to the landscape, formerly of production and now of devastation, in Red Baker's working-class community. The bars and the restaurants there have value because that's where friends meet and renew an unspoken, an unspeakable, compromise with market and place. When Red visits an old girlfriend, now a widow who owns a bar, she tells him that she's moving to Florida, although she's afraid to move away:

> "I grew up here. I know everybody, but there's nothing left, Red. You can't live on memories."
> "I know we don't see each other much, Ruby, but . . . well, I like knowing you're here. I mean . . . hell, you know what I mean." (P. 46)

Far from abolishing memory by pastiche and other anti-narrative techniques, postmodernism implicitly acknowledges that the appropriation of space and time is one of the central issues confronted by culture today. The ability to appropriate artifacts of the past now belongs equally to processes of social reproduction attached "mechanically" to place (Updike's Pennsylvania, Iron City, working-class Baltimore) and social differentiation "organically" derived from economic and cultural markets (as in the "literary gentrification" of *Bright Lights, Big City* and the postmodern city of *Less than Zero*).

Whether the material landscape will be completely made over by demand for the latter sort of consumption depends on how economic change is mediated by architecture and urban design. The liminality of the inner landscape finds an echo in the city's production of liminal space, incorporating areas that used to be tightly defined by social limits into market culture. Spaces of production recede into the historic vernacular; more than ever, the urban landscape relies on image consumption.

3   The Urban Landscape

> Last night . . . more than 1,200 guests gathered to cele-
> brate the opening of the Place des Antiquaires, New York's
> newest antiques center. . . . Cecile Zhilka was the chair-
> woman of the evening, which benefited the Metropolitan Op-
> era and was marked by the distinct accents of New York and
> Paris. . . . "I just want to know where I am: in Paris, in New
> York, or in a new city floating in between them," said Am-
> bassador de Margerie.
>
> *New York Times*, November 19, 1987

We owe the clearest cultural map of structural change not to novelists
or literary critics, but to architects and designers. Their products, their
social roles as cultural producers, and the organization of consumption
in which they intervene create shifting landscapes in the most material
sense. As both objects of desire and structural forms, their work bridges
space and time. It also directly mediates economic power by both con-
forming to and structuring norms of market-driven investment, production, and consumption.

A major result of this cultural mediation is now a blurring of distinctions between many categories of space and time that we experience
every day: when the leisure of home life is invaded by well-designed
machines, cities appear more alike, and Saturday traffic jams connected
with shopping are worse then weekday morning rush hours. In general,
spaces that used to stand alone—representing "pure" nature or culture in people's minds—now mix social and commercial functions,

Battery Park City, New York (1989). Photo courtesy Battery Park City Authority.

sponsors, and symbols. Times that were perceived as distinctive, because the social experience connected with them was either finite or lasted "forever," are now condensed and combined. Although David Harvey has tried to capture these experiences in terms of a modern "time-space compression" that begins in the Enlightenment, intensifies around the time of World War I, and reaches extreme proportions in the current global economic reorganization, he leaves a lot about these unsettling experiences unsaid. An especially open question is how the visual economy of landscape mediates market culture.[1]

Here Victor Turner's concept of liminality again comes into play. Instead of social groups experiencing moments of liminality, however, the liminal experience of the market is broadened so that new urban spaces are formed, permeated, and defined by liminality. All such spaces stand "betwixt and between" institutions, especially the sacred sphere of culture and the secular world of commerce. Zones where business is transacted and public roles exchanged, liminal spaces institutionalize market culture in the landscape.

Heavily influenced by market norms, liminal spaces no longer offer an opportunity for the kind of creative destruction Turner describes. In the nonmarket and preindustrial situations that he observed, groups were rejuvenated and refreshed by liminality, and social values reaffirmed. Even in the late-nineteenth-century European cities Walter Benjamin wrote about, urban spaces carried a potential that hesitated between conformity and utopia, a world of commodities or of dreams.[2] Today, urban places respond to market pressures, with public dreams defined by private development projects and public pleasures restricted to private entry. Liminality in the landscape thus resembles the creative destruction that Schumpeter described, reflecting an institutionalized reorientation of cultural patrons, producers, and consumers.

Creative destruction works both for and against architects and designers. They confront conditions in a new market culture quite similar to those that have challenged the autonomy of traditional manufacturers: abstraction of value from material products to images and symbols, global markets, and a shift in the major source of social meaning from production to consumption. Not only do they adapt to these changes, they tailor their products to them; they give visual form to Schumpeter's "perennial gale" of capitalist innovation.

ARCHITECTS AND THE LANDSCAPE OF POWER

The two cultural products that most directly map the landscape are architecture and urban form. Because they shape both the city and our perception of it, they are material as well as symbolic. Like the rest of the built environment in a market economy, design and form relate to space in different ways: as a geographical (or topographical) constraint, as a terrain of potential conflict or cohesion, and as a commodity. They tend, therefore, toward constant change and rapid obsolescence. Without neglecting the enormous part played by architecture and urban form in the symbolic attachments of place, we must emphasize how much they are influenced by markets. What buildings and districts look like, who uses them, their diversity or homogeneity, how long they last before being torn down: these qualities reflect the spatial and temporal constraints of a market culture.[3]

While architects today work mainly under corporate patronage, urban planners, real estate developers, and city officials work within a matrix of state institutions and local preferences. Both are neither free nor unfree from market forces and the attachments of place. Although architects most often produce designs for an individual client rather than "on speculation," with the idea of offering them for sale, the business clients who are sources of most commissions impose market criteria by demanding more rentable space in less construction time. Increasingly, these clients are national and international investors (especially Canadian, British, and Japanese). There is thus a practical connection between architecture and urban forms and "multinational capitalism."[4]

New architecture and urban forms are, moreover, produced under nearly the same social conditions as consumer products. They increasingly follow similar patterns of both standardization and market differentiation. Variations are imposed by local real estate markets and the local built environment. Diversity is also encouraged by the incorporation of older urban forms for "sentimental" or aesthetic reasons, in the economic process that David Harvey describes as "flexible accumulation."[5] Regardless of these precious artifacts, it has become practically impossible to separate the perception of urban form from the effects of internationalized investment, production, and consumption.

After 1945, the process of suburbanization demanded centralized control over finance and construction even while it rapidly decentralized housing and shopping malls, with their anchor stores, controlled environment, and inner streets of shops, and destroyed the commercial viability of many central business districts.[6] From 1973, however, centralized, multinational investment supported both continued decentralization of commercial development and a reconcentration, with enhanced stratification, of urban shopping districts. The same products and ambiance came from multinational corporations in New York, France, Japan, and Italy. Within a few years, both products and ambiance could just as well be found in shops on upper Madison Avenue or Rodeo Drive as on the rue du faubourg St. Honoré or the via Montenapoleone. When local merchants were displaced by the higher rents these tenants paid, they correctly blamed the showplace boutiques whose rents were subsidized by their parent multinational corporations. In a subtle recapitulation of earlier transformations, more international investment shifted shopping districts from craft (quiche) to mass (McDonald's or Benetton) production and consumption.[7]

McDonald's and Benetton epitomize the connections between international urban form and internationalized production and consumption. Their shops are ubiquitous in cities around the world, giving strength to the parent firms' strategy of international expansion. An executive at Benetton's U.S. headquarters has even identified the two corporate strategies. "We consider ourselves the fast food in fashion," he says. "We want to be everywhere, like McDonald's."[8] The companies do differ in the way they run their worldwide operations. While McDonald's sells traditional franchises to local operators, Benetton neither invests in nor collects franchise fees from Benetton stores. Instead, Benetton licenses the right to sell Benetton clothes in individually owned Benetton stores. Further, McDonald's managers buy their food supplies locally. Benetton managers must buy their entire inventory from Benetton.

Both chains maintain uniform standards by other corporate policies. These include rigorous training of store managers; insistence on adherence to company standards for quality and service, and, at Benetton, for decor and window display; and frequent on-site inspections by visitors from company headquarters. Despite the differences in the types of products that they sell, both Benetton and McDonald's owe their growth in part to organizational innovation. Much of their advance centers on production and distribution. McDonald's honed to a fine point the "robotized" operations of fast-food cuisine; Benetton developed cheaper methods for softening wool and dying colored garments, as well as investing in computerized manufacturing and design and real robots for warehouse operations. In the process, both chains developed a total "look" that merges product, production methods, a specialized consumption experience, and an advertising style. As their "classic" mass-produced sweaters and burgers link consumers around the world, these multinational corporations become more significant players in each domestic economy. McDonald's voracious demand for beef inflicts damage up and down the food chain in cattle-raising countries of Latin America. By contrast, Benetton's new U.S. factory in North Carolina provides (automated) employment to textile workers.[9]

Benetton and McDonald's are landmarks on many local scenes. Yet the social process that supports their production confirms the three structural shifts that we consider important: abstraction, internationalization, and the shift from production to consumption. Significantly, their profits reflect both production of basic goods—clothes and food—and less tangible economic factors of land rent, marketing, and the organization of distribution.

In contrast to the marketing of mass-produced consumer goods, the marketing of architecture has a higher profile. Even though individual buildings have become more standardized, their designers claim to offer their owners more distinction. Professional architects continue to theorize an underlying aesthetic or social program, especially the faux populism that adheres to many postmodern styles. This demotic urge facilitates architects' acceptability to corporate patrons. By means of architectural patronage, corporations gain public acceptance. New "user-friendly" architectural styles for corporate and regional headquarters distinguish the companies that adopt them from those that inhabit the glass boxes commercially adapted from modernism from the 1950s through the 1970s.[10]

Developers who sell office space are less intellectually constrained. "My buildings are a product," a building developer says. "They are products like Scotch Tape is a product, or Saran Wrap. The packaging of that product is the first thing that people see. I am selling space and renting space and it has to be in a package that is attractive enough to be financially successful." As if to confirm Schumpeter's dour prediction about the decline of entrepreneurs, he adds, "I can't afford to build monuments because I am not an institution." The architectural critic Ada Louise Huxtable turns this comment around in her criticism of the monumentally sized, egregiously individualized new skyscrapers that are especially common in New York City. "In the last five years," she says, "a new kind of developer has been remaking the city with something called 'the signature building,' a postmodernist phenomenon that combines marketing and consumerism in a way that would have baffled Bernini but is thoroughly understood by the modern entrepreneur." [11]

Signature or "trophy" buildings link the cultural value of architecture with the economic value of land and buildings. This linkage has been propelled, in recent years, by the entry of new property investors, especially foreigners, and inflation in property values. The growth centers are in the bicoastal economy: New York City, Washington, D.C., Boston, San Francisco, Los Angeles, which are also major sites of postmodern architecture. Trophy buildings have a dual value to corporate owners. These buildings are identifiable corporate images, and they are salable. As corporations restructure, reducing their work force, they sell their buildings to foreign investors. Thus Citicorp leased space in its slanted-roof headquarters, which cuts the Manhattan skyline, to Japanese investors, and moved a major part of its work force to a new building in Queens. [12]

An emphasis on individualized products that can be identified with individual cultural producers is inseparable from intensified market competition in an age of mass consumption. The "Egyptoid" character of postmodern skyscraper design was paralleled, in the 1920s, by the "Mayan" pyramids of speculative office buildings competing in a real estate boom. [13] Similar competition among Hollywood film studios for audience loyalty to their products encouraged individual directors to make the "signature film." * In architecture, as labor costs have increased and craft skills have atrophied, the burden of social differentiation has passed to the use of expensive materials and the ingenuity of the design itself. And like Hollywood directors, architects assume and even become commercial properties. Philip Johnson is selected as the architect of AT&T's corporate headquarters or Kevin Roche is chosen by the boards of General Foods and the Metropolitan Museum of Art because these architects are already identifiable brand names. As Calvin

---

* Just as Ada Louise Huxtable recognizes the developer's role in producing the signature building, so major film producers, and specific studios, are recognized as much as directors for having created signature films of the 1930s and 1940s. In the 1950s and 1960s, the attempt by noncommercial critics to theorize the director's role and/or deemphasize the commercialism of Hollywood production led to writing about the director as the film's *auteur*.

Tomkins slyly remarks of Philip Johnson's market savvy, they have the potential to outlive their buildings.[14]

Architects have always been chosen on the basis of both their names and their work. But recently there has been a heightening of both the subjective and objective use of individual architects. Choice of an architect legitimizes a building's sponsor, and offers that sponsor a competitive advantage. By the same token, as architectural design is more broadly diffused, it gains both economic and cultural value. Magazines have joined their coverage of fashion with surveys of new architecture and design; museums have established architecture departments; and architects' drawings have begun to sell at high prices as works of art. Interior design is similarly routinized as an element of both cultural literacy and social distinction. Under these conditions, a larger number of people may be impressed by architects' names than actually know their buildings.[15]

Saying that architects, especially postmodern architects, have adopted the rhetoric of stylistic differentiation because they are aesthetically dissatisfied with modernism tells only part of the story. They also face increasingly stiff competition for corporate commissions. Major architects maintain quasi-corporate offices like those of much larger major law firms. They thus depend on corporate clients to support their practices. There is no automatic correlation between an architectural career path and market differentiation. It has often been noted that Philip Johnson turned to postmodernism during the 1970s after an illustrious 40-year career as a prime exponent of modernism, and now varies his style for each project. After Michael Graves was roundly condemned by architectural colleagues in the early 1980s for turning to postmodernism, he began receiving highly visible corporate and public commissions. By the same token, the visibility of its idiosyncratic late modern building behind the opening credits of the television show "Miami Vice" helped establish the Miami firm Arquitectonica. The speculative real estate boom of the 1920s, like that of the 1980s, suggests that stylistic differentiation among architects supports their commercial expansion. By the 1920s, architects supervised much larger offices and crews than they had before. The costs of land acquisition and construction made them "become as much a part of Big Business as the engineer, the legal counsel and the financier."[16]

Paradoxically, as architecture and design have become more professionalized, with special educational requirements and licensing procedures restricting entry to the profession, their concerns converge with those of their patrons. On the one hand, architects and designers mingle socially with wealthy and famous elites. On the other hand, an emphasis on culture to enhance the commercial values of product and property markets incorporates architects and designers into the landscape of power.

As cities try to lure new capital investment, especially from the high end of business services, they refashion their commercial districts by commissioning new buildings and urban plans. Traditional downtowns were decimated by the flight and decline of industry, and the competition from new shopping centers in the suburbs. Seeking to restore—or create—a vernacular lustre, local interests hire "name" architects, whose reputations should minimize financial risk. Yet these architects work under a dual market constraint: that of their client and that of their firm, both of which demand a distinctive, salable product. Consequently, architects place their own signature on the landscape, and repeat it wherever they are hired.

Superstar architects create a standardized form that they move from place to place. They also create buildings that look stupendous from a distance—on the city's skyline—but fail to fit in with local "context." This makes an architecture that is less risky for investors but also less evocative of a sense of place.[17] "Suddenly," a Boston architect complains about Fan Pier, a major new project on the waterfront, "the demand for the 'name' architect, often overcommitted elsewhere, has placed these architects and their products side by side." This threatens the historic waterfront with looking like that of any other city.[18] Because of their cultural commodities, superstar architects mediate the leveling of local and regional distinctions by transnational economic investment.

Superstars could be interpreted as a modern version of the Renaissance cult of genius. In the early fifteenth century, Brunelleschi designed palaces and public works for the aristocracies of Florence, Pisa, and Mantua, far surpassing the achievements of local architects. He became "so famous," Vasari writes, "that those who needed to commission important buildings would send for him from great distances to provide his incomparable design and models; people would make use of friends or bring strong influences to bear to secure his services."[19] But the rise of the superstar architect today reflects market competition. It indicates the desire by major corporations in the services to recoup value from long-term, large-scale investments in product development—their buildings. The superstar architect is produced by the same market conditions as the superstar rock group and TV anchor.[20]

From about 1880 to 1930, modern architecture was also spurred by real estate development that demanded constant innovation in the urban landscape. In 1905, when Henry James returned to New York, he deplored the destruction of the city that he knew. He blamed the imminent demise of Trinity Church—sold by its own wardens for real estate development—on "the universal will to move—to move, move, move, as an end in itself, an appetite at any price." In this period, the average longevity of an office building in New York shrank to only twenty years. By the 1920s, production of commercial buildings depended on speculators whose financing got a project underway, architects who could "draw . . . an imposing picture of a skyscraper; if it is several stories higher than the Woolworth Tower, so much the better," and newspapers that eagerly published "pictures of high buildings, real or imagined, because . . . readers have a weakness for them."[21]

COMMERCE AND CULTURE

As in architecture, the visual image that designers create has been integrated into the landscape of power. The growth of a service economy extracts design from the system of material production and makes it a symbol of the power of ideas. Because design can be responsible for a product's success, designers have also become superstars. They are valued for their ability to connect commerce and culture.* When the French interior designer Andrée Putman attracted an audience of about a thousand people at the annual meeting of the Los Angeles furniture design industry in 1987, she spoke about the extraordinary recent growth of the design industry. "I don't think 15 years ago it would have been possible to talk to so many people," she said. "There's a kind of fascination and passion internationally for new ideas, and a strange hunger for signatures. Designers are gurus of today, an overly respected animal." They are also public figures and media celebrities. When the French *haute couture* fashion designer Christian Lacroix appeared at a New

---

* The Japanese language, for example, has imported *deezainah* without attempting to translate it, along with such terms as "advertising copywriter" and "project coordinator," which have no indigenous equivalent (*Business Week,* July 13, 1987, p. 51). Industrial designers become more important when competition among manufacturers turns from sheer cost to product quality—a point much appreciated in current U.S.–Japanese competition (*Business Week,* April 11, 1988, pp. 102–17).

York clothing store to introduce his first "mass-market" ready-to-wear collection, he was mobbed by shoppers asking for his autograph.[22]

The new cultural value of designers to some degree reflects the general upward reevaluation of the economic significance of high-level services. Historically, however, the role of design in architecture began to overshadow construction as early as the seventeenth century.[23] In the early twentieth century, architects from Le Corbusier to Frank Lloyd Wright designed furniture and objects to further their building designs. Only recently, however, has the architect's talent for design been appropriated by a large number of commercial commissions in other fields. Architects are now prominent in marketing small consumer goods, including birdhouses, wrist watches, coffee pots, and dinner plates. The increase in architect-designed furniture, moreover, represents a burgeoning market. The "authentic" reproduction of work by early twentieth-century designers has even benefited Andrée Putman, who manufactures and distributes the work of Eileen Gray.[24]

The most commercially successful architects are the most sought after designers of consumer goods. But this spiral of success constrains architectural designers to meet more market criteria. The risk of mixing bad aesthetic and commercial judgment is suggested by the forced retirement of the fashion designer Halston, who "lost his name" when he lost a franchise to sell fashion to the masses at J. C. Penney. On the other hand, the value of a "name" designer reflects the acumen of his or her business partner at least as much as the quality of design.[25]

Interior, furniture, and fashion designers have also gained value through department store promotions. Introducing a new product, stores will often identify and commercialize an entire "genre" of design, so that the promotion creates a new linkage between designers, mass consumers, and wealthy patrons of high culture. At the high end, as Debora Silverman observes so well, a department store like Bloomingdale's conceives a promotion around imported goods that are designed in New York, mass produced overseas in low-wage plants, and exhibited in a central place in the flagship store as though in a museum. In fact, the promotions that Bloomingdale's organized at the beginning of the 1980s, at the time of Ronald Reagan's first presidential election, were scheduled to coordinate with thematic exhibitions at the Costume Institute of the Metropolitan Museum of Art. Bloomingdale's and the Met thus shared an interest in the cultural consumption of antique Chinese robes and current Chinese imports, French *haute couture* as designed by Yves

Saint Laurent, and equestrian costume as marketed by Ralph Lauren. Silverman believes that the revaluation of "aristocratic" taste promoted by both department store and museum promoted the wealthy elites that supported conservative president Ronald Reagan, "a consumerist power elite."[26] But the mix of patronage to include both the rich and the famous and department store customers, framed by high culture institutions and commercial establishments, indicates a much broader value of design. Design links the mass public and private elites in a visual organization of consumption.

Department stores have always used design to market the products they sell. But since the 1980s, the competitive need for product differentiation has fostered a reliance on design to shape the whole space of consumption. Department stores have undergone multiple reconfigurations into theme or designer boutiques; lavishly orchestrated promotions celebrate a design motif extracted from history, current films, and regions of the world. Once the emphasis shifted from product to design, social patrons of both fashion and the arts found department stores a receptive context for their special events. The department store sponsors charity galas, receptions for nonprofit cultural institutions, and promotions of work for sale by designers—all in one event, for the same people. By lowering the barriers between commerce and culture, and private patronage and mass consumption, the department store creates a liminal urban space.

Beyond a single store's four walls, new waterfront shopping centers expand a zone of liminality downtown based on visual consumption. Usually built on disused piers in older cities with declining ports, they present shopping as a means of enjoying urban culture. This type of project includes the redevelopment of Boston's Faneuil Hall, Baltimore's Inner Harbor, and South Street Seaport in New York City, all of which used historic preservation laws to subsidize commercial construction. From the 1970s to 1987, federal tax laws supported historic preservation by making it financially advantageous for investors to reuse old urban forms for commercial revitalization. Changes in the tax code in 1986 reduced these advantages and made them more relevant to smaller investors. Aesthetically, however, historic preservation often mobilizes support for the commercial redevelopment of downtown for consumption uses among those groups that previously opposed urban renewal, highway construction, and large-scale demolition. The principled refusal to destroy old urban forms contrasts with the use of modern architecture, in the 1950s and 1960s, to assert the commercial district's viability. In those years, developers and city governments replaced historic low-rent structures with standardized, "internationalized" office buildings. In a changed sentimental climate after 1965, this high-rise construction suggested alienation. Smaller scale, respect for context, and mixed uses of space were proposed as a way of restoring a visual sense of place.

Shopping centers have replaced political meetings and civic gatherings as arenas of public life. Despite private ownership and service to paying customers, they are perceived as a fairly democratic form of development. Moreover, they are believed to "open" the downtown by creating a sense of place. Downtown developers derive a theme from former economic uses—the harbor, the marketplace, the factory—and offer consumers the opportunity to combine shopping with touristic voyeurism into the city's past. The ambiance of authenticity is important to establish the critical mass of shoppers vital to retail competition. In some downtowns, where a high density of business services creates demand, even an artificial sense of place enhances consumption. In other cities, however, the downtown is still too tied to industrial uses to encourage the liminality of a consumption space.

In the process of revitalizing the waterfront, old piers and Main Streets were turned into emporia of mass consumption. Beneath the image of locality these places project, they are really marketplaces for goods that are not locally produced. "Gourmet foods" and croissant shops were at least initially imported, and the chains of retail clothing stores that fill these urban shopping centers sell mainly imported apparel. Tourist items are nearly always made outside the country. Even products like Samuel Adams beer, which is associated with Boston, and Vermont butter are either produced out of state (the beer in Pittsburgh) or with out-of-state materials (milk for the butter from dairies outside Vermont). Projects like Faneuil Hall are, moreover, developed by national firms and financed by New York money center banks. Like the high-class shopping street, these shopping centers unify international investment, production, and consumption.[27]

PRIVATE CONSUMPTION AND PUBLIC SPACE

The museum, department store, and waterfront shopping center create liminality by opening public space to private consumption. A more provocative example of this liminality is the State of Illinois Center, designed in 1986 by the architect Helmut Jahn. In a variety of large buildings that he previously designed for both the private and the public sectors, Jahn eclectically used architectural elements from every period—the so-called historical references of postmodernism. But the new state office building in Chicago merits attention less for style than for the way it uses space. Under its atrium/rotunda, the eighteen-story public building surmounts a three-level shopping center, with public-access spaces interspersed among the stores. This combination of public and private uses has struck critics as *submerging* public place to private markets. It takes to an extreme the liminality between public and private urban spaces that began in the nineteenth century.

From the 1880s on, the increasing use of new mechanical inventions for transportation and telecommunications forged hybrid public-private cultural forms. Telephones provided men and women with both accessibility and distraction. Newspapers achieved mass circulation as means of both intimacy and information. Railroads bridged the scale of the journey and arrival in the city with the liminal transparent tunnels of great railroad stations built of iron and glass.[28] From this time, urban form has increasingly been defined by the public use of private space. In contrast to the decline of public space for civil society, this sense of place has grown together with means of market consumption.

Social life in modern cities often depends on expanding once exclusive means of market consumption to a broader public. From the 1860s on, coffee houses, tea rooms, and restaurants, which sometimes began as a refuge for middle-class teetotalers, became general places for meeting and entertainment. Department stores, which began as shopping havens for unescorted women, expanded into general bazaars. And hotels, striking "the note of the supremely gregarious state" that Henry James found so typical of America, began as marketplaces of sociability for a wealthy upper class.[29]

James's observations on the grand hotel—the milling crowd, the ladies buzzing with tea-time conversation, the shops providing a cornucopia of rare imported goods, the whole unlike anything seen in Europe—foreshadow Fredric Jameson's description of the Los Angeles Bonaventure, one of the atrium-hotels built by the architect-developer John Portman during the 1970s. Like James, Jameson is struck by the coherence and "publicity" of the hotel's interior world. Unlike James, however, Jameson calls it postmodern that "the *Bonaventura* [*sic*] as-pires to being a total space, a complete world, a kind of miniature city, . . . [to which, moreover, there] corresponds a new collective practice, the practice of a new and historically original kind of hyper-crowd." For Jameson, Portman's selection of architectural elements marks the creative destruction of modernism's monumental, although readily comprehensible, scale. Ironically, Jameson neglects to compare the naturally lighted, abnormally high interior central space of Portman's hotels to the architecture of late-nineteenth-century department stores like the Bon Marché (1876). In his view, Portman's atrium expands volume beyond human capacity to experience it; the elevators and escalators extend and accelerate, but also confine, human movement beyond "that older promenade we are no longer allowed to conduct on our own."[30]

Yet Henry James had already sensed in "the universal Waldorf-Astoria" the entrapment of "the great collective, plastic public" by "the great glittering, costly caravansery." No less than Jameson in the atrium, James sees "the whole housed populace move as in mild and consenting suspicion of its captured and governed state, its having to consent in inordinate fusion as the price of what it seemed pleased to regard as inordinate luxury."[31]

There is a direct line of visual consumption from Henry James at the Waldorf Astoria in New York in 1905 to Fredric Jameson at the Los Angeles Bonaventure. But the public use of private space *inside* the hotel only symbolizes change in the surrounding city. Urban form has been especially vulnerable in recent years to an asymmetry of power favoring the private sector. Since the 1970s, because of the withdrawal of federal funding and the aftermath of local "fiscal crisis," city governments have become more dependent on pleasing private investors, including holders of municipal bonds, property developers, and directors of large banks and corporations. In a small number of cities—New York, Cleveland, Yonkers—nonelected committees drawn from the leadership of large financial institutions have exercised veto power over the city budget since 1975. (Cleveland's Financial Planning and Supervisory Commission was eliminated in 1987; New York City's Municipal Assistance Corporation has assumed new responsibilities for financing, and demanded reorganization of, the transportation and education systems.) Even when new mayors come into office with populist bases or the support of ethnic and racial minorities, as in Chicago and Denver, the city administration's public works are coordinated with private developers.[32]

Constrained both institutionally and ideologically, cities face "a shrinking of the realm of the possible and a shrinking of the realm of the public, simultaneously."[33] The material landscape created by the joint efforts of speculative developers, elected officials, financial institutions, and architectural designers responds to these conditions by merging public places and private markets, often under the management of a quasi-public urban development corporation. Significant public life moves inside from the streets.

Following Schumpeter, creative destruction in the economy changes the nature of demand and fosters the deployment and differentiation of capital along new lines. Architectural design and urban form suggest that creative destruction in culture is a similarly directed process. The primacy of visual consumption in the twentieth century fosters the social production of image-makers, whose imagination is ruled by the economic value of both public and private display. The social context of cultural patronage, production, and consumption reduces producers' autonomy from both patrons and consumers. It also drives the transformation of previously bounded institutions—department stores, museums, hotels—into disorienting liminal spaces for both market and nonmarket cultural consumption.

For these reasons, it is impossible for the art museum to be "the domain in which to express the moral brake on conspicuous consumption"; the museum truly "becomes the extension of the department store and another display case for the big business of illusion making"[34]— but it does so for its own "cultural" goals. While these processes enhance the role of culture in social differentiation, they also equalize perceptions of cultural production "for the market" and "for art." This is the conundrum of postmodern culture.

By the same token, the urban landscape gives both material and symbolic form to the opposition between *market* and *place*. The market's constant pressure to reproduce variety contradicts the constant pressure on place to reproduce stability. While most people really want to enjoy the pleasures of fine buildings, good stores, and beautiful urban spaces, the processes that create them make the city more abstract, more dependent on international capital flows, and more responsive to the organization of consumption than the organization of production.

Five Twentieth-Century Landscapes

The following five chapters explore an array of familiar American landscapes that span twentieth-century experience, reflecting the interplay between market economy and market culture.

These landscapes begin with a fairly narrow focus on the economy, looking at a company town (Weirton), an industrial city (Detroit), and an affluent suburb that has become a corporate headquarters location (Westchester County). Reflecting the growing influence of culture in the economy, the landscapes then become less tied to production and more concerned with the organization of consumption. The fourth and fifth landscapes describe the expansion of downtown by means of gentrification in New York, Chicago, and Boston, and the re-creation of urban form in Miami, Los Angeles, and Disney World, postmodern resort colonies or cities of dreams.

Each landscape is being transformed, as lives are lived and business is done, by the internationalization of the economy, the increasing abstraction of value from productive labor, and the transfer of the dominant source of social meaning from production to consumption. The series thus presents ideas about space, time, and economic power. It also emphasizes the importance of such "contingencies" as social relations of work and community, changing patterns of consumption, national politics and ideological climate.

Most important, however, the landscapes document a moment in space and time when local social relations are transformed on the basis of change in larger social and economic institutions. So they take to heart Joseph Schumpeter's call to study how capitalist forms are created and destroyed, rather than how they endure.

Charles Sheeler, *American Landscape* (1930). Oil on canvas, 24 × 31 inches. Collection, Museum of Modern Art, New York. Gift of Abby Aldrich Rockefeller.

4 Steeltown: Power and Autonomy in Weirton, West Virginia

Nor has the subject which occupied the earnest attention of politicians in Queen Elizabeth's time ceased to be of interest; for, after the lapse of nearly three hundred years, we find the smith and the iron manufacturer still uppermost in public discussions. . . . The strength and wealth of nations depend upon coal and iron, not forgetting Men, far more than upon gold.

SAMUEL SMILES, *Industrial Biography: Iron Workers and Tool Makers* (1863)

But there is a mystique involved in the steel industry that makes it a symbol of economic strength all over the world. The great industrial economies that emerged in the nineteenth century were built on steel, and wars were won with it. For more than a century, both politicians and economists have regarded steel capacity as a measure of industrial progress and a source of geopolitical power. The shock of steel's crisis, therefore, is out of all proportion to the actual figures involved.

Business Week cover story, September 19, 1977

No industry has a more powerful image than steel. Its symbolic weight in the national economy reflects a host of material factors: the brute force required to make steel, the volume of capital investment in a mill, the size of the work force engaged in smelting, pouring, casting, and shipping, and the omnipresence of steel in all modern structures, from rail trestles and bridge girders, to auto bodies, skyscrapers, airplanes, and ships. Steel has power because it has been the lifeline of industrial society.

But social life revolving around steel production has always exuded power. For thousands of years, the manufacture of basic metals upheld an almost mystical relation between power and community. Iron spearheads made it possible for a small group of people to defend their homes or conquer new lands; iron plowshares enabled them to cultivate food crops and build permanent settlements. Over the ages, practical minds improved upon traditional technologies. As metalworks grew larger, secretive masters and experienced hands jealously guarded the formulas of production they had developed in the furnace and the pit. Long before steel was produced by capital and labor in giant, steaming mills, it combined alchemy, destiny, wealth, and power. Ironmasters truly commanded these elemental forces. And individual ironmakers in turn transformed the economic specialization of their local communities into a dominant position in global markets.

During the eighteenth and nineteenth centuries, cast steel production brought new life to the dying English town of Sheffield. Iron and steel works later helped Pittsburgh grow from a trading center into an industrial city. After the Civil War, when Pittsburgh's employment in coal and glass doubled, it tripled in iron and steel. In the twentieth century, new fiefdoms of steel production were created around the world. The steeltown of Gary, Indiana, was privately built in 1906 by U.S. Steel and named for the company's president, Judge Elbert Gary. Three years later, Ernest T. Weir established a smaller steeltown in Weirton, West Virginia. The steel plant there became the core of National Steel when that corporation was established under Weir's presidency in 1929.

More than any other local industry including computers and automobiles, steel has historically enjoyed national stature. Steel is linked upward to the national government by warfare and international trade, and downward to the local manufacturing community as an emblem of economic power. After World War II, the governments of France, Italy, Japan, and Korea placed a new generation of integrated steel mills in coastal locations. Around them they built new communities, or rebuilt agricultural and fishing villages as steel communities.

By fact as well as symbol, steel signifies masculine power. The industry's raw materials are valued for their hardness, its finished products for their indestructibility. Until the recent mechanical age, lifting the weight of semifinished steel slabs demanded the muscular strength

and coordination thought characteristic of men. The heat and noise of
the blast furnace are, moreover, both elemental and infernal. The various "cooking" processes used over the years in melting metal and casting steel impose a demanding rhythm on working time. In the past,
firing techniques in an open hearth required workers to tend a single
batch of product around the clock. Throughout this century, shift work
has kept steel mills in continuous operation. Production is carried out
by night crews and overtime workers while wives and children sleep.
Only recently have women won the right to be trained and hired for
steel employment. Rosie the Riveter got inside the steel mills during the
domestic mobilization of World War II, a temporary inroad that was
not renewed until the 1970s, when the pressure of equal employment
opportunity laws permitted small numbers of women to become steelworkers. Automated production technologies now promise to make
steelwork easier for both women and men. However, the work force is
still predominantly male.

New recruits to the work force have usually taken the most arduous
jobs in the industry. In North America, Slavs provided a mainstay of
unskilled labor, replacing immigrant English ironmasters during the great
waves of immigration and rationalization in the second half of the nineteenth century. From the end of World War I until the Great Depression, African-Americans were employed in the least skilled jobs and as
strikebreakers. During the Depression, blacks and Chicanos lost disproportionately more work than white steelworkers. Those who remained
were given the hardest, most dangerous jobs in the coke ovens and blast
furnaces.[1]

Steelworkers and employers inhabit a male production culture. Since
the days of Andrew Carnegie and Henry Clay Frick, owners and managers have been brusque, forceful, often violent. If the worker was a
"man of steel," he faced no less an adversary than the "steel baron,"
surrounded by his hired security guards and hand-picked elected officials. In the famous strike that Frick incited in 1892 by banning all
labor unions from Carnegie's steel mill in Homestead, Pennsylvania,
hired Pinkerton guards shot down company workers and community
residents as they demonstrated in the streets. That incident set a standard for confrontation in the industry. Much of the force behind confrontation derived from the rough equality that steelworkers traditionally felt with their employers. The legacy of iron manufacture was a
craft-dominated production process in which highly skilled workers ac-

cumulated power on the basis of know-how and technique. When a monopoly of ownership confronted a monopoly of skill, the resulting power struggles centered on the privileges of craftsmanship.

"The road to Homestead," a historian says, "was clearly marked out by a single-minded intention to usher in the age of steel by burying once and for all the champions of the age of iron." As iron manufacture yielded to steel, owners took the opportunity to break men's wills by breaking apart the production process. Dividing the coherent craft of steel production into segmented, highly specialized tasks, they reduced the social difference between unionized craftsmen and unorganized, unskilled laborers. And by integrating the various stages of steel production on a single plant site that they controlled, they consolidated their authority over the entire work force.[2]

Even in public statements and negotiations with government officials, steel owners have always been more overtly confrontational than the leaders of other industries. Historically, they headed larger firms and directed bigger plants than other industrialists. Men confronting men in the first modern, large-scale production enterprises, with managers recruited—until the 1970s—for their knowledge of production: all this created a social context for steel's machismo. It also created an aura of autonomy. The local production site, an archetypal company town, was often isolated from other settlements and industries. While it was close to suppliers of raw materials, mainly coal and iron-ore mines, transportation nodes, and steady customers in local markets, the steeltown was a world in itself.

The key problem in all company towns, noted a 1931 article in the *Encyclopedia of the Social Sciences,* was the unified control concentrated in the employer's hands.[3] As the builder and owner of all housing in the town, the employer made housing tenure contingent on employment. Furthermore, as the investor in both housing and production, the company paid little attention to the amenities of town planning. As benefactor and moral authority, moreover, the company controlled such community institutions as churches and schools, and also compelled workers to buy exclusively from company stores. The employer's political control extended to judges, mayors, city councils, and the entire police force. A company town was closed to peddlers, labor unions, and any other employers who could possibly compete for the captive work force. Steel enforced the nineteenth-century landscape of paternalistic industrial power. Most company towns followed the model set by Pullman, Illinois, where only rental housing was made available to company workers. In the steel industry, however, companies encouraged workers to buy a home as early as the 1890s. Homeownership in a company town closed the circle of debt. It bound workers to a mortgage, but it also encouraged a sense of individual autonomy.[4]

The integration of all stages of production in the larger steel plants supported a real autonomy from nonsteel institutions. The self-sufficiency of an integrated plant, with on-site port and rail facilities, foundries, furnaces, coke ovens, and machining operations, provided the model for River Rouge, Henry Ford's industrial complex in Dearborn, where the Eagle boat, the Model T, and the Fordson tractor were all produced. Like the integrated steel mills, River Rouge represented the quintessential landscape of modern economic power. The way it dominated the landscape, as well as its technology and organization, suggested the very image of mass production.[5]

This image was widely diffused in its time. As early as 1908, the Pittsburgh Survey, financed by the Russell Sage Foundation, commissioned artist Joseph Stella to document conditions in the city's steel mills. Instead of the loss of human dignity that had been shown by photographer Lewis Hine in coal towns and textile mills, Stella showed the power and beauty of steel's large-scale facilities. This set a model for artistic representations of twentieth-century economic power. Fifteen years later, the photographer Edward Weston—now known for his detailed studies of natural forms and nudes—documented the buildings of the Armco Steel Plant in Ohio. In 1927, Elsie Driggs sketched the stacks and blast furnaces at Jones and Laughlin, which she turned into the painting *Pittsburgh*. From the late 1920s until 1936, Margaret Bourke-White made dramatic formal studies of industrial sites. Her photographs of Otis Steel, Rome Wire, Studebaker Company, the Aluminum Company of America, and pipeline and dam construction from Colorado to Magnitogorsk were widely seen in such new mass-circulation magazines as *Life* and *Fortune*.[6]

Commissions to Charles Sheeler and Diego Rivera resulted in an extraordinary amount of visual documentation of the industrial site at River Rouge. The fact that the Rouge became the most visible symbol of U.S. industrial power reflected the Ford family's modern style of patronage, which developed together with mass print media like *Life, Time,* and *Fortune* magazines and the advertising on which they relied. Sheeler was in fact recommended to the Fords by their advertising firm,

N. W. Ayer. Thanks to the Fords, and the artists they commissioned, the integrated auto plant emerged at the cusp of mass production and mass consumption.

Sheeler's painting *American Landscape* (p. 58) presents an exterior view of the Rouge in a horizontally layered panorama that recalls seventeenth-century paintings of the Dutch countryside. Like the plant itself, this view integrates most of the activities of production in a single, nonhierarchical landscape. In the foreground, barges deliver coal for the coke ovens and railroad cars take the finished steel away. Behind the rail lines are the sheds, the foundry, the stamping plant, and the bleeder stacks, built in various sizes and forms during the 1920s. Sheeler's paintings and photographs stress strong horizontal planes. Without a human figure in sight, they nonetheless convey a sense of the sheer scale of the works and the incessant movement of men and materials. This movement stretches outward beyond the bounds of both plant site and artistic representation: the steel plant suggests a world in itself, but one that is hardly self-contained.

The lateral movement in these landscapes contrasts with the verticality in Sheeler's photographs of the cathedral of Chartres, which were taken around the same time. They present a strikingly different image of power. A precisionist who admired the machine aesthetic, Sheeler viewed both Chartres and River Rouge as Gothic cathedrals. This led him to emphasize the similarity of their architectural forms. But his study of the intersection between chimneys and silo at the Rouge ("Criss-Crossed Conveyors," 1928) is much more dynamic than its formal counterpart at Chartres ("Flying Buttresses at the Crossing," 1929). Significantly, although he was surely no conceptualist, Sheeler submitted "Criss-Crossed Conveyors" to *Vanity Fair* as a "portrait" of Henry Ford.[7]

While Sheeler and most other artists of his time used exterior views to show the spatial and aesthetic forms of industrial production, the muralist Diego Rivera painted scenes inside the plant, on the shop floor and the assembly line. Yet the frescoes Ford commissioned from Diego Rivera convey the same sense of power as Sheeler's earlier photographs, which Rivera probably never saw. Diego Rivera's multi-paneled mural of the blast furnace at the Rouge (1933) is an interior landscape of economic power. It tells the story of steel production as we might imagine it:

In the fresco . . . the furnace has been tapped and the molten metal rushes out into an open sand trough and is diverted to a metal dam which separates the slag which floats on the top from the pure molten iron underneath. The slag and iron are diverted into two different sand troughs and captured in slag buggies which run on railroad tracks for transport. . . . The two workmen in the fresco hold long metal rods used to adjust the dam, pull metal gates to change the flow of the metal, and take samples of the molten iron. The drill used to bore into the furnace to release the metal is shown. . . . The flowing molten iron casts an orange light on the lower section of the furnace. The furnace is not altered in design or scale, nor are the billows of smoke and color exaggerated. Once the actual tapping process is observed, its similarity to a volcano is immediately recognized.[8]

There could be no stronger image of the immanent power of steel production. Control over the elemental force of fire is historically submerged in control over men and materials, transforming a chaotic topography into a coherent landscape of economic power. In this image, moreover, landscape and vernacular are one: the capital of the steel barons is inseparable from the force of labor and the culture of the local community. This *was* and *is* the landscape of Pittsburgh, or Youngstown, or Gary.

Behind this image of steel, however, lies an unresolved tension between power and autonomy. It foreshadows the question of who bears responsibility for the eventual decline of the U.S. steel industry. Does a powerful business like the steel industry really enjoy autonomy? Who is autonomous from whom, for which purposes, and for how long? Although we live in a time when place is subordinated to market forces, these forces may be mediated by noneconomic factors that curtail the autonomy of market actors.

Relative to those of other countries, the U.S. steel industry has always enjoyed great autonomy. The state never exercised direct control over the industry either by massive capital grants or by outright nationalization. Nor was output rigidly set by economic planning. Today, there is still no official industrial policy to expand the industry's share of domestic and foreign markets. And in contrast to steel producers in the European Community, the U.S. industry is not subject to supranational controls. Yet autonomy vis-à-vis government planning just fits market culture as it has developed in the United States. Steel producers also confront other elements of market culture—abstraction, globalization, and the shift from production to consumption—with which to some degree they have actively colluded.

As early as the 1880s, industrial elites in the steel city of Pittsburgh had already abstracted social and cultural power from the economic power of the landscape. They were eager to overcome their industrial origins by building the cosmopolitan culture of civic clubs, museums, and parks that they associated with great cities like Paris and New York, and integrating their children into national networks of the upper class.[9] Even the precisionists' aesthetic interest in steel mills may be understood as an *abstraction* of the economic landscape. It symbolized the beginning of the "postindustrial" denial of material production many years before industrial and financial elites articulated it.

Throughout its history, moreover, domestic steel was critically affected both by shifts in the state's fiscal and financial policy and by governmental scrutiny. Beginning with the trust-busting strategies of Progressive politicians, nearly every decade of the twentieth century brought new conflict between steelmakers and national political leaders. Government periodically chastised the steel industry because of its concentrated market structure, refusal to expand capacity, high wages (from the mid 1950s on), and noncompetitive pricing strategy. Perennially concerned about competition in overseas markets from international cartels, the steel industry lost out when Presidents Truman and Eisenhower aided the reconstruction of national steel industries in Western Europe and Japan.[10]

There is, all together, an enormous discrepancy between the steel industry's economic and cultural power over *place*—defined as a company town, a mono-industrial region, or the "social community" of the industrial sector—and its clear lack of autonomy from global *markets*. Thus the structured coherence of the modern industrial landscape has always reflected a fragile equation between autonomy and power.[11]

"FRAGMENTING" THE INDUSTRIAL LANDSCAPE

Between the 1880s and the 1920s, people took it for granted that steel output determined the strength of the national economy. Until 1901, in fact, the industry grew together with the nation's railroads and banking system. By virtue of close ties with firms in those two fields, steelmakers enjoyed unlimited access to capital. Capital was used both to expand production and to finance mergers and acquisitions in the industry. During this period, moreover, the steel industry had practically no competition from newer materials like cement and tile, which were still too untested to replace steel in construction. In terms of size, complexity, integrated facilities, and geographical isolation, the steel industry represented the totality of American manufacturing at a time when the power of the national economy became synonymous with industrial power. On a global as well as a local scale, a powerful steel industry was equated with national autonomy.

Yet even at the height of its growth, steel was never completely autonomous. A steeltown's local community was entwined with the growth of the national economy. Not only did the local community's survival depend on demand for basic steel products in other sectors and regions, but the firm that owned a steeltown also depended on finance capital and public policy. Each firm required, moreover, a stable work force in the locality and a regional network of steady customers and suppliers.

Government criticized steel for too much capacity in the early 1930s and for too little capacity ten years later, before American involvement in World War II, a shift that contributed to a "background of paradoxical experiences." [12] Uncertainty was deepened by steelmakers' mistrust of President Truman. After winning the presidential election in 1948, he espoused both populism and internationalism, leading to more public pressure on steel. Truman simultaneously threatened to nationalize the industry for lack of competition and pressed it to expand capacity. But he also insisted on global markets.

Since the 1950s, the social, political, and cultural base of the steel industry's autonomy has been eroded. Since the 1960s, and more drastically after 1973, the decreasing autonomy of steelmakers in product and capital markets has fragmented both the material power of the industry and its cultural power over place. In the United States, the phasing out of large-scale government construction of bridges and highways reduced domestic demand for steel. Overseas, fully competitive foreign-owned mills supplanted U.S. exports. In many products, steel was replaced, moreover, by cheaper, more flexible materials such as aluminum and plastic. In another process of substitution, domestically produced capital goods that utilized steel were themselves replaced by cheaper imports. With fewer U.S. makers of transportation vehicles, machine tools, and farm equipment, the market for domestically produced steel was further reduced. At the same time, commercial and investment bankers deserted the industry, pulled by the increasingly hectic pace and worldwide scope of their financial operations.

Since 1977, much of the U.S. steel industry has been downsized, diversified, become dependent on tariff protection, or filed for bankruptcy. Shutdowns have boarded up steeltowns across the Middle West from Buffalo to Pittsburgh, from South Chicago to Detroit. The industry work force, most of whom are represented by the United Steel Workers' Union, has steadily diminished: from 627,000 in 1970, to just over 500,000 in 1981, and somewhat more than 300,000 in 1983.[13] Almost each reduction in the industry has appeared as a historic trough. During the recession of 1974, for example, the May 27 issue of *Business Week* announced that steel employment had reached its lowest point since 1939.

In contrast to the troubles of large, integrated steel producers, mini-mills have prospered. These facilities usually specialize in the middle stages of steel production, eliminating both coke and iron ore production, as well as the fabrication of finer finished products. Most mini-mills are located in nontraditional steel markets of the Southeast, Southwest, and West. Since their origins in the 1960s, they have enjoyed the advantages of a lower cost structure and more "flexibility" than integrated plants. Mini-mills installed the most efficient new technology in electric arc furnaces, bought cheap, often imported, scrap, and paid lower rates, including production quotas and bonuses, for nonunion labor. This evidence of operating "lean and mean" attracted equity capital. Under public stock ownership, a multilocational mini-mill like Nucor has over the years aggressively expanded its plants and product lines to compete directly with larger producers.[14]

Signs of change have crept slowly into market culture. The work of the economist Simon Kuznets first shifted emphasis from the *production* of steel to its *consumption*. Not the former but the latter, according to Kuznets, indicates a nation's industrial strength. By the end of the 1940s—despite the period of heavy reconstruction that followed World War II—British economists had further challenged steel's structural role. Yet a full generation later, during the international economic crisis of the 1970s, U.S. Steel's president, David Roderick, complained that Americans were still so used to thinking of steel as the country's dominant industry, they couldn't face reality. "We're a $36 billion business in a trillion-and-a-half dollar economy," he said. "Now industries like autos and petroleum dwarf us."[15]

PUBLIC AND FINANCIAL PRESSURES

While steelmakers continued to attract publicity after 1973, much of the initiative in their sector had clearly passed to government, financial institutions, and steel consumers. As early as 1964, most people both within and outside the industry began to see that basic steel could be imported more cheaply than it was produced by the largest domestic firms that had historically controlled the U.S. market.[16] This realization changed the pressure on Big Steel—mainly from the federal government—both to expand capacity and to lower "administered" prices considered artificially high.[17] For years, many people in the public sector had thought that more steel mills and less concentration of ownership and production would lead to lower prices. Now, however, while the issue of expanding capacity was effectively mooted by international competition, lower prices were still very much on the public agenda.

Big Steel saw the agenda differently. As they saw it, the five or six largest firms in the industry could respond to international competition in one of two ways. They could either start a crash construction program to build more modern plants or diversify into nonsteel investments. Public discussion still blamed the steelmakers for refusing to lower prices to the level of imports. Nonetheless, Big Steel's strategy was also constrained by "outside" forces. The autonomy of industry leaders was limited by financial institutions on the one hand and by existing obligations on the other. During the 1960s, steelmakers grew increasingly dependent on banks and other financial institutions, like insurance companies, for short-term loans. These lenders were not keen to build more steel mills in the United States because they could get a better rate of return from other investments, including industry overseas. Nor did Big Steel itself find it easy to break free of precedent. A web of obligations mediated by the state—including the companies' financial obligations to labor, industry leaders' social obligation to set an example of toughness and tradition for the rest of the industry, and the ideological obligation to defend "free enterprise," which was readily shouldered by industry spokesmen—inhibited steelmakers from seeking to change the system.

But the big steelmakers did want some change. For a number of years, they had wanted to reduce rather than expand capacity. Since the mid 1950s, they had also toyed with the idea of diversifying—first by adding coal and iron-ore suppliers to their corporate organization, and then by shifting investment out of steel. Steelmakers were unable to downsize to the degree they desired, however, until import levels rose to crisis proportions. As in other countries, diversification outside steel was constrained, moreover, by industry tradition. Production-oriented managers stuck to steel as a source of both local and national economic power.[18]

By the mid 1960s, capital markets also tended to downgrade steel. Financial markets in these "go-go years" could practically name the conditions for capital placement. While assets controlled by financial markets increased, so did corporate debt, direct overseas investment, and loans to municipal, state, and federal governments in the United States and to foreign governments. Steel companies followed the trend toward increasing debt. At the same time, however, their ability to attract equity investors dimmed. This certainly constrained modernization. Nor could financial analysts and industry leaders reach an understanding on diversification. The decline in the U.S. steel industry's ability to raise capital partly reflected financial analysts' disillusionment. A worldwide recession had lowered foreign steel prices in 1958, and a three-month strike in 1959 cut domestic production. Partly too, however, the withdrawal of investors reflected lower rates of return on equity. Stock values in steel had already begun to decline.

The need to compete for external capital by offering high dividends caught steel firms in a vise. Global competition lowered profit rates on the one hand and demanded more flexible pricing structures on the other. "The world steel map," wrote the industry journal *Iron Age* at the end of 1959, "is going through an era of marked change. Possibly not since the rise of the U.S. as a manufacturing nation has there been a comparable period of shifting of the balance of power in steel production." Under these conditions, the autonomy of steel managers receded before that of financial institutions.[19]

The increasing costs of, and diminishing returns on, capital must have daunted steelmakers too.* Did this make steel investments less

---

* One of the long-standing problems with analyzing the steel industry—or for that matter, any business enterprise—is the reluctance of its leaders to make full disclosure of business data. As late as 1960, according to the economist Gardner Means, neither the industry nor individual firms had adequate data-gathering, forecasting, and planning methods. In

cost-effective, or did it merely intimidate corporate boards of directors and prevent them from taking risks? Through 1960, steel firms consistently outspent other domestic manufacturing sectors on capital improvements. Yet instead of going all out by building modern "greenfield" plants, they mainly "satisficed" by "rounding out" existing facilities. No single factor explains their failure to adopt innovative technology. Doubts about the efficacy of the new basic oxygen furnace may have influenced most firms to stick to the entrenched open-hearth technology. Or steelmakers may have been immobilized by their own power—in terms of the sheer size of assets frozen in existing plant. They would in any case think very hard about the high capital costs of building new greenfield plants for integrated steel production. These costs might be so high that they could never really be recouped by either lower operating expenses or increased profits.[20]

Because steel firms divvied up existing U.S. markets, they were able to justify forgoing investment in new technology by referring to specific market expectations. This circularity prevented markets being broken up by the construction of new integrated plants in the older industrial regions. In 1951, for example, industry leaders managed to destroy one of the very few proposals for modernization to come from outside the industry—a suggestion to build an integrated coastal plant in New England. The industry's reasoning was recapitulated in a feasibility study performed by an "independent" engineering firm. On the one hand, a new plant would merely rob market share from both the Bethlehem Steel plant in Baltimore, at Sparrows Point (where the fictional character Red Baker worked), and small producers throughout New England. On the other hand, a new plant would not be able to build up a critical mass of local customers, for nearby metalworking plants tended to spread their orders among different suppliers. According to conventional wisdom, it would be cheaper to install new plant in an existing firm. Tax laws on plant depreciation, market structure, and financing all favored the status quo. A New England steel mill was never built. Although regional political interests had lined up federal subsidies for construction from the Reconstruction Finance Corporation, the New England Steel Development Corporation was not strong enough to upset the veto power of industry leaders.[21]

1980, the steel analyst Robert Crandall notes, there were no published data on the costs of operating a new integrated carbon steel plant in the United States, making it difficult to evaluate steel companies' claims.

A slight window of opportunity for investment in modernization opened in the early 1970s before the 1973 recession. Under the Nixon administration, import restrictions and a currency devaluation gave U.S. producers more control over domestic markets. President Lewis Foy upgraded Bethlehem Steel's relatively modern plant at Burns Harbor, Indiana. The president of U.S. Steel, Edgar Speer, announced plans to build a huge new steel mill in Conneaut, Ohio. But the financial sector blocked these plans. Bethlehem's project was criticized in the business press. Several feasibility studies by financial institutions came to a negative conclusion on Conneaut, so that U.S. Steel could not raise the $4 billion required for construction. Perhaps the financial sector did not want to encourage the company to return to steel from its tentative efforts at diversification. Even this early, in the 1970s, U.S. Steel was deriving an increasing share of its revenues—at that point, around 40 percent—from activities outside of steel.[22]

While modernization faltered, and imports continued to gain market share, the steel companies faced paradoxical, periodic shortages of output. Their loss of control over product and capital markets, in a fragmented political climate, led them to modify their confrontational strategy toward labor. This strategy had inspired strikes throughout the postwar period, in 1946, 1952, 1956, and 1959. From 1960 on, however, the large unionized companies reached an expensive accommodation with the United Steel Workers' Union on wages and benefits. They did not match foreign firms, however, especially the Japanese, in cutting the labor time required for each ton of steel. U.S. steelmakers may have left work rules unchanged because of premonitions of labor unrest. Indeed, at the beginning of the 1970s, the steel and auto industries experienced a wave of both wildcat and planned local strikes. Within the steelworkers' union, the established leadership faced radical rank-and-file opposition.

This period proved fortuitous for labor demands. Contracts expired just when import competition eased and demand for steel increased. Further, the leadership of the steelworkers' union enjoyed a new legitimacy because of new national collective bargaining arrangements instituted after the long 1959 strike. On both sides, management and union leaders found it advantageous to attempt to achieve long-range peace through a "human relations" approach. In 1973, steel companies and the steelworkers' union adopted an Experimental Negotiating Agreement (ENA) that banned strikes in the industry. During this time, steelworkers enjoyed the fruits of apparent prosperity. Hourly steel wages rose more rapidly between 1968 and 1983 than those of any other U.S. manufacturing sector. Yet wages and dividends did not reflect real control over markets, for in this period domestic steel companies became dependent on government-imposed import controls.[23]

By the mid 1970s, the global market in steel made the loss of autonomy in national industry abundantly clear. Profit rates were decreasing, bottoming out in 1977. Production workers' hourly compensation, though rising everywhere, always looked cheaper somewhere else. Above all, in the United States, imports were taking a larger share of the market for all steel products, from structural steel and plate for construction to hot and cold rolled sheets for automobiles and appliances, and steel bars that could be put to many uses.[24] Despite their success in lobbying for import controls, the steelmakers were shaken by new governmental limits. They didn't like the price controls imposed by a Republican administration under President Nixon in 1973–74. Nor were they fond of new antipollution regulations that demanded expensive equipment. To some degree the competitive internationalization of steel production instituted similar constraints on all national steel industries. Even in Japan and Western Europe, traditional smokestack regions sought new means of preserving their way of life in a global market culture.[25]

But strategies chosen by foreign steelmakers were politically and ideologically barred to American companies. On the one hand, mergers to save money by consolidating facilities—the perennial proposal of the industry—were intensely scrutinized by the U.S. Justice Department, and were usually denied for violating antitrust regulations. On the other hand, capital infusions by the state—in the form of either equity capital or direct investment—were rejected by both steelmakers and politicians as a violation of free enterprise norms. Nor did government loans to finance modernization get unqualified approval. Unlike their colleagues in the Department of Housing and Urban Development (HUD), Commerce Department officials never supported these loans, and big steelmakers opposed them because they aided smaller firms. Under these conditions, relief from import competition by means of negotiated quantity restraints (1968) and controls based on "trigger" pricing (1978) represented the least costly resolution.[26] Some people criticized the steelmakers severely for becoming dependent on the federal government. Those who took the workers' side blamed corporate managers for insufficient modernization, little attention to marketing or product quality, disregard for customer service, and pricing that failed to compete with that of overseas producers.[27]

The consensus in the financial community, finally, was that if U.S. steelmakers persisted in producing steel, they were simply doomed. Steel profits were boxed in by cyclical swings in demand, imports, pollution controls, and heavy debt. Financial wisdom dictated a way out by diversification, as U.S. Steel had already begun to do in related fields. But this strategy demanded institutional reforms among steelmakers, reforms that would convert the material power of the industry into financial power. And this was chancy. "Steelmen are better industrialists than businessmen," the vice-chairman of Pittsburgh National Bank, in the heart of the traditional steel region, said. "Moving mountains turns them on more than making money."[28]

NATIONAL STEEL

If Wall Street couldn't change the industry, it would change the steel men. Finance capital would mediate the internationalization of the steel economy by means of low profit rates, disappearing dividends, and a relative scarcity of investment capital. This had to affect change at the very top of the industry. Executives of the major steel firms, whom the financial and political communities had seen for years as "arrogant, narrow-minded or just plain inept," were replaced by new CEOs. To enjoy the continued confidence of their boards of directors, who were responsible to both lenders and investors on Wall Street, these chief executive officers were expected to emphasize finance over production. From some points of view, even traditional steel barons had always paid too much attention to the bottom line. The switch in executive recruitment, however, shifted perspective. Now steelmakers were supposed to raise profit margins by decreasing their commitment to steel.

At National Steel, which by 1980 was the fourth-largest integrated steelmaker in the United States, the new CEO was Howard Love. Love, a sales executive with a Harvard MBA, had been raised in the old-line steel-and-auto network. His father had been vice-chairman of the board at National and chairman at Chrysler, one of National's major customers. Howard Love himself spent his whole career at National Steel. His colleagues David Roderick at U.S. Steel and Donald Trautlein at Bethlehem rose to the CEO's position from their firms' accounting departments. These three were generally discussed in the business press as bringing the new financial perspective into the industry.[29]

In 1980–81, his first year as CEO, Love enjoyed outstanding success. He persuaded the work force at the Weirton Division to give up their premium wage without a walkout. Independently organized since Ernest Weir's time in their own labor union, steelworkers at Weirton were paid more than United Steel Workers' members in other plants. Love may have modeled the rest of his program around the career of David Roderick at U.S. Steel. Roderick had ensured his promotion at the larger firm by ordering a feasibility study of potential shutdowns. This study led to the permanent or partial closing of fifteen plants and the elimination of 13,000 jobs at U.S. Steel. Love also announced a strategy of diversification and selective disinvestment from steel at National in order to provide competitive dividends to equity investors. But he publicly regretted that National chose this strategy "five years too late."

The financial strategy for managing National Steel nevertheless resulted in a 1982 plan to shut down the Weirton Division and a 1984 proposal to sell off half of Great Lakes Steel, National's division in Detroit. Weirton, of course, was the historic core of the firm. Although it provided about a quarter of corporate revenues, no one thought it could attract a buyer. By contrast, the fairly efficient facilities (by U.S. standards) at Great Lakes Steel, as well as its midwest location, attracted a buyer in Nippon Kokan, a large Japanese steelmaker that wanted to establish a production site in North America. National's new divestment strategy reaped early rewards. By 1983, the firm had reduced annual capacity from twelve to six million tons and eliminated 5,000 out of 16,000 employees. At that point, National was the only major U.S. steelmaker to report an operating profit. Significantly, the work force at National hadn't been this small since 1932. Love's ability to take the firm out of steel without a social upheaval impressed Wall Street. By 1984, when Love was praised as a "dazzling asset shuffler," steel contributed less than half—down from 80 percent—of National's revenues. In 1986, National again followed the example of USX (originally U.S. Steel), choosing a new name: National Intergroup.[30]

The path of National's last few years in steel is worth tracing in detail. In the corporation's 1981 annual report, officials described a familiar pattern of inadequate capital investment. The company budgeted only $1.3 billion in expenditures on its plant, mainly for replacement of existing equipment and mandatory environmental controls. This resulted in an investment "shortfall" of $360 million. Nor is it easy to find a real effort to develop either new markets or new products. National did announce that from 1982 on it would offer customers in the auto industry in Detroit new technical support services. But in light of poor prospects for flat-rolled steel, this must have been a temporizing gesture. Nor was National building up exports. Only 1–2 percent of all its shipments—mainly tin mill products from Weirton—were sold overseas. Furthermore, like other steel companies, National spent little on R&D. The company devoted just 1 percent of total sales to research and development in 1979, 1980, and 1981. Moreover, National showed the same pattern of desultory experimentation with nonsteel investments as in the rest of the industry. National had done a little joint marketing of coal with several other steel firms since 1951, dabbled in aluminum production since the mid 1960s, and distributed some products in steel service centers—that is, wholesale distribution points—since the 1970s. National also announced plans to build a new plant for aluminum foil production—in Europe—and sponsor some exploration for oil and gas.

Once it ventured outside traditional heavy industry, however, the company began to seem more dynamic. In 1980, National became a provider of financial services by buying United Financial Corporation of California for $241 million in cash. UFC doubled in size in 1981 by acquiring two savings and loan associations, in New York City and Miami Beach. That year, according to National's annual report, the company's long-term debt-to-equity ratio decreased from 36 to 31 percent.[31]

As National freed itself from being a steel producer, it even began to show a profit. With $300 million in its coffers from the sale of half of Great Lakes Steel to Nippon Kokan, and another $300 million available in tax credits, National became friskier in seeking acquisitions. Yet the merger that management offered stockholders in 1985 featured a takeover of National by the smaller Bergen Brunswig, a pharmaceuticals company from California, in return for only an exchange of shares. Howard Love justified this merger in the context of defending National from a hostile takeover attempt by Leucadia National Corporation, a maverick investment and insurance partnership.*

* An interesting feature of the merger, in light of the story of McLouth Steel in the next chapter, was the proposal for a "golden casket"—that is, a high-level death benefit sup-

Although Bergen Brunswig eventually withdrew from the merger offer, Love's defensive strategy in the proxy fight against Leucadia drew him into an equity-based alliance with Wesray, a private investment firm established by former U.S. Treasury Secretary William Simon. In this new deal with Wesray, National acquired the Permian Corporation, a crude-oil shipping company based in Texas. In return, however, National granted Wesray existing shares of stock as well as options on a significant number of newly issued shares. The deal made Wesray a 14 percent owner of National in 1986. Wesray also took two of the eleven board seats. In the maneuvering, National sold its 81 percent equity in First Nationwide Financial Corporation, which was doing well, to Ford Motor Company. Ford justified the acquisition as complementary to the auto business.[32]

Liberation from the constraints of steel production meant closer ties with the financial community. From this perspective, National's experience contrasted dramatically with that of the steeltown it left behind.

LOCAL COMMUNITY

By 1980, the steel industry's problems had changed in two key dimensions. For the first time, they were depicted as "structural" rather than caused by a cyclical "slump." The industry's problems were also individualized in terms of the steel-producing regions and towns whose reliance on a single, failing industry doomed them to extinction.[33] Attention focused on the Rust Belt of the Middle West. Within this area, a landscape of devastation was centered on the steel valleys around the Ohio, Monongahela, and Mahoning rivers in Ohio and southwestern Pennsylvania, the city of Buffalo, New York, and the dunes in northwestern Indiana. By contrast, steeltowns in the northern Great Lakes region retained some degree of cohesion because of their strategic location. They were located near iron-ore deposits and transportation, yet far enough away from ocean ports to lessen the impact of import competition. While communities in the Mon Valley now succumbed to Big

---

posed to act as a financial inducement to persuade Howard Love, then chairman of the board, and the president of National Intergroup to stay with the new firm, Bergen National, for the next ten years.

Steel's chronic underinvestment in modernization, the future of Great Lakes steeltowns looked somewhat less bleak.[34]

Between 1977 and 1980, steel companies shut down 5 percent of capacity. Although archaic plants were concentrated in just a few areas of the country, shutdowns affected them badly. Alan Wood Steel closed in Conshohocken, Pennsylvania. Bethlehem Steel closed plants in Johnstown, Pennsylvania, and Lackawanna, near Buffalo, New York. U.S. Steel both reduced capacity and shut down its plant in Torrance, California. Youngstown, Ohio, lost plants owned by Youngstown Sheet and Tube (part of the Lykes Corporation), U.S. Steel, and a newly merged Jones and Laughlin and LTV (Lykes-Temkin-Voigt). The human effects of these shutdowns were well documented in the business press, the national media, and radical newspapers. Mass firings, most without prior notice, idled thousands of steelworkers and reduced their families to living off welfare checks or spouses' lower earnings in jobs outside steel. Family quarrels, alcoholism, and violence, including suicides, mounted. Some observers noted that unemployed steelworkers utilized their skills in an endless renovation of their homes. No less immobile than most production workers, local managers now found themselves unable to keep up their leadership roles in local elites. Like the fictional country club in Western Pennsylvania that Rabbit Angstrom joins, elite institutions in steeltowns sought new infusions of capital by admitting townspeople who would not have been encouraged to apply before. While no large businesses moved into the shadow the blast furnaces still cast, many unemployed workers were eventually hired in the service sector, or went off on their own to do part-time work. In any case they had a net loss of income, which in turn increased demand on local social services.[35]

At the end of the 1970s, Youngstown represented in acute detail the array of problems a steeltown faced. A somewhat chaotic pattern of corporate ownership of Youngstown's steel mills indicated three factors behind simultaneous massive shutdowns. Corporate owners had engaged in trans-sectoral accounting that robbed steel to pay for diversification into oil and gas. Absentee control had minimized any regard for the locality. And multi-locational investment strategies had starved Youngstown's old plant to feed other facilities. Nor did the local community communicate effectively with the corporate world. While attention centered on the community's opposition to the shutdowns, it was difficult to establish negotiations between these remote, yet adversarial, bargaining partners. Neither side understood the local situation the same way. While the local community believed that at least one of the steel plants would survive because it made a profit, corporate leaders looked at things from another perspective.[36]

But local disappointment at Youngstown was transformed into local action. Grassroots protests against the shutdowns developed new forms of community mobilization. An initial long phase of trying to "save our plant" as a means of production segued into efforts to "save our valley" as a means of consumption. These efforts went beyond the organizational limits of labor union locals. Organizing "the community" meant mobilizing unemployed and retired production and maintenance workers, local management and sales staff, small business owners, local and regional banks, church groups, and spouses. Mobilization on the basis of local culture thus had an even greater effect than economic or workplace ties. Reminiscent of the great strikes of the nineteenth and early twentieth centuries, before labor unions were legalized, these community mobilizations against plant shutdowns expressed vernacular power.

Although supported by radical critics of the government and the capitalist economy, the local community rarely attacked capitalist institutions. In the Mon Valley near Pittsburgh, Pennsylvania, workers did boycott a local bank for not investing in the region. Peaceful community protest against a shutdown was supported by almost the entire panoply of Youngstown's elected officials, regardless of political party. Furthermore, local and regional members of Congress, representatives of "urban" interests, and liberal politicians with a national constituency all advocated aid to the steelworkers of Youngstown.

Officials in the most pivotal roles, however—the Democratic president, Jimmy Carter, leaders of the United Steel Workers' Union international, and municipal politicians—were either unable or unwilling to come to the steeltown's aid. Their absence from the Youngstown crisis contrasted with the key role played in the Chrysler bailout, around the same time, by the White House, the Treasury Department, and the United Automobile Workers' union.[37]

While the new awareness of structural crisis in the steel industry surely affected the form and degree of official involvement, other factors were also key. In Youngstown, each element of potential institutional support for the survival of the local community was too weak in some ways and too strong in others. While workers were fairly united on the goal of community ownership of the steel mills, neither the federal government nor local political organizations could accept this. Furthermore, as the community protest against shutdowns developed into a wider challenge to corporate control, it ignited hopes across the country. Yet for this very reason it failed to establish its legitimacy with the people and institutions who could make it work.[38]

The reasons are instructive. The community effort to save the Campbell Works, one of three steel plants in Youngstown due to be closed down, fell victim to competition between federal agencies and conflicting mandates within them. On one side, the Economic Development Agency (EDA) in the Commerce Department was mandated by Congress to guarantee and also provide small business loans, but it always ran the risk of being criticized, especially by big business, for aiding smaller firms that deserved to fail by market criteria. On the other side, HUD, the Department of Housing and Urban Development, which was more community-oriented, could provide limited investment capital for economic development through the UDAG (Urban Development Action Grant) Program. But HUD was always pressured by competing local interests. In the Youngstown crisis, HUD commissioned an economist, Gar Alperovitz, a critic of deindustrialization, to do a feasibility study of community ownership of the Campbell Works. HUD officials also expressed an interest in setting up a demonstration project for redeveloping obsolete industry in Youngstown. But HUD's authority was soon contested by EDA. In 1978, facing structural crisis in the steel industry, Congress had set up a $500 million loan program for smaller steelmakers and put EDA in charge. Continually pressed by congressional critics to take a tough stand against "marginal" firms, however, EDA got tough on Youngstown. The agency elbowed HUD out of its mandated control over UDAG grants and then rejected Youngstown's application.

The United Steel Workers' Union also failed to save Youngstown's steel plants. On the plant level, the union local at the Campbell Works opposed a community and worker takeover of the steel plant because it was "socialistic." A militant USW local at another plant, Brier Hill, failed to win support from the international union leadership. During the struggle over the Campbell Works, an ecumenical coalition of local religious organizations took the main organizational role from the steelworkers' union. But this coalition lost momentum after the withdrawal of two key denominations: the largely working-class Roman Catholics and the management-based Presbyterians.

Nor did local elected officials provide unequivocal support for community and worker ownership. In Youngstown, the local Democratic party and the business community both opposed a takeover of the Campbell Works. Similarly, in more highly urbanized South Chicago, where a series of three steel plant shutdowns shortly after the Youngstown crisis racked the community, white ethnic politicians and local union officials were either ineffectual or unwilling to reverse their traditional support for plant owners.[39]

Community opposition to the shutdown of U.S. Steel's Youngstown Works developed an interesting and partly effective strategy in litigation. The community sued U.S. Steel for violating their First Amendment rights by refusing to consider selling its property to the community. The community also sued the corporation for breach of contract in reneging on an agreement to keep the plant open if it showed a profit. At the end of the trial, the community scored when the judge counterposed the right of free enterprise, or *markets,* to the abiding obligations of *place.* In a novel statement from the bench, the judge issued the opinion that a community that depended on a single industry had its own property rights. These rights were broader and at least as historical as the owners'. "Everything that has happened in the Mahoning Valley," the judge said, "has been happening for many years because of steel[,] and schools have been built, roads have been built. Expansion that has taken place is because of steel. And to accommodate that industry lives and destinies of the inhabitants of that community were based and planned on the basis of that institution: Steel."[40]

The community's right was "perhaps not a property right to the extent that can be remedied by compelling U.S. Steel to remain in Youngstown," the judge continued, acknowledging the power of capital mobility. Yet U.S. Steel was not completely autonomous. The corporation could not simply "abandon" the community, because their entwined histories gave the community certain vested rights. This position lost on appeal. The appeals court upheld a dismissal of the property claim for lack of precedent. It also upheld a dismissal of the breach-of-contract claim because it was not "reasonable" for the workers to rely on a promise that mills would be kept open if they made a profit.

At bottom, Youngstown's survival was not a legal matter. It was both an economic and ideological challenge to existing market culture. A community buyout could not proceed without either reform in the ranks of capital or greater accommodation within the community to market norms. On the one hand, a community buyout needed capital to pay the seller, U.S. Steel, and no capital was forthcoming from either the U.S. government or the financial community. On the other hand, U.S. Steel did not find a community buyout either credible or desirable.

Yet only two years later, after National Steel had turned itself into National Intergroup, the community of Weirton, West Virginia, survived because of a worker buyout. When the work force bought the Weirton Division of National Steel on January 11, 1984, they saved roughly 7,000 jobs in a town population of 26,000. This was the first worker buyout in the U.S. steel industry, as well as the largest ESOP (Employee Stock Ownership Plan) of its time. The newly independent firm, Weirton Steel, immediately became the ninth largest steelmaker in the country.

How was Weirton able to maintain a landscape of economic power? Weirton, Youngstown, and South Chicago were all rooted in the same steeltown vernacular. Both the local community and the plants in all three places contained a large number of white ethnic groups whose grandparents and great-grandparents had come from Italy, Poland, Czechoslovakia, and England. Each town had, moreover, a similar local merchant community, whose business depended entirely on the steel mills' payroll. And each plant had a mainly unionized group of workers and a local management who shared the same production culture. Although Weirton was able to overcome the structural and institutional constraints on a steeltown's survival, it did so by accepting the same loss of autonomy that plagued the industry. This was not a choice offered Youngstown or South Chicago—or one they would necessarily have taken.

WEIRTON

Weirton's viability depended on two important factors that Youngstown and South Chicago lacked: a docile work force and a good investment banker. These created both the climate in which a worker buyout was doable and the conditions, both publicized and unspoken, of the deal itself. Whether they also worked to the community's long-term advantage remains to be seen.[41]

Workers at Weirton were doubly captive, but not underprivileged. During the paternalistic regime of the town's founder, Ernest T. Weir, a company union had been set up in the 1930s to prevent the work force from joining a more radical organization, the United Steel Workers' Union, which eventually became the industrywide bargaining agent. The Independent Steelworkers' Union represented the Weirton workers for fifty years, with neither labor strife in the plant nor rank-and-file dissidence in the union. Two reasons for the apparent harmony, as in southern textile towns, were job security at the mill and labor recruitment from a fairly tranquil working-class population. Despite the prior history some Weirton families had in West Virginia's turbulent coal-mining industry, both English and Slavic households contributed to the stability of the working-class community. Wages were another reason for stability, for Weirton workers had higher hourly wage rates than members of the national union. For these reasons they were regarded around the USW headquarters in nearby Pittsburgh as "Weirton Scabs."[42]

The Weirton work force were able to sustain a comfortable life. Many of them enjoyed homeownership, hunting in the countryside, and, until the 1970s, a social life typical of one-paycheck postwar households in which the male breadwinner drew a family wage. Before the worker buyout, production workers at Weirton earned between $35,000 and $45,000 a year, or $22 an hour. Sons often joined their fathers and uncles in the mill. Prior to the early retirements Howard Love negotiated in the early 1980s, the plant employed as many as 11,000 men from Weirton and its neighboring town across the Ohio River, Steubenville, Ohio.

Neither the town of Weirton nor the Upper Ohio Valley appears a likely candidate for postindustrial transformation. Throughout the buyout period, West Virginia had an unemployment rate of 19 percent, the highest of all fifty states. Coal mining—not an expanding industry— had seamed the land and piled up slag in the surrounding counties. A shopping mall some miles to the west of Steubenville had drained both that town and Weirton of most commercial activities—which were now limited mainly to the local dime store, coffeeshop, and bank. With 7,000 employees just before the buyout, the Weirton Division was the largest employer in the state. The town of Weirton is, in short, an archetypal industrial landscape. The chimneys of the steel plant's four blast furnaces dominate one end of Main Street, and viewed from the bridge across the Ohio River at the other end, the plant dominates the entire town.

Although the society of the Upper Ohio Valley was formed by industry, over the past thirty years this influence had begun to wane. As in most older industrial regions, both the occupational and the gender structure of the work force have shifted. While more than 47 percent of everyone who worked in Weirton and Steubenville had a manufacturing job in 1960, only 43 percent worked in industry in 1970 and 39 percent in 1980. During the same period, moreover, the number of men employed declined, and women entered the local work force in greater numbers. Between 1970 and 1980, women's share of employment in Weirton and Steubenville rose from 25 to 35 percent. Most women worked, however, in the slowly growing sectors of health care and education. Despite a slight shift of the entire occupational structure toward service-sector jobs, there were few managers and professionals, only around 5 percent of the work force. Even fewer jobs, around 3 percent, were in finance, insurance, and real estate. There has been, however, a steady increase in the number of technical, sales, clerical, and other service workers. This shift to lower-level service-sector jobs parallels the partial feminization of the local work force and the relative, as well as absolute, decline in industrial labor (both skilled and unskilled).[43]

In this landscape, a worker buyout of the steel mill can be viewed from two different perspectives. From a populist point of view, it is "part of a peculiarly American myth—a movie like Frank Capra's 'It's a Wonderful Life' . . . in which a town is threatened with calamity and the citizens band together to save it." This vision includes a July 4 demonstration down Weirton's Main Street in favor of buying the plant, whose publicity value was appreciated by Lazard Frères, the labor union's investment banker.[44] From a more conflictual point of view, however, a worker buyout is contradictory. The workers negate their class interest as producers by buying their employer. The source of capital for both buying and running a worker-owned plant remains borrowed funds from the financial community. Management retains control over day-to-day operations as well as a dominant voice on reinvesting profits. Especially when most worker buyouts in the United States impose wage concessions, boards of directors who are not controlled by worker-shareholders, and dependence on cross-class support from the local community, a worker buyout is a sellout of workers' interests.[45]

The Weirton buyout both avoided and repeated these generic patterns. It was from the outset a product of the 1980s mania for business restructuring. But while demands for capital mobility forced other firms toward wage restraints, asset sales, layoffs, and leveraged buyouts solely by investment banks or managers, the Weirton work force were able to use these pressures to save jobs without a loss of self-esteem. Under new ownership, Weirton even reversed National's pattern of cuts in capital spending. Referring to the total reorganization that simultaneously lowered the cost structure of the firm and freed National from its fixed investment, a management consultant from McKinsey and Company who worked on the Weirton buyout expresses admiration: "They've done what Continental Airlines [and many other firms] would like to do." Weirton is both like and unlike other firms. Although the new Weirton was among the first steelmakers to impose significant wage reductions in the 1980s, it was the first to do so by a worker buyout. Like leveraged buyouts by management in other fields, this worker buyout immediately resulted in new leadership in both management and the labor union local. But unlike many other cases of corporate restructuring, it led to a moderately happy ending.

What made Weirton exceptional was finding a golden mean: a general strategy for revitalizing the firm based on an "equality of sacrifice."* In the process, the buyout relied on both an economic and a political strategy. On the one hand, the reorganization of Weirton involved a calculation of how to cut costs with the greatest effect. On the other hand, it included a change of attitude from worker to investor that enabled most employees to acquiesce in the new firm's financial policy. An attorney from Willkie Farr and Gallagher who worked on the Weirton buyout refers to the development of this dual strategy as "a major educational process" for all concerned. "It was a big step," one of the investment bankers adds, "for the labor union to accept an *economic* basis rather than a *job* basis of decision making." This shift from a producers' to an investors' role is confirmed by the new president of the labor union, who was elected just as the buyout negotiations began. "This was the first time the union knew what things cost," he says, implying that sharing the company's financial information was a crucial step in broadening the workers' perspective.†

---

* This term, which most Americans would identify with Lee Iacocca's campaign for federal government loan guarantees for the Chrysler Corporation, initially derives from Felix Rohatyn's coordination of the fiscal restructuring of New York City's government in 1975. It thus affirms that variant of corporate restructuring associated with liberal Democrats whose advocacy of "industrial policy" implies no desire to do away with private capital markets.

† Just as he was elected because he was more in tune with the buyout strategy than the former head of the union, this president was himself replaced in 1988 when he backed management's plans to reformulate the terms of the ESOP.

The buyout process was lengthy and complex compared to most other acquisitions. Both work force and lenders had to be convinced. The terms of sale not only included the usual basic contracts between seller (National Steel) and buyer (the new Weirton Steel Corporation), but also projects for corporate governance through an ESOP, control of costs by means of wage and benefit reductions, and control of uncertainty for all parties—especially the lenders and the work force—by guaranteeing loan repayment and pension benefits. No matter how unconventional these arrangements were, preserving *place* at Weirton promised minimal disruption of underlying *market* forces.

THE DOABLE DEAL

The amount of cash that actually changed hands in the Weirton buyout was fairly small. To acquire all the assets of the old Weirton Division, with a book value of $386.2 million, the new Weirton Corporation paid National Steel $193.9 million, but it paid only $74.7 million right away. A note for a second payment installment of $47.2 million was due ten years later, with a final note for $72 million due in another five years, in 1998. The inflation rate at the time of the sale was high enough to make these payment terms compare favorably with a bank loan, especially since Weirton secured an interest rate of only 1.5 percent over prime. The lenders set up a revolving loan fund of up to $120 million. This was guaranteed by the new firm's agreeing to maintain at least $40 million in operating capital during the first year, and increase it later. The lenders also held liens on the firm's property and business assets.

The lead bank in the financing was Citicorp Industrial Credit, a Cleveland-based division of Citicorp. It was joined in the lenders' syndicate by regional banks in Pittsburgh and Detroit. One of the new firm's first actions was to draw $55 million out of the "revolver" to pay National as described above. An additional $35 million was withdrawn for start-up operating capital. An extraordinary feature of these loan arrangements—considering the financial prognosis for old plants in the steel industry—was that they required no government participation. Unlike Youngstown's failed attempt at a community buyout, the worker buyout at Weirton was done purely by "conventional" banking arrangements.

Less conventional were the noncash exchanges. With the age structure of the Weirton work force weighted toward middle age, pensions were a major cause of concern. Although National owed the workers a total of $770 million in pension benefits, the company had funded only $350 million of its obligation. This was an especially shaky period in the steel industry's pension situation. Other firms—notably the troubled Wheeling-Pittsburgh and LTV, which filed for Chapter 11 bankruptcy protection in 1987—did not face the crisis of underfunding well. They threatened to withdraw federal government funds from the Pension Benefit Guaranty Corporation, an agency that ensured retirement benefits. But Weirton and National resolved this serious problem themselves by exchanging future obligations. Weirton assumed $192.3 million of National's liability; National agreed to pay pension benefits if the new Weirton failed within the first five years. National also agreed to buy a fixed share of Weirton's sheet steel (for use at Great Lakes Steel) in return for supplying some semifinished slabs.

There was no way to know in advance whether these terms would be accepted by either party, or whether—in contrast to Youngstown—financial institutions would be willing to get involved. High levels of risk and uncertainty made each step of the negotiations both more onerous and more dramatic. These conditions reinforced the importance of the outside consultants hired to advise the work force. Practically the first question that emerged when a buyout was suggested was whom to hire and who would exercise control. All sides were aware that experienced consultants could end up in the driver's seat, controlling those who had hired them. Hiring consultants was done by a Joint Study Committee that represented the buyer in the deal. This committee was made up of the labor union's executive committee and Weirton Division management. Forming a joint labor-management committee alone shook previous alignments at the plant.

The idea to sell Weirton to the work force was apparently born as a follow-up to Howard Love's divestment strategy. This strategy, insofar as it affected Weirton, was publicly announced after a National board of directors meeting in March 1982. After Love announced that all investment in Weirton would cease, he went immediately to West Virginia to consult with Governor Jay Rockefeller. After the meeting, Rockefeller flew to Weirton with three of his aides to offer the services of the state's director of economic development as a liaison to National. The next day, J. G. Redline, Weirton Division president, suggested to the labor union that they form the Joint Study Committee.

Through Redline, National's board of directors communicated to the work force at Weirton that the board had three choices. First, National could shut Weirton down—which would be feasible, but expensive, given federally mandated shutdown costs. Second, National could sell the plant—if there were only a buyer. Third, National could keep the plant open by either "milking" it for cash or turning it into a finishing mill, which would eliminate about 6,000 of the 8,000 jobs. Faced with these alternatives, the labor union and division management joined together to study a worker buyout. This was, in fact, the choice preferred by National's management consultants. The two-step buyout procedure lasted eighteen months, from March 1982 to September 1983. The first step, after months of negotiations, set the terms of the buyout deal between the Joint Study Committee and the parent firm. The second and final step was taken when the work force voted on whether they should accept these terms.

No decisions could be taken by the Joint Study Committee entirely on its own. National's management consultants, who had advised the corporation to sell the Weirton Division, also recommended that the Joint Study Committee begin by hiring its own consultant. They suggested Alan Lowenstein, an attorney from northern New Jersey, who had shepherded the worker buyout of Hyatt Clark from General Motors. But Lowenstein lasted only a couple of weeks at Weirton. The reasons for his dismissal influenced negotiations as well as the future shape of the deal.

Significantly, Alan Lowenstein alienated the labor union by suggesting that he didn't see his role as working for it. He wanted to work instead for the new firm's board of directors, which he thought he should select himself, together with Governor Rockefeller. He also insisted that the new firm needed new management, although this was a difficult step for both union and management to take right away. The most unacceptable condition for the union, however, was Lowenstein's ultimatum that the workers forgo voting rights on the stock each of them would acquire through the ESOP. Lowenstein insisted on "pass-through" (i.e., compulsory proxy) voting for the first ten years, during which time the board of directors would exercise full control. Nearly as unpalatable was his suggestion that the company didn't need its own coke plant (a source of jobs that ultimately became the subject of lengthy negotiations), as well as his proposal to transform Weirton from a steel mill to a service center for the German firm Thyssen Steel. The final straw, as far as the union was concerned, was Lowenstein's failure to disclose his full financial and personal relations with National Steel.

Dave Robertson, the Weirton-born local attorney for the Independent Steelworkers' Union, decided that the Joint Study Committee had to strike out on its own. Robertson called on friends and acquaintances, his reading of the business press, and recommendations he gathered during a trip to New York City. By means of these efforts, the Joint Study Committee ultimately chose McKinsey and Company as its management consultant and Willkie Farr and Gallagher as its legal consultant. Finally, after a well-placed contact said, "If you have cancer and are willing to admit it publicly, go for Felix Rohatyn," it appointed Lazard Frères as its investment banker.

Hiring outside consultants was a crucial departure in the grassroots strategy for Weirton's survival. While locals took some time to digest the hefty fees charged by these "New York firms," the consultants individually and collectively provided the credibility, political strategy, and publicity on which the entire deal relied. McKinsey is a distinguished international management consulting firm, which had already recommended to British Steel that it reduce steelmaking capacity. But the McKinsey team that went to Weirton was committed to both the plant's survival and the long-term viability of U.S. industry. Willkie Farr is a large corporate law firm with expertise in mergers and acquisitions. Its attorneys were also committed to Weirton's survival. Lazard is a case by itself. Senior partner Felix Rohatyn became an unofficial spokesperson for liberal Democratic industrial policy during the Carter administration. Since that time, his advocacy of restructuring for domestic industry has always included three elements: downsizing capacity, increasing capital spending for rebuilding (private) plant and (public) infrastructure, and fostering mutual accommodation between capital and labor. In a calmer, less risky atmosphere than currently prevails, much of the restructuring Rohatyn envisions could be financed by private capital markets. Similarly, in his view, less volatile capital markets go hand in hand with a more stable international economic order.[46] While Rohatyn himself never met with Weirton representatives, his general views on the industrial economy appealed to the Joint Study Committee. Consequently, the image of Rohatyn shaped the worker buyout—and gave it, from the moment Lazard was hired, a certain *éclat*.

Lazard's representatives at Weirton worked with Rohatyn. Eugene

Keilin, who had assisted him in setting up the Municipal Assistance Corporation in the 1970s to manage the fiscal crisis of New York City, was eventually elected to the new Weirton's board of directors. Josh Gotbaum, who had worked under Rohatyn for a year and a half, had previously been a member of the domestic policy staff at the White House during the Carter administration. In that role he had some experience with Youngstown and Wisconsin Steel in Chicago. Keilin and Gotbaum thought Weirton's market opportunities were fairly positive. The company had a good reputation for high-quality tin plate and galvanized steel products, and it had a decent share of the domestic market for them, along with U.S. Steel and Bethlehem. The problem was that these markets were generally declining, with newer materials rapidly being substituted for steel. Moreover, profit rates were low. In seven of the ten years preceding the buyout, the Weirton Division had made a profit, but profit levels were not high enough to pay for modernization. For four of these ten years, in fact, National had shifted the costs of capital improvements at Weirton to other divisions. Around 1980, while National was deciding to stop further investments in Weirton, the division's annual profit margin was roughly 1 percent. (At the time, profit margins in the steel industry averaged around 3 percent.) In hot and cold rolled products, which were sold to the auto, construction, and appliance industries, Weirton suffered from the one-two punch of structural decline. On the one hand, it lost market share to midwestern and overseas competitors; even National allocated more of these orders to Great Lakes Steel than to the old Weirton division. On the other hand, decline in domestic makers of capital and durable goods reduced Weirton's potential market.[47]

All in all, despite the absence of other buyers, Lazard believed the workers' bid to purchase Weirton should attract a commercial lender. Weirton's plant was sufficiently modern to produce competitively—although it needed about $1 billion in additional capital investment, beginning with pollution control devices, relining its four blast furnaces, and installing a second continuous caster so that all its steel could be continuously cast. Lazard also thought the plant generated adequate cash flow to meet a lender's criteria. Nevertheless, neither the Weirton work force nor their advisers could afford to take a chance that no lender would appear. As one of the Lazard representatives points out, the effort to save Weirton had three strikes against it. It was in the steel industry. The plant was under new management. And it featured a worker, rather than management, buyout.

While Lazard "played the Rohatyn card," "gloomed and doomed it" with the work force to avoid raising their expectations, and drew the national media to Weirton to document local community support, the consultants from McKinsey hit upon the necessity of making a dramatic gesture. In its feasibility study, which was the first consultants' action to have a real impact on the work force, McKinsey demanded that the workers take a 32 percent cut in financial compensation. Otherwise, the McKinsey team insisted, the new company just wouldn't stand a chance. Besides the specific cost structure of the plant, the capital structure of other steelmakers, and Weirton's market situation, McKinsey's calculations took in three strategic factors. First, it looked at the industry leader, U.S. Steel, and figured that Weirton had to come in *on the low end* of U.S. Steel's cost structure across the *whole range* of its plants. Second, it thought the new firm would have a better chance to succeed if the workers didn't take *halfway measures;* in other words, it had to avoid fairly tolerable wage cuts of 10 or 15 percent, which might generate insufficient savings and thus cause the new firm to fail. Third, in a strategy dovetailing with Lazard's calculated appeal to potential lenders, McKinsey thought that a heretofore *unprecedented wage cut* of 32 percent—or a reduction from, say, $20 to $14 an hour— would have a tremendous *political* effect. It would shock the work force into realizing the seriousness of their situation, and make them that much more committed to both a worker buyout and the new firm. In more objective terms, McKinsey defended this attack on financial compensation because labor costs represented "the *only* category of Weirton's steelmaking costs that was large enough and controllable enough to provide the margin of improvement needed" for cash flow and an equity base.[48]

As things worked out, financial compensation was reduced by only around 20 percent. But the symbolic effects of *announcing* a 32 percent cut were just as dramatic as the consultants had planned. "The big difference between Weirton and Youngstown," says one of the investment bankers, "is the [Weirton] workers' willingness to sacrifice. At Youngstown, the feasibility study [done by Gar Alperovitz] was completely unrealistic *because it said the workers wouldn't have to sacrifice anything.*" Not for nothing did the McKinsey team consider themselves the "shock troops" of the Weirton buyout. Workers did exchange present financial benefits for future power in the ESOP. But this power was heavily contingent on the new firm's survival, and also on moderation, gradualism, and the desire to filter the workers' interests through appropriate channels. As an investor, the labor union had to work through its executive committee, which sat on the Joint Study Committee, and eventually through labor's three representatives on the new board of directors. As wage earners, however, the work force could continue to press demands through the union.

Alan Lowenstein, the short-lived consultant at Weirton, had initially suggested that the ESOP feature pass-through voting. The eventual ESOP proposal ironically did just that, but limited it to only the first five years. At that point, the ESOP stock would be distributed to all participants who requested it, and a one-person / one-vote referendum would be held on whether the stock should be sold to anyone other than a Weirton employee (i.e., whether the company should "go public"). The work force would not enjoy full voting rights to elect the ten to fourteen members of the new board of directors. Instead, a feature of pass-through voting was that the ESOP trustees who held the stock also chose most of the board. Only three directors would be nominated by the union, and another director's seat would be taken by the CEO. The company could issue seven million shares of stock, with six and a half million acquired right away by the ESOP trust, which would essentially own the firm.

Nor would all workers and employees own equal shares of Weirton. Although Lazard, Willkie Farr, and the Joint Study Committee all began by supporting distribution of equity on an *equal* basis, they were led by the tax laws on ESOPs and financial considerations to support a *proportional* distribution of stock according to level of compensation. Thus employees who earned higher salaries—management, in short—would own more shares of the ESOP trust. The influence of the wage hierarchy reflected the provisions of the 1974 congressional legislation that established ESOPs as a special sort of pension plan. According to ERISA (the Employee Retirement Income Security Act), a company can deduct from its taxable income the entire amount of money it pays—both in principal and interest—to acquire stock on an ESOP loan, but it can only deduct up to 25 percent of the payroll. This percentage is not calculated on the entire, aggregate payroll. Instead, it is calculated on the basis of the lowest compensation. Therefore, the attorneys from

Willkie Farr concluded, Weirton would have to follow the example set by all other ERISA buyouts except Hyatt Clark. For the new corporation to take maximum advantage of an ESOP's tax-sheltering benefits, the buyout had to be structured in a hierarchical way. So the original rallying point at Weirton, equal ownership, was converted into the far more subjective concept of equal sacrifice.

Countering these conditions was another, more positive contingency. As long as Weirton made a profit, and had a net worth of $100 million, profit-sharing could begin in two years, as early as 1985. At that point the work force could choose to distribute 33 percent of the profits to themselves. And when net worth reached $250 million, as much as 50 percent of annual profits could be paid out as dividends. These provisions on profit-sharing, relatively high for an ESOP, would assuage the work force for the wage reduction proposed by McKinsey.

Despite all these complicated assurances, it was not easy to attract a commercial lender. Publicity surrounding the local community's support helped a great deal, especially when Lazard emphasized that local donations paid its consultant's fee of over a million dollars. (A small portion, $125,000, was also paid by the Economic Development Administration of West Virginia; before this money was found in the state budget, Governor Jay Rockefeller had personally guaranteed it.) Negotiations with several banks finally resulted in the major share of the deal being taken by one of Citicorp's units for leveraged buyouts and asset-based loans, although it did so, according to another participating commercial banker, "for public relations reasons." This banker expressed worry that his own regional bank "could get in trouble" for loaning money to Weirton. Whether he was expressing a banker's prudence or a preference for going with the flow of international economic power, he thought industrial loans should support a global regime of free trade. At that moment, in his view, "employment in South Korea [was] more important than employment in Weirton."

But the banks did have solid financial reasons for accepting the Weirton deal. As in all risky cases, they insisted on issuing an asset-backed loan. On the lookout for "controls" in case of failure, they would be able to seize the firm's assets—cash, buildings, materials—and get out. In the short run, the banks demanded the right of daily review of cash-flow figures. If the cash flow fell below an agreed-upon point, the banks could declare the loan forfeit. In the long run, assurances to the banks included controls on labor: notably, a no-strike clause and a wage freeze during the term of the labor contract. Most important, while the collective bargaining agreement was to remain in effect for the new firm's first six years, the loans were extended for only five—ensuring that labor conditions remained the same throughout the term of the loans. Loaning to an ESOP trust was, finally, good business for a bank. According to the 1984 Deficit Reduction Act passed by Congress shortly after the buyout vote, banks can deduct 50 percent of the interest payments on ESOP loans from their taxable income.*

Most of the work force found these terms more satisfactory than risking their underfunded pensions or their jobs to oppose the worker buyout. National news stories featured local people—a hairdresser, a pensioner, the wife of a laid-off worker—marching to support the buyout under the slogan "We Can Do It." But between March 1982, when Howard Love strongly pushed Weirton workers to buy the firm, and the vote on the buyout in September 1983, nearly unanimous community support confronted uncertainty within the work force, dissidence, and even lawsuits against the Joint Study Committee.

A dissident Rank-and-File Committee worked out of people's houses and a community legal services office in Steubenville. This fifteen-man group included both white and black workers, and both production workers who had been laid off and others who were still actively employed. Over the year and a half of buyout discussions, they articulated dissatisfaction with the buyout procedure, disaffection from both local management and the union, and some radical criticism of racism, politicians, and the capitalist system. They were conscious that all the national publicity put them "in a pivotal position" and convinced, moreover, that a worker buyout was tantamount to "political suicide" for the working class. While they didn't mind being described as radicals, as a member who worked on the pouring platform in the steel mill says, the Joint Study Committee and the outside consultants saw them as just a small, intransigent group fighting over spurious issues.

The Rank-and-File Committee formed to express opposition on three strategic points. They wanted to express disappointment that the labor union had relinquished an adversarial position vis-à-vis National and division management. They also thought there should have been more critical discussion of the ESOP and less rah-rah community mobiliza-

---

* Continuing the precedent set by ERISA in 1974, this law also excluded dividends paid on stock held in ESOP trusts from corporate taxes and extended other tax benefits to various stock transfers that an ESOP may do.

tion. If the ESOP passed, they wanted to ensure maximum benefits for workers marginal to the new firm—that is, laid-off workers and those who would take early retirement. Furthermore, the rank-and-file dissidents called for preliminary polling of the entire labor force prior to the final referendum on the buyout. They sought more public disclosure of financial data and projections—especially the proprietary model of industry analysis from which McKinsey derived the proposal for a 32 percent pay cut. In general, the Rank-and-File Committee thought the work force had come out badly on the deal: paying too much for National's old assets, letting National walk away from pension liabilities, and giving up too much in wages and benefits.

The committee's "modus operandi centered on getting more information out to the workers," a member says, and also on delaying the buyout procedure by litigation. Not only did this challenge the strategy pursued by the Joint Study Committee, it also lengthened an already time-consuming process. During 1982 and 1983, one of the legal consultants recalls, there were presentations and discussions at fifty-five meetings in the plant and one meeting held at a large arena. All this, as the dissidents implied, built up to a single denouement programmed by the Joint Study Committee: the final buyout vote in September 1983.

While the dissidents won none of their three lawsuits or the appeals, they felt they won on the political issues. One case, *Gregory v. Bish,* resulted in extension of the right to vote on the buyout to laid-off workers who had a right to be recalled to the plant. Another case, *Bauman v. Bish,* publicized the demand for greater disclosure of McKinsey's data. The third case, *Gilliam v. Bish,* concerned full disclosure of the terms of the new collective bargaining agreement—although Walter Bish, who was then the new president of the Independent Steelworkers' Union, and the attorney Dave Robertson say that the entire agreement was not yet ready for inspection. After this suit was filed, the union nonetheless released a thirty-page description of proposed contract changes.

Other lawsuits—filed by individual workers Sutton, Bruno, and Dahrer—went to the heart of the pension question as it affected both union and nonunion workers. The national steel industry had for some years accepted two norms of eligibility for retirement benefits in extraordinary business circumstances. The "70/80 Rule" and the "Rule of 65" potentially increased retirement benefits, or made them available, when jobs were eliminated—but only in case of a shutdown. Under the 70/80 Rule, employees could enhance their seniority status by adding their age to their years of service. Under the Rule of 65, the shutdown of an entire plant or even a department would permit a worker at retirement age to draw a full pension; until the age of 62, an employee whose employment was severed under these conditions would receive a monthly shutdown supplement of $400. Consequently, Weirton workers who were close to retirement age before the buyout wanted to leave the firm—but only on condition that the sale of the plant was legally construed to be a shutdown. Because 3,000 workers and employees had sufficient age and service to qualify for retirement according to the 70/80 Rule or the Rule of 65, this lawsuit posed a worrisome challenge to the new company's fragile financial resources. Again, however, the plaintiffs won neither the trial nor the appeal.

In September 1983, the work force voted by a seven-to-one margin to buy the plant. As in many cases of corporate restructuring, one of the first steps was to dismiss the old division president. The former CEO was held responsible for bad shopfloor labor-management relations, and he was considered to be too committed to Weirton's traditionally conservative marketing strategy. The new board of directors chose Robert Loughhead, who had been president of the Copperweld Steel Company in Warren, Ohio, to be the new CEO. Loughhead immediately launched a new "participative" management style, much in keeping with both the spirit of the Weirton buyout campaign and a national trend in heavy industry toward more cooperative labor-management production committees. In another innovation, Loughhead recruited production workers to make sales trips to potential customers. And he even installed a telephone hot line for workers' complaints.

Despite a new management style, a worker-dominated ESOP, and a consensus on cutting labor costs, the union faced hard negotiations on job issues typical of the 1980s. While job classifications were not changed, as Dave Robertson says, there was a good deal of "salary compression." Work rules, moreover, remained a most sensitive area of negotiation. Weirton workers were well aware that crew sizes were being cut everywhere in the steel industry, and that, according to the McKinsey report, which they had adopted, they had to continue cutting costs *more* than their competitors. So changes in work rules were carefully hedged. According to the 1984–89 collective bargaining agreement, if management eliminates a job with four incumbents, it has to offer workers the option of early retirement. The labor union retains the right to demand arbitration on changes in the work rules. Yet while these rules, and national norms like the 70/80 Rule, will stay intact, the union has no assurance that it can win in plant negotiations on either crew size or job elimination. Nor has the union won any of the cases on work rules that it has brought to arbitration since 1980.

Another major problem Weirton workers faced was capital investment for modernization. For the most part, the new Weirton management planned to fund an investment program of $100 million a year for the first five years by reducing operating expenses. (Toward the end, National was investing only $34 million a year at Weirton.) The company had to buy new equipment to comply with federal antipollution regulations, and modernize the hot strip mill (which alone would cost $225 million). It was initially proposed, moreover, that Weirton should buy a new, second continuous caster, at a cost of $250 million, in order to compete with planned modernization at Bethlehem and Inland Steel. But when Robert Loughhead was replaced as CEO by Herbert Elish in 1987, the new president decided merely to upgrade the 20-year-old caster, at a savings of around 80 percent. Another choice concerned whether to reopen Weirton's coke plant, with the possibility of restoring at least 300 jobs, or buy cheaper coke from abroad.

Another key goal was building up an equity base in order to attract future lenders, as well as provide returns on the ESOP investment. McKinsey's estimate of the equity or net worth that would be required was $200 million. Yet when the company reached a net worth of $250 million in 1988, the 50 percent profit-sharing arrangement went into effect. The average bonus came to $9,000 a worker, and the degree of profit-sharing now seemed to management to be out of line with capital spending requirements. This combination of factors, in addition to the company's liability to buy back stock that workers might want to cash in, led the Elish management to propose unexpected changes in the ESOP. CEO Elish, who had been placed on the board in 1984 as an outside director, insisted upon cutting back capital spending by not buying a new continuous caster. He also proposed cutting profit-sharing back to 33 percent of profits and selling up to 20 percent of equity on open financial markets. Finally, management wanted a 12 percent reduction in the plant's 8,000 jobs, to be accomplished by means of attrition.

Such business problems as capital spending, marketing, and developing a flexible product mix to compete with plastics and aluminum, now occupied the foreground of labor-management negotiations. These issues tie the work force as investors more directly to the plant than ever before. Yet as employees, they have neither permanent job security nor control over management decisions. Any attempt to resolve the economic problems of the firm brings stronger ties with private market forces. This is especially true because of the company's continued dependence on financial markets, where Lazard Frères continues to act as a mentor.

All the outside consultants made Weirton workers aware of the importance of giving the financial community "guarantees." But there are no guarantees about the effectiveness of continued investment, and continued sacrifice, in the steel industry.

Will the new Weirton keep enough operating capital to satisfy the lenders and stay afloat?

Will management use its daily, operational control to fire workers or otherwise subvert their interests as producers and wage earners in order to gratify their interests as capital investors?

Will workers, for their part, press demands they know will alienate financial institutions?

If Weirton fails, what will happen to workers' pensions?

If workers are eased out of their majority share in the ESOP, what will happen to cooperative labor-management relations and productivity?

And in the regional context, would the state of West Virginia—suffering continued job loss in coal mining, glass, and chemicals—be devastated by layoffs at Weirton, the largest employer in the state?

THE NEW STEEL LANDSCAPE

By the time the Weirton buyout was voted in 1983, wage concessions had become a normal part of the industry pattern. No other worker buyouts of steel plants were being planned. Within two years, National Intergroup had almost completely divested itself of steelmaking facilities; Great Lakes Steel was run mainly by the Japanese. By this point, both U.S. Steel and Weirton were buying semifinished slabs from overseas mills. These conditions suggested a very limited autonomy for U.S. steel producers.

In a moderately happy ending at Weirton, however, the firm finished its first year under worker ownership with a sizable profit. Weirton made the second highest annual profit in the industry, after U.S.

Steel. In 1985, it achieved its goal of increasing net worth to $100 million—the kick-in point for distributing 33 percent of annual profits. The company has continued to make a profit every year since then. And net worth, as we have noted, reached $250 million in 1988.[49]

Weirton's profitability contrasts with National's failure. National Intergroup did show a profit in both 1983 and 1985, with the latter credited to oil and gas (via the Permian acquisition). From that point, however, the diversification strategy—into financial services, then oil and gas, and finally wholesale pharmaceuticals distribution—cut profits to zero and piled up debt. Institutional investors and investment bankers forced several changes. Howard Love was no longer chairman of the board by 1990, although he remained CEO. A new outside director with few ties to Love—the former chairman of the board of Westinghouse—became a serious "inside" critic of all corporate decisions. National continued to attract attention as a potential takeover target. Yet all the corporate raiders insisted that the corporation sell National Steel, which they saw as a permanent drain on profits. This pressure resulted in a transfer of more equity to NKK of Japan in 1990.[50]

For the outside consultants, the Weirton buyout aided careers. The new board of directors at Weirton included the union attorney Dave Robertson and Eugene Keilin from Lazard. At Willkie Farr, the lead attorney on the Weirton buyout was promoted to partner. *Institutional Investor* named the Weirton buyout one of the deals of the year in December 1983. And the public relations firm Hill & Knowlton Inc. named the labor-management program under Loughhead one of the nation's best.

While workers at Weirton didn't notice any great change in life at the plant, especially in shopfloor participation, they felt they had secured the paramount goals that Dave Robertson describes. First, they didn't lose their pensions. Second, the real estate values of their homes didn't decline. And third, the worker buyout kept their families together. Significantly, these achievements are all connected to workers' roles as *consumers*. By the end of the first five-year labor contract, however, the Weirton work force were still trading off their interests as producers to satisfy investors' demands. This could be justified, as management was likely to do, by distinguishing between the workers' short-term interest in recouping five years of wage concessions and their long-term interest in the firm's, and the community's, survival. Maintaining employment levels required maintaining the firm's viability in financial markets. In this the work force had to follow the lead of the global financial institutions integrally connected with Weirton's corporate strategy as lenders and members of the board.

Significantly, the federal government did not play an instrumental role in saving either the steel plant or the local community. From the outset, Weirton's consultants shied away from direct federal involvement. Following National's divestment decision, Governor Jay Rockefeller did play a supportive role. He may have been helpful because of his Democratic party affiliation, or because he wanted to run for the U.S. Senate. He arranged an early meeting on Weirton in the state capital, where elected officials from the area promised all their help. Yet in the end, neither they nor the state's congressional delegation—which included the then Senate Democratic leader, Robert Byrd—provided substantive aid. At the time, of course, despite finally supporting steel import quotas in 1984, with an explicit requirement of capital investment in modernization, the conservative Republican administration of Ronald Reagan wanted troubled industries to submit to "market" criteria. This meant that government wanted some firms to fail.

Besides import quotas, Weirton benefited from three subsidies that did not require direct government expenditure. The West Virginia Economic Development Agency wrote special legislation that was passed by the state legislature, reducing Weirton's taxes by the amount of the ESOP contributions. This resulted in an annual savings of half a million dollars. By forgoing these taxes, the state of West Virginia subsidized the workers' purchase of equity in the new company. Further, the regional Air Control Board of the federal Environmental Protection Agency allowed Weirton to delay installing new antipollution equipment, calculating the plant's noxious emissions according to the more lenient "bubble" formula. At the expense of breathing polluted air—hardly a unique trade-off in Weirton's history—the community subsidized the plant's operations.[51] Finally, in contrast to Youngstown's unsuccessful applications, Weirton got small UDAG and EDA grants from the federal government.

At neither Youngstown nor Weirton was there any discussion, even in theory, of transforming the industrial landscape into a landscape of consumption. No suggestion arose of trying to compensate for the loss of manufacturing jobs by growth in the service sector. In no sense was it felt that the local community didn't *need* the jobs or the capital investment that steel provided. Among needy plants, however, Weirton stands out for what its financial consultants accomplished. They established the reliability of a labor union vis-à-vis financial institutions.

Four other factors were also important in saving Weirton. First, the chairman of National, who was undoubtedly tempered by both exposure to Youngstown and a wave of leveraged buyouts in American industry, was ready to sell a plant to the work force. Unlike U.S. Steel, National needed money. Nor did Howard Love mind leaving a "competitor" in place, instead of closing down a plant, because he planned to leave steel entirely. At any rate, he found the Weirton work force to be a credible buyer—on the proposal of his management consultants and in the situation.

The governor of West Virginia also showed early support for a worker buyout. By doing so, he legitimized the ESOP effort. Having an independent labor organization at Weirton was also important because it prevented the worker buyout from having direct ramifications across the industry. While the Weirton buyout did put pressure on the United Steel Workers' Union to alter its opposition to worker buyouts, it could not create a precedent within the union because Weirton was not in the union. Finally, as Lee Iacocca did in the Chrysler bailout, the Weirton work force dramatized the virtue of sacrifice. Collectively, they were a Schumpeterian entrepreneur.

The Weirton buyout demonstrates that power at any level—even the power of self-determination—is often acquired at the cost of a loss of autonomy. In a capitalist economy constrained by market forces, the place of steeltown only survives if both the work force and the local community submit more directly to markets enforced by financial controls. In the past, of course, no steeltown was ever completely autonomous from outside forces: a steeltown produced for the national market and paid off loans from the New York banks. Yet as Weirton shows, the survival of this place depends on its subordination to market forces.

Global markets have continued to fragment the landscape of economic power based on steel. The first year after the Weirton ESOP went into effect, import levels were only restrained by another round of voluntary restrictions. In 1989, Congress and the Bush administration extended these restrictions for only two and a half years. Meanwhile, Weirton's competition in Big Steel pursued both more aggressive financial strategies and more modernization. USX, whose annual investment in R&D was modest by international standards, still invested more than other U.S. steel firms. Yet under pressure from major stockholder Carl

C. Icahn—who had threatened a takeover in 1986—USX told the financial community that it planned eventually to sell its steel operations. Under these conditions, the national basis of industrywide collective bargaining started to erode. Managements of individual firms decided they they could get a tougher deal by negotiating labor contracts locally.

Not surprisingly, the symbolic landscape of the steel industry also faded. In Pittsburgh, only sixty miles from Weirton, a neon sign of a steelworker pouring metal, which had been a local landmark, was turned off, because steel was no longer poured within the city. Nor was a steelmaker still the largest employer: it was the University of Pittsburgh.[52] The steel city was now a different place. An urban redevelopment plan depended on a coalition between the largest corporate owners of both plants and real estate, who forged a new landscape dependent on the service sector. In Weirton, however, steeltown seemed to be the same old place. Neither deindustrialized nor postindustrial, Weirton just became a more subtle, and ever less autonomous, landscape of economic power.

5 Motown's Steeltown: The Power of Productive Labor in Detroit

Detroit isn't a very exciting place. Big chimneys. Black smoke.

GARY COOPER to MARLENE DIETRICH,
Desire (1936)

As a general rule, the people now making a lot of money were not producing things, and the people who were producing things were not making a lot of money.

DAVID HALBERSTAM, *The Reckoning* (1986)

The worker buyout of Weirton Steel had special characteristics—a docile labor union in a company town and an ingenious investment banker. The resurrection of McLouth Steel in Detroit, however, took place in a considerably different local landscape. McLouth is smaller than Weirton, privately held, and fiercely organized by the United Steel Workers' Union. It has one of the most modern integrated steel plants in the United States. And the city that surrounds it—Detroit—is larger, more diversified socially and economically than Weirton. It is also dependent on the U.S. automobile industry, which is more financially astute than steel and more closely linked to international production.

Yet since the early 1970s, an influx of imported cars and a failure to meet qualitative changes in consumer demand had played havoc with Detroit, the auto city. Periodic layoffs stretched into massive unemployment, with fortunate laid-off auto workers driving taxis in the city. J. L. Hudson, the major department store, was bought by the Dayton Company of Minneapolis in 1969 and closed in 1983, leaving parts of

Catherine Redmond, *Afternoon Light: Simultaneous and Sequential* (1987). Oil on canvas, 72 × 84 inches. Collection, Butler Institute of American Art, Youngstown, Ohio.

downtown in its wake shuttered and abandoned. Many houses were either emptied or torn down for lack of prospective buyers. Those who could afford to move left the area, especially young people who saw no future there in steel and autos. It was as though Detroit were the Weirton of America's big cities.

Beside the general disinvestment, rebuilding downtown and mounting large urban renewal projects seemed quixotic. These efforts were backed by the city's corporate wealth and power. But they failed to generate the street-level traffic and small business start-ups that cities require. While Ford Motor Company bankrolled the silver and glass towers of Renaissance Center, General Motors displaced homeowners in midtown to build a hotel, offices, and a shopping-center complex; and the Stroh Brewery developed a corporate office, shopping, and performing arts complex called River Place on the waterfront site of the 1904 Parke-Davis pharmaceuticals plant, a registered historic landmark. Mayor Coleman Young built a downtown convention center and sports arena. He also tried, and failed, to get the city's voters to adopt legalized casino gambling. By the late 1980s, Detroit's unemployment rate was realistically estimated at 36 percent, in contrast to 12 percent unemployment in the metropolitan region and 6–7 percent in the country as a whole.[1]

The city's famous industrial suburbs begin downriver, past an area near the city limits that in the 1950s was Detroit's only racially integrated entertainment district. Their names are synonymous with the history of America's smokestack production. There is Dearborn, site of the integrated Rouge Steel works owned by Ford; Ecorse, home of Great Lakes Steel; Trenton, where McLouth's facilities for producing hot-rolled steel—including basic oxygen furnaces and continuous casters—and offices are located; and Gibraltar, where some of McLouth's raw steel is pickled, annealed, cut, and otherwise turned into cold-rolled sheet and strip before being shipped.

Spread out along the Detroit River, great chimneys alternate with the hyperbolic towers of cement and power plants. An individual plant site may stretch half a mile, its black-painted chimneys, turrets, ladders, and pipes a city of metal against the sky. While the landscape was formed by heavy capital investment, the vernacular is still composed of strong labor unions and Democratic municipalities. They represent the organized power of productive labor that followed the auto industry's accommodation with labor unions in the 1940s due to wartime mobilization and the surge in consumer goods manufacturing after World War II. The vernacular downriver was also constructed by white ethnic households that own their homes (despite the many black workers drawn into the city's auto industry from rural areas of the South), blue-collar families recruited from downstate farm country or Appalachia after both world wars, and the descendants of nineteenth-century European immigrants. And, of course, the automobile. The avenues and boulevards of the center city quickly widen into highways that commemorate the founders of the auto city—Fisher Freeway, Chrysler Freeway, Edsel Ford Freeway—and their products. In downriver communities, everyone drives everywhere. Streets are marked by shopping centers and gas stations; distance is noted in miles, not blocks. Many steelworkers' families drive two cars and a recreational vehicle to go fishing or to a vacation home in Michigan's Upper Peninsula. Unlike in other U.S. suburbs, most cars are American. Here cars are not just a means of transport: cars mean jobs.

The entire socio-spatial structure of Detroit and its inner suburbs depends on cars. Shifting landscapes of production, consumption, and devastation reflect the regional dominance of a single industry, an industry that itself depends on decisions made by three giant companies. As early as 1939, these companies began to decentralize production from Detroit around the United States. As a result, auto employment grew more slowly in the city of Detroit than in either the rest of the country or rural areas of the Middle West. Even while automakers prospered, between 1960 and 1978, they did not increase production jobs in Detroit.[2]

Dependence on the auto industry is mediated not only by Detroit's socio-spatial structure but also by the kind of supplier network that links GM to McLouth. As domestic auto manufacturers have disinvested from U.S. production, they have become more exacting about the quality and price of the steel they do buy. McLouth lost half its sales after 1977, when GM cut its usual order. Like other steel suppliers, McLouth had to compete with steel imports, inter-regional outsourcing, automobile imports, and plastics, which were substituted for steel in auto bodies. Joint ventures between U.S. and Japanese auto makers only increased competition, for they tended to favor Japanese suppliers.[3] In this situation, the power of productive labor paled in autos, steel, and downriver's industrial communities. Big plants like BASF and Firestone Steel were closed. District 29 of the United Steel Workers'

Union, with contracts at 400 downriver plants, lost almost half its membership between 1979 and 1986. And business at McLouth declined.

In 1981–82, McLouth Steel Corporation was plunged into bankruptcy by its creditors. Unlike Weirton, the company was reorganized during a long battle in federal bankruptcy court. Acquired at the last minute by an independent entrepreneur, McLouth made a fresh start under a new managerial regime. Again unlike at Weirton, however, production lagged, morale declined, and the new owner failed to turn the plant around. In 1987, the company was saved by means of a worker buyout. The Weirton strategy of labor concessions, managerial mobilization, and product diversification also appeared downriver. But this time, McLouth was saved by means of extraordinary state and labor union intervention: in other words, the creative destruction of a landscape.

LITTLE MCLOUTH

Like Weirton, McLouth Steel Products Corporation is a relatively small firm that looms large on the local landscape as both a taxpayer and an employer. The company holds 1–2 percent of market share in the domestic steel industry and 3–4 percent in flat-rolled steel. With 2,000 employees producing 2,000–3,000 tons of steel a day, McLouth is the eleventh-largest steelmaker in the country. The work force is highly paid and mostly male. It is also predominantly white; the first black worker was hired only in 1962.[4]

Although it had a place in the *Fortune* 500 list (as McLouth Steel Corporation) while under public ownership from 1956 to 1983, McLouth has always been too small to be included in triennial pattern bargaining between the USW and Big Steel. As a "me-too" firm, however, McLouth has traditionally taken the national collective bargaining agreement as a base, and then added higher hourly wages, more fringe benefits, and more lenient work rules. Despite premium conditions similar to Weirton's, the work force at McLouth has often expressed discontent. Beginning in the early 1970s, a history of adversarial labor-management relations generated a company reputation for slowdowns and wildcat strikes.

Secured creditors from the U.S. financial community tried to put the firm out of business in 1981 by calling a technical default on their loans. The consensus at that point among both managers at competing steel firms and labor leaders in the USW was to let McLouth die. Competitors—including nearby Great Lakes Steel—saw a shrinking worldwide market that demanded plant closings and reduction of capacity. Labor leaders feared that if McLouth survived by means of concessions and give-backs, it would create a dangerous precedent in the industry. The work force at McLouth, however, were of two minds. Afraid of losing their jobs in the economic crisis they saw all around them, they nonetheless distrusted the firm's management and bitterly resented proposed cutbacks in wages and benefits. Until management actually filed for Chapter 11 bankruptcy protection, workers refused to believe the company would close down.

Yet from the mid 1970s on, McLouth was not well run. Bad shop-floor relations between workers and supervisors merely accentuated the profile of a "ham-handed," mean, and inconsistent senior management, in the labor unions' view, and a series of bad investment decisions. No less than the workers, management was myopic about the place of the firm in new steel markets. During bankruptcy proceedings the secured creditors expressed shock that management had spent scarce cash to feed the deer at the firm's upstate executives' retreat, but this was only the tip of the iceberg. Management insisted that McLouth was brought down by external sources: crisis in the steel and auto industries, import competition, and a heavy debt burden. The view from outside, however, blamed internal factors. This critical view was shared by the secured creditors, the business press, and the firm's investment bankers at Lazard Frères, who were hired in March 1982 at the secured creditors' demand to pursue a liquidation of assets.

One problem was that the company had invested during the late 1970s in upstream integration, mistakenly believing that the price of iron ore and coke would go sky high. Instead, it paid more for its ownership of the Ironton and New Boston Coke companies and Empire Mining Partnership than it would have paid for raw materials on the open market. The $60 million loan it took out to buy a coke plant added to its financial burdens, and bringing these facilities up to federal environmental standards also cost more than the company could afford. Another problem concerned investments in unnecessary modernization. McLouth had done extremely well with its early innovations—the basic oxygen process for producing steel, continuous casters, single stack annealing furnaces, and the U.S. industry's first completely automated hot mill and stainless steel sheet line—but the A-O-D (Argon-Oxygen-Decarburizing) process it installed at the Trenton plant in the late 1970s was never fully utilized. Nor did the firm derive as much flexibility in production as its computer-controlled equipment would have allowed.

McLouth was also overly dependent on the auto industry. While the company had reduced its supplier relationship to GM from a half to a third of total sales, more than 70 percent of its output still went to the auto industry in one form or another. Such a restricted customer base didn't permit McLouth to recoup sales in 1979 when auto orders declined. Nor did it benefit the firm when the quality of its products failed to meet car makers' criteria.

McLouth's management, moreover, was guilty of sloppy, or even fraudulent, accounting procedures. The use of equity accounting to include the profits of the Jewell Coal and Coke Company among Mc-Louth's profits was investigated and litigated by the Securities and Exchange Commission in 1981. McLouth was also accused of reporting shipments of goods that were never made.

McLouth suffered, further, from the desultory diversification strategy so typical of the U.S. steel industry during the 1960s and 1970s. An attempt to diversify saddled McLouth with three trucking companies that management couldn't figure out how to use, especially after federal deregulation. (These were sold during the bankruptcy reorganization in 1982.)

Between 1976 and 1982, the company cut nearly 2,000 jobs, or half its work force, contributing to the general economic crisis downriver. Its 1976 profit of $10.8 million, or just over 2 percent of sales—twice the profit rate of Weirton—was considered a "paltry return" in the industry. In contrast to Weirton, however, McLouth was regarded as a likely takeover target because of its modern equipment. At least, that remained a viable option until the steel and auto crisis of 1979. Profits evaporated, with a loss of about $15 million in 1977 and, after regaining normal levels in 1978 and 1979, a swift plunge downward. The firm lost nearly $100 million in 1980 and 1981, and long-term debt amounted to $166 million.[5]

Since the 1950s, McLouth had owned three separate production sites: the original Detroit plant, founded in 1934 by Donald McLouth, which now had a modern stainless steel production line; the main Trenton plant, built on swampland beside the Detroit River between 1948 and 1954; and the Gibraltar plant, another greenfield facility along the river, completed in 1955. Without new financing, however, these plants were questionable assets. Structurally, the firm had exhausted the advantages of its first-generation equipment, but it was too small to invest significantly in R&D.

The "angel" that had enabled McLouth to invest in advanced technology in the 1950s still had deep pockets, but was no longer available. In the early years, McLouth had acquired its basic oxygen furnaces with General Motors' money. GM bought $25 million of McLouth's preferred stock in order to finance a modern plant in the Detroit area that would compete for GM orders with Great Lakes Steel. McLouth was thus intended to act as a control on both price and quality. By the late 1970s, however, a more globally minded GM had little interest in bailing out McLouth, although GM did send a $13 million check to the secured creditors via one of McLouth's attorneys at the end of 1981 to buy the company a little time.

All in all, McLouth suffered from the same management syndrome as GM's competitor, Ford. As David Halberstam described the automaker in 1979, its "costs were out of line, its products lacked quality, and they had lost their appeal."[6] All the vital business signs suggested McLouth should fail.

The local labor market already groaned under layoffs, shutdowns, and unemployment. A University of Michigan study of the ripple effects of a probable closing at McLouth in January 1982 found that a shutdown would cost the state 14,645 jobs (at both McLouth and its suppliers), $278 million annually in personal income, and $25 million a year in state and local taxes. At that point, the state's unemployment rate of 16 percent was nearly double the national average. Panic was sharpest in the downriver municipalities of McLouth's plant sites, where the company contributed the major share of taxes and most of the work force lived. Riverview, whose 1981 school tax revenues fell 42 percent behind budget because of McLouth's payment arrears, feared that it would have to close its school system if the plant shut down. The mayor of Trenton threatened to turn off McLouth's water supply. Even the electric company, Detroit Edison, had reason for both anger and fear. McLouth owed Detroit Edison $15 million when it filed for Chapter 11 bankruptcy protection, and its $1 million weekly energy bill made it that utility's third-largest customer. After the labor unions' pension funds,

Detroit Edison and Michigan Consolidated Gas were McLouth's largest unsecured creditors.

Despite the structural similarities between McLouth and Weirton as small steelmakers in a downsizing industry, marked contrasts between the firms and their local contexts affected their chances for survival. Not only did McLouth's financial situation look much more dismal than Weirton's, but the way McLouth entered into bankruptcy proceedings cast a bleak light on that firm's future. Instead of a willing seller like National Steel, which sought a relatively inexpensive exit from Weirton, McLouth was pushed into bankruptcy proceedings by secured creditors who were determined to liquidate assets. Bargaining with them just to keep both Trenton and Gibraltar plants open made it impossible to argue over terms. Furthermore, the militant work force at McLouth were conditioned by the USW's local history and past grievances against management. They could be expected to resist the two most important elements of the Weirton buyout: sacrifice and cooperation with management.

Less certain in its effect was the complex industrial political economy of the Detroit area and the entire state of Michigan. Downriver seemed to suffer from a bad case of deindustrialization, and with so much at stake, the state would be forced to play an instrumental role. Once the secured creditors thrust the firm into bankruptcy court in 1981, federal bankruptcy law limited the state's ability to intervene. But the conditions of the second restructuring from 1986 on, and the reelection of a governor with some claim to an industrial policy, made it easier for the state to act. Circumventing the cultural and institutional barriers to "bailouts," the Michigan Commerce Department was able to play a crucial "facilitating" role.

Yet success was never assured. If labor concessions made the first restructuring "unique" in the industry, according to one of the firm's attorneys, the second restructuring by worker buyout was "a miracle," the financial vice-president says.

BANKRUPTCY REORGANIZATION, 1981–82

McLouth's bankruptcy reorganization is rooted, in a sense, in the early 1950s, around the same time that the Trenton plant was built. Those years were important in the lives of four adversaries who struggled over the bankruptcy and the future of the firm, for that was when they began their careers:

Milton Deaner, who took over as CEO in 1981 to try to straighten out
   McLouth's management, worked in Latin America for a company
   that constructed steel plants, building mills that would later compete
   with U.S. steel producers;
Harry Lester, who was elected downriver district director of the USW
   in 1979, moved to Detroit from a coal-mining family in West Virginia, and got a job as a locomotive engineer at McLouth;
James Toren, who led the secured creditors' attack on McLouth as the
   representative of Prudential Insurance, developed the financial expertise that later helped Prudential cut its ties to troubled firms; and
Cyrus Tang, who bought McLouth's plants and inventory in 1982 because he wanted to own a steel mill, emigrated from Shanghai to
   Chicago, and got a job in the stamping plant at Temple Steel.

Socialized in the expanding markets and self-regarding world of postwar heavy industry, these men knew what manufacturing at a steel plant was worth. But they had also learned firsthand about the crisis of the steel and auto industries during the 1970s. As adversaries in bankruptcy proceedings, the financial representative, the labor leader, the self-made entrepreneur, and the steel manager played out the limits of a restructuring of this type. Bankruptcy confirmed the power of financial institutions over U.S. industry, limited the state's role to applying federal law, and prevented the labor union from taking an innovative directing role in either negotiations or postcrisis management.[7]

Throughout 1981, as losses at McLouth mounted for the second straight year, the company's ten secured creditors repeatedly issued waivers to delay repayment of their loans.* They thought that Milton Deaner had a 50–50 chance of turning the firm around, and they knew General Motors supported him. At a meeting on November 30, 1981, however, McLouth's auditors advised the board of directors to get professional advice on bankruptcy. Two days later, egged on by the banks, all the secured creditors called a technical default on their loans. Ironically, this default was incurred by an action on McLouth's part to raise

---

* These secured lenders were the Prudential Insurance Company of America, Metropolitan Life Insurance Company of New York, Mutual Life Insurance Company of New York, New York Life Insurance Company, National Bank of Detroit, Detroit Bank and Trust Company, Manufacturers National Bank of Detroit, Manufacturers Hanover Trust Company, AmeriTrust Company, and Harris Trust and Saving Bank.

cash to cover operating costs. According to conditions the creditors had imposed in March 1981, for a restructuring of the $166 million they held in long-term debt, the company was required to maintain a tangible net worth of $107.5 million. Most of this was provided by property and equipment, including the Detroit mother plant, the 320-acre plant in Trenton, and the 850-acre plant in Gibraltar, which had, according to Lazard Frères's later estimate, a total book value of $151 million. Yet when in October 1981 the company sold its stainless steel plant in Detroit to Jones & Laughlin for $23.5 million, its net worth fell below the threshold of creditors' demands.[8]

A week after receiving the default notice, management filed for Chapter 11 bankruptcy protection. No advance notice was given to either the work force or suppliers. Consequently, the USW local fell into a state of shock. Some workers had 20–25 years in the plant, and saw their pensions, or retirement under the advantageous union conditions of "30 and out," going up in smoke. McLouth's corporate attorneys, from the Detroit firm of Dickinson Wright, Moon, Van Dusen & Freeman, tried to calm all the creditors, but the secured lenders appeared to be the only ones with a plan. Their strategy was to liquidate the firm and wipe out the shareholders and "unsecureds," including the labor unions, so that they themselves would get all of McLouth's assets.

The financial institutions made cooperation among the creditors impossible and treated McLouth's two labor unions as pariahs. Although the USW was elected to the creditors' committee at a bankruptcy court hearing soon after the Chapter 11 filing—by virtue of the firm's $16 million pension commitment—the secured creditors refused to speak with union representatives. Even when a union delegation flew to New York to attend a creditors' meeting in June 1982, the secured creditors let them into the meeting room only after heated argument. Nor would the secured creditors speak with labor and management together. (The bankruptcy court ultimately permitted several of the major unsecured creditors to join an enlarged, 17-member creditors' committee; the unsecured creditors were also allowed to form their own informal group.)

The labor unions almost immediately began to negotiate financial concessions with McLouth's management. This was surprising, not only because of their roiled history, but also because of the inconsistency with which top management had approached labor concessions throughout 1981. Management's ultimate withdrawal of demands for wage reductions had curiously culminated in all-round raises at the troubled firm. This did not convince the work force of a need to sacrifice. Nevertheless, labor-management negotiations that lasted through the month of December led to ratification of a one-year concession agreement that reduced wages by 10 percent and annulled certain fringe and pension benefits. Negotiations with management over further concessions and changes in work rules continued through the rest of the new year, until another labor contract was signed with Cyrus Tang in November 1982.

The first few months of 1982 were marked by a series of "drop-dead" agreements with the creditors. These were 30-day extensions of debt that permitted McLouth to operate the plant till March, then May, 1982. Management argued with the secured creditors to keep the plant open as long as possible so that the raw materials on hand could at least be processed into more valuable steel. Additional economic factors blunted the secured creditors' stated desire to "shut the blast furnaces down." First, it is costly both to restart a blast furnace once it has shut down and to shut it down in compliance with federal environmental regulations. Shutdown also requires a firm to settle pension and insurance obligations, which can cost as much as $60,000 per worker. And settling accounts on unfunded liabilities brings a firm into conflict with the Pension Benefit Guaranty Corporation in Washington, D.C.

Meanwhile, the major problem at McLouth was how to maintain the level and pace of production. Workers' morale had sunk so low they didn't want to work at all, but the continuous casters still demanded a steady flow of steel. The lower the output, the less the plant earned. At this point the secured creditors urged the firm to hire an investment banker to cultivate potential buyers of assets. On their recommendation, management hired Lazard Frères in New York, which supplied different associates from those who worked on the Weirton buyout. The corporate attorney in Detroit also brought in a "boutique law firm" from lower Broadway in New York that specializes in bankruptcy cases. The New York attorney remembers how strange it was to work on McLouth because "there was no client." Unlike at Weirton, where around the same time the Joint Study Committee of labor and management was negotiating with National to buy the firm, no actor at McLouth could take responsibility for the future of the company.

Visible evidence of the lack of internal leadership was that managers started to desert the firm. But the bankruptcy attorney from New

York devised what he thought was an ingenious solution—an Incentive Bonus Plan for executives—to stop their flight. This temporary measure would last until the beginning of June, when the second drop-dead agreement expired. It paid ransom, in effect, to hold managers at the firm, with payment proportional to managers' financial compensation. Judge George Woods called this "blackmail" in bankruptcy court, and the USW district director, Harry Lester, termed it a case of "golden handcuffs," but the judge, Lester, and the secured creditors all accepted a total payment of $700,000 as the only way McLouth could retain its management. The judge, moreover, awarded an equal payment to the USW local, which used it for one-week paid vacations and some pension benefits that had been cancelled.

While Lazard prepared a prospectus on the firm for potential buyers, the bankruptcy hearings continued. Assets like the coke plant and the executive jet were put up for sale. Yet meetings continued in an effort to gain support for the firm's survival from creditors, local elected officials, and federal authorities in Washington, D.C. Michigan Senator Donald Riegle pleaded with secured creditors to keep McLouth open and even canvassed potential buyers. No support came, however, from the federal government.

In 1980 Ronald Reagan had given an ambiguous speech downriver in which he expressed support for U.S. industry. But his conservative Republican administration adamantly opposed bailouts to troubled firms. When Labor Secretary Raymond Donovan visited downriver in March 1982, the angry wife of a McLouth steelworker challenged him. Donovan told a labor union delegation they would "all be better off when the sick plants close." A month later, the union marched on Washington. After meeting with Commerce Secretary Malcolm Baldrige about their pending application for an EDA loan, they read Baldrige's reply in the *New York Times:* "There will not be a bailout." The USW delegation also failed to obtain a meeting with President Reagan set up by Michigan's two Democratic senators. According to the union, Reagan cancelled the meeting because he decided that they would only use the occasion to denounce his administration.

Without either federal support or a potential buyer in view, Harry Lester, the USW district director, proposed a new strategy. Why not copy Weirton and firms outside the steel industry, and set up an ESOP to run McLouth? No one found this appealing. The secured creditors did not take Lester's idea seriously. For their part, the workers in District 29—where Lester had run for director in 1979 on a platform of "No Concessions"—were skeptical about what they would gain. The ESOP's most serious opposition, however, arose within the national committee of USW district directors. Not only did they fear the precedent that workers' concessions in an ESOP would set, but unlike the more progressive UAW, the USW had no interest in worker ownership.

Lester remembers the meeting at which the USW Executive Committee finally gave him permission to negotiate an ESOP as the worst experience he ever had. Several district directors urged him to let the plant go under because if he didn't, he would have too many problems later. They also thought the price of concessions would be too high. But Lester convinced them to help fund a feasibility study of an ESOP for McLouth by arguing that the firm was too small to set a precedent in national bargaining. (In fact, the chief labor negotiator for U.S. Steel never let the USW forget that it permitted members to negotiate lower wages at McLouth than at other firms.) Significantly, Lester's position was upheld by the international USW president, Lloyd McBride, whose battle for the presidency Lester had strongly supported against the dissident Ed Sadlowski.

Although the two union locals at the plant liked the idea of saving their jobs with an ESOP, they did not have access to capital to buy the plant themselves. Nor did they want to accept the sacrifice an ESOP involved, for the ESOP feasibility study proposed cutting hourly wages for production workers from $18 (the level reached by two consecutive 10 percent concessions) to $15. The secured creditors ultimately turned the ESOP proposal down. But Harry Lester believes they used the calculations in the feasibility study to lure Cyrus Tang, who unexpectedly appeared as a buyer in July 1982.

Tang's motives for buying McLouth were as opaque as the other parties claimed to find his "inscrutable Oriental" bargaining style. Yet he already owned an empire of midwestern steel service centers, distribution points into which McLouth's production could feed. Although both the secured creditors and Lazard initially doubted Tang's financial ability, they were persuaded by annual revenues of $200–$300 million at Tang Industries, Tang's credit line at Continental Illinois (which was not affected by the bank's eventual financial troubles), and the bargaining style of Tang's Chicago lawyer. At any rate, Tang had been recommended to CEO Milton Deaner by an executive at GM. When the bankruptcy broke, in 1981, he had expressed interest in buying the stainless steel operations that Jones & Laughlin eventually acquired.[9]

Under bankruptcy conditions, Tang was able to buy McLouth on very advantageous terms. He selectively acquired the best parts of the firm and used them to form a viable business. Tang bought the inventory "at fire sale prices" of just over $30 million in cash, the former corporate attorney says, and took out an income debenture note to pay most of the purchase price of $46.5 million on plant equipment and property. The debenture note would be paid from the new firm's eventual profits. This allowed the new McLouth—now called McLouth Steel Products Corporation—to pay for operations and maintenance, expansions in inventory, and receivables, before making payments on either principal or interest. The remainder of the purchase price was leveraged by a note on the assets themselves.

With two minor partners, including the owner of a coke company that supplied McLouth, Tang paid only a fraction of the plant's net worth. He did not acquire the old company's debts or pay off its shareholders. Nor did he turn over any money to the secured creditors, who agreed, once they accepted Tang, to extend the long-term debt, now reduced by about $50 million. Tang's $30 million in cash went directly into operating capital for the new firm. Cyrus Tang was also able to reduce the cost structure of the new McLouth. His attorney negotiated a 60 percent reduction in property taxes from the city of Gibraltar, saving $3 to $4 million a year. The new firm had a tax carryforward from the old McLouth that it could use to reduce federal taxes. The restructured debt, moreover, reduced interest payments. Prior to filing for Chapter 11, according to the old firm's corporate attorney, McLouth had the highest debt service in the steel industry.

But wages and benefits were still the largest element in the cost structure, and the unions continued to argue with Cyrus Tang over concessions throughout the summer. Older workers approaching retirement voiced special concern. Because pensions were calculated on the basis of their last year's wages, they risked lowering their pension payments by accepting wage concessions. At one point, the president of the USW local offered to trade back the concessions Tang had already made to the district director—a compromise ESOP consisting of a 15 percent share of both equity and pretax profits—for higher wages and benefits. Having come this close to an ESOP, however, Lester vetoed trading these rights away.

In return, Tang offered production workers an incentive of fifty cents an hour, which was termed an insult by the union. He then proposed implementing the incentive in only one shop in the plant, which was rejected by the union as impractical. At the same time, Tang eliminated the pension system for middle management, which led to angry meetings with them, too. Morale and production dropped so low that when Lester called Tang to a meeting in September, he warned the new owner he was driving himself out of a mill. "I'm a rich man," Tang replied. "I can shut the mill down."

Significantly, labor was the only adversary left with a major grievance. The secured creditors felt somewhat assured that their loans would be repaid. The bankruptcy specialist, the investment bankers, and the former corporate attorney brought several months of negotiations to "a very highly successful conclusion," in the bankruptcy attorney's view. After spending the summer locked in a series of confrontations, Tang and Lester finally reached agreement on workers' concessions. A new labor contract was signed on November 14, 1982, and Tang closed the deal for the purchase of the firm three days later.

The new total hourly labor cost for production workers was $18, higher than the $14 Tang had bargained for. Payment of the COLA was deferred until 1985, dental and optical insurance plans were dropped, and three paid holidays were eliminated. Two areas of contention remained as at Weirton and throughout the industry: work rules and contracting out on maintenance work. While many of the work force loudly complained about the contract, most workers at McLouth, according to CEO Milton Deaner, really favored the deal. But they may have been a silent majority, for concessions were negotiated over their heads.

Deaner was optimistic about McLouth's chances for success during 1983 and 1984. The company broke even on sales of about $500 million a year, and Tang committed himself to a modernization program. To help finance a small part of the five-year plan for capital investment, EDA approved a $15 million loan guarantee in August 1983. This was to be used for relining one blast furnace, building iron desulphurization equipment, refurbishing the continuous casters, replacing the annealing facilities, improving the hot mill control system, and several smaller items.

Old McLouth had filed its initial loan guarantee application five years earlier, in 1978, when EDA (under the Carter administration) was more lenient toward troubled firms. At that time, EDA negotiated informally with applicants before they actually found a lender. The high default rate of 30–40 percent on these loans, and the Reagan administration's negative orientation toward EDA—which was nearly cut out of every annual budget after 1980—made it much harder for new McLouth to get a loan guarantee. Here again, however, a member of Congress from Michigan intervened. Responding to interest expressed by Congressman John Dingell's staff, EDA approved McLouth's application. The agency, as usual, took priority over all other creditors. Jim Toren and the other financial representatives did not readily accept this change in the secured creditors' status. Besides insisting on an asset-backed loan that subordinated the secured creditors' claims, EDA imposed three conditions on the firm: locking in a cheap iron-ore supply, ensuring a stable market share, and keeping peace between management and labor.

Management now stepped up its sales efforts. Expanding the sales staff, it added 75 new customers. It also counted on increasing sales to Cyrus Tang's service centers from 2–3 percent to 10 percent of output. In 1983, Deaner spoke optimistically of capturing "a meaningful market." But some of these sales were achieved by undercutting the competition and skimping on quality. Although Tang invested the $70–$80 million he promised for modernization, neither output nor productivity improved. Using semifinished Brazilian slabs did not work out as hoped, and after a couple of profitable years, McLouth resumed its lethargy.

Relining the blast furnaces continued to loom as a costly item. A mini-relining cost over $15 million; a full-scale relining cost three times as much. With this and rising energy costs in mind, Deaner reduced electricity bills by running the hot mill at night, when rates were lower.

Many problems at the firm still concerned labor. While the new labor contract lowered total hourly labor costs for production workers from $23 to $18, and for laborers from $12 to $8, arguments over work rules and safety conditions continued. Workers doubted whether management wholeheartedly accepted the new participatory style, or whether it treated the work force fairly. Supervisors especially were "the Achilles' heel" of the firm in the view of a consultant who closely followed the Quality of Work Life program at McLouth. But Deaner was also inconsistent as CEO. Generally regarded by labor as much too kind to his managers, he was apt to fire off an angry letter to a worker if something irked him at the plant.

Even after business losses, lackluster productivity, and bad labor relations forced Milton Deaner to leave, worker dissatisfaction grew. Workers' concessions had enabled the firm to survive bankruptcy and acquire a new owner. Yet their failure to produce—which was, after all, the workers' basic role—confirmed the new steel firm's inability to tap the continuing power of productive labor.

WORKER OWNERSHIP, 1987–88

By 1986, McLouth had suffered two straight years of business losses and again owed back payments on local taxes. Desertions among managers and highly skilled workers began in earnest, with some of them applying for jobs at Mazda's new Flat Rock plant, which was due to open in 1987. Worst of all, the steel mill failed to meet the production level that McLouth needed to break even—approximately 3,000 tons a day—because the workers had started slowdowns. By this point the work force had no trust in management's competence. Nor did they believe Cyrus Tang's commitment to keep the steel plant open. Workers questioned the "arm's-length" distance Tang had pledged to maintain between McLouth and his other corporate businesses. They suspected he was buying McLouth steel at artificially low prices and shipping it to his own service centers. They also doubted that he had really invested the promised $80 million in capital improvements.

Harry Lester was worried enough about the plant's survival to take an unprecedented action. Since 1981 he had been committed to keeping McLouth going no matter what it cost in labor concessions. But Lester was convinced that the main problem with McLouth was management. He criticized the firm's managers as "retreads" from other steel companies and "country-club management." So in 1986, shortly before Governor James Blanchard's campaign for reelection, Lester initiated a heart-to-heart talk with him about the future of McLouth and its 2,000 jobs. Over the next few months, Harry Lester persuaded the governor that the state had to get involved in McLouth's survival. With Blanchard unable to act until after the November election, Lester also initiated contact with two of McLouth's major iron-ore and coke suppliers: Cleveland-Cliffs Inc. and Elk River Resources (a division of Sun Oil). Surprised, at first, to be contacted by a USW leader, executives at these firms were eventually won over by Lester's pleas and arguments that they should also involve themselves directly in McLouth's internal affairs.

Governor Blanchard quietly promised the aid of the Michigan Commerce Department and its director, Doug Ross. A former state senator from Detroit, Ross had been allied with Harry Lester and the USW in election campaigns stretching back to his youth, in the Kennedy years, when he first became interested in politics. On this basis of trust—and Lester's explicit promise not to embarrass the governor into keeping the plant open if the business prognosis was bad—the labor union developed a dual strategy: replacing Cyrus Tang with workers' ownership and creating a management more responsive to both market and place.

Yet few of the actors could be counted on to play their parts. The suppliers, heavily dependent on McLouth's orders, were wary of telling the firm what do to. The state Commerce Department, which had already been approached by McLouth's management for an infusion of funds, was determined "not to throw money" at troubled firms. Nor did the rest of Michigan's state government roll over at labor's request. State Treasurer Robert Bowman, who ultimately controlled government funds, demanded that Harry Lester "do his part" by getting labor in line on new concessions. Business conditions, moreover, did not bode well for Lester's agreement with Governor Blanchard. Hired to study the firm toward the end of 1986, the management consultants Touche Ross doubted McLouth would be able to survive in the continued absence of a serious business plan. At that point, the work force engaged in a wildcat strike.

Staff at the Michigan Commerce Department felt that McLouth would stand or fall on "attitude." Unlike segmented production lines in the auto industry, they liked to explain, an integrated steel mill works like the human body; the production process in the entire plant is driven by a single heartbeat. If that heartbeat—attitude—could only be improved, output would rise, and the company would have a fair chance of survival. This perception was the source of their willingness to undertake a limited rescue operation. Doug Ross in particular made a special commitment. Like Harry Lester, he privately decided not to let McLouth die. In contrast, however, to the West Virginia coal miner's son, Doug Ross saw himself as one of the last proponents of 1960s-era optimism. John Kennedy and Lyndon Johnson had shown his generation that an energetic, committed government could accomplish nearly any goal. The goal he had in mind was not the "industrial policy" discussed from 1979 to 1984, for Walter Mondale's decisive defeat in that year's presidential election eliminated this option from the political agenda. Doug Ross did not favor government directly controlling, or even taking an equity share in, troubled industries. Instead, he vowed to use his considerable energy and the staff at his command to get inside the steel mill, motivate its work force, and lead "roundtable discussions" with management, the labor unions, and suppliers until they reached agreement on saving the company. It probably did not hurt his sense of mission that Ross contemplated resuming his career as an elected official by running for higher office.

Ross and his staff sent a mailing to McLouth employees urging them to "all pull together" and asking for specific complaints. They believed the work force were so used to thinking of themselves as management's victims that they were incapable of taking constructive action. To their surprise, however, they received 259 detailed responses from the firm's 2,000 workers and employees. As many as a dozen workers complained that others in the plant were abusing drugs or alcohol on the job, and thus jeopardizing safety conditions. An equal number asked for more trust and cooperation between management and the unions. Suggestions from 24 workers focused on the need for better preventive maintenance of equipment. Other individual comments proposed specific improvements in the production process.

Contrary to its initial desire, the Michigan Commerce Department did invest some money in McLouth. It paid Touche Ross for its management study and the development of a business plan. (Commerce contributed half of Touche Ross's $200,000 fee; the other half was paid by the USW and the company.) Commerce also persuaded the Michigan Department of Labor to finance a $300,000 study on social relations at the plant. This study ultimately confirmed that the work force suffered from overwhelming, self-defeating fear. The workers, in Doug Ross's view, were like the Detroit Lions football team, stuck forever at the bottom of the league. Ross used this analogy—in an effort at reverse psychology—in weekly meetings he began to hold with workers at the plant.

Within five months, by April 1987, output increased, and the roundtable composed of Harry Lester, McLouth's suppliers, and the Commerce Department drew up the terms of deal they wanted to pursue. These conditions were more important than "attitude." First and foremost, the company's finances had to be restructured by converting outstanding debt to equity. This move would enable the firm to get a new infusion of capital. Second, labor relations had to be improved.

But third, the sine qua non of restructuring, in Harry Lester's view, was taking ownership of the company away from Cyrus Tang.

Tang was in fact an absentee owner. Although day-to-day operations were still decided by management, the company's future was being decided not by Tang but by a "corporatist" roundtable representing local government (including officials of several downriver municipalities), the labor unions, and McLouth's suppliers. Indeed, the suppliers and the labor unions had deepened their involvement. Cleveland-Cliffs and USW headquarters each loaned a management analyst from their organization to work at McLouth and prepare a business plan. Faced with this direct intervention and mounting losses, Cyrus Tang gradually decided to relinquish ownership. But Tang wanted to choose both his bargaining partner and the pace of his withdrawal.

His discussions with Harry Lester were mainly confrontational, especially when the district labor leader threatened to probe Tang Industries' finances so deeply—another participant recalls—that he would "pierce the corporate veil." Tang clearly preferred to deal with Doug Ross and the state of Michigan rather than Lester and the USW. While Tang told Ross in early 1987 to go ahead and "take the company," negotiations nevertheless dragged on for another year.

Labor was again the keystone of restructuring. Although a (second) new labor contract had been put into place in July 1986, the ESOP required still more financial concessions in order to lower costs. But the significant discovery McKinsey had made at Weirton was even more relevant at McLouth: in order to attract financial institutions, the work force had to give tangible evidence of a willingness to sacrifice. The ESOP's supporters argued that worker ownership would make a difference, so that new wage concessions would raise productivity. Not everyone who had to make concessions agreed.

Under pressure from Harry Lester and job insecurity, the exhausted work force accepted another wage reduction of 10 percent in return for 85 percent worker ownership in an ESOP. This left Cyrus Tang and his partners holding 13 percent of the firm. Workers were also assured that the existing pension system would be maintained, although this point was eventually negotiated by the firm and the Pension Benefit Guaranty Corporation.

Neither the work force at McLouth nor the USW Executive Committee dropped the resistance to worker ownership that they had shown in 1982. For the work force, the new concessions—even with an ESOP—

went down "like Castor oil." But Lester argued that the ESOP was a no-lose situation. If the steel plant closed, workers just faced unemployment—and that they were facing anyway, under Cyrus Tang. But if, on the other hand, the plant stayed open and made a profit, they "could walk away with a lot of money." Not only would workers recoup their wage concessions by means of productivity bonuses and eventual profit-sharing, they could also sell their shares back to the company in five or ten years, when many of them would have enough years of service at McLouth to retire. Thus the combination of old and new forms of collective bargaining—nationwide USW rules and ESOP terms at the plant—would ultimately protect the workers' interests.

Lester faced an Executive Committee of his fellow district directors that was just as skeptical as it had been in 1982. In the earlier bankruptcy crisis, the committee had warned him that trying to save McLouth by making concessions would cost him his union career. They tried to make him understand that he would never win reelection as district director when his first five-year term expired. This time, however, in 1987, the Executive Committee was more supportive. Once again with the backing of Lloyd McBride, the USW's president, Lester received the committee's approval to keep McLouth alive. Following that meeting, the new labor contract was finally ratified in fall 1987.

During the summer, the crucial arrangements began to restructure debt and develop a business plan. The company was under special pressure to do so because it had recently lost its source of operating capital. This was, in fact, the immediate reason behind management's approach to the Michigan Commerce Department in 1986. The financial institution that held $130 million in loans for McLouth's operating capital had decided to sell its commercial loan business to AmeriTrust of Cleveland, on the condition that AmeriTrust could give back certain problem loans that were deemed uncollectible within a year. One of these problem loans was McLouth's.

Long-term debt to secured creditors had already been reduced to the relatively small amount of $11 million. But Michigan State Treasurer Bob Bowman cautiously refused to get involved before all financial restructuring was completed. Bowman also demanded that McLouth hire an investment banker who would provide credibility vis-à-vis financial institutions. Through his connections, and those of McLouth's major suppliers, the firm hired the financial restructuring group at Shearson Lehman Hutton in New York City in July 1987. Shearson was asked to draw up the long-awaited business plan that management still hadn't devised. This plan would be presented to potential lenders.

Not surprisingly, Shearson's investment bankers found "less than total sophistication" at McLouth, one of them says. Defeatism took the form of "a strongly held view that the state had to help" McLouth. Furthermore, as at Weirton, there was "a deep cultural antipathy to New York financial types." Distrust was compounded by a suspicion that Lazard Frères, the firm's investment banker during the bankruptcy crisis, had done nothing to help it. (Unlike in the case of Weirton, Lazard's representatives had indeed proceeded on the assumption that McLouth would fail.) However, despite this reluctance on the part of both management and the USW, the state government insisted that they fully cooperate with Shearson. Unlike Lazard, Shearson did not think McLouth "was a goner." The Shearson team of three spent a lot of time at the plant in Trenton. They focused especially on labor. Using a fairly standard restructuring model, they aimed to "tell a story" about Mc-Louth that would interest potential lenders. This scenario included the important elements of cash flow projections, tax obligations, and the profitable consequences if the company could just be taken public (i.e., if equity were converted to public ownership by selling shares on the stock market).

The Shearson team also tried to buy the company time. Suppliers, persuaded by their presentation and still dependent on McLouth's business, agreed to freeze past liabilities as long as the company kept up payments on current bills. The local tax authorities and the PBGC were willing to go along. Greater resistance arose from the financial institution that held the income debenture and one of McLouth's trade creditors. Significantly, Shearson delayed meeting with the secured creditors—who were so determined to shut the plant down in 1982—until all the other creditors had agreed to its conditions. By that point, and with the assistance of NBD, a local bank, Shearson convinced the secured creditors to accept a stretch-out of the firm's debt from three to five more years. The secured creditors were already a somewhat different group. Jim Toren had retired from Prudential, and Manufacturers Hanover's even more vociferous representative was no longer involved.

On Shearson's advice, McLouth converted debt to equity by persuading holders of the $130 million in debt for operating capital to convert it to preferred stock. The firm also managed a reverse stock split, converting ten old shares to one new share of common stock and issuing enough shares to the ESOP trust to cover 85 percent of equity. To provide cash for additional working capital, Shearson negotiated a new revolving credit agreement for $60 million from Congress Financial Corporation, a subsidiary of a Philadelphia-based bank-holding company that specializes in high-risk loans to troubled firms. It took almost a year to conclude these arrangements. Final negotiations ended in May 1988.

The restructured McLouth is run on both a more egalitarian and a more corporatist basis than ever before. It thus contrasts not only with other U.S. firms but also with the worker buyout at Weirton Steel. A major difference is that the distribution of shares in the ESOP at McLouth—an important indicator of social power—is based on both wages and hours worked. Like everything else at McLouth, this distribution scheme reflected some hard bargaining. While management had argued for a hierarchical distribution based entirely on wages, as at Weirton, the USW insisted on including the number of hours individuals actually worked. Yet against older workers, who wanted to base ownership shares entirely on seniority, the union held out for the compromise yardstick of hours and wages. This was, in Harry Lester's view, the most equitable balance between both labor and management and experience and productivity. Unlike the norm of "equality of sacrifice" that was used at Weirton to compensate for social differences in the allocation of ownership, McLouth's formula reinforces social differences in the firm. In our terms, Harry Lester consciously used *market* measures to strengthen commitment to *place*.

The ESOP at McLouth also contrasts with Weirton's because it avoids the distributional mechanism of profit-sharing. McLouth's ESOP distributes bonuses in the form of shares of productivity gains. Lester estimates that workers will work less and recoup more by these arrangements than they gave up in wage concessions. Productivity bonuses to ESOP shareholders are also supposed to create "a self-directed work force." While Lester approves, he admits that under the ESOP, supervisors may find motivated workers "frightening."

Under the new regime, McLouth is making a more serious effort at participatory management than in 1982. While managers are still preoccupied with financial and operating problems, they now aim at consistency and teamwork in labor relations. Yet this orientation to some degree follows the mildly participatory management style also initiated by larger steelmakers (including Bethlehem, Inland, National, and

LTV) and even by McLouth's supplier, Cleveland-Cliffs. In July 1988, McLouth hired a new CEO from Great Lakes Steel, McLouth's closest competitor. Ironically, he was one of the local steel executives who had called Harry Lester in 1982 and urged him to let McLouth go under.

The new board of directors institutionalized the corporatist participation of labor unions, local government, and suppliers that underlay the restructuring process. During the first fifteen years of the ESOP, the worker-owners have only pass-through voting rights. But the board of directors includes four seats for creditors (including, on the first go-round, Cleveland-Cliffs, Elk River, and Detroit Edison); three seats for USW delegates, personally selected by Harry Lester (including former UAW president Douglas Fraser, the USW's ESOP attorney, and Lester himself); one seat voted by the salaried workers (who chose the treasurer of downriver Wayne County, whose spouse is a McLouth employee); two seats for public members (the Michigan Commerce Department's director, Doug Ross, and a former president of National Steel); and the CEO. These directors want to be "a hands-on board." Significantly, they consider their biggest challenge to be arranging the financing for future capital improvements in the plant. Although Cyrus Tang did invest $70 or $80 million in new and upgraded equipment, these costs continue to stir great concern. On the agenda for McLouth are upgrading the continuous casters, relining the oxygen furnaces, and installing new finish equipment for potential customers. We know that these are costly operations.

On the workers' side, too, concessions at McLouth have fostered big changes. The company now has the lowest total hourly labor costs in the steel industry, by about $2.50. The new labor contract reduced plant size by 10 percent, bringing the work force below 2,000. New rules, moreover, finally established flexible work crews whose members are interchangeable and accept a variety of assignments as required. Although Harry Lester took the greatest amount of criticism from union members on this flexibility, it is the area in which McLouth comes closest to an emerging industrywide norm. The production workers' hopes ride heavily on Harry Lester. Without a strong local leader to challenge him, Lester wields great power as both district director of the USW and member of the board of directors.

By the middle of 1987, before the ESOP and the labor contract were even put into final form, conditions in the steel industry began to change. Because of reduced capacity and import quotas enacted in 1984,

McLouth and Great Lakes Steel were able to sell all the steel they could produce. Weirton, Bethlehem, and U.S. Steel (the steel division of USX) planned to sell improved steel cans to the beverage industry. The increase in demand for domestic steel altered the sluggish trading of steel companies' shares on the stock market. Bethlehem Steel, whose stock values in recent years tended to decline every time the company announced it was investing in capital improvements, sold an entire new issue of stock equity. The largest steelmakers, including Bethlehem and U.S. Steel, actually made a profit from their steel operations.

This rising tide seemed to lift all boats. In fact it reflected the continuing use of constrasting strategies in a much smaller steel industry. The giant, diversified USX continued to shut plants down, inducing a 39 percent cut in capacity and a 50 percent reduction in employment. Bethlehem continued to drive for more efficiency in the use of existing technology. Nucor, the mini-mill company, invested heavily in advanced technology for making thinner steel, and also established a joint venture in Arkansas with a Japanese steelmaker.[10]

McLouth still bled from a high rate of labor turnover, losing 80 of 400 salaried employees in 1987 alone. Yet four straight months of productivity gains resulted in cash bonuses being paid to the work force. It looked as though by means of productive labor, McLouth was going to survive again.

MCLOUTH AS A NEW LANDSCAPE OF POWER?

An ESOP, as Lazard's investment bankers taught folks at Weirton, is not an anticapitalist revolution. But it does represent both a material change in economic ownership and a symbolic change in social roles. Just as the core work force now bear the major risk for the financial performance of their firm, so they also shift the form in which they bear this risk from wage labor to investment. At best, when workers in durable goods and transformative industries save their jobs, they assume a double burden. Not only do they have to cope with more automation and more "self-direction" in their jobs, they also have to support their employment with the direct investment of their pensions and reductions in earning levels.

Worker buyouts, therefore, represent a mortgage on the future. Except for rare experiments like Lucas Aerospace in Britain, they remain a peculiarly American experience, harnessing the world's most diversified financial institutions to the richest pension system. Yet worker buy-outs are just a last resort for firms when they can raise no new capital from either private markets or the state. They can only be an interim solution to problems of raising capital for industrial renewal. Neverthe-less, when corporate takeovers and junk bonds wane, ESOPs find favor in the financial community as a socially acceptable means of both en-forcing labor productivity and raising capital.[11]

Both ESOPs and EDA loan guarantees are caught between the Scylla and Charybdis of market criteria. Workers who would be impoverished by losing their jobs are nonetheless "rich" enough to buy their plant. Similarly, if a company were "rich" enough to pay back a loan, as an EDA official says, it wouldn't need to apply for a loan guarantee in the first place. And if a company was too "poor" to be a good credit risk, it would surely default. McLouth was in fact the only firm that did not default on EDA loan guarantees issued under the special 1978 program for smaller steelmakers. Both LTV and Wheeling-Pittsburgh, bigger companies that were considered better credit risks, eventually filed for Chapter 11 bankruptcy protection. By contrast, the element that distin-guished McLouth—besides its modern plant and Detroit location—was support for the firm in the local vernacular. McLouth and Weirton dramatize the same success factors researchers on worker ownership found in the 1970s—but these now occur in a context of downsized industry, intensified global competition, and labor concessions.[12]

While each potential shutdown causes tremors to run through the local business and political communities, McLouth stirred real commit-ment on the part of its corporate attorneys, its local bank, and the Michigan Commerce Department. Each actor was determined not to let the company fail, and they all collaborated in this interest. The work force, for their part, were orchestrated by Harry Lester, who directed the unions' strategy from outside the USW local, much as the attorney Dave Robertson did at Weirton. Lester turned the local's militant tra-dition into a means of corporate mobilization. Thus the docility of Weirton's company union does not seem to be a decisive factor. What is important, however, is a situation in which "entrepreneurial" local forces are not blocked by market institutions.

Many players who took part in restructuring McLouth and Weir-ton—especially those from the financial community—emphasize that the work force must show a "willingness to sacrifice." But two addi-tional factors are also important. Representatives of financial institutions must really commit themselves to the viability of the firm and act accordingly. This degree of commitment was shown by all the outside consultants at Weirton and in the *second* restructuring of McLouth. It was notably absent during McLouth's Chapter 11 bankruptcy reorganization. Another important factor is the absence of a barrier in the form of a giant corporation that will neither sell nor keep a plant open. This is a major contrast between Weirton and McLouth, on the one hand, and Youngstown, Lackawanna, and Alan Wood Steel, on the other.

Even by these standards, McLouth's survival in 1982 was really a fluke. The secured creditors attacked the firm with all the financial power at their control. They literally saw no future for a small, independently owned domestic steel mill. No one could have predicted that they would fail to shut the firm down. Yet for all the incompetence of the old ownership, whose equity was spread out among "widows and orphans," and "ham-handed" or "country-club" management, McLouth managed to retain the autonomy of place over market forces. Harry Lester would probably not have got so far in 1982 in a different local landscape—in South Chicago, Buffalo, or Conshohocken, Pennsylvania—where Big Steel held sway over labor markets.

By contrast, again, with Weirton, the political economy's complex dependence on heavy industry aided McLouth's survival. During the firm's bankruptcy reorganization in 1982, eleven other plants represented by District 29 of the USW filed for Chapter 11 bankruptcy protection. Five years later, during the ESOP negotiations, the largest machine tool manufacturer in Detroit, Snyder Tool and Die, shut down. There was neither labor nor community mobilization in that case to save the plant. Was it the strength or weakness of productive labor at McLouth that permitted the vernacular to change and survive?

The way McLouth was saved contradicts both the adversarial history of the U.S. steel industry and the Schumpeterian tradition of the individual entrepreneur. From the 1950s through the 1970s, General Motors behaved toward McLouth like a Japanese industrial bank. Its financial commitment to the steelmaker permitted McLouth to make long-term investments in new technology. After GM excluded McLouth from the nexus of supplier dependency, McLouth's own suppliers, with the labor union's prodding, forced the company to restructure. This recalls the strong social networks we associate with Japanese suppliers and the government of Japan. The state of Michigan also acted like the Japanese MITI or the central government of a European state by forcing labor and management to seek consensus. Unlike their foreign counterparts, however, Michigan officials did not play explicit or well-defined institutional roles. Unlike private financial institutions, moreover, they acted from self-interest, but not for the sake of immediate profit. The version of market culture from which they extemporized their roles utilized, rather than destroyed, the norms of place.

For all the foreign-sounding innovation, these arrangements reflect an "internalized corporatism" typical of the market culture of U.S. economic actors. Harry Lester, after all, promised the governor of Michigan that he would not embarrass him. State Treasurer Bob Bowman, whose job and connections fostered cooperation with the financial community, relied on Lester to keep the labor unions in line. Lester and the Michigan Commerce Department's director also had a long-term political alliance. And the raw materials suppliers who pressed for the second restructuring were dependent on the firm. The more regional industry downsized, the tighter that bond grew. These changes are not foreseen by those who advocate combating industrial disinvestment through either worker ownership or local control.

In the long run, however, the local landscape of economic power can not count on being reconstituted by auto and steel production. A look at the shifts in employment around Weirton and downriver Detroit confirms national trends toward job growth in services and a female work force, especially in health care, schools, and retail trade. Generational and household changes reflect these shifts. In the family of one steelworker at McLouth, for example, the men are downwardly mobile across three generations. The husband, in his forties, is a union activist whose father was also a highly skilled worker; the son, a young steelworker, was laid off in 1980. But the wife has a public-sector administrative job, and a daughter works in a nearby retail store. This is a typical household at McLouth and many other manufacturing firms, where wage and benefit concessions and layoffs have sent more wives and daughters into the work force. More jobs of this type will be created in the deindustrialized landscape of the future.[13]

Metropolitan Detroit promises to be a divided landscape. If firms like McLouth can survive on the basis of productivity and new technology, they only do so by continuously retraining an aging work force (subsidized by the state) and drastically curtailing new hires. The old community network that provided access to the labor market, passing steel and auto jobs from one generation to another, has been broken. Its informal vernacular has been replaced by bureaucratic control over such qualifications as computer literacy and formal skills. Yet in that segment of productive labor that can adapt to these new norms, the vernacular will survive. Indeed, the upgrading of highly automated industry downriver in Detroit, and in other Michigan suburbs and rural towns, preserves the white ethnic blue-collar vernacular at a continuing cost to that of the impoverished, mainly African-American, inner city of Detroit. In the Great Lakes region, especially in lakefront cities like Detroit, black male production workers are more likely to be displaced by both shutdown and automation than any other category of the work force, and also less likely to benefit from job growth in high tech industry.[14]

Even downriver, however, the landscape is divided. McLouth is considering the sale of 500 acres, more than half its Gibraltar site, to a Baltimore real estate developer who plans to build a major tourism and entertainment complex like Inner Harbor. There is already another yacht facility nearby, and a former B. F. Goodrich plant is being converted into a marina. Rail transport on tracks along the river ended some years ago, but the waterfront that was so crucial to downriver's industrial development will be shared, temporarily, by two contrasting economic landscapes: those of steel plants from the industrial age and postindustrial pleasure boat basins.

Maintaining the corporate office and shopping-center landscape typical of other Detroit suburbs, in Fairlane and Oakland County, may also pose problems. Under the surface of job growth and new construction lies the issue of eventual overdevelopment. This issue will become more dramatic as more middle-class blacks move to the suburbs. The industrial suburb of Dearborn, for example, was long shielded from racial diversity by Ford Motor Company's segregationist town-planning policies. Yet in the 1980s Fairborn was confronted by a lawsuit filed by the National Association for the Advancement of Colored People seeking equal access to public places like municipal parks. To the north, Oakland County already has a growing black population. Preserving steel plants like McLouth, or the more highly automated auto manufacturers, may retain jobs for the relatively small number of blacks who already work in such plants, in contrast to the greater number of blacks who work in repetitive production jobs. But the rest of Detroit's black population will not have an adequate economic base for their suburbanization. The economic and social institutions with long-range presence on which the vernacular relies are lost.

I. M. Pei, IBM facility, Somers, New York (1989). Photo courtesy IBM.

6   The Mill and the Mall: Power and Homogeneity in Westchester County

> Nestled amid rolling hills brimming with glorious years-old trees, country flowers, a cascading waterfall and tall, proud grass, is the nature-kissed town of Cheshire, Connecticut. Now the home of Bloomingdale's By Mail Ltd. new Executive Offices and Distribution Center, the charm and tranquil beauty of Cheshire literally swept us off our feet. . . .
>
> The town is rich with history, not the least of which was copper mining, begun in 1712. Today, the town is a suburban village to New Haven and Hartford commuters as well as a composite of industrial homes, from one-man machine shops to major corporations.
>
> Bloomingdale's Christmas catalogue, 1987

The divided landscape around Detroit and most other large American cities indicates a major reversal of meaning between the city and its suburbs. Until quite recently we thought of cities as the economic heartland whose vast wealth nourished a surrounding, and clearly subordinate, regional culture. The city had smokestacks; the suburbs had tract housing developments. The city had sleek office towers; the suburbs had poky commuter trains. The city had theaters and concert halls for original performances; the suburbs had mass culture's derivative shopping centers and drive-in movies. This socio-spatial differentiation repeated the pattern of form following function, with "suburbanism" considered a form of consumption derived from the city's productive functions. More critical, however, is the fact that the city has always financed the suburbs. Investment by the city's banks builds highways and shopping centers. Employment in the city's offices pays mortgages on suburban homes. And the concentration of "social problems" in the city fuels the exodus outward into the suburbs of all those people who can afford to move away. Even in the glossiest cultural representations, it was never imagined that the suburbs would compete with the city as a source of productive wealth, a landscape of economic power.

Yet Westchester County, whose vast greensward and rolling hills form the northern border of New York City, from the Hudson River to Connecticut, is one of the major corporate headquarters locations in the United States. Westchester was farmed by English immigrants before the Revolutionary War. At the end of the nineteenth century, the Hudson Valley properties that their descendants still owned attracted buyers from the city—William Rockefeller, John D. Rockefeller, Jr., Jay Gould—who built Gilded Age villas, horse farms, and country clubs: a landscape of consumption for a metropolitan as well as a national elite. Westchester was still "three-quarters . . . untouched" by either urban or industrial development at the start of the Great Depression. But between 1950 and 1985, so many corporate headquarters and other offices were built along the Cross Westchester Expressway between Tarrytown, New York, and Greenwich, Connecticut, that the highway was called the "platinum mile"[1] (see map 1).

The creative destruction of Westchester County reflects a familiar array of factors. These begin with deindustrialization—that is, the decline or takeover of local manufacturers in the southern towns of the county and a failure to attract new industries. They include the decentralization of corporate offices outside New York City to suburban towns and villages like those along the "platinum mile." This relates to a reorganization of corporate functions that has been speeded up in recent years by the high costs of labor and office space in city centers, changes in tax laws, and mergers and acquisitions. All this has occurred quite independently of Westchester County. But real estate development guided by zoning laws and urban plans always implies the hidden hand of local place-based elites. So the landscape of Westchester County also reflects the countywide coordination of public and private economic power. The result of these processes of creative destruction is a prototype landscape of consumption. In contrast to previous suburban landscapes, however, consumption spaces coexist with corporate offices that finance and contextualize the distinctive upper-middle-class mode of

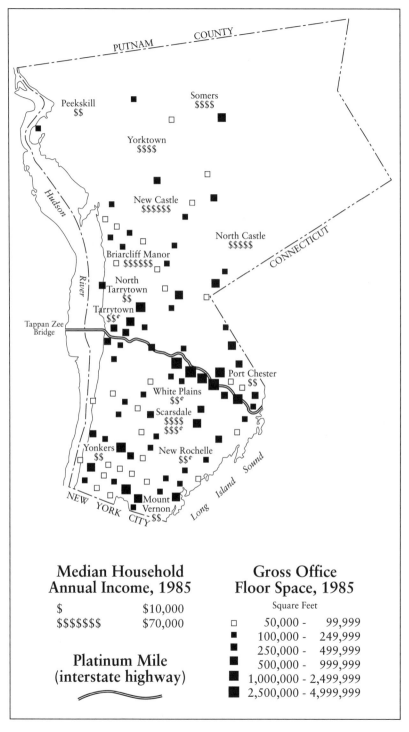

Map 1. Commercial development and median annual household income in Westchester County towns (Westchester County Department of Planning, 1986).

residential real estate development. Integrated into the transnational service economy, Westchester County also provides a perspective on maintaining traditional social class and racial distinctions in a new landscape of power.

If we looked only at deindustrialization and corporate headquarters location, the creative destruction of Westchester County would appear to be just a microcosm of market forces or macroeconomic trends. Yet the ability to create a landscape of such striking homogeneity also represents the conscious, long-term efforts of local actors with enormous power over place. Early in the twentieth century, Westchester's landed elite realized the high stakes of socially homogeneous property development that would exclude industrial uses. The setting they created appealed to the financial and organizational strategies of cash-rich corporate leaders after World War II. And like residents of many nineteenth-century bourgeois suburbs in England and the United States, Westchester's growing population of affluent consumers consciously sought to exclude lower classes from their state of grace.[2]

Westchester County also represents a midpoint in our series of five twentieth-century landscapes. Originally organized for both mill town production and country house consumption, Westchester based its modern growth on a new landscape of consumption accessible to a growing upper middle class. In part the county's landscape looked back to nineteenth-century suburbs, where owners of villas consumed "nature" in country clubs, on parkways, and the grounds of their own estates. But Westchester also looked forward to more crowded twentieth-century suburban landscapes, where homeowners, shoppers, and corporate employees consumed "culture" in commercial centers, parking lots, and offices. Thus economic development strategies led to an interesting paradox. While *visual* homogeneity was fairly easy to maintain, the construction of *social* homogeneity posed continual problems.

THE SUBURBAN LANDSCAPE

For at least 100 years, "urbanization" has included both a steady growth of cities and a parallel decentralization of economic activity to the suburbs outside them. From the 1850s, factories began moving out of the most developed urban cores into unbuilt farmland on the suburban fringes. Forming an eventual decentralized concentration, the industrial suburb has existed as a distinct American socio-spatial form since 1910.

Unlike its earlier counterparts in Europe, the U.S. industrial suburb at its best developed in a different landscape. U.S. companies often chose to surround their plants with a spacious, natural environment that gave their wooded "campuses" the same pastoral quality residents chose in exurban housing. At this stage, suburban industry relied on both railroads and trucking. After 1925, however, as local highway builders and large property owners struck alliances with state legislators to fund road construction, trucking became more common. Once a nationwide system of highways was planned by the U.S. Congress, almost all new industrial construction took place in the suburbs.[3]

Cheap land, transportation, and room to grow: these were the roots of the suburbs' manifest destiny. The alternative was urban congestion, high taxes, and labor strife, all the impediments *place* imposes over time on *market* forces. By the beginning of the twentieth century, older American cities represented a highly specialized and somewhat limiting socio-spatial structure for both place- and market-based entrepreneurs—that is, those who dealt in land and those who appropriated labor. Older subway systems—notably, New York's—had expanded to the limits of profitability by 1910. This condition restricted the possibility of developing more subway lines, which in turn would have opened up more areas of the city to intensive industrial and commercial development. Consequently, large landowners who wanted to capitalize on place focused on centrally located speculative office development that paid the highest rents. Partly because of real estate speculation, the high price of urban land made assembly of large sites difficult—and made the construction of new industrial sites practically impossible.

The same development of cheap transport and good communications that enabled the annihilation of space by time on a global scale also opened the suburbs to a variety of uses. By the same token, the centralization of capital in fewer corporate hands concentrated office employment in a small number of major cities, while rationalizing the maze of railroad lines that linked these cities and surrounding residential suburbs. Against this large-scale backdrop, local landowners played out their financial strategies. A far-sighted landed elite would try to harness public power to advance their private speculative interests. In any milieu they tended to develop and control town-planning institutions. But in the suburbs they also relied on the traditional political fragmentation of towns and villages to provide space for action. Town and village governments were usually unable to oppose large-scale development projects (e.g., housing, roads, and regional shopping centers). Beyond these small local units, however, the countywide scale of relatively open country offered developers and landed elites the opportunity to construct a new landscape of power.[4]

But the residential development that had opened U.S. suburbs to middle-class housing during the 1920s reached an impasse during the Great Depression. Local landed elites who wanted to pursue development sought to merge their interests with those of the federal government. As a result, the massive federal aid to suburban development that began during the 1930s subjected intensive spatial reorganization to norms of social homogenization. From 1933, federal homeownership programs consistently undervalued the central city and favored the suburbs. At the same time, federal guidelines tacitly ceded public housing to the inner city, while reserving publicly subsidized private housing development for the suburbs. Federal agencies excluded nonwhite families from such subsidies as government mortgages and mortgage guarantees. They also endorsed racial covenants that prohibited white suburban homeowners from selling to nonwhites. When the Federal Housing Authority instructed local employees on how to measure the quality of an area, the FHA emphasized "economic stability" and "protection from adverse interests." These were understood to be code words against the city's social, especially racial, heterogeneity.[5]

By the same token, the post–World War II influx of white working-class and middle-class households into many suburbs—including Westchester County—was rigidly controlled by town zoning laws that favored relatively large lots and developers' legal latitude to reject would-be homebuyers. In much of the rest of the United States, however, opening the suburbs to massive residential development spatially defined a new market culture. Suburbia's socio-spatial patterns typically anchored in *place* the *market* arrangements of the postwar period. Moreover, mass suburbanization offered a macroeconomic solution to prewar problems of underconsumption. Buying a house, at least one car, and domestic equipment integrated households into a national landscape of mass production and consumption. Indeed, 85 percent of new U.S. housing after World War II was built in the suburbs.[6]

HOMOGENEITY AS A LANDSCAPE OF POWER

Despite the heterogeneous uses to which suburban land was put, both the material and symbolic landscapes reinforced an image of homogeneity. In the built environment, the sheer amount of suburban space devoted to consumption—from new housing and public schools to country clubs and shopping centers—and the unprecedented scale on which these facilities were built created a singular material contrast with the city's multiple landscapes of consumption and production. The overwhelming presence of white residents, moreover, and the restriction of new suburban homeownership to those social classes that could afford to live there, symbolized the elimination of the city's divided landscapes of affluence and devastation.

The suburbs' symbolic landscape was also defined by the double mobility—both geographical and social—of the many new suburban homeowners who held managerial jobs in major corporations. Their mobility reflected the growth of national business organizations staffed by nationwide internal labor markets. Rising within one of these internal labor markets often required a transfer between corporate divisions, and a corresponding move from one region of the country to another. One of the most widely read books about the 1950s described the suburban corporate employee—"the organization man"—as "the man who leaves home."[7]

While the organization man's personality was almost wholly formed by his job, he and his wife were also social pillars of "the new suburbia." They may have grown up in the city or a small town. But the move to the suburbs represented a step up in social class, a step taken by so many at one time that it supported both the structural mobility of an entire generation and a transcendence of the very idea of social class. The socially homogeneous material landscape of the corporate suburbs, in other words, represented a middle-class image of classlessness. This was the symbolic landscape most people associated with postwar suburban development.

If this landscape was marked at all as a landscape of power, it was surely the power of individuals in America to make their own destiny. Yet continued development of the suburbs testified to the presence of large-scale, bureaucratic economic power. The suburbs grew by the efforts of major real estate developers and financial institutions, the federal government, and national corporations. Their economic power created not only corporate suburbs but also "corporate malls" and "corporate strips." Much maligned for their standardized architecture and "decentered" social life, commercial strips and shopping centers are nonetheless significant liminal spaces. They are both public and private—privately owned, but built for public use. They are both collective and individual—used for the collective rites of modern hunting and gathering, but also sites of personal desire. They are, further, liminal spaces between the intimacy of the home, car, and local store and the impersonal promiscuity of chain stores, name brands, and urban variety. Shopping centers, moreover, are both material and symbolic: they give material form to a symbolic landscape of consumption. Their imagery seduces men and women to believe in the landscape of a homogeneous mass consumption by masking centralized economic power in individual choice.[8]

Beneath the image, however, suburban homogeneity reflects three overlapping processes of creative destruction: de-gentrification, deindustrialization, and corporate office relocation.

In a process of *de-gentrification,* modern suburbs are created when developers acquire property from earlier residents who are wealthier and often more socially prominent. As time goes on, the "landed gentry" who buy suburban homes own smaller lots and more standardized housing designs than their predecessors. This does not necessarily affect the economic value of a suburban home, which keeps pace with general inflation and the pursuit of social homogeneity.

Westchester County was first de-gentrified in 1880–1900 when New York City financiers bought property from descendants of colonial elites. The nouveaux riches of the Gilded Age had great economic power. Property owner Jay Gould, for example, owned the New York Central Railroad, so he could go to his office in the city by flagging a passing train. Yet this class was less socially distinguished than that of the old, prerevolutionary families. By the end of the 1920s, another wave of de-gentrification occurred, when the mode of development shifted to large houses built on relatively small plots of land. Because of the automobile, this housing was often located deep in the county, far from the railroad stations. Although new residents were poorer and less socially prominent than the Rockefellers, they were hardly members of the working class. In 1930, almost the same proportion of Westchester County residents worked in banking and finance as residents of New York City.[9] During this time, housing developers preserved Westchester's verdant landscape. In upper-income residential communities such as Bronxville, Scarsdale, and Tuxedo Park, developers followed the natural topography by saving trees and building winding roads, and only sold large lots. Bronxville, for example, developed by William Van Duzer Lawrence in the 1880s, offered grand houses in a variety of styles—Tudor, Romanesque Revival, Italianate—an early "postmodern" marketing decision.

In the 1950s, members of this prewar suburban gentry mourned the demise of *their* suburban way of life as "ticky-tacky" houses on quarter-acre lots encroached upon their horse farms, woods, and golf clubs. In a footnote to *The Organization Man*, William H. Whyte, Jr., tells an anecdote about one such couple, who sold some property in eastern Pennsylvania to a developer, who built tract houses for managers of the nearby Bethlehem Steel Plant. The couple then criticized the president of Bethlehem Steel, a personal friend, for recruiting managers who lacked aesthetic taste and had wives who spoke with a midwestern twang.

In Westchester County, also, the de-gentrification of the 1950s brought both desired and unwelcome changes. When, on the one hand, the United Nations built its headquarters in New York City after World War II (on land bought by John D. Rockefeller, Jr., and donated to the world organization), many U.N. embassies bought estates in Westchester. This undoubtedly saved some of them from decay, property tax defaults, and demolition by avid developers. But when, on the other hand, relatively affluent middle-class communities began to expand in Westchester in the early 1950s, amid corporate office relocations from New York City, many of the older gentry were dismayed. Despite new additions to the tax base, a vocal antidevelopment group formed in the county, with the most aggrieved residents moving northward toward Putnam County. Differences of opinion regarding de-gentrification were so intense that a local writer warned of the social partition of the county under the tongue-in-cheek title "The Coming Crisis in Slobovia."[10]

Another process of creative destruction in older suburbs is *deindustrialization*. Unlike in the downriver suburbs of Detroit, however, most people view Westchester's deindustrialization as a desirable transformation, because "obsolete" industry is replaced by new service jobs. Industry has for the most part, moreover, been segregated in Westchester's southern towns. Their ethnic and blue-collar populations are the most directly affected by the loss of industrial jobs. Nor has this been a cataclysmic process. Local industries have been shutting down in West-chester for most of the twentieth century. Although manufacturing jobs in the county continued to grow after 1899, the light industry that had built up the southern towns began to disappear between the two world wars. The county became even less geared to industry after World War II. Westchester in the late 1940s got the lowest share of new plant value in New York State—a smaller share of new industrial investment than Manhattan. But while manufacturing jobs in most of the county's major industrial sectors dramatically declined between 1942 and 1951, employment in services and construction boomed. Metal fabrication lost almost half its jobs, employment in the lumber industry declined by 25 percent, and there were 20 percent fewer workers building transportation equipment. At the same time, however, construction jobs grew by over 200 percent, financial jobs increased by 500 percent, and employment in business services expanded by more than 600 percent. If this was a case of deindustrialization, it was a case nearly everyone seemed to approve.[11]

During the 1960s, both deindustrialization and de-gentrification continued remapping the landscape, with paradoxical results. On the one hand, while employment opportunities in manufacturing rapidly dropped, the pressure for housing from working-class households, especially African-Americans living in the southern cities, began to affect nearby residential areas. On the other hand, although the influx of corporate offices and corporate residents enhanced the tax base in towns and villages from Armonk to Scarsdale, it brought Jewish and other minority executives into virgin WASP territory. Paradoxical or not, the effects of creative destruction were bound to please both place- and market-based entrepreneurs. The expansion of the service sector fed a voracious appetite for real estate development.[12]

These processes of change subtly altered the symbolic landscape of Westchester County. De-gentrification by means of new residents and business activities made Westchester more socially heterogeneous than ever before. Until 1960, for example, registered Republican voters far outnumbered Democrats, and Republican victory was assured in all elections. By 1968, however, registered Republicans in the county outnumbered Democrats by only two to one. Democratic candidates began to win local offices, and votes for Democratic presidential candidates steadily rose from 1960 to 1984.

Yet deindustrialization countered this social heterogeneity with spatially homogenizing effects. After 1950, as traditional industries declined and public housing began to be built, most of the industrial working class, especially blacks and Hispanics, became more deeply concentrated in the southern towns and old manufacturing centers. At the same time, corporate office relocations transformed elite residential areas into affluent commercial suburbs. These suburbs now had a dual advantage. The combination of upper-class residents and high-status white-collar employees allowed them to retain a sleek image of homogeneity. By contrast, the homogeneity of the economically troubled southern towns reflected their concentration of lower-class residents and blue-collar workers. By the 1980s, economic power divided Westchester County into *two* homogeneous landscapes: a landscape of affluence based on consumption and a landscape of devastation based on industrial production.[13]

The homogeneous landscape of Westchester County can therefore be viewed from three overlapping economic perspectives: deindustrialization, corporate relocation, and de-gentrification or real estate development. Each perspective reflects the consequences of structural change as well as individual action, producing both a "natural" and a socially constructed landscape.

DEINDUSTRIALIZATION: FROM OTIS ELEVATOR TO IBM

Until quite recently, Westchester was one of New York State's major industrial powers. In 1909, its industrial production trailed that of New York and Erie counties. (Erie surrounds the industrial city of Buffalo.) As late as 1954, Westchester's industrial employment was exceeded only by New York's, Erie's, and Nassau County's (on Long Island). The city of Yonkers remained Westchester's key industrial center throughout this time. Since the 1970s, however, Yonkers has been plagued by factory shutdowns, fiscal crisis, and disorganization in the face of economic decline on the part of local elected officials.

Yonkers has the landscape of devastation that Westchester County planners abhor. It reminds them of the Bronx, whose decline some white residents of Yonkers fled. During the 1980s, moreover, the Yonkers City Council chose to defy federal court orders to enforce racial desegregation of public housing location and public schools. Yet from the seventeenth to the early twentieth centuries, Yonkers supported a vigorous manufacturing economy. Its vernacular working-class community represented a middle ground between the density of production in the city and the nonworking landscape of Westchester's landed elite.

While early industrialists simply used the Hudson and Saw Mill rivers' abundant water power to run lumber and sugar mills, a later generation of factory owners were more entrepreneurial. Making—and often losing—fortunes, they developed both new goods and the technology to produce them. Indeed, the careers of Yonkers factory owners in the late nineteenth century were cast in the very image of the industrial entrepreneur. John Waring's family, for example, manufactured a kind of wool hat for which Yonkers became known and also developed the hatting machinery to produce it. Alexander Smith, owner of a carpet factory that in the 1880s was the city's biggest employer, invented a better power loom for making tapesty, moquette, and Axminster carpets than the famous Bigelow loom of Massachusetts. Charles Otis, the city's most famous entrepreneur, developed the passenger elevator from a simple safety-catch improvement, and established the Otis Elevator Company in Yonkers in 1852. Leo Baekeland, a Belgian immigrant, invented Bakelite in his Yonkers laboratory; this plastic was widely used in the twentieth century in radio sets, toilet seats, and weapons systems.[14]

The mutually reinforcing growth of invention and industry was fed by two sources of power: strong local banks and steam, both controlled by the city's industrial elite. Around 1900, it must have looked as though they would enjoy unlimited growth forever. In retrospect, however, the city's industrial future was limited. Besides the usual number of fires and bankruptcies, the largest firms in Yonkers tended to monopolize technological initiative and bank credit. While this may have strengthened their industries—brewing, machinery, carpet weaving, and printing—it probably did so by limiting others. Many Yonkers firms, moreover, depended on a local market. This made them vulnerable to competition from bigger firms in New York City.[15]

When Charles Otis died in the 1860s, the Otis Elevator Company employed only eight or ten men and was worth just $5,000. The firm prospered in the building boom that followed the Civil War, but lost half its capital in the depression of 1873. Ten years later, however, success was assured. The firm employed 350 men in the Yonkers plant and an equal number in on-site installation. The country's industrial and urban expansion fed demand for Otis products. In 1854, the firm built five or six elevators; in 1883, the plant produced six hundred, including hydraulic, steam, and "belt" elevators, which were attached to other building machinery. Business success confirmed its position in the local community. "On the whole," says the author of a history of Westchester published in 1886, "the Otis Brothers have been for years a power in the business, social and religious life of Yonkers and of the county at large."[16]

Otis Elevator continued to grow both by developing new technology and by expanding markets. Building booms in the 1920s increased elevator sales, and the trend toward taller buildings required more sophisticated products. The growth and branching of department stores also increased demand, and Otis responded with safer, streamlined escalators. In the 1940s, moreover, when apartment and office building owners tried to cut overhead by replacing elevator operators with self-service cars, Otis developed the new automated technology.[17] Beginning with the Otis elevator installed in the Eiffel Tower in 1889, the company found a worldwide market for its products. Eventually Otis opened plants overseas. By the 1980s, Otis Europe had over 5,000 employees on twenty-four sites throughout France, most of them in the industrial suburbs of Paris. In North America, production was carried out in several regional locations.[18]

Although Otis had bought up other firms throughout its history, it was itself acquired by the larger United Technologies Company in 1975. UT first bought 70 percent of the outstanding shares in the firm for $276 billion, and then, in an unwelcome maneuver, made Otis a wholly-owned subsidiary. By that point, Otis was the world's largest manufacturer of elevators and escalators, building and installing 20,000 new pieces of equipment a year. Continuing the pattern set in 1883, Otis concentrated its core business equally in manufacturing and service contracts. Being part of United Technologies promised some advantages. While UT's core business was building aircraft and engines, in 1978 the corporation bought and merged several electronics firms, which gave Otis access to microprocessors for more flexible elevator technology. In the early 1980s, UT's Building Systems division, which included Otis, Carrier Air Conditioning, and some smaller units, accounted for a quarter of the corporation's $13.8 billion in sales and a third of its operating profits of about half a billion dollars.[19]

From 1852 until 1976, Yonkers benefited from the Otis Elevator Company's continual expansion. Generations of Yonkers residents worked in the Otis plant. Managers were drawn from both local residents and outsiders, but production workers came mainly from traditional Irish and Italian working-class neighborhoods on the West Side of the city. This work force was racially integrated by affirmative action in the early 1970s, providing unionized jobs to African-American residents. Nearly 1,300 local residents were employed at the four-story, red-brick mother plant in 1968, when management asked the city government's help to expand into new facilities. Otis played on the relation between a local plant and the local community. And the city was desperate to retain one of its few remaining large industrial employers. Local officials put together a package of $13.9 million in public development funds, part of which was contributed by the federal and state governments and part by the city of Yonkers. The federal and state funds were used to acquire and clear a nine-acre site adjacent to the original Otis plant, midway between the declining downtown and the railroad station. The city government relocated sixty businesses and several hundred families from this site, and then sold it to Otis for only one-tenth the cost. Otis paid $539,000 to the city and promised to spend $852,000 on site improvements. The company spent a total of $10 million to build the new plant, which opened in 1976. At that point Otis was taken over by United Technologies.[20]

Six years later, the Otis management announced the shutdown of the new Yonkers plant. Employment had already shrunk from 1,300 to 375, but management made no demands for a wage cut, gave no advance notice, and entered into no negotiations with the International Union of Electrical Workers, the collective bargaining agent of Otis employees. Although the mayors of Yonkers who held office during these years were not keen on either United Technologies or the Otis expansion—one mayor, Angelo Martinelli, owned a printing plant that had to be relocated from the Otis site—the city government was determined to keep the Otis jobs. Not unreasonably, city officials insisted that recent public investment in the plant entitled them to expect some longevity. Neither the labor union nor the previous mayor took the initiative, so Mayor Martinelli, who served one term from 1974 to 1979 and another from 1982 to 1987, approached Otis management to try to negotiate. For months prior to the formal announcement of the shutdown in November 1982, management rebuffed the mayor's offers and denied it was really thinking of closing down.

Like Chicago and New Bedford, Massachusetts, where local officials also faced factory shutdowns after investing public funds, the city of Yonkers tried to sue United Technologies for breach of contract. But no formal contract had ever guaranteed the plant's longevity, and the city manager had even signed a release to the effect that UT had fulfilled all the terms of the urban renewal grant. Searching for another legal strategy, the city's attorneys examined the terms of the urban renewal plan to determine whether the city government could prohibit UT from leasing the plant to another firm. These attorneys were joined on a special Otis task force by representatives of HUD and the New York State Urban Development Corporation, as well as by corporate attorneys from the private sector, who donated their time *pro bono,* and staff from the County Clerk's and Mayor's offices. (Until 1982, both officials were Democrats and inclined toward governmental activism.).

For publicity, Mayor Martinelli led a caravan of demonstrators to United Technology's corporate headquarters in Hartford, Connecticut, and held a candlelight vigil outside the Yonkers plant. He also asked the state legislature to enact a bill requiring advance notice of factory shutdowns, six years before the U.S. Congress finally passed a similar law. Despite sympathetic coverage in the press, and a number of supporting statements by law professors on a company's obligation to stay in town after receiving public assistance, the city government did not succeed in keeping the Otis plant in Yonkers. City officials did not even win a lawsuit to recover property taxes that had been forgone as part of the urban development grant; that suit was dismissed on a technicality. Nor did higher elected officials from the state or the federal government offer to aid the Yonkers city government in the Otis case.

At any rate, Yonkers was unique among Westchester towns in using urban development funds to promote manufacturing. Since the mid 1960s, when the city of White Plains, capital of Westchester County, undertook a massive rebuilding of the downtown, practically all urban renewal funds had been used to build offices. But Yonkers had no choice. There was relatively little industrial construction in Westchester. And from the 1960s on, the lion's share of all new office construction was drawn not to the south but to the central part of the county, in and around White Plains. In contrast to that bustling city and its satellite shopping malls, the center of Yonkers, just a few miles away, was dotted with commercial vacancies. Yonkers' only attraction seemed to be the edible ethnic heritage—the kugelach, sfogliatelle, Polish Easter bread, and Napoleons—that Mayor Martinelli lauded to the *New York Times.*[21]

Although parts of Yonkers suggested a Rust Belt landscape of devastation, the reasons behind the Otis shutdown are still unclear. The decision to phase the plant out was made as early as 1973, before the expansion was even completed. The 1972 recession and the oil crisis of 1973, and a resulting slump in office construction, surely lowered demand for new Otis products. Yet other Otis plants did not shut down, and managers were transferred after 1982 from Yonkers to plants in Ontario, Canada, and Bloomington, Indiana. It is also possible that management simply made a huge mistake, drawing up an expansion plan that was prematurely outmoded. On the one hand, microprocessor technology for elevator mechanisms may not have been incorporated into the new Yonkers plant. On the other hand, the company may have decided after starting construction to automate a larger share of the production process. Or foreign-made elevator components could have been imported more cheaply than they would have been made in Yonkers. Around the same time, in 1984, Otis justified to the National Labor Relations Board a decision to end its research and development activities in New Jersey and move them to its offices in Connecticut— without bargaining with the labor union that represented its New Jersey employees—because of significant business changes.[22]

During this time, moreover, United Technologies was engaged in an ambitious, expensive mergers and acquisitions program under the impetus of CEO Harry Gray. The new Otis plant in Yonkers may have been affected by the corporate parent's financial pressures, including problems in the aircraft industry, which also resulted in layoffs at UT's Pratt & Whitney plants in Connecticut. In any case the entire Otis subsidiary was not at risk, for only three years after the Yonkers plant shut down, the company agreed to set up new manufacturing plants in China.

Significantly, the city of Yonkers was in the same position as all the old industrial towns of Westchester County. Their manufacturing plants existed in isolation from both small start-ups using new technology and distant corporate parents with global concerns. All the old industrial centers were losing their last major industrial employers, and confronting vacant plants or conversion to new residential properties. When management closed the original Life Savers plant in Port Chester in 1985, it blamed declining demand for hard sugar candy among calorie-conscious Americans. Nevertheless, it kept production going in newer Life Savers plants in Michigan, Puerto Rico, and upstate New York. In contrast to the unused Otis plant, however, Life Savers' corporate parent, Nabisco, sold the 1920 Port Chester factory to a Connecticut real estate developer. He turned it into residential condominiums, preserving the illuminated, seventeen-foot-long metal replica of a Life Savers roll that "floated" from the plant's facade.[23]

In North Tarrytown, on the Hudson River, the oldest existing General Motors assembly plant, opened in 1900 by the Maxwell Company, was scheduled to shut down in 1982. The shutdown would have displaced 4,000 employees, as much as half the town's population. Most of the work force, as in Yonkers, had followed parents and grandparents into the plant. Both the town and the auto plant were made up of Italian, Slavic, and Hispanic ethnic communities. Because the Hispanic community was the largest in Westchester County, moreover, it attracted undocumented Central American refugees. North Tarrytown already suffered from an array of inner city problems: overcrowded housing and jails, and not enough low-skill employment.

While GM blamed the shutdown decision on a decline in new car sales, local costs also appeared to be important. These included the $170 million price tag on building a new body paint shop to eliminate federal environmental violations, expensive utilities, and financing road or railroad improvements to provide clearances for shipping cars on the Conrail Hudson River Line. In this case, local and state governments took effective action. They were clearly inspired by the Otis shutdown in Yonkers, the dearth of other industrial employers in the county who could absorb the GM work force, and memories of a 22-month-long layoff at the North Tarrytown plant in 1973. Three years of negotiations resulted in a subsidy package for GM that recalls Weirton and McLouth. New York State reduced electricity costs, built the rail clearances, and reduced property taxes. The local industrial development agency bought the plant site from GM, and then leased it back to the company for a nominal $1 a year. The town government, moreover, accepted rent payments in lieu of property taxes, and set them equal to the annual interest on the bonds issued by the industrial development agency to pay for building GM's new paint shop. The U.S. Commerce Department also designated part of the local airport a free-trade zone, saving GM nearly $2 million a year in duties on imported parts.

The effort to preserve industrial jobs in North Tarrytown led to significant ironies. The federal government aided the auto industry's strategy of outsourcing by setting up the free-trade zone. On the state's part, Governor Mario Cuomo offered GM cheap nuclear power from a plant on Lake Ontario, although he fought bitterly to prevent the start-up of a nuclear power plant at Shoreham, on Long Island. And, of course, in real estate terms, the economic value of preserving industrial sites in Westchester County was far less than converting them to commercial and residential properties.[24] Yet in contrast to Yonkers' experience with Otis, this arrangement was successful. Two years after an agreement was signed, the work force at the auto plant rose to 4,500, and GM agreed to produce a new line of mini-vans in North Tarrytown, ensuring employment there through the 1990s. Unlike in Yonkers, local and state agencies were able to do a deal with GM. And unlike at Otis, the UAW work force showed the same spirit of union-management cooperation as the workers did at Weirton. A joint union-management group lobbied GM to build the mini-van in North Tarrytown, and the UAW local—like the USW at McLouth—accepted new work rules for flexible teams.

Surprisingly, the Otis shutdown did not end with the new plant's vacancy and abandonment. The Otis site was turned into an industrial facility for building transportation equipment by means of the extraordinary resources of the Port Authority of New York and New Jersey, a public superagency that oversees the region's major airports and mass transit systems. Yet while this intervention revived a major local industry that dates back to the early twentieth century, the firms involved are Japanese. After renovating the plant for prospective manufacturing tenants, and installing a new rail line on the site, the Port Authority leased part of it to a joint venture of Kawasaki and Nissho, which started producing new and refurbished railroad cars in 1986. The Port Authority also got a $250,000 federal grant to retrain local workers who had lost their jobs in plant shutdowns.

This experience of industrial renewal is limited. It was not the result of a statewide or even a local industrial policy. The Port Authority's effort is limited to this site, and its clout is contingent on its procurement budget. The Japanese were only persuaded to locate in Yonkers, moreover, by the conditions Port Authority imposed on its request for bids on equipment, which basically required successful bidders to produce it in the region. Few local agencies have this clout. Port Authority's industrial commitment also reflects a personal decision made by the former executive director. Redeveloping the Otis site for industrial use would lose its priority under a different director, more serious fiscal constraints, and pressing plans for alternative kinds of development or projects in other parts of the region.[25]

Yonkers' manufacturing economy suffers in general from other institutional limitations. On the one hand, industrial property in most of the county, including Yonkers, has a higher economic value as commercial space than as a production site. On the other hand, New York State's economic development policies are directed to large firms rather than the small and medium-sized businesses found in Yonkers.[26] These factors inhibit keeping space in industrial production. In any case, so many manufacturing facilities disappeared from Westchester County between 1954 and 1975 that its economic base was completely transformed.

In 1955, twenty manufacturing plants were listed among the thirty-seven major private-sector employers in the county. Besides Otis and General Motors, local industries included two multi-plant dairies and three multi-plant bakeries, multi-plant manufacturers of health equipment and electrical supplies, the largest nut and bolt factory in the world, two cable and wire plants, and several smaller industries. Most of this manufacturing activity was concentrated in Yonkers. At the same time, however, Westchester County was already the site of several corporate headquarters. Older ones included Otis, Life Savers, and the Reader's Digest Association. But between 1950 and 1955, new corporate headquarters had also been built in the county by such major national and international firms as General Foods, Nestlé, Standard-Vacuum Oil Company, and General Electric. These all immediately became major employers. AT&T's Long Lines Division, which moved into a new building in White Plains around this time, was also a major employer.[27]

By ten years later, no new major industrial employers had appeared. The biggest new business presence in the county in the 1960s was IBM, which opened several different office and research and development sites in the mainly undeveloped central and northern parts of the county.

IBM, with 10,400 employees, was Westchester County's largest private-sector employer in 1975. It was followed by federal (6,900), state (4,100), and other (32,500) public-sector employers. These in turn preceded an array of services and offices and a small number of manufacturers: New York Telephone (with 4,010 employees), the corporate headquarters of General Foods (3,200), AT&T's Long Lines Division (2,800), the Reader's Digest Association (2,500), Consolidated Edison (2,400), the GM assembly plant at North Tarrytown (2,200), Union Carbide research facilities (1,600), the plant and offices of Technicon

Instruments (1,400), the plant and corporate offices of Otis Elevator in Yonkers (1,350), Pepsico's corporate headquarters (1,350), the County Trust Company (1,330), Penn Central Transportation (1,280), Yonkers Racing Corporation (1,060), offices for the Swiss pharmaceutical firm Ciba-Geigy (1,050), Westchester Rockland Newspapers (1,025), and Gleason Security Services (1,000). The remaining large manufacturers were generally limited to between 500 and 1,000 employees.[28]

These shifts were accentuated after 1975. By 1988, Westchester County's largest employers were IBM (with 13,000 employees), the county government (8,000), AT&T's Long Lines Division (4,064), the GM assembly plant at North Tarrytown (4,000), the U.S. Postal Service (3,700), New York Telephone (3,300), the corporate headquarters of General Foods (2,740), NYNEX, the former New York Telephone (2,700), the Yonkers City School District (2,484), Reader's Digest Association (2,307), Consolidated Edison (2,300), the city of Yonkers (2,000), Pepsico's corporate headquarters (1,811), the Bank of New York (1,596), the Franklin D. Roosevelt Veterans' Administration Hospital (1,530), Metro North Commuter Railroad Company (1,422), New Rochelle Hospital Medical Center (1,290), Ciba-Geigy offices (1,217), and the plant and offices of Technicon Instrument Corporation (1,200).[29]

Significantly, no major private-sector employer had located in the industrial parts of the county since World War II. Aside from IBM's dispersed locations, all corporate headquarters, banks, and utilities clustered in the central part of the county, in and around White Plains. Not surprisingly, therefore, Yonkers exported its residents' labor, mainly to service jobs in other areas of Westchester. This marked a great change in the landscape.[30]

CORPORATE RELOCATION: IBM AND MORE

Just as the suburban landscape was changed by corporate reorganization in the industrial economy, so it also reflected the decentralization and recentralization of corporate offices. An increasing number of *Fortune* 500 firms moved their headquarters out of New York City to office campuses in the suburbs. While the city remained a corporate headquarters center, especially for financial firms, new office construction took place in Bergen and Middlesex counties in northern New Jersey and the Westchester-Fairfield county complex linking New York and Connecticut along the platinum mile.[31]

New office construction throughout the United States partly followed the decentralization pattern set by manufacturers half a century earlier. Giant urban centers—New York, Chicago, Dallas, Houston—kept most business services in downtown areas. By the 1960s, however, an increasing number of offices, even corporate headquarters, were being built in the suburbs. In Boston, Pittsburgh, Los Angeles, Philadelphia, Detroit, and other cities with large suburban populations, there were more office jobs in the suburbs than in the central business district. Not until the 1970s did the extent of suburban office growth across the nation attract attention. By that point, the fairly small budgets of suburban towns confronted unexpected costs of growth: traffic congestion, diminishing water supply, and inadequate garbage disposal facilities. Yet the increase in business services continued to attract high-income, white-collar employment, more traffic, and some commercial amenities. These added to the new suburban landscape.[32]

Economists who studied New York City's financial sector during the 1950s had already drawn attention to financial firms' potential for mobility. In contrast to those who assumed that Wall Street would never die—or disperse to the suburbs—the authors of *Money Metropolis: A Locational Study of Financial Activities in the New York Region* predicted that external economies would eventually persuade large offices to move outside the center city. These researchers focused on financial firms moving from Wall Street to midtown Manhattan. But they denied that traditional factors—either attachment to the city or face-to-face interaction of corporate elites—would weigh more heavily, in the long run, than economic costs. "The fact remains," they wrote, "that inertia and tradition hold firms in the financial district only so long as there are no strong reasons for them to go elsewhere. . . . When those reasons clearly show themselves, a shift eventually occurs, regardless of sentiment. It may take the form of building up major branches outside the main financial district, or even creating a second 'headquarters' office. So sentiment compromises with economics."[33]

The technological revolution that brought computers into every large and medium-sized office by the end of the 1960s had a direct effect on the landscape of Westchester County. Computers made possible a much greater and more rapid decentralization of corporate activities than even the most astute economists had imagined. They also supported IBM's expansion. During the 1960s, the computer manufacturer grew larger, and also changed its corporate strategy to sell rather than lease new machines for interactive data processing. These two changes increased the company's need for geographically linked facilities. This in turn led IBM to become the biggest developer of multiple office locations in Westchester County.[34]

Suburban corporate location like IBM's depended on more than just a cheap supply of available land. It also responded to corporate reorganization that separated manufacturing from headquarters, marketing staff, and research and development; public investment in highways and planning; and private developers who were ready to move into office campus development. Corporate strategy played, moreover, on social and cultural differentiation within the middle class, which had not been so fully expressed since before the Great Depression. Male professionals sought new family housing near, but not in, large cities. Technicians and engineers were likely to stay around universities. Middle-class women who had graduated from high school or college often held only part-time jobs or worked until they had children. From another perspective, however, corporate relocation from the city paralleled the pursuit of the cultural values of suburban homeownership: visual consumption of nature and social exclusivity. Like many residents, corporate executives also wanted their place of work to flee the city's urban blight, its racially and ethnically heterogeneous labor force, and its dirty, though costly, space.

General Foods Corporation undertook the first major corporate headquarters relocation to Westchester County in 1951. GF executives had, however, begun thinking about moving out of New York City as early as 1937. Their offices near Grand Central Terminal suffered from "the discomforts caused by dirt, dust, noise, and the ever-increasing problem of traffic congestion." Yet they were reluctant to leave New York City because of face-to-face business contacts, a large labor pool, and banking connections. By contrast, however, Westchester County offered "excellent" banks, schools, churches, and recreational facilities. For a peacetime, white-collar work force, in short, "the whole area is *a community of American homes*—a desirable place to live."[35]

But housing a work force in Westchester County was terribly expensive. Even in 1950, when General Foods and several other firms were moving in, county planners pointed out that half the county's residents couldn't afford to buy a new home there. Nor were there many apartment houses in Westchester County, or mass transit besides the north-south commuter trains. Yet countywide planning officials supported the corporate relocations. "If the trend to the county continues," said the same planning document that noted a lack of affordable housing, "Westchester may become as well known for offices among the trees as Hartford [Connecticut] is for insurance or New Jersey's Union and Hudson counties are for oil refineries." Similarly, the 1961 edition of *This Is Westchester* praised the "snowstorm of park-type plants [that is bringing] . . . a resettlement of skills and brains into the county." There is no longer any mention of antidevelopment passion.[36]

To guide this new mode of development, the Westchester County Association, a private-sector business group with ties to major corporations and New York City's Regional Plan Association, was founded in 1950. Unlike the Westchester County Planning Department, its public-sector counterpart, the Westchester County Association assumed the dominant role in land-use decisions. It thus controlled the major source of change. Unlike the traditional Westchester Chamber of Commerce, moreover, the Westchester County Association from the outset represented large corporations. Countywide planning therefore tended to downplay the interests of the smaller local firms that made up the bedrock of the local economy.

While in the 1950s some corporate CEOs lived in Westchester County or exclusive nearby suburbs like Greenwich, Connecticut, most of their employees lived in New York City. Several companies that moved to Westchester at this time offered employees inducements to move up from the city with them—for example, subsidizing mortgages and providing daily bus service from New York. IBM made no cash payments to employees, but most of its work force did move to Westchester when several divisions were relocated there after 1961. IBM's Home Guarantee Program offered employees who were relocated assistance in selling their old homes and purchasing new ones. At General Foods, most employees commuted from New York City after the corporate headquarters moved to Westchester in 1954. GF's chairman of the board, however, lived in Bronxville.[37]

That there were mixed feelings within the corporate community about relocating to Westchester is shown by the tentative pattern of most of the early moves. Each corporation hesitated before making a final consolidation in Westchester County.*

---

* After the company moved to Westchester, a former honorary chairman of the board of General Foods said that it should send a van back to New York City to transport the intangibles, too: the quality of the city, human contacts, fairness, and tolerance. And after

General Foods just couldn't find adequate office space near Grand Central Terminal. By 1944, the company was renting offices outside its corporate headquarters at 250 Park Avenue, in two buildings on Madison Avenue. It expected growth to continue after the war and complained—in those days before computer networks and fax machines—of "a serious loss of working efficiency" because of the need to move papers among its multiple office locations. GF undertook "an exhaustive search on the fringes of the metropolitan area" for a greenfield office site, rejecting areas in New Jersey and Nassau County because they were too industrial. It clearly rejected Park Avenue north of Grand Central Terminal, too, although other firms were relocating to new corporate offices in that area. It finally bought forty-four acres of land in White Plains in 1950 or 1951, announcing that it would build a new "nerve center of [its] farflung" plants spread out among 100 U.S. towns and cities. When the move was completed in 1954, the corporation's annual report announced it as one of the year's major business developments. It was surely a profitable property transaction, exchanging a valuable site in midtown Manhattan for cheaper land in Westchester.

General Foods' new corporate offices were handsome, freestanding, and isolated on the brow of a hill. Employees found them cheerful and comfortable. The low-rise, three-building office complex was prominently featured in newspapers and architecture reviews because of its stunning whiteness and dramatic modern design by John Dinkeloo and Kevin Roche. The architects were severely constrained, however, by town planning laws in White Plains, which limited buildings to three-story height. Of General Foods' 1,500 employees, 1,200 chose to follow their jobs to Westchester. Some were persuaded to do so by the company's six-month trial offer and a financial bonus.

By the mid 1980s, General Foods had built on four separate sites in the county. While the original corporate headquarters in White Plains was renovated and converted into a divisional headquarters, GF built a new corporate headquarters in 1983, one year before being acquired by Philip Morris. Again, it commissioned the most modern architectural design. The new headquarters was located in the wealthy village of Rye Brook, close to the Connecticut border. GF also built a new technical center on a Hudson River site in 1957, and moved its central laborato-

the chairman of the board, who lived in the county, retired, he became director of the Economic Development Council in New York City; at that point he said that GF's move to the suburbs had been a mistake.

ries to Westchester from Hoboken, New Jersey, home of the mother plant of Maxwell Foods. This time, unlike in the 1930s, there were no complaints about the inefficiencies of multiple sites. Corporate reorganization and computerization made separate facilities more feasible, especially when each dominated its part of the suburban landscape.

While General Foods was the first large corporation to build a corporate headquarters in Westchester, IBM has had the greatest influence on the county's socio-spatial structure. IBM eventually had three to five times as many employees in Westchester as General Foods and built even more corporate campuses throughout the county. In 1955, a year after General Foods moved into White Plains, IBM bought a large property in nearby Armonk, on the Connecticut border, and held it for future development. While the corporate headquarters remained in Manhattan, in 1957 the company moved its research center south from Poughkeepsie, in Dutchess County, to leased facilities in Ossining and Cortlandt, in the northern part of Westchester County. This represented a deliberate separation of IBM's research activities from its manufacturing plant.

During the same period, IBM moved its data-processing division headquarters to leased office space in White Plains. This division included the development, manufacturing, and marketing of most of IBM's large business products. At the time, this was the primary focus of the entire corporation. (White Plains, meanwhile, was the focus of intensive urban renewal discussions among Westchester County planners.)

IBM reorganized the data-processing division in 1959, splitting it into three separate divisions for product development, manufacturing, and marketing. Shortly thereafter, IBM announced that it would finally build on the Armonk property it had bought several years before. This was to be the site of the headquarters for the newly created data systems and general products divisions. The reorganized data-processing division, which was to remain in White Plains, was now only responsible for marketing and servicing the company's large commercial business product line.

In 1961, IBM's research operations also made a symbolic move, from leased space in northern Westchester to the company's new Thomas J. Watson Research Center in Yorktown Heights. Named for IBM's founder, the new research center was designed by a famous modern architect, Eero Saarinen. It was widely reviewed in newspapers and architectural magazines, like the corporate headquarters of General Foods, because it had a Japanese garden, a three-story natural stone facade, and floor space equivalent to eight football fields. Almost half the 700 men and women employed in this building were professional scientists.

In 1961, IBM began an experiment to see whether Westchester would be a viable corporate headquarters location. Several hundred headquarters employees were tentatively relocated to the Watson Research Center from IBM's building at 590 Madison Avenue in Manhattan, including the offices of the president and chairman of the board, Thomas J. Watson. Later that same year, despite the reverse commuting to the suburbs required of nearly all employees, IBM selected Armonk for its new corporate headquarters site. The original plan for the Armonk property was converted to accommodate corporate headquarters operations. Redesigned from 250,000 to 420,000 square feet, the new corporate headquarters that opened in 1964 featured Skidmore, Owings and Merrill's architecture and a sculpture garden by Noguchi. For the divisional headquarters that were supposed to move to Armonk, IBM bought the former Standard Vacuum Company Building in Harrison.

In contrast to General Foods and IBM, which from the 1960s on maintained only regional sales offices in New York City, the Union Carbide Corporation hedged its decision to move. After World War II, like GF and IBM, Union Carbide bought a large property in Westchester. But it also built a new corporate headquarters on Park Avenue, north of Grand Central Terminal, in Manhattan, in the very area that IBM and General Foods fled. Union Carbide moved just its research and development operations to Westchester. At the end of the 1970s, however, it sold its building on Park Avenue and built a new corporate headquarters in Danbury, Connecticut, not far from Westchester County.

If a move to White Plains or Armonk seemed a good corporate strategy during the 1950s, twenty years later—during New York City's fiscal crisis—a move farther from the city, to northern Westchester or Connecticut, was even more highly regarded. Olin Corporation had moved to Fairfield County, Connecticut, in 1968, followed by American Can Corporation (later renamed Primerica) in 1970. And during the 1970s more than twenty-five *Fortune* 500 companies relocated their corporate headquarters to a swath of Fairfield County between Danbury and Stamford, Connecticut.[38]

IBM lists three reasons for its suburban relocations: to create a better working environment for employees, make commuting to work easier, and offer its work force more leisure time to spend with their families. But, as we have noted, most IBM employees did not live in Westchester County prior to the corporate relocations. New housing in the county was also expensive. There are clearly other reasons why firms like IBM developed a suburban strategy.

Especially before restaurants and shopping centers spread throughout the Westchester-Fairfield region, few amenities distracted corporate employees from work. Suburban corporate offices thus exerted greater social and spatial control over employees than they could do in the city, particularly when employees spent their entire day on the corporate campus. Executives at GTE, for example, which moved from New York City to Stamford in 1970, and Singer, which moved in 1979, happily reported that employees arrived at the office earlier than in the city and left later in the day. They also spent their lunch hour in the company cafeteria and came to work on Saturdays. "When people are on the payroll," said the chairman of the board at GTE, "we want to monopolize their time."[39] A change in corporate fortunes and capital markets may also have suggested a suburban move. The burst of suburban office development after World War II coincided with both a buildup of cash reserves in many major corporations and a search for investment projects outside central cities on the part of major financial institutions. In this postwar period of corporate expansion, the primal economic act was to buy land in the suburbs. Another reason for a suburban office location was to enhance corporate security. Isolated, parklike suburban settings are easily fenced and guarded.

A suburban office location also contributes to the symbolic landscape. A firm poised for growth—like General Foods in 1950 or IBM ten years later—wants to show its market power by making a dramatic impact on space. Architecture plays an important role in fulfilling this desire. Just as some corporations built tall buildings in midtown Manhattan after 1950, so others opted to create a low-rise, campus environment. With lower taxes, land values, and construction costs in the suburbs—even Westchester County—companies got a bigger symbolic impact for their investment. They created a new, more controllable landscape of power.

The cost and quality of the labor force steadily became more important. As early as the 1950s, General Foods reported that it had to interview far fewer applicants to fill jobs in Westchester than it did in New York City. Texaco, which moved its corporate headquarters from New York City to Westchester in the 1970s, is widely regarded as having sought an educated, but docile, clerical work force of white middle-class women. Researchers in other areas of the country have suggested a nationwide corporate flight from urban minority-group or foreign-born employees.[40]

Nevertheless, the lack of affordable housing in Westchester and Fairfield counties continues to make the recruitment of a suburban labor force problematic. In 1987, a family in Westchester with a median income of slightly over $38,000 a year could afford only 42 percent of the median price of a house. Indeed, many houses in this area routinely sell for between $300,000 and $3 million. IBM recruits its Westchester employees from as far away as lower Fairfield and Rockland counties, and NYNEX has trouble getting employees to travel south to jobs in White Plains. In annual business surveys conducted by the Westchester County Association over the past twenty years, executives from all the major Westchester corporations have reported that their work forces live farther away.[41]

Over time, corporations have developed their own socio-spatial node in Westchester County facilitating and legitimizing head office decentralization. One way to look at this new landscape of economic power is in terms of the gradual development of suppliers' networks that anchor them to their location. Another way is to focus on the attraction of CEOs to affluent residential suburbs—or to suburbs where they themselves live. But since continuous corporate relocation to the suburbs requires *transforming* the landscape, a basic social process of intra-elite cohesion is involved. Corporations develop a spatially based social network by means of overlapping memberships on their boards of directors. In addition to labor factors and external economies, these high-level intercorporate ties give coherence to the socio-spatial structure.[42]

Although the numbers involved are small, and may reflect individual or social as well as geographical choices, boards of directors of corporations whose headquarters are in Westchester County develop more ties over time than might be expected for the usual business-sector reasons. Indeed, as corporate headquarters in Westchester increased from 1955 to 1985, so did interlocking directorships between them, as well as the number of directors who "migrated" between boards over time (see fig. 1). While it would be difficult at this point to say that a tie between the 1955 boards at General Foods and General Electric persuaded them both to move to Westchester County, by 1975 a number of ties developed among boards of directors whose corporate

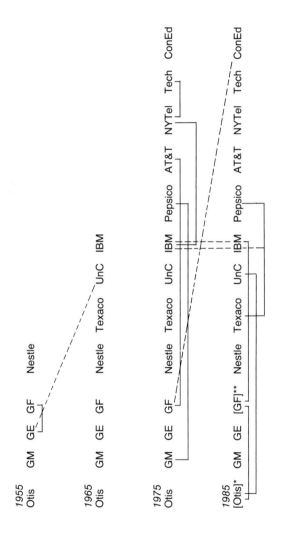

Figure 1. Overlapping memberships on boards of directors of major corporate employers in Westchester County, 1955–85. Corporations: AT&T, Consolidated Edison (ConEd), IBM, General Electric (GE), General Foods (GF), General Motors (GM), Nestle, New York Telephone (NYTel), Otis Elevator, Pepsico, Technicon Instrument (Tech), Texaco, Union Carbide (UnC). (Data from Westchester County Association, Moody's Industrials, and Standard and Poor's.)

——— Simultaneous memberships   * Acquired by United Technologies 1976; now board of Otis Group
- - - - Migration between boards   ** Acquired by Philip Morris 1984; now board of Philip Morris

headquarters were already there. Not surprisingly, IBM plays a key role in this network.

Frank T. Cary, CEO at IBM in the 1970s, had become a member of the Pepsico and Texaco boards by 1985. In 1975, moreover, the IBM board of directors was also linked to the board of New York Telephone, as were Union Carbide, General Foods, and AT&T. Board members of big corporations are often linked to local utilities in a growth machine. But in Westchester County, interlocking directorates also link corporations whose only common feature is their Westchester location. CEO Harry Gray of United Technologies served on the board of UT's subsidiary, the Otis Group, and in 1985 was also a director of Union Carbide. In the same year, John S. Reed of Citibank, another member of the Otis board, was also a director of General Foods, now part of Philip Morris.

Corporate leaders play a disproportionately big role in planning the future of the county. They are brought together not only by overlapping corporate boards but also by membership in the Westchester County Association, where their leadership is ensured and even required. The WCA recruits executives from the largest corporations to chair both the organization and the various task forces that prepare recommendations for regional planning. With "local actors" like IBM, General Foods, and Union Carbide, business planning in Westchester is permeated by companies with global concerns. So far, these global actors are content with their location. The percentage of executives who rate the county an "excellent" business location doubled between 1976 and 1984. By that point, the major reason they gave for possibly moving out of Westchester was expansion beyond their present location. Yet the growing number of mergers and acquisitions since 1984, and corporate reorganizations, including filing for bankruptcy protection, represent an even stronger threat to "the corporate footprint" across the platinum mile.[43]

Westchester's corporate legitimacy feeds the market for more upper-class real estate development. Although that conflicts with employers' needs to ensure housing for their work forces, as well as the requirements of light manufacturers and warehouse owners, it is the main focus of place-based elites.

REAL ESTATE DEVELOPMENT: THE HIDDEN HAND OF
COUNTY PLANNERS

Few localities in this day and age are able to keep the social or spatial qualities that attracted early residents. Yet Westchester County has remained a striking contrast to both suburban sprawl and urban blight. The continued visual homogeneity of this landscape reflects a carefully crafted commitment to the kind of planning that keeps property values high. These in turn safeguard the county's social homogeneity—at least outside the former industrial towns. Unlike many other places, Westchester County explicitly contradicts the idea that suburbs don't plan their growth. It also stands out for the precision with which county planners hit their target.

Were it not for the planners, the degree of continuity between old and new landscapes in Westchester County would seem truly providential. A 1955 planning department publication lists these attributes as the county's major residential attractions:

> It's green with trees and grass.
> It isn't cluttered with run-down factories.
> It has few slums.
> It's a good place for children.
> Manhattan is easily reached.
> The parkways make driving pleasant.
> The schools are unexcelled.
> The stores sell practically everything.
> Government is clean and progressive.
> Citizens are actively interested in the county's future.
> The air is fit to breathe.[44]

Thirty years later, after the hectic period of growth related to corporate headquarters location, the very same qualities head a list of "values to be saved" drawn up by the Westchester 2000 Steering Committee, a planning group run by the Westchester County Association. Thinking of Westchester, the committee members picture:

> A typical suburban neighborhood with 6 to 8 housing units per acre; lots of grass and trees.
> An advanced looking classroom.
> A rural vista in northern Westchester . . .

A long view of the Hudson.
A well-swept, graffiti-free street in White Plains.
Shoppers on a village street buying from a charity-sponsored bake-
    sale table . . .
Dressed-up people attending Summerfare [an annual music festival
    on a local college campus sponsored by Pepsico].
Historic preservation, e.g., Philipse Manor . . .
Mixture of people, downtown New Rochelle.[45]

Since the late nineteenth century, when New York City financiers moved into their Hudson Valley estates, planning in Westchester County has been dominated by the private sector. Patrician residents joined the Republican political "machine" in local and countywide planning bodies, which engaged in constant public education and legislation. While they publicized the economic and aesthetic benefits of zoning laws, and emphasized the dire consequences of a failure to enforce them, they also promoted the development of infrastructure—dams and reservoirs to preserve the county's lakes, highways, and parks—in order to raise property values. They worked in tandem with the Regional Plan Association, a private organization that studied, and issued recommendations for, overall development of the New York metropolitan region. This cooperation was influenced by the Rockefeller family's strong support of both planning organizations. The family's interest in turn reflected a desire to protect the value of its property holdings throughout the region.[46]

Under Republican "Boss" William Ward, who ruled Westchester from the turn of the century to 1933, the building of major infrastructure coincided with, and aided, a boom in housing construction. Although much of this development also coincided with the industrial development of the county's southern tier from 1880 to 1900, the explit long-term goal of public-private planning efforts was *not* to encourage manufacturing, but to raise land values.[47] The prehistory of formal planning in Westchester dates to 1900–1910, when an ad hoc commission was formed to examine a proposal for building the Bronx River Parkway. This early grouping of landed and political elites found a common interest in infrastructure—sewers, highways, and parks. Over the years, infrastructure maintained its importance as both a focus of development strategy and a core of future planning organization. Joint public-private planning of infrastructure formed the basic link between the county's natural topography and its socially constructed landscape.

Like the contemporary New York City "power broker" Robert Moses, the builders of Westchester's parks and highways shaped future development in a practically autonomous way. Even after the elected office of county executive was formed in the 1930s, the Westchester County Parks Commission remained independent of any other public authority. Moses was in fact influenced by the planning of the Bronx River Parkway. In 1922, while contemplating building a highway through Long Island, he read a newspaper account of the unique landscaping being developed for the Westchester County road, which was still under construction. Said to be "the most beautiful road in America," the Bronx River Parkway eliminated traffic lights and intersecting traffic by building crossroads above the level of the primary roadway. The parkway's designers also covered the overhead bridges with stone to match the scenery and landscaped the parkway on both sides of the roadway. Aesthetically, they extended the "natural" landscaping of nineteenth-century suburban developers to the age of the automobile.[48]

This road in fact set the standard for all Westchester's major traffic arteries. While they offered a leisurely, picturesque experience of driving through the landscape, their curves and narrow widths were dangerous for crowds of either commuters or Sunday drivers. They thus restricted access to the county. Here again, Robert Moses took a lesson. Like Moses, moreover, the Westchester planners laid down the principles of public power that underlay the suburb's terrific growth. They overrode the vernacular interests of local elected officials with the "nonpolitical" interests of those who had the economic resources to construct a countywide landscape.[49]

After the Bronx River Parkway was designed, influential people in Westchester began to express a preference for formal countywide planning. Correctly anticipating increased demand for suburban housing by upper-income households, and wishing to block industrial expansion from Yonkers and North Tarrytown, where Otis and GM were based, large property owners in the county pressed for the passage of the first zoning law in 1920. Six years later, on the urging of staff from the Regional Plan Association, the same alliance of public and private interests established the Westchester County Planning Federation. During these years, large property owners in New York City were also developing zoning ordinances and studying land use patterns with the Regional Plan Association. The RPA relied on zoning and highway construction to coordinate development of the regional economic base. Fifty years after it began, an RPA publication pointed out, "Westchester's development follow[ed] the pattern recommended by the Regional Plan Association more closely than that of any other county in the Region."[50]

To manage this homogeneity of land use, private interests tried to control public policy on the model of the railroad. Since the nineteenth century, the building of railroad lines had shown the practical benefits of public-private alliance. While the privately owned railroad lines made development possible, public investment in their construction directly enhanced the value of the lands they owned on either side of the tracks. Like the railroads, the development of public parks and parkways in Westchester County from 1890 to 1930 had a direct effect on land values. And as with the towns developed along railroad tracks, the sale of concession rights for gas stations and refreshment stands along the parkways also raised revenues for Westchester County. This cash flow eased the tax burden for property owners, who surely believed the costs of the county's ambitious highway construction program would have an impact on their tax bills. Although that program had "started with some hesitancy only a few years ago," concluded a 1932 RPA publication, it rapidly became "one of the most significant undertakings, from an economic point of view" in the metropolitan area. Despite costing the county authorities over $62 million for land acquisition between 1921 and 1931, highway construction raised land values in Westchester from less than $700 million in 1921 to nearly $1.7 billion in 1929.[51]

The planners were terribly concerned about maintaining the aesthetic and recreational qualities of the landscape that boosted property values in the undeveloped parts of the county. For this reason, they stressed "the undesirability of mixing large-scale industry with comparatively high-cost residence, recreation, and water supply," and urged preservation of the natural topography. By the Great Depression, the planners made "the decision to recommend only such industrial expansion as is necessary for, and intimately related to, the dominant use of residential occupancy."[52]

Not all the early infrastructure proposals in Westchester County were accepted so quickly. Although building small airports for executive travel was encouraged, discussion of a plan to extend Riverside Drive from Manhattan to northern Westchester dragged on until 1937. It was challenged politically by small factories in Yonkers and other Hudson River towns. It was also plagued by construction problems due to existing rail lines. When the Hudson River Parkway was eventually built, it bore modifications planners were forced to accept, and it never became the throughway they had hoped for.[53]

Another issue that bitterly divided pro-growth advocates after World War II involved the location of a new United Nations Headquarters in the northern part of the county. Earlier this chapter referred to the location of the UN in Manhattan as a boon for Westchester's landed elite. Like the corporate headquarters that followed several years later, however, the UN was a bone of contention among them. After 1945, when the world organization sought a permanent home, its site selection committee considered such major U.S. cities as Philadelphia, San Francisco, and New York. But committee members opted for a suburban location, ruling that the site should be located between twenty-five and eighty miles from any large city. This eliminated two New York City sites from consideration: all of Manhattan, and the 1939 World's Fair grounds in Flushing, Queens. When Westchester residents learned that three sites in the county were under discussion, they tended to be either overjoyed or outraged.

Among those who welcomed the UN project was Otto E. Koegel, a wealthy attorney who owned a 1,200-acre farm in Granite Springs, near the northern town of Somers, one of the competing sites. Koegel claimed to support progressive international causes and oppose atomic power. Building the UN headquarters at Granite Springs, he claimed, would bring economic growth to northern Westchester while aiding world peace. Other local boosters included wealthy owners of large estates near Somers, real estate brokers, and the Chamber of Commerce. But outraged local opponents included 1,300 families who would be displaced from their homes by the UN construction, fruit growers whose livelihood would be disrupted, and organizations like the Scouts and churches. For more than six months in 1946, while the UN site selection committee narrowed its choices to five—three sites in northern Westchester and two in Fairfield County—citizens of Somers held protest rallies to "save homes." By September, however, after promises of aid for relocation were received, most local groups shifted from opposition to welcome. Koegel, who chaired a countywide committee to bring the UN to Westchester, which was endorsed by the county executive, offered to donate his farm to the United Nations.

All this local mobilization was abruptly curtailed by an announcement that appeared in New York City newspapers in December 1946.

The press reported that John D. Rockefeller, Jr., had decided some time earlier to buy an East River site in Manhattan, assembled by the developer William Zeckendorf, for $8.5 million, and present it as a gift to the United Nations. If the UN did not accept Rockefeller's offer, he vowed, he would donate his Westchester estate at Pocantico Hills to the world organization. That he announced the latter offer after the United Nations had accepted the East River site aroused some skepticism among proponents of the Somers location—especially Otto E. Koegel.[54]

Was this a no-lose situation for Westchester County, or merely for the Rockefellers? Rockefeller apparently engaged in some high-level lobbying to ensure the United Nations would take the East River site. With the world organization occupying such a large, prime parcel of midtown land, commercial competition for the tenants of Rockefeller Center was reduced. This seems to be the last time, at any rate, that the Rockefellers' commercial property interests in Manhattan conflicted with the desires of their landed neighbors in Westchester County. During the next decade, David Rockefeller—"Junior" 's son, president of Chase Manhattan Bank, and Westchester County planning board member—actively encouraged corporate headquarters development there.

Even in cases where the Rockefellers were not directly involved, battle lines were drawn between "locals" and corporate elites. Pepsico's 1967 plan to build a new corporate headquarters on a former polo field in Purchase, in the town of Harrison, reversed the forces of opposition. In this case, the nearest residents who would directly suffer the negative impact of corporate development were owners of large estates. Lower-income town residents lived farther from the Pepsico site. Consequently, estate owners mobilized to stop Pepsico from getting the land rezoned for office construction. At the same time, lower-income residents and elected officials supported the arrival of a corporate taxpayer with deep pockets. The estate owners tried every political stratagem to oppose the Pepsico plan. But Pepsico appealed for public support by playing the underdog against them, and also hired President Nixon's Wall Street law firm, Mudge Rose & Guthrie. Eventually Pepsico won.[55]

As long as they didn't live close by, Westchester's place-based elites generally liked shopping centers, new parkways, and centers of activity like Yonkers Raceway that drew a paying crowd. Against other residents' continual objections to traffic congestion and noise pollution, the large property owners who dominated the planning process defended these projects because they raised land values. Place-based elites thus spoke glowingly of the integrated social life shopping centers fostered: "It will be . . . possible for the young matron to assemble her spring wardrobe and arrange for her daughter's tonsillectomy without a change of parking place." Indeed, this development strategy integrated the landed elite's property investment with a middle-class investment in individualized mass consumption.[56]

County planners nonetheless admitted by the mid 1950s that Westchester was on "the horns of the dilemma" of growth. They asked themselves whether continued business development would raise the tax base or the tax rate. And they were unsure whether more development would sooner or later make life in the county unpleasant, and county land less valuable for further development. The planners showed keen awareness of the costs of losing their grip on homogeneity.

For the most part, this grip relied on town zoning laws, which controlled both the extent and aesthetics of growth. Zoning, as we saw with General Foods, limited the height and density of all commercial construction, shaping the campuslike corporate headquarters that became so influential. Zoning in most Westchester towns and villages also mandated rather large lots—a minimum size of 7,500 to 10,000 square feet in "closely built" areas. This basically eliminated small businesses, as well as low- and middle-income households, from any *legal* possibility of building in most of the county. Such uses of public power led, not surprisingly, to "the limited and highly selective character of the recent in-migration of industry." In other words, public power shaped both the visual and social homogeneity of commercial development.[57]

By 1971, when Westchester County had a new landscape of power, the planners had grounds for self-congratulation. The percentage of county residents employed in jobs in the county was continually increasing. Between 1959 and 1967, the proportion moved toward 80 percent. Furthermore, the social status of these jobs was continually rising. Professional, technical, and managerial jobs grew faster than clerical employment. By the year 2000, county planners thought, more than half of all office jobs in Westchester would be on corporate headquarters staffs. The planners hoped that the continued growth of such high-level jobs would spin off two socio-spatial developments. It should stabilize the local labor pool of relatively highly skilled young secretaries, whom corporate executives preferred. And it should also stabilize the downtowns in the southern cities against commercial competition from shopping centers.[58]

The future of the downtowns had long worried county planners, because they posed a threat to countywide postindustrial development. As early as 1950, planning documents showed a concentration of substandard housing in downtown Yonkers, Mount Vernon, and Port Chester. The planners asked whether it would be better to fight poverty and racial discrimination by aiding the downtowns' existing uses— manufacturing and working-class housing—or bring the poor and the minority groups who lived downtown "into the mainstream" by offering them better education *and building subsidized housing outside the area where they now lived.* Foreshadowing the Yonkers desegregation conflicts by at least fifteen years, Westchester planners confronted the dilemma of how to help the poor and rebuild the county's downtowns without jeopardizing land values.[59]

Urban renewal programs provided the tools for downtown redevelopment in the suburbs as in the city. Just as urban property elites had seized the subsidies offered by the Housing Act of 1949 to renovate downtown commercial centers, so Westchester elites in the early 1950s oriented their urban renewal projects to the commercial redevelopment of White Plains, the county seat. Their choice more or less coincided with the selection of White Plains as a headquarters site by several large corporations. White Plains did have a large ethnic and racial minority population. But because it was not so heavily industrial as Yonkers, it lacked strong manufacturing interests. Furthermore, it was located closer to the center of the county and farther from the Bronx. Absent from White Plains, moreover, was a heavily urban political machine such as that entrenched in Yonkers. White Plains—with plenty of manufacturing land and buildings that had lost their economic value—would pose few barriers to building a new landscape of power.

Urban renewal in White Plains began in 1954 with a plan for a new downtown. Federal government funds were approved in 1965, and the land was acquired the following year. County planners would demolish houses, stores, warehouses, and lofts on 130 acres, replacing them with modern office buildings on larger lots, and widen the streets for easier driving. All this required relocating 1,700 households, 10 percent of all households in the city, mainly to subsidized housing. Only 170 households were able to relocate themselves to publicly unassisted housing in White Plains. Significantly, many others were sent to Yonkers and Mount Vernon, increasing the number of poor and minority residents in those towns.[60]

By contrast, White Plains benefited from a concerted influx of public and private investment. More than $67 million in federal urban renewal funds, $22 million from New York State, and $1 million in Community Development grants was spent on downtown redevelopment. Throughout the urban renewal period, crucial liaison work between public and private sectors, and between local, state, and federal government agencies, was done by New York State Governor Nelson Rockefeller, who still kept an eye on the family's interests from the estate at Pocantico Hills. Atypically, his lieutenant governor, Malcolm Wilson, also came from Westchester County.

During the 1970s, another master plan was developed to control land use in White Plains until the year 2000. Financed, again, by federal funds, the master plan was drafted by consultants over a six-year period and fine-tuned in sessions with the business community. The liaison work in this case was done by the Westchester County Association. The new master plan signaled developers that the county's political and landed elites still favored White Plains as the commercial center of Westchester County. It also indicated no interruption in the planners' strategy of hands-on control. The continuation of selective planning, in a period of corporate expansion, resulted in continuous increases in property values. Between 1965 and 1981, the assessed value of properties in the White Plains urban renewal area increased from $9.8 million to $51.3 million, over 400 percent. So many new offices, stores, and hotels clustered in White Plains that town planners made no attempt to attract new projects.[61]

The mode of development in White Plains that proved so successful for elites contrasts dramatically with that in Yonkers, Mount Vernon, and Port Chester. New housing in those downtowns is often publicly assisted, and the relevant agencies for commercial development are not planning departments or business groups, but lower-status community development and industrial development agencies. People in these city agencies say that Yonkers, Mount Vernon, and Port Chester lack "the right aesthetics" for business growth. Their mix of social, ethnic, and racial groups contradicts the image of homogeneity of the rest of the county.[62]

Since the mid 1950s, planners have stated that they want affordable housing, less traffic congestion, and the power to plan on a countywide scale.[63] So far, however, only the power to plan has been fully implemented, and the mode of development that it has supported over the past eighty years is founded on the opposite goals. Higher land values have made housing less rather than more affordable. More office buildings and employment have brought more traffic congestion. This is bound to perpetuate the "dilemmas of growth" that set planners' teeth on edge. Planning in Westchester has, moreover, utilized strategies of deindustrialization and corporate relocation generated in other areas of the economy. Whether a landscape of economic power can outlast these strategies—or can flourish against the global interests of major local actors—poses additional, unacknowledged dilemmas.

A POST-INDUSTRIAL SUBURBAN LANDSCAPE?

In Westchester County, there is an unusually broad convergence between landed and corporate elites. The economic robustness of markets reflects strong social and cultural values of place. Yet there are also serious contradictions between place- and market-based economic values, which imply limits to the "growth machine" that has worked until now.

Since 1900, Westchester's mode of development has been both conceptualized and legitimized by a pro-growth coalition dominated by major financial interests. Although most of their business activities focus on the financial markets of New York City, these companies are also global producers of goods and services and local property owners in Westchester County. Their interests, in short, bridge geographical scales. Moving their corporate offices to Westchester not only reflects attraction to a specific locality, it also makes a significant statement about the socio-spatial process of redeveloping that local landscape as a global marketplace.

Like upper-class and upper-middle-class residents, global investors are drawn to homogeneity. They capitalize on both the visual homogeneity of nature and the social homogeneity of upper-middle-class culture in the suburban landscape. Furthermore, corporations that chose to invest in Westchester County after 1950 found a relatively open socio-spatial structure that contrasted with the city's overdetermined landscape. The suburbs offered a landscape on which the corporate "footprint" could easily be imposed. In particular, corporate property owners could reorganize space while rebuilding a labor force. They were welcomed, moreover, by local landed and political elites. Unlike real estate interests, politicians, and labor unions in the city, suburban elites were amenable to corporate planning. As both a market for corporations and a place for landed and political elites, Westchester County legitimized the new suburban marketplace.

Yet the creative destruction that underlies this landscape reflects divided patterns of growth and decline. On the one hand, social pressures build in local communities—notably, Yonkers—still mired in the old vernacular of a lower-status, racially segregated homogeneity. On the other hand, economic pressures build in housing markets that have been inundated by affluent corporate employees and developers. Most new office construction in Westchester still occurs in areas with the highest median household income, reinforcing social and spatial inequality.

The newest IBM facility in Westchester, pictured in the illustration to this chapter, continues this pattern. In the late 1970s, IBM bought 640 acres in Somers. Additional purchases brought the total to 750 acres by the mid 1980s. At that point, the company decided to consolidate operations from eleven different sites that it leased and owned in the county by building at Somers, which was convenient to all its various facilities in Westchester, Dutchess, and Putnam counties. Consolidation also fit corporate goals of streamlining and cutting costs, which became more important with sharper competition in the computer industry after 1985. Originally only planned for headquarters staff, however, the Somers complex—designed by architect I. M. Pei—was instead developed for all personnel of the company's lines of business and divisional headquarters. Thus when the Somers site opened in 1989, it provided office and computer space for high-level coordination of IBM's manufacturing and development activities. This magnified corporate influence at Somers. Much of the social pressure facing towns like Somers arises from the very mode of development IBM and local planners prefer. New corporate offices raise land values, and these make it difficult to draw a middle- and lower-middle-class work force to office and service jobs. Westchester's development is thus torn between market and place. Should local and business elites use their economic power to create more, or less, social homogeneity?*

Corporate executives in the county oppose policies that would spread the benefits of postindustrial development at the expense of business

---

*Galloping land values also make life inconvenient for wealthy residents, who find it harder either to keep horses at their estates or to find horse farms in the county (*New York Times*, December 23, 1989).

climate. Though they admit that affordable housing for their labor force is a significant problem, they refuse to support either rent control laws or housing construction subsidies from the public sector. To the degree that they affect planning through the Westchester County Association, they preserve Westchester's precious homogeneity.[64]

Even under the "best" conditions, Westchester suggests that postindustrial development in the suburbs creates an uneven flow of benefits. A special burden for many men and women is the disparity between service-sector wages and rising land values. House prices in Westchester County are so much higher than median income that most new housing is really "unaffordable." Yet wage rates in new service jobs are actually reducing average wages in the county. The most rapidly expanding employment category in the county is not jobs for high-level executives or managers, but clerical positions paying between $5 and $7 an hour—a far cry from the income required for Westchester's suburban lifestyle. Ironically, Westchester residents who commute to work in New York City generally have better jobs at higher wages than their suburban counterparts who work in Westchester.[65]

Deindustrialization and corporate decentralization served the elites' interest by raising property values through most of the county. But they also created unemployment and visible misery in the southern cities. When, in the 1980s, affluent corporate employees and professionals were attracted to the better old houses in Yonkers, they found property values—as they conceived them—threatened by the low degree of social integration in the area. Significantly, the corporate elite who live in Yonkers have formed community groups that favor racial and social class integration, in contrast to highly publicized mobilization against integration by working-class and lower-middle-class white residents. In this case, the cultural values of markets contrast with those of place.

The culture of corporate mergers and acquisitions also threatens place. During the 1980s, Texaco was penalized by a $3 billion settlement with Pennzoil because it acquired another oil company that Pennzoil had already wooed. Additional payments to Carl Icahn and other stockholders to avert a takeover attempt pressured Texaco into sales of assets and managerial reorganization. These financial pressures could have affected its Westchester corporate headquarters location. By the same token, after General Foods was bought by Philip Morris, it was merged with Kraft, another acquisition, in 1989; the new division—Kraft General Foods—has headquarters in Illinois.

With the decentralization of corporate headquarters throughout the suburbs, the landscape of economic power has spread out geographically, but has not been reversed. The selective affluence of Westchester's postindustrial economy reflects structural trends of disinvestment and deindustrialization that have been aided and abetted by local institutions. The production-based culture of the southern towns has been submerged into an upper-middle-class consumption culture. Dangerously, the homogeneity of the visual order hides the volatility of transnational corporate consolidation in a service economy.

Cesar Pelli, Winter Garden, World Financial Center, New York City (1988). Copyright © 1988, Peter Aaron/ESTO. Photo courtesy Olympia & York Companies (U.S.A.).

7   Gentrification, Cuisine, and the Critical Infrastructure: Power and Centrality Downtown

I think this was the last year for nouvelle cuisine, thank God. It's not food; it's landscape, made to be framed, not eaten.

ANDRÉE PUTMAN, interior designer,
New York Times, December 31, 1987

She was an art director, which apparently meant some kind of designer, . . . in Manhattan. To Kramer that suggested an inexpressibly glamorous life. Beautiful creatures scampering back and forth to taped New Wave music in an office with smooth white walls and glass brick . . . a sort of MTV office . . . terrific lunches and dinners in restaurants with blond wood, brass, indirect lighting, and frosted glass with chevron patterns on it . . . baked quail with chanterelles on a bed of sweet potato and a ruff of braised dandelion leaves. . . . He could see it all.

TOM WOLFE, *The Bonfire of the Vanities*

The diffusion of economic power outside central cities is not the only process to create a new landscape of power in recent years. Each moment of growth and decline—the decline of U.S. manufacturing and the growth of business services—is also etched into the built environment at the center. The uneven ebb and flow of investment "frees" some spaces for creative destruction while pushing others into denser, higher, newer, ever costlier construction. More than other landscapes, the city center offers an explicit commentary on structural change and business

179

cycles. As the central image and image of centrality of the modern city, downtown is also the site of a paradoxical struggle between economic and cultural values. At the same time it gives material form to the symbolic rupture between development and disinvestment.

Like the bedroom suburbs that now sprout corporate towers, the downtowns of many American cities have undergone a reversal of meaning that challenges most of the social and spatial assumptions of the past fifty years. Unlike most suburbs, however, downtown is not virgin territory. Both densely built and historically layered, downtown is the "urban jungle" that pits the cultural hegemony of economic power against its alternate image of social diversity. Each segment of downtown is already a coherent landscape that comments on the others without claiming to represent the whole. The ethnic ghettos, the financial district, the department stores, city hall, skid row: alone, each suggests an autonomous development, but as an ensemble they assume the characteristics of a single landscape, whose value varies with a change of perspective.

Viewed from "uptown," downtown is market commerce and market culture, high-rise buildings, the daytime regime of "white man's" work. Viewed as a skyline, however—as we commonly enter a city, these days, from the airport or expressway—downtown is synonymous with the city itself. Whether it is a material landscape or a symbolic representation, downtown legitimizes the assertion of power at the center. Deindustrialization, corporate decentralization, and real estate development are responsible for downtown's recent creative destruction. Unlike in Westchester County, however, they interact not to build a new landscape that looks different from what went before, but to impose a new perspective on it. They incorporate downtown's segmented vernacular into a coherent landscape on the basis of *cultural* power. This time, too, the process of creative destruction links a new organization of production and consumption, a reorganization of power at the center.

Images of the city always wrestle with the relation between downtown's geographical centrality and its concentration—or loss—of economic power. From architecture to the basic urban disciplines of sociology and geography, those who define the city tend to assume that centrality is a spatial paradigm of social domination. This only seems confirmed by the social power that underlies gentrification—that is, the conversion of economically marginal and working-class areas of the central city to middle-class residential use beginning in the 1970s.

CENTRALITY AS A LANDSCAPE OF POWER

Throughout the twentieth century, writing about the modern city has stressed the taut rapport between centrality and power. While orthodox ecologists see spatial concentration as an unproblematic social fact, urban critics view it as a source of paradox and contradiction.

Geographers in the first third of the century developed central-place theory to explain spatial patterns of urban and regional dominance. Looking at cities in terms of size, density, and economic function, the theory described fairly evenly distributed spatial hierarchies that radiated outward from a central core. Central-place theorists tended to ignore social processes other than those market or quasi-market transactions between cities that formed and reformed structures of functional domination. Nor did they examine the social inequities of central power. By contrast, in the 1920s, the Chicago School of urban sociologists graphically defined central cities in terms of symbolic power and material deprivation. Their empirical research within cities—especially Chicago—juxtaposed ethnographic reports of the lower depths of society and its commanding heights. The Chicago sociologists portrayed a gallery of "urban types" in their "ecological" milieux: the more these groups deviated from an accepted social norm, the closer they were to the cultural and geographical center of the city, and the farther from economic power. Yet culture and power—urbanism, in short—radiated from the center.

Chicago's topography led these sociologists to visualize the contrast between landscape and vernacular as a series of concentric circles. Between two homogeneous landscapes—the high rents and amenities downtown and rich suburban mansions—lay the segmented vernacular of the Black Belt, Little Sicily, Chinatown, Deutschland, the Jewish ghetto, stockyards, factories, rooming houses, and railroad tracks. As capital migrated outward, we would now say, the downtown citadel was surrounded by vernacular zones that the center was anxious to control, though from a distance.[1]

Writing after the Great Depression and World War II, the urban historian Lewis Mumford showed greater appreciation of centrality's contradictions. Like the Chicago School, he didn't distinguish between urbanism and capitalism in the modern city, or between the social power concentrated in modern cities and the economic system's centralized power. Mumford showed the same disdain for the congestion and hyperactivity of city life that the Chicago School had inherited from Georg Simmel's German sociology, "the loss of form, the loss of autonomy, the constant frustration and harassment of daily activities, to say nothing of gigantic breakdowns and stoppages." More critical, however, of "an expanding economy, dedicated to profit, not to the satisfaction of life-needs," he despised the "new image of the city, that of a perpetual and ever-widening maw, consuming the output of expanding industrial and agricultural production, in response to the pressures of continued indoctrination and advertising." New technology offered the potential to overcome this voracity. Yet Mumford found in economic power the source of both the diversity and perversity of the city center: it was a machine for both production and consumption, where pleasure was joined with social control. Mumford, therefore, confronted a power of centrality that he believed had "no precedent in history. Though the metropolitan container has burst, the institutional magnets still maintain to a large degree their original attractive power."[2]

Mumford's eclectic view suggests the outline of future ecological as well as radical perspectives on the city. A dominant mainstream approach to cities from the 1950s, urban ecology emphasized the center's capacity to drain power from the surrounding region, even while residents flee and manufacturers leave. Viewing suburbanization as an individual process of flight, ecologists failed to see the complex attenuation of central power—by means of investment in the suburbs, outlying regions, and overseas. Nor did they consider the ideological struggle between landscape and vernacular that dominated real city centers during this time. On the one hand, the material landscape at the center was fragmented into a fairly small, high-class downtown and the expanding, physically dilapidated, low-rent inner city inhabited by racial and ethnic minorities. On the other hand, the symbolic landscape separated the public world of work downtown at the city's productive core from the private world of families, kids, and household consumption in the suburbs.[3]

These ideological divisions concerned radical social critics. The "urban struggle" they described from 1973 on refers not only to specific, daily assaults on the city-dweller's integrity, but also to the general disintegration of economic and cultural values under a modern capitalist system. Fault lines in urban housing and labor markets clearly affect the social institutions of place, including family, gender, race, and community. And much of the urban struggle involves the use of space. If cities are a socio-spatial matrix of the market economy, then the way their spatial structures are produced continually destroys and re-creates the social inequities of the entire economic and political system. Centrality as such is not an issue. But the social exclusions and hierarchies constructed in space—by means of property rights and rents, zoning laws, transportation systems, and other, more symbolic forms of control—imply that central positions are not mere artifacts. No less than the suburbs, they are carefully crafted landscapes.[4]

Dominant economic institutions carve their imprint on the center by producing what the French sociologist Henri Lefebvre calls "abstract space." This space is delineated and defined by capital investment, corporate headquarters, and prestigious governmental projects. They brutalize and dominate the city, tearing apart the familiar "cradle of accumulation, site of wealth, subject of history, center of historic space." Like Mumford, Lefebvre identifies the central city with a historic concentration of crowds and commerce, sights and acts. And writing in the 1970s, he underlines the tensions beneath the city's concentration of economic power: "Those who say 'urban spatiality' also say center and centrality, existing or potential, saturated, broken, assaulted, whatever; that is to say, a *dialectical* centrality."[5]

Although centrality's contradictions are rooted in the *accumulation* of economic and political power, the major contradiction for Lefebvre is the *fragmentation* of urban space. It is simultaneously specialized and boring, ghettoized and homogeneous—the condition, by the 1970s, of most downtowns.[6] But a more explicit economic reading relates growth and decline in central urban space directly to processes of capital accumulation. As David Harvey has often described it, the play of economic value through urban forms and spaces creates simultaneous pressures to both create and destroy. Economic values are perennially and potentially highest at the city's geographical center. Yet these values are often absorbed by "unproductive" uses—banks, government offices, parking garages—that can either meet or evade landed elites' expensive demands. Thus the brutalized use of the center, in Harvey's view, does not determine its value; instead, use follows shifts in value. When return on investment in the center falls below the rate of return in other areas, new construction and high-status tenants move to the suburbs. The periodic decline in the economic value of capital in the center leads to its temporary abandonment as a landscape of power.[7]

The geographical play of investment parallels the social and spatial centralization of capital. On the one hand, fewer economic actors with control over investment capital tend to concentrate their investments in a small number of specific spatial clusters. On the other hand, a cluster of their investments at the center of the city reflects a concentration of their social power.[8] Until the mid 1970s, however, downtown remained a patchwork of social uses and economic values. It included sedimentary concentrations of capital investment from the past, empty lots that formed a holding pattern—often under the aegis of publicly sponsored urban renewal—against the loss of economic value, and low-rent quarters for local, déclassé, and traditional ethnic uses. These were all excluded from the landscape of economic power.

THE DOWNTOWN LANDSCAPE

Nowhere is the dialectic of concentration and exclusion, power and vernacular, more visible than from the elevated subway train crossing the East River between Manhattan and Brooklyn over the Manhattan Bridge. The bridge spans two downtowns: downtown Brooklyn, once the center of an independent city, and downtown Manhattan, which as center of New York City absorbed Brooklyn by annexation in 1898. From the look of them, these are entirely different scenes of landscape and vernacular.

Facing the Statue of Liberty, on the Manhattan side of the bridge, tall towers of steel, concrete, and glass create a layered panorama of twentieth-century finance. The neo-Gothic minarets of the Woolworth Building—the world's tallest skyscraper when it was completed in 1913—delicately point to the World Trade Center's mammoth modern boxes, built for Wall Street's global expansion during the 1960s. These are flanked in turn at mid-height by the large, postmodern structures of the World Financial Center and Battery Park City, whose decorative mansard roofs and indentations fill the remaining pockets of cloud and sky.

As the subway rushes from the earth, smaller buildings loom in the foreground. The red-brick tenements of Chinatown, built in the 1880s for Italians and Jews, testify to a still active immigrant presence. Windows level with the train open on Chinese-run garment shops, while in the streets below spill stands of green cabbages and scallions, purple-skinned eggplant, and oranges. Incongruously stolid, between the elevated track and red-character banners spanning the street, is the gray and white ashlar facade of the First Chinese Presbyterian Church.

The middle ground holds the earliest vestiges of Manhattan's working waterfront. Once the dockside offices of fish merchants, more recently pre-dawn haunts like Sweet's Restaurant and Sloppy Louie's that catered to patrons of the wholesale fish market on the water's edge, these pastel-painted, eighteenth-century buildings on Schermerhorn Row stand partly "restored" but mostly empty, awaiting new stores and restaurants consistent with the waterfront's commercial rebirth. From the middle of the bridge they look like dollhouses.

Facing the red-brick shopping center of South Street Seaport, these remnants of the mercantile era are dwarfed by Wall Street's leviathans. At night, with windows lighted by part-time workers and cleaning staff, the buildings of downtown Manhattan are punched out against the darkness like huge electric chessboards.

The Brooklyn side of the water is guarded by red-brick hulks of empty warehouses and a few brightly painted sheds along the piers. In contrast to Manhattan's immanent landscape of economic power, entry to this "city across the river" is marked by a red-white-and-blue sign that says, "Brooklyn Works!" Here the East River slaps against rotting stumps that outline the shadows of former docks. Twelve stories above the empty riverfront street, a majestic clock tower presides over a large loft building that has been renovated into offices for the New York State Department of Labor. A building next to the clock tower still bears the painted legend "Sweeney Manufacturing Co. / Nickelware . . . Hardware." As the subway rushes past blocks of commercial lofts, a backward glance reveals a giant rooftop sign heralding the future transformation of this area into a "Landmark Waterfront Business District." Soon we shall find on the Brooklyn waterfront a replica of downtown Manhattan, a movement outward of the central image of power.*

Because space is mutable, "the assumption of centricity," as David Harvey calls it, is not a fact. It is a social process, a spatial imposition of centralized economic and political power, a problematic relation between use and value.[9] Yet centrality also reveals a cultural process. If architecture can abstract power, the built form of downtown—sleek,

---

*No sooner were these words written than an editorial in the *New York Times* announced, "New York City's central business district is finally crossing the East River to downtown Brooklyn, to the benefit of all New Yorkers" (March 19, 1988). The editorial went on to congratulate local elected officials for leasing a very large site not far from the Brooklyn waterfront, in the new public-private Metrotech development, to a computer-operations branch of the securities industry.

dense, tall—embodies the growing outreach of capital investment and the enormous concentration of authority where investment decisions are made. Downtown skyscrapers also separate the present from the past. Their verticality replaces an earlier, horizontal civic ideal, forcing a change of both the landscape and perspective.[10] At their feet, the very paving stones of the center indict both "civilization" and its decay. Changing over time from hewn stone to asphalt, from smoothness to trolley tracks to potholes, the streets possess a memory of the center's creative destruction.

Downtown is in fact as well as image a collective memory of objective achievement and sentimental attachment to place. It marks the oldest ring of continuous settlement (despite the relative youth of North American cities), and the place where the tallest structure of each era is built. Centrality is simultaneously a spatial link with history and a temporal link with economic and political power. The individual occupies a special place in this landscape. For some people, downtown represents continuity with a family firm or family property. Centrality in that case may mean membership in the patrician families that support the city's major cultural institutions and often own the largest share of urban land. Others merely aspire to enjoy the extraction of wealth in the center. In this case, centrality may exert a terrifying power. "Within the history of capitalism," John Berger writes, "Manhattan is the island reserved for those who are damned because they have hoped excessively."[11]

Since the late 1960s and early 1970s, there has been a noticeable shift of investors' interest into this inferno. Not only Manhattan, but also the downtowns of Philadelphia, Chicago, Boston, and many smaller cities have been restructured by both commercial property development and new homeownership in townhouses, condos, and lofts. Furthermore, downtown has become a creative mecca. This refers less to the survival of the old bohemian fringe than to its expansion in size, its consolidation in certain downtown areas by collaboration with major cultural institutions, and its colonization by the marketing of cultural innovation. Gentrification is part of this socio-spatial reorganization. The movement of people and investment downtown by gentrification is simultaneously a distancing from the traditional middle class and an aspiration to power. Gentrification is an effort to appropriate downtown's centrality—and also, by consuming it, to enhance its economic and cultural value.

GENTRIFICATION AS MARKET AND PLACE

Gentrification refers to a profound spatial restructuring in several senses. It refers, first, to an expansion of the *downtown*'s physical area, often at the expense of the *inner city*. More subtly, it suggests a diffusion outward from the geographical center of downtown's *cultural* power. Ultimately, gentrification—a process that seems to reassert a purely *local* identity—represents downtown's social transformation in terms of an *international* market culture.

Gentrification is commonly understood in a much narrower sense. Not only does it generally refer to housing, especially the housing choice of some members of a professional and managerial middle class, it usually describes this choice in individualistic terms. Yet the small events and individual decisions that make up a specific spatial process of gentrification feed upon a larger social transformation. Each neighborhood's experience of gentrification has its own story—yet every downtown has its "revitalized" South End (in Boston), Quality Hill (in Kansas City), or Goose Island (in Chicago). Regardless of topography, building stock, and even existing populations, gentrification persists as a collective effort to appropriate the center for elements of a new urban middle class.*

The notion of gentrifiers as "urban pioneers" is properly viewed as an ideological justification of middle-class appropriation. Just as white settlers in the nineteenth century forced Native Americans from their traditional grounds, so gentrifiers, developers, and new commercial uses have cleared the downtown "frontier" of existing populations.[12] This appropriation is coordinated, logically enough, with a local expansion of jobs and facilities in business services. While some of these jobs have decentralized to the suburbs, the city's economy as a whole has shifted toward finance, entertainment, tourism, communications, and their business suppliers. Yet neither corporate expansion nor gentrification has altered a general trend of urban economic decline, decreasing me-

---

* Race poses the most serious barrier to all new private-sector capital investment, including gentrification. During the 1970s, as housing prices continued to climb and the housing supply failed to keep pace with demand, white gentrifiers became "bolder" about moving into nonwhite neighborhoods, or more tolerant of the costs in security and services such residence imposed. Only when gentrification risks displacing people of color—notably, in Harlem—is there even a chance of mobilizing against it. Even then, as in industrial displacement, the victims are either bought out or permitted to buy into the new structure—in this case, the improved housing stock.

dian household income, and income inequality. Instead, gentrification makes inequality more visible by fostering a new juxtaposition of landscape and vernacular, creating "islands of renewal in seas of decay."[13]

Reinvestment in housing in the center relies on capital disinvestment since 1945 (or, more accurately, since 1929) that made a supply of "gentrifiable" building stock available. But it also reflects a demand for such building stock that was shaped by a cultural shift. This in turn represents a "reflexive" consumption that is based on higher education and a related expansion of consumers of both high culture and trendy style: these are potential gentrifiers.[14]

The private-market investments of gentrification effectively took over the role of clearing out the center just at the point when public programs of urban renewal ran out of federal funding and alienated supporters from every racial group and social class. Gentrifiers, moreover, often used noninstitutional sources of capital, including inheritance, family loans, personal savings, and the sweat equity of their own renovation work. Gentrification thus constituted a transition in both the mode of downtown development—from the public to the private sector, from large to small-scale projects, from new construction to rehabilitation—and the source of investment capital.

At the same time, the entire political economy of the center city was changing, the result of a long structural process of deindustrialization and cyclical decline in property values. Large manufacturers had moved out of the center since the 1880s, arguing that the multistory arrangement of the buildings and congested streets was functionally obsolete. Dependent on horizontal layout of production processes, truck deliveries, and automobile commuting, manufacturers preferred new greenfield plants in suburban locations. Suburban land prices, taxes, and wages also exerted an appeal. But the small manufacturers who remained in the center, often concentrated in late-nineteenth-century loft buildings downtown, paid rents so low they seemed anachronistic. Although they had been hit severely during the 1960s by competition from overseas production and import penetration, such centrally located activities as apparel manufacturing and printing continued to thrive in low-rent clusters near customers, competitors, and suppliers. In New York, they also benefited from mass transit lines that connected downtown and midtown Manhattan to more distant working-class areas where low-wage, often immigrant and minority workers lived.

Despite their economic viability and historic association with downtown areas, these manufacturers lived under the gun. They were perceived as interlopers by the growth machine of landed elites, elected officials, and real estate developers. Their socially obsolete vernacular posed a barrier to expanding the downtown landscape of economic power. During the 1960s, simultaneously with urban renewal programs on the one hand and new office construction in the suburbs on the other, many city administrations turned to reforming mayors who formed a new coalition with corporate business and banking interests. Mayor John Lindsay in New York, for example, shed City Hall's New Deal alliances with small business and labor unions for a more favorable orientation toward the financial sector, including real estate developers. From Lindsay on, New York's mayors backed a growth machine that explicitly focused on service-sector expansion throughout downtown Manhattan.[15]

Provided businesses had a need or desire to be located downtown, the price of property there was by this point relatively low. While a "rent gap" reflected the cyclical loss of economic value at the center, some private-sector institutions—mainly banks and insurance companies, the offices of foreign-owned corporations, and financial services—remained committed to a downtown location for its symbolic value.[16] Yet downtown had never completely excluded "upscale" use. A small number of patrician households had always remained in Boston's Back Bay and Beacon Hill, and Philadelphia's Society Hill and Rittenhouse Square.[17] Small areas such as these, which never lost economic and cultural value, served as springboards of "revitalization" in the center.

With one eye on redevelopment contracts and the other on property values, the patricians who owned downtown land were in an ideal position to direct a new mode of development that increased economic value. They also controlled the sources of investment capital, city government authorizations, and cultural legitimacy that are needed for a massive shift in land use, because they shaped the policies of banks, city planning commissions, and local historical societies. New York may have been an exception, for the patricians with property in downtown Manhattan—who now lived uptown or in the suburbs—pressed only for new building and highway construction until 1973.

In Philadelphia, however, the upper-class residents of Society Hill and their associates in banking and city government started a fairly concerted effort at preservation-based revitalization in the late 1950s. From house tours of Elfreth's Alley, they proceeded to government subsidies for slum clearance of nearby neighborhoods and new commercial construction. Twenty years later, just in time for the bicentennial celebration of the Declaration of Independence, their residential enclave downtown near the Delaware waterfront was surrounded by a large area devoted to historic preservation, tourism, new offices for insurance and financial corporations, and not coincidentally, gentrification in nearby Queen Village. The displaced were small businesses, including manufacturers, and working-class, especially Italian and Puerto Rican, residents.[18]

In downtown Manhattan, by contrast, the displacement of low-rent and "socially obsolete" uses from around 1970 was part of the politics of culture. Specifically, the landscape of downtown Manhattan was shaped by an unexpected triumph on the part of an artists' and historic preservationists' coalition. Formed to defend living and working quarters that cultural producers had established in low-rent manufacturing lofts, artists' organizations protested the demolition of these areas by the growth coalition. They also claimed the legal right to live and work in buildings zoned for manufacturing use alone, on the basis of their contribution to New York City's economy. Since the 1960s, nontraditional forms of art and performance had indeed attracted a larger, paying public. Their gradual concentration in downtown lofts connected these spaces with a downtown arts economy.

In a competition over downtown space between the arts producers, manufacturers, and real estate developers, which lasted until 1973, the artists emerged as victors. Yet they could not have won the right to live in their lofts without powerful allies. Their political strategy relied not only on the growing visibility of artists' clusters, but also on the patronage of some landed and political elite members who otherwise would have supported the growth coalition. Saved by the cultural values of historic preservation and the rising market values of an arts economy, the lofts of downtown Manhattan were transformed from a light manufacturing into a cultural zone. This process ran parallel, we see with hindsight, to gentrification.[19] The legitimation of "loft living" in downtown Manhattan marked a symbolic as well as a material change in the landscape. Cleared of "obsolete" uses like manufacturing by an investment flow apparently unleashed "from below," downtown space demanded a visual, sensual, and even conceptual reorientation. Just as the new mode of development downtown reflected a new organization of production, so many of the gentrifiers' cultural practices related to a new organization of consumption.

At the outset, gentrifiers' fondness for restoring and preserving a historical style reflected real dismay at more than a decade of publicly sponsored urban renewal and private commercial redevelopment, which together had destroyed a large part of many cities' architectural heritage. The photographic exhibit (1963) and book on *Lost New York* (1967), for example, documented the handsome stone, masonry, and cast-iron structures that had dominated downtown Manhattan from the Gilded Age to World War II. Most of these buildings were torn down in successive periods of redevelopment as downtown commerce moved farther north. For a long time, demolition signified improvement. But the destruction in the early 1960s of Pennsylvania Station, a railroad terminal of the grand era whose soaring glass dome was replaced by a mundane office building, dramatized the loss of a collective sense of time that many people felt.[20]

The photographic exhibitions that were mounted for *Lost Boston*, *Lost Chicago*, and *Lost London* showed a nearly universal dissatisfaction with slash-and-burn strategies of urban redevelopment. Criticism ranged from aesthetics to sociology. The journalist Jane Jacobs, whose family had moved into a mixed residential and industrial area in the oldest part of Greenwich Village, argued for the preservation of old buildings because they fostered social diversity. She connected small, old buildings and cheap rents with neighborhood street life, specialized, low-price shops, and new, interesting economic activities: in other words, downtown's social values. Studies by the sociologists Herbert Gans and Marc Fried suggested, moreover, that for its residents, even a physically run-down inner-city community had redeeming social value.[21]

The rising expense and decreasing availability of new housing in the center worked in tandem with these developing sensitivities. Meanwhile, new patterns of gender equality and household independence diminished the old demand for housing near good schools, supermarkets, and neighborhood stores, at least for those families without children or with adequate funds for private schools. While they couldn't afford Park Avenue, or wouldn't be caught dead on the Upper East Side, highly educated upper-middle-class residents viewed the center in light of its social and aesthetic qualities. Equally well educated lower-income residents—notably, those who had chosen cultural careers and those who lived alone, including significant numbers of women and gays—viewed the center in terms of its clustering qualities. Relatively inexpensive building stock in "obsolete" areas downtown provided both groups of men and women with opportunities for new cultural consumption.[22]

New middle-class residents tended to buy houses downtown that were built in the nineteenth century. They painstakingly restored architectural detail covered over by layers of paint, obscured by repeated repairs and re-partitions, and generally lost in the course of countless renovations. The British sociologist Ruth Glass first noted their presence in the early 1960s as an influx of "gentry" into inner-city London neighborhoods. While the new residents did not have upper-class incomes, they were clearly more affluent and more educated than their working-class neighbors. The neighbors rarely understood what drew them to old houses in run-down areas near the center of town. Since that time, however, gentrifiers have become so pervasive in all older cities of the highly industrialized world that their cultural preferences have been incorporated into official norms of neighborhood renewal and city planning.[23]

With its respect for historic structures and the integrity of smaller scale, gentrification appeared as a rediscovery, an attempt to recapture the value of place. Appreciating the aesthetics and social history of old buildings in the center showed a cultural sensibility and refinement that transcended the postwar suburban ethos of conformity and kitsch. Moreover, moving downtown in search of social diversity made a statement about liberal tolerance that seemed to contradict "white flight" and disinvestment from the inner city. By constructing a social space or *habitus* on the basis of cultural rather than economic capital, gentrification apparently reconciled two sets of contradictions: between landscape and vernacular, and market and place. On the one hand, gentrifiers viewed the dilapidated built environment of the urban vernacular from the same perspective of aesthetics and history that was traditionally used for viewing landscape. On the other hand, their demand to preserve old buildings—with regard to cultural rather than economic value—helped constitute a market for the special characteristics of place.[24]

Yet as the nature of downtown changed, so did gentrification. The concern for old buildings that was its hallmark has been joined, since the early 1980s, by a great deal of new construction. Combined commercial and residential projects near the financial district—like Docklands in London or Battery Park City in New York—exploit the taste for old buildings and downtown diversity that gentrifiers "pioneered." By virtue of its success, however, we no longer know whether gentrification is primarily a social, an aesthetic, or a spatial phenomenon.

Small-scale real estate developers slowly awakened to the opportunity of offering a product based on place. "You find a prestigious structure that is highly visible, and built well, preferably something prewar," says a housing developer who converted a neo-Gothic Catholic seminary in a racially mixed neighborhood near downtown Brooklyn to luxurious apartments. "You find it in a neighborhood that still has problems but is close to a park, a college, good transportation—something that will bring in the middle class. And almost by the time you are through, other buildings around it will have started to be fixed up."[25]

Downtown loft areas formed a more specialized real estate market because they had a special quality. Their association with artists directly invested living lofts with an aura of authentic cultural consumption. If the artist was "a full-time leisure specialist, an aesthetic technician picturing and prodding the sensual expectations of other, part-time consumers," then the artist's loft and the surrounding quarter were a perfect site for a new, reflexive consumption.[26]

Markets are not the only arbiters of a contest for downtown space between landscape and vernacular.[27] The key element is that the social values of existing users—for example, working-class residents and small manufacturers—exert a weaker claim to the center than the cultural values of potential gentrifiers. Gentrification joins the economic claim to space with a cultural claim that gives priority to the demands of historic preservationists and arts producers. In this view, "historic" buildings can only be appreciated to their maximum value if they are explained, analyzed, and understood as part of an aesthetic discourse, such as the history of architecture and art. Such buildings rightfully "belong" to people who have the resources to search for the original building plans and study their house in the context of the architect's career. They belong to residents who restore mahogany paneling and buy copies of nineteenth-century faucets instead of those who prefer aluminum siding.

Gentrifiers' capacity for attaching themselves to history gives them license to "reclaim" the downtown for their own uses. Most of them anyway tend not to mourn the transformation of local working-class taprooms into "ye olde" bars and "French" bistros. By means of the building stock, they identify with an earlier group of builders rather than with the existing lower-class population, with the "Ladies' Mile" of early-twentieth-century department stores instead of the discount stores that have replaced them.

Mainly by virtue of their hard work at restoration and education, the urban vernacular of ethnic ghettos and working-class neighborhoods that were due to be demolished is re-viewed as Georgian, Victorian, or early industrial landscape—and judged worthy of preservation. "In this new perspective [a gentrified neighborhood] is not so much a literal place as a cultural oscillation between the prosaic reality of the contemporary inner city and an imaginative reconstruction of the area's past."[28]

The cultural claim to urban space poses a new standard of legitimacy against the claim to affordability put forward by a low-status population. Significantly, cultural value is now related to economic value. From demand for living lofts and gentrification, large property-owners, developers, and elected local officials realized that they could enhance the economic value of the center by supplying cultural consumption.*

In numerous cases, state intervention has reinforced the cultural claims behind gentrification's "market forces." New zoning laws banish manufacturers, who are forced to relocate outside the center. Since 1981, moreover, the U.S. tax code has offered tax credits for the rehabilitation of historic structures. Although the maximum credit was lowered, and eligibility rules tightened, in 1986, the Tax Reform Act retained benefits for historic preservation. Every city now has procedures for certifying "landmark" structures and districts, which tend to restrict their use to those who can afford to maintain them in a historic style. But when landmarking outlives its usefulness as a strategy of restoring economic value at the center—as it apparently did in New York City by the mid 1980s—local government is capable of shifting gears and attacking the very notion of historic preservation.[29]

Gentrification received its greatest boost not from a specific subsidy, but from the state's substantive and symbolic legitimation of the cultural claim to urban space. This recognition marked cultural produc-

---

* However, when investment in new projects is viable, economic claims to the center take precedence over cultural claims. The absolute failure of a historic preservation movement in Hong Kong is the exception that proves the rule. " 'In New York, London, Paris or Rome, none of this [demolition] would ever have been allowed to happen,' said David Russell, an architect and the founder of the colony's Heritage Society, which disbanded five years ago after losing three major preservation fights in a row" (*New York Times*, March 31, 1988).

ers as a symbol of urban growth. While storefront art galleries and "French" restaurants became outposts and mediators of gentrification in specific neighborhoods, cities with the highest percentage of artists in the labor force also had the highest rates of downtown gentrification and condominium conversion.[30]

Yet the aesthetic appeal of gentrification is both selective and pliable. It can be abstracted into objects of cultural consumption that bear only a distant relation to the downtown areas where they were once produced. "Before Fior di Latte," reads an advertisement for a new brand of "fresh" cheese mass marketed by Pollio Dairy Products Corporation, "you had to go to *latticini* [dairy] stores in Italian neighborhoods to buy fresh mozzarella. Store owners made the delicious white cheese daily and kept it fresh in barrels of lightly salted water." The point is that it is no longer necessary to go the ethnic neighborhoods downtown to consume their heritage; international trade and mass distribution can reproduce a historically "authentic" product. "To capture this fragile, handmade essence of fresh mozzarella," the ad continues, "Polly-O uses methods and equipment imported from Italy. We even pack each individual serving of Fior di Latte in water to keep it moist and fresh up to 25 days." No need for *latticini* when fresh mozzarella is sold in supermarkets.

The organization of consumption thus has a paradoxical effect on downtown space. Initially treated as unique, the cultural value of place is finally abstracted into market culture.

DOWNTOWN AS LIMINAL SPACE

In the new era of capital reinvestment in the center, downtown emerges as a key liminal space. Institutionally, its redevelopment straddles public and private power. Visually, the redevelopment process eliminates or incorporates the segmented vernacular into a landscape of power. Since the 1970s, downtown has graphically mapped the forms of social control that we have identified as part of the inner landscape of creative destruction. These include both entrapment and fragmentation, as well as a sense of unlimited power. Downtown mediates the social transformation initiated by capital flows and public policy.

The reassertion of power in the center is shaped by the narrowness of streets and the historic gathering functions of the core, the jigsaw of social uses that reflect uneven economic values, and over all, the density of the built environment that permits markets to generalize the products of a highly specialized place—and to communicate them through a larger market culture. Downtown ironically recapitulates the destiny described by urban ecology, but it does so in a changing economy.

Experience with gentrification shows that new downtown markets are formed in stages. We first find a change in the uses of space: from manufacturers and a working class who are absorbed in material production to a professional, managerial, and service class that spends considerable energy on cultural production and consumption. We then find a change in perspective, or people's relation to the space. The way they view it re-forms the urban vernacular—with its diversity of low-rent quarters—into an aesthetically or historically homogeneous landscape. Finally, we find a change in the nature of space itself. Downtown becomes larger and more expensive, its old structures are joined by new construction, and its social meaning is transformed from "in" to accessible, and therefore "out" of fashion. At that point of liminality between "in" and "out," downtown space becomes too expensive for some of the initial gentrifiers.

We clearly see the effects of this socio-spatial restructuring in the demise and reshaping of vernacular landmarks, including the death of the cafeteria and the birth—in all its guises—of the downtown club.

The death in 1986 of Philip Siegel, 85-year-old owner of the Belmore Cafeteria in Manhattan, marked the definitive end of downtown's cafeteria era. For most of Siegel's lifetime, cafeterias were not only a restaurant genre where a cup of coffee was served in heavy china and still cost less than a newspaper. More important, cafeterias were a cheap public space downtown.

> Mr. Siegel bought the cafeteria, on Park Avenue South at 28th Street, in 1929. Over the years, he expanded the dining area from 100 to 500 seats and, in the late 1970s, he installed fashionable track lighting and put potted plants in the front windows.
>
> He never dropped the Belmore's slogan—"New York's most fabulous restaurant"—and he never disposed of the turnstile that discharged a little ticket to each customer who entered.
>
> Until Mr. Siegel closed the Belmore and sold the building for a condominium complex in 1981, it was serving about 5,000 people a day on weekdays. It was particularly popular

with cab-drivers, students and elderly people on fixed in-comes. Scenes for the movie "Taxi Driver" were filmed there.[31]

From the 1960s, however, the downtown cafeteria became as so-cially obsolete as most downtown manufacturers. Its disappearance did not reflect lack of demand for cheap food served quickly and without ostentation. Far from it: Bickford's and Horn and Hardart's were only replaced by McDonald's and pizza stands. But in contrast to cafeteria habitués, as Isaac Bashevis Singer has often described them, dawdling, dreaming, and arguing over their trays, the clients of fast-food outlets are trained to regard restaurants as a market for eating rather than a place. These are high-rent, high-volume outlets that sell highly stan-dardized food. They are as different from the automat as the lack of formality and absence of novelty that surround them. Familiarity is pro-vided by institutional context rather than social interaction: the form of consuming is vital, not the cultural activity of consumption.

New economic values make it too expensive to preserve the cafete-ria's cultural values. Who at any rate is left to mourn the loss? Just as condominium conversion has removed many habitués from their apart-ments and places of work, so Philip Siegel's survivors have dispersed throughout the metropolitan region or retired to Florida. As downtown expands its landscape of economic power, vernacular landmarks lose meaning and vanish.[32]

This change in the material landscape parallels a change in the way downtown is viewed. From a messy space sporadically supervised by institutions of the public sector—jails, courthouses, and public housing projects—rises a renewed grassroots perspective on downtown as the incubator of cultural innovation. The new symbolic landscape is marked not only by art galleries, but also by downtown nightclubs and central railroad stations. Liminal spaces in themselves, they cross night and day, *haut monde* and underworld, cultural monuments and commerce. They also represent the landmarks of a downtown liminal zone.

Michael Musto, a *Village Voice* reporter, has chronicled the birth and death of this downtown liminality during the 1980s.[33] The East Village, the clubs, and the underground network really worked at the beginning of the decade, when they "attracted a vivid bunch of Euros, downtowners, and rich kids who really mixed amid the Busby Berkeley-style theme changes." Once the whole varied ensemble was perceived "as a stepping stone to bigger things," however, the vernacular scene was finished. Certainly the conspicuous idleness and illegal drug consumption of downtown club denizens "and the snobbery of some doormen" had made this scene far from "idyllic." Yet for little economic cost, downtown offered "glitter, innovation, and raw talent." This downtown was inhabited by those who lived off government grants for the arts, inherited wealth, the new service industries, the informal sector (including drugs), and the wages of celebrity.

Of "three hot clubs" in the 1980s—Area, Limelight, and Danceteria—one "[died] a natural death," the second survived with a less artistic clientele, and the third "[gave] way to expensive office space." "The biggest factor in downtown's demise is," Musto decides, "the high cost of living in Manhattan." * "Parasites who happen to be real estate developers" exploit and explode the downtown scene. Yet it is the change of perspective focusing on cultural values that makes downtown accessible to potential investors. And this in turn enhances property values. "Now you have uptown coming downtown and Wall Street coming uptown," the owner-designer of a new "surf-theme" restaurant says to Musto, "but that's what makes the city grow."

The life cycle of clubs suggests how property investment re-forms the urban vernacular away from liminality toward a landscape of power. Instead of artists, rich kids, and literary emigrants who comment with an air of detachment on market culture, downtown is taken over by another kind of market culture, one made by real estate speculators, institutional investors, and big-time international consumers. From Musto's perspective, this real estate market destroys the neighborhood, the artist's community, the *place* that he sees downtown.[34] What Michael Musto regards as "the death of downtown" keynotes, however, the expanding organizational field of central power. By standardizing and replicating cultural forms that originate in the center, and attracting new, often international investment, downtown's liminal space mediates the dialectical tension between centrality and power. Downtown works "best" in this role when new capital, uses, and urban forms subvert and bury the unique vernacular of the downtown scene. By contrast, this dynamic works "worst" where old industrial structures are

---

* Despite the later recognition that AIDS had ravaged downtown art and design communities, Musto eventually claimed that the sex scene in downtown clubs had been reborn ("Wild in the Clubs," *Village Voice*, December 20, 1988). The following year, another local newspaper declared that New York nightclubs were more diffuse and less exciting, both too expensive and too tightly regulated by the city administration ("For Night Crawlers, Are City's Glamour, Excitement Fading?" *New York Observer*, December 11, 1989).

most entrenched, where shopping cannot replace the jobs and income lost in corporate reorganization, where the urban vernacular remains both structurally and institutionally embedded in the downtown core.[35]

The expansion of both artists' communities and business services since 1975 has made downtown Manhattan an avatar of liminality between commerce and culture. Yet the reassertion of a landscape of central power is constantly tested by resurgence of the urban vernacular, especially by the presence of homeless men and women. Homelessness is a recurrent problem for makers of landscape. Before Central Park was formed at the end of the 1860s, squatters had to be removed from shacks in the middle of the swamp. Years later, during the Great Depression, homeless people built shantytowns in Riverside Park. Again, after 1980, the expansion of the homeless population spilled over from the Bowery downtown to midtown's Port Authority Bus Terminal. Parks, streets, subway stations, and nearly all public space downtown brought the ambivalent nature of liminality in a market economy to the fore: could public space be appropriated by *everyone* and *anyone,* or should its use be defined solely by private development?

Grand Central Terminal during most of the 1980s continuously remapped the boundary between respectability and homelessness, landscape and vernacular. Under the bright blue, gold-starred dome of the arrivals and departures hall, commuters and office workers shared a reasonable landscape of power. Ticket booths, stores, newspaper kiosks, and food stands filled the white marble expanse, where music students performed chamber pieces at lunchtime. The homeless slept downstairs, next to the tracks and in the labyrinth of tunnels. They also filled the waiting and rest rooms. An uneasy truce over these territorial divisions was policed by the city administration and the New York Civil Liberties Union. One compromise involved locking the doors of the terminal every night at 1 A.M. so that more homeless men and women wouldn't pour in through the night. By 1987 a clearer division between commercial public space and areas where the homeless slept was desired. The Metro-North Commuter Railroad, the quasi-public authority that owns Grand Central Terminal, developed an architectural plan to renovate the station. As the president of Metro-North said, "We want to put the grand back in Grand Central."

Later that year, the New York City government intensified its efforts to remove the homeless from desirable commercial and residential areas. The most infirm among them were to be removed from public streets, for their own safety, to public hospitals and shelters. But the key to removal was geographical: the homeless were only to be removed from public spaces in the downtown area. The way the downtown was defined, moreover, made it significantly larger than was commonly perceived. Not only did the homeless sweep affect the traditional landscape of downtown power—Wall Street, midtown, and the Upper East Side—but it also expanded the locus of centrality to those areas of Manhattan that had recently been reclaimed by gentrification. Thus the organizational field of central power now extended from West 110th Street and East 96th Street down to the southern tip of the island. The issue of the homeless dramatized the fact that "public space" was no longer open to the public without conditions.[36]

The return of business investment downtown during the 1980s not only changed the face of the center; it made the center larger. In Chicago, the map the Chicago School described around 1920 no longer holds true. The Loop, as the historic central business district is known, has multiplied fourfold in size. The new "super Loop" contains luxury apartments, office lofts, nightclubs, chic restaurants, art galleries, and a continuation of the upscale shopping district for which Michigan Avenue is known.[37] As a result of this expansion, the concept "downtown" no longer has geographical limits.[38] When a reporter asks the singer Madonna to name her favorite downtown store in Manhattan, she mentions one on the Upper West Side. Branching and replication of stores have in fact eliminated the need to "go downtown" in search of a special product. And mass distribution—as with "Fior di Latte"—makes the point of consumption equally convenient to everyone. Downtown now becomes a fluid space, whose abstraction of cultural values into consumer goods makes shopping a significant social experience. As *New York* magazine put it in a special double issue on downtown Manhattan, "Downtown is a style, a sensibility, a state of mind reflected in the art world, fiction, restaurants, fashion, and the way people live."[39]

While gentrification and downtown expansion have not "integrated" the center of the city, they have overcome its traditional segmentation. On the one hand, mixed uses have rendered obsolete the old barriers of space and time—skid row and the manufacturing districts that most people avoided after nightfall, the entertainment districts of gay bars and secret lives, and tawdry streets of low-price shops—and made downtown a high-profile, night-and-day landscape of consumption. On the other hand, the sensual opportunities densely produced in downtown space—Musto's clubs, avant-garde art, the smell of fresh bread being delivered in *Bright Lights, Big City*—have shifted downtown's social meaning from production to consumption.* "In a sense, we are redefining the function of the central city," the city planning director of Chicago says. "It was always the center for banking, government, education and health care, but that is becoming even more the case. And now we are adding housing, too, which puts people back on the streets and gives us the possibility of a city that is open 18 hours a day." Re-creating downtown as a liminal space enhances economic values. When Moody's Investor Service upgraded Chicago's bond rating to A, it cited fiscal retrenchment on the part of the city administration and "also downtown development and the gentrification of a number of neighborhoods." There is no clearer indication of the synergy between economic and cultural values.[40]

Yet Michael Musto has already declared in print that "downtown" is dead.[41] What he means by this is nothing other than the hallmarks of current structural transformation: the internationalization of investment, a shift in social meaning from production to consumption, and an abstraction—in this case—from cultural to economic values. The "death of downtown" also highlights differences in spatial organization between production and consumption. Production units function best in clusters of customers and suppliers. Historically these clusters gave downtown its specialized aura of variety and innovation. But consumption units are increasingly spread out, diffused, standardized, and reproduced. Decentralization reduces the power of consumption spaces; it requires conscious action to restore their specific meaning.

Under these conditions, mediating the dialectic of power and centrality depends on a critical infrastructure for cultural production and consumption. Here I am thinking of men and women who produce and consume, and also evaluate, new market-based cultural products. Like artists, they both comment critically on, and constitute, a new kind of market culture. Their "inside" view opens up new spaces for consump-

---

* The novel *Bright Lights, Big City* offers an object lesson in this sort of transformation. The poor and the misfits intrude on the narrator only as objects of consumption—the peddler who sells him a fake Rolex on the street, the mother in the outer boroughs who exists in front-page tabloid headlines. Similarly, he gets the fresh bread that offers him new life at the end of the novel from a trucker who is unloading a bakery delivery, "a man with a family," he thinks, "somewhere outside the city." In most cases, the bakery that produces this bread is also located outside the city, especially outside Manhattan.

tion. They enhance market values even when they desperately want to conserve the values of place.

Gentrification takes older cities into a new organization of consumption based on cultural capital. One of the interesting aspects of this organization of consumption is that it is spatially specific: consumption markets (clubs, housing) are attached to places that claim to be unique. It also provides extensive variety and 24-hour-a-day availability of goods and services. So it strengthens spatial concentration and generates part-time work. New products, and new practices of consumption, require a labor force that can deal with cultural capital. Artists, actors, and graduate students are often mobilized to fill these roles. Neither servile nor professional, restaurant waiters and boutique sales clerks interpret cultural goods to potential consumers. They help constitute the experience of consumption.[42]

For a college-educated generation, the wide array of goods now available requires more carefully considered, *reflexive* consumption. We saw in chapter 3 how this is mediated in some fields by architects and designers. But increasingly selective consumption is more broadly mediated by those who communicate information about new consumer goods and services. These men and women perform several important social roles. They form a highly visible wedge of gentrification in specific cities. They staff the new service careers in publishing, restaurants, advertising, and cultural institutions on which downtown's economy depends. And by means of their creative products—especially their reviews—they provide an aesthetic critique that facilitates upscale consumption. They supply the critical infrastructure for downtown's transformation.[43]

The critical infrastructure undeniably rests on a wider base of consumer demand. Outside the nexus of food stamps, unemployment, and the minimum wage lies another world where people eat to read and read to eat. While it becomes harder to feed a low-income family a nutritious diet, more affluent, choice-ridden consumers are increasingly preoccupied by new means of consumption—and new anxieties about how to choose between them.

A newspaper column by Russell Baker marks the change in behavior "just recently when the consumption of high-priced victuals became a national craze. Since then," he writes,

> it has become almost impossible to find a good dinner conversation because your companions—people who grew up just like you, thinking real olive oil on the salad dressing was the essence of elegant eating—constantly interrupt to criticize the comestibles.
>
> The conversation moves happily toward a delicious divorce scandal when—just a minute now!—someone is exasperated by the endive. The endive is not quite as crisp as the best endive should be.
>
> Which reminds someone else of the best endive she ever tasted.[44]

Not just a shift in taste, but a shift in the way taste is produced accounts for the rise of reflexive consumption. The aesthetic and sensual side of gentrification reflects the "Orwellian" norms of redemption, critical distance, and astonishment,[45] but it also requires a shift in mediation from personal protocols to impersonal arbitration.

In Edith Wharton's novel *The House of Mirth*, for example, the character Selden "learned with amusement [from his upper-class New York friends in Monte Carlo] that there were several places where one might miss something by not lunching, or forfeit something by lunching; so that eating actually became a minor consideration on the very spot consecrated to its rites." The quality of food, at the end of the Gilded Age, is clearly secondary to the social space of consumption. " 'Of course one gets the best things at the *Terrasse*—but that looks as if one hadn't any other reason for being there: the Americans who don't know any one always rush for the best food. And the Duchess of Beltshire has taken up Bécassin's lately,' Mrs. Bry earnestly summed up."[46]

While a taste "for the best food" doesn't compensate for "whom one knows," it nonetheless substitutes today for hierarchies based on personal networks and social position. In a mass-produced and mass-distributed culture, a taste for "the real thing" becomes a strategy of social differentiation. Yet the real thing refers to two quite different sorts of goods. It refers to goods that offer the authenticity of the past and those that suggest the uniqueness of new design.

Today cultural consumption follows the lead of several mediators:

the artist, the primary consumer, and the designer, who interpret desire and direct the consumer to equate awareness of consuming with awareness of life; and the line producer in new service industries, catering to a jaded consumer "who yearns for homespun to ease the chintz."[47] This yearning is satisfied by a juxtaposition of very old ("historic") and very modern ("state-of-the-art") products. Just as a gentrified neighborhood is a repository of collective memory, so it is also a site of individualized, high-technology household consumption. The emergence of new tourist regions reflects a similar combination. While by day we visit archaic landscapes, like the aristocratic country house and the eco-museum, by night we comfort ourselves in a country inn with good ("French") food. The point is not that such attractions exist, but that we think enough about them to combine them in a single practice. "After my first trip to America," Milanese designer Ettore Sottsass calmly recalls, "I knew that a new culture of consumerism was not the answer. Rather, I wanted to make the consumer aware that he *is* consuming." This shift of perspective is the principal product of the critical infrastructure.[48]

The critical infrastructure resolve three contradictions that underlie a new organization of consumption. By means of their product—an object of cultural consumption like gentrified housing or nouvelle cuisine—they mediate the opposition between authenticity and design. Because they both produce and consume the city, they also encourage a re-viewing of the nondescript, segmented vernacular as a coherent landscape of power. And finally, by means of their labor—part self-provisioning and self-employment, part volunteer activity, part wage work—they help transform the qualities of a specific place in the built environment into a market for a wide variety of consumer goods. Producers of critique, they play a critical role in a new organization of consumption.

The growth of a new type of regional tourism, based, like gentrification, on recapturing an experience of the past, suggests how this organization of consumption derives from shifts in both production and consumer demand. Withdrawal of capital investment from local industry leaves old production sites intact instead of promoting their modernization. Once these old places are depopulated, decayed, and abstracted from the organization of production, they take on the appealing aura of the "sublime." For reasons of eccentricity or pleasure, the newly perceived qualities of place generate new markets. Old textile mills become eco-museums; country house hotels and inns replace the local Marriott's or Howard Johnson. These shifts in demand lead to the decline of some established tourist regions and the new popularity of others. New England, for example, has become an economically viable tourist region both in the old industrial interior (except, perhaps, for north Berkshire County in Massachusetts) and along the savage Atlantic coast. While to some degree the region's commercial viability reflects the incorporation of unused factories and nonworking waterfronts into the built landscape of culture, it also represents a tendency to re-view the less developed parts of the seacoast as nature. Similarly, in Britain, "part of this trend has been an increased tendency to visit the seaside, but much of this increase went not to 'organized' resorts where a kind of [mass] culture dominates nature but to relatively 'unspoiled' (that is, more natural) parts of the coastline."[49]

Because of simultaneous disinvestment and new development, tourists can view an entire "living panorama" of industrial history and contrast it with their own everyday environment. Living antiquity attracts tourists today in Williamsburg, Virginia, or Newport, Rhode Island, the way it did 100 years ago in Paris, Rome, and Athens. When Henry James observed Americans scurrying from site to site in Rome, he thought that it must be Roman architecture and style of life—the omnipresence of art in the streets—that created a vast entertainment zone. But today we see that living antiquity inspires the generic tourism that requires the help of a guide. "Italy was," in short, as art historian Barbara Novak says, "the *didactic* museum of the past."[50]

A similar didactic quality pervades both new tourist regions and urban neighborhoods that emerge as "ripe" for gentrification. But today the guide is provided by the critical infrastructure. Walking tours through old neighborhoods are staffed by volunteers who have "discovered" their cultural value. Restaurant reviews point out the little bistro one would never find by oneself on the far side of town.

In her studies of low-wage immigrant workers in New York City, Saskia Sassen points out that the new consumption practices of gentrification are labor-intensive.[51] She indicates the English nanny required to watch the children of a two-income family, the Salvadoran maid who cleans their apartment, the Ethiopian or Haitian livery service driver who brings a hard-working spouse back to the nest late at night, the Dominican home-workers who hand knit sweaters for expensive Seventh Avenue designers, the delivery boy from the local Chinese restaurant, and the family of the Korean greengrocer who keep the fruit stand open twenty-four hours a day. Just as important, however, is the labor of the critical infrastructure. Not only are they high-culture artists and performers; they are also the work force in service organizations. They are museum curators, advisers to corporate art collectors, and members of art gallery staffs. They sell cheese at the local gourmet food store. They are restaurant waiters as well as chefs and owners; they are also the restaurant critics whose reviews are eagerly read for vicarious cultural consumption.[52]

GENTRIFICATION AND CUISINE

Gourmet food—specifically, the kind of reflexive consumption beyond the level of need that used to be called gastronomy—suggests an organization of consumption structurally similar to the deep palate of gentrification.

The labor force that produces gourmet food in new "French" restaurants illustrates the hierarchy of social classes in the new, service-oriented urban population. While they may produce a version of French cuisine more authentic than the "continental" menu that was so popular in the 1950s and 1960s, these restaurants contrast with real French establishments, which are usually French-owned and run according to a traditional professional standard. At the bottom, where French employees would begin an apprenticeship in restaurant management, low-skilled, mainly immigrant, employees work as busboys and sometimes cooks. The kitchen, and even the lesser service stations, which are traditionally the realm of apprentice and master chefs, are staffed by college graduates and degree-holders from culinary arts schools. Generally recruited—in contrast to France—from the middle class, they need restaurant experience to begin a chef's career or open their own establishments. Waiters and waitresses in new "French" restaurants are recruited from the critical infrastructure. So many underemployed actors, artists, and writers have been drawn into part-time restaurant employment, at least in Los Angeles and Manhattan, that the hiring process now resembles a casting call.[53]

Alongside the actual consumption of restaurant food, another set of producers satisfy a need for vicarious consumption. Among the specialized magazines that began publishing in the 1970s and 1980s, a burgeoning "gourmet" press caters to the gentrifier's intellectual curiosity. Over the years these magazines have become more professional, with greater attention to "authentic" ingredients, the careers of chefs, and regions of food production (some of which, like California wine country, have been developed into tourist regions). At the same time, a large number of trade books published for display on the coffee table feature luscious photographs of sushi, grapes, or cheese, organized around exotic themes. (Alexander Cockburn once called this literary genre "gastro-porn.")

Certainly these forms of vicarious consumption are related to older means of communication, especially newspaper journalism and television. We can hardly underestimate the didactic effect of Elizabeth David's and Jane Grigson's writing about food in the English press in the 1950s and 1960s, Julia Child's U.S. television series on French cooking during the 1970s, and the "home," "style," and "weekend" supplements that daily newspapers have published since the 1970s. Increasingly, however, vicarious consumption of gourmet food abstracts, rather than reproduces, cuisine's cultural values: many upper-middle-class devotees of television cooking shows today never go into the kitchen.[54] Restaurant consumers of gourmet food run the same gamut as those who participate in gentrification. New "French" restaurants draw both rich gourmets who know about the food and middle-class pretenders who know about the place. Thus we have a simultaneous increase in restaurants with "four-star" cuisine and those that merely feature modish, trendy, or "theme" menus.

Three main kinds of gentrifiers, moreover, parallel the consumers who patronize gourmet food stores. Gentrifiers are either former urban residents who seek to recapture an old ethnicity, aspirants toward a higher level of cultural consumption, or small-scale investors in housing development. Similarly, "we have a blend of three kinds of customers," the president of a regional chain of discount gourmet food stores says. "Those who grew up where the product was sold and are familiar with it, those who are interested in establishing a higher quality of life for themselves, and those who are the bargain-hunters."[55]

These preliminary notes suggest that, like gentrification, the social organization of gourmet food consumption cannot be adequately explained by demographic changes, the pursuit of positional goods for social differentiation, or the economics of market segmentation. These days, gourmet food takes many forms. Between mass-market prepared dishes and traditional French cooking lies the landscape of nouvelle cuisine. Like the downtown landscape, nouvelle cuisine represents a basic restructuring of socio-spatial power. It also reflects change in a landscape of central power—that is, the production and consumption of classical French cuisine.

THE LANDSCAPE OF CUISINE

In 1972 readers of the magazine section of the Sunday *New York Times* were treated to their first in-depth visit to the Lyonnais restaurant of Paul Bocuse. No less an authority than Waverley Root, the American author of *The Food of France,* described for *Times* readers the restaurant that Bocuse had built down the road from his father's traditional, family-run establishment. Root described so readers could taste it Bocuse's signature dish of baked *loup en croute.* He also wrote about the chef and his wife's attention to the "locals" who frequently called.[56] Only fifteen years after Root made this regional chef a household name among readers of the *New York Times,* Bocuse was integrated into a new global organization of gourmet food consumption. He became part owner, along with two other "three-star" French chefs, of a 230-seat French restaurant at Epcot Center, Florida, which they leased from Disney World. With 200 employees, the restaurant Chefs de France fed between 2,000 and 4,000 visitors a day, many of them tourists from around the world.[57]

In the intervening decade, *Times* readers were treated to periodic views of Bocuse and other innovators of French cuisine as they flew into New York to cook dinner at a charity event or to Tokyo to give a week of cooking demonstrations. These chefs also published illustrated cookbooks to communicate their new, "simplified" manner of cooking and presentation. Like the food itself, these cookbooks were both complex and luxurious. Roger Vergé, for example, one of Bocuse's chef-partners at Epcot Center, published a conceptually austere vegetable cookbook whose color photographs, arranged by season, reached toward a high degree of sensual fulfillment. Yet key ingredients and preparation routines were not in most American readers' reach.

The worldwide expansion of cuisine as a new form of cultural consumption had important economic effects. On one level, the chefs' expeditions around the world enhanced the economic value of their restaurants as well as the more general production of French cuisine. On another level, by expanding the social and entrepreneurial repertoire of professional chefs, they established the economic value of cuisine as a new service institution. Not only did their own licensing arrangements and cookbooks prosper, but cooking schools in Paris drew an expanding and revitalized clientele, especially from the United States and Japan. Furthermore, within the occupational structure of French cuisine, the best apprenticeships now took young chefs from France to grand hotels in North America and Southeast Asia instead of circulating them among the provinces. The experience of Paul Bocuse's generation of chefs suggests the extent of structural transformation in classical French cuisine. On the one hand, a top culinary career in France now relates to the exercise of global, rather than regional, cultural power. On the other hand, the diffusion of the individualized, signature products of a relatively small number of nouvelle cuisine chefs reflects a new centralization of cultural power.

It is important to remember that the preparation style and ingredients basic to globally hegemonic "French cuisine" are really rooted in local cooking traditions. The area around Paris called the Île-de-France is where both French cuisine and French *political* culture were formed. Just as local powers from the Île-de-France historically imposed their rule over other French regions, so the court they established imposed its cooking on the rest of France. To this day, as Waverley Root points out, the national butter-based cuisine that originated in the Île-de-France represents the standard for national culture, even while it coexists with other regional cuisines (and agrarian ecologies) based on olive oil and pork fat.[58]

To the spread of cuisine by military and political rule, we must add the forceful effects of social and cultural power. All the world's great cuisines were spread at some point by adoption or imitation of courtly norms. Thus "culinary culture" in both Europe and Asia historically depended on social hierarchy. A local style of cooking is universally transformed into cuisine if it appropriates food by means of both an inter-regional or international distribution and a market-based agricultural production. It also requires a fairly broad elite in society outside the initial nucleus of aristocratic demand, an elite that has, moreover, an inquiring and aesthetic—a reflexive—attitude toward food consumption.[59]

After 1973, the consumption of nouvelle cuisine spread not by military rule or cultural imitation but by market power. Chefs of Lyon, heirs of a celebrated, but essentially domestic, regional cooking tradition, had previously produced great food *in situ*. By the 1970s, however, the restructuring of the global economy generated a broader elite with an interest in the reflexive consumption of classical cuisine that the Bocuse generation supplied. People around the world saw their kitchens as the primal scene of a global culture. Consequently, the "nouvelle" cooking of the Lyonnais region was transformed into an international norm.

This process of change indeed marked a structural transformation. Like gentrification, nouvelle cuisine—especially as practiced in the United States—depends on a new supply of market-based agricultural production, an inter-regional and international system of fresh food distribution, a change in consumer demand, and, most important, the melding of segmented vernacular cooking traditions into a homogeneous landscape of culinary power. Classical cuisine, in the process, was turned inside out.

Cuisine has first and foremost always implied a rigid set of rules. The elaborate procedures of food preparation based on the hierarchy of the kitchen are paralleled by an elaborate etiquette of eating that reflects a general social hierarchy. A good description is offered by A. J. Liebling, Waverley Root's friend and fellow trencherman among American journalists in Paris between the two world wars. Liebling's account of a memorable dinner he enjoyed with a French gastronome, the somewhat ailing M. Mirande, fondly but ironically sums up the rule-bound nature of classical cuisine. "After the trout," writes Liebling,

> Mirande and I had two meat courses, since we could not decide in advance which we preferred. We had a magnificent *daube provençale,* because we were faithful to *la cuisine bourgeoise,* and then *pintadous*—young guinea hens, simply and tenderly roasted—with the first asparagus of the year, to show our fidelity to *la cuisine classique.* We had clarets [i.e., wines from Bordeaux] with both courses—a Pétrus with the *daube,* a Cheval Blanc with the guineas. Mirande said that his doctor had discounseled Burgundies.[60]

Rule-making in cuisine incorporates external regional or social differentiations—for example, between "home-style" *cuisine bourgeoise* and the "classical" cuisine of the Île-de-France, between Bordeaux and Burgundy, between housewives' cooking *("la cuisine des femmes")* and the products of professional male chefs—into an internal cultural differentiation. The categories of cuisine in turn become the foundations of cultural ritual. Nouvelle cuisine as practiced by the chefs of Lyon simply began as an effort to rearrange this internal differentiation. But processes of global economic restructuring quickly swept aside all traditional, ritualistic constraints. Which ingredients went with what, the sequence of courses, the aesthetic balance of a dish, the new attention to extrinsic (e.g., nutritional) factors: nouvelle cuisine seemed to break all the established rules. This discontinuity was even more obvious in the organization of consumption that supported nouvelle *American* cuisine.

In France and Italy as well as the United States, a return to fresh goods from freezing and other, technologically advanced means of food preservation was perceived as part of the pursuit of culinary "authenticity." Because consumers were willing to pay for this special taste, both regional production and national distribution systems changed. Paul Bocuse himself said on a visit to the United States in the 1980s, "When I first came here in 1967 you could not find fresh chervil or tarragon anywhere, and now you can buy ingredients like that in the supermarket." The pursuit of local sources of supply, moreover, enhanced the cultural value of regional cooking traditions. Most of these traditions had died out during the period of mass industrialization from 1880 to 1940, when new food production technologies were developed and imposed, and national networks standardized procedures of food distribution. But new sources of supply in the 1980s not only reflected the revitalization of small-scale regional agriculture. They also relied on both the expansion of imports and local farmers' willingness to try new agricultural techniques.[61]

New products enabled consumers to choose from a highly varied menu, borrowing from archaic local traditions as well as distant cuisines. The chef at the London Chop House in Detroit, for example, offered customers such dishes as grilled salmon with mustard greens, "bringing together native salmon, cattails, and mustard greens flavored with imported olive oil and balsamic vinegar." Even the use of simple foods proved a dramatic innovation. "Where it used to be standard Midwest cooking [here]," a restaurant consultant in Kansas City attests, "people are now going wild over grilled fresh fish."[62]

Just as products and protocols in the kitchen were altered, so was the social production of professional chefs. The new American cooks have college training and considerable travel experience before they ever enter a restaurant kitchen. If they reach the rank of executive chef or pastry chef in Manhattan, they may earn up to $100,000 a year. These conditions could not contrast more with the traditional, formal apprenticeship system in which real French chefs are trained.

Discontinuity in the social production of chefs is illuminated by the disagreements that surfaced during a recent discussion among French-trained and new American chefs, all of whom work in good restaurants in New York. When an American chef says that if she wanted to, she could produce Japanese cuisine, Jean-Jacques Rachou protests that while she may be able to imitate it, she "can't really do it right." For Rachou, chef-owner of the elegant restaurant La Côte Basque, authentic cuisine reflects the continuity of classical tradition: a totally predictable fulfilling of expectations, a subdued individuality, the whole the result of rigorous training. "Now see," he says,

> it took me 10 years just to become a junior chef. Young chefs today come from the Culinary Institute and after six months, one year, they are junior chefs. You give them a chance to be in charge; they stay long enough to learn my system. Then they go and become chefs somewhere else. This is normal. Then they learn another system, then they go in business or are chefs by themselves. And they call what they do American cooking. But it's not. (What is it then?) It's French.[63]

While an American and a French chef assert that since "there was no old American cuisine, . . . there cannot be any new American cuisine," the woman chef supports the idea that American cuisine is synonymous with appropriation and innovation. "I do not believe that we should limit ourselves," she says. "Why can't we take the best of everything and make it even better? It's all been done before. We're just taking one step in front of another, hoping that something fabulous comes out of it." This indeed recalls the original idea of cuisine, when the center of an empire appropriates the best elements of various local traditions.

New American cuisine, like gentrification, is built on appropriation and subversion of segmented vernacular traditions. On the one hand, local ingredients and preparations—poblano chilis, blackened fish—are incorporated into new "classical" cuisine at the center. On the other hand, new regional cuisine develops in commercial restaurants rather than the home; and it submits local elements to the formulas (or recipes) of cultural power. Los Angeles and New York serve as the two centers of new American cuisine. In both places, long and wildly incon-

gruous restaurant menus are a noticeable result of vernacular appropriation. A typical menu may blend elements of known or resurrected
cuisines—like Cajun and Creole—with local products flown in from
distant shores (e.g., Maryland crab cakes, Virginia ham, wild mush-
rooms from Oregon or Michigan, Minnesota wild rice). It may also
synthesize local preparations in a newly named regional cuisine. Such a
cuisine is no longer "Tex-Mex," but the "southwest" cuisine of New
Mexico, Texas, and Arizona. Similarly, when arugula and goat cheese,
fresh vegetables, and game are sold in restaurants in Chicago, they constitute "midwest" cuisine.

Sometimes the culinary consequences are more provocative than
tasty. "My fellow diners couldn't decide which was worse," Bryan Miller
writes in a review of the restaurant America in Manhattan,

> the so-called hot and spicy homemade alligator sausages, which
> had all the flavor of a pocketbook, or the "dry-cured Virginia
> ham scrapple," an oversalted mound of mush that would bring
> tears to a Philadelphian's eyes. The only edible appetizers en-
> countered were the Buffalo chicken wings, which were little
> more than fried chicken with bleu cheese dressing and hot
> sauce, and the char-grilled wild mushrooms.[64]

Another ironic consequence of appropriation by the center is not
the re-creation, but the de novo creation of vernacular cuisine. In Texas,
where one had always thought Tex-Mex cooking was born, regional
chili cook-offs have been created as part of a national trend. New modern standards of taste—such as the tenderness and quality of the meat—
count more in these contests than traditional local criteria that have to
do with peppers and spices. The style of showmanship of the cook,
moreover, and the names of the creations are at least as important as
the edible results. Significantly, participants in these cook-offs are not
local talent; they come from all over the United States. Nor are the
cook-offs themselves local fiestas. Instead, they act as drawing-cards to
other events sponsored by local social groups.[65]

The career of Alain Dutournier, chef-owner of a *grand restaurant*
in Paris, suggests that the same processes of structural transformation
are altering the landscape of French culinary power. Dutournier started
out as the *patron* of a pleasant neighborhood restaurant that featured
the Gascon cuisine of his home region in southwestern France. Au Trou

Gascon was located outside the center of Paris, in the XIIe arrondisse-
ment. It captured restaurant critics' attention for the serious quality of
Dutournier's cooking, the authentic ingredients he brought to Paris, and
his attention to decor. Dutournier's original "regional" repertoire combined "his famous Gascon *pastilla* [a North African term]—a delicate,
sealed croustade of pigeon, foie gras, grapes, pine nuts, and baby cabbage—and an Indian-spiced, stuffed *cul de lapereau,* his grandmother's
escalopes de foie gras de canard au vinaigre, and a remarkable salmon
baked with cabbage." And success was predicated on attracting a nonlocal clientele. "He wanted to discourage the kind of locals [in Paris!]
who came for Sunday lunch—one old lady and her poodle to a table,
no wine, and half a bottle of mineral water."

A decade and several Michelin stars later, Dutournier owned a chain
of franchised wine bars in addition to Au Trou Gascon. At that point
he opened a luxurious *grand restaurant* in the most expensive part of
the center of Paris. The menu featured dishes that were "authentically
southwest," the wine cost 25 percent more than at Au Trou Gascon,
and the clientele, as the *patron* always wished, was devoutly international. Alain Dutournier had mapped the new landscape of culinary
power.[66]

A LANDSCAPE OF CONSUMPTION

Both gentrification and new cuisine represent a new organization of
consumption that developed during the 1970s. Both imply a new landscape of economic power based, in turn, on changing patterns of capital
investment and new relations between investment, production, and
consumption. A new international division of labor, greater trade and
more travel, the abstraction or removal of traditional activities from
local communities: all these consequences of the global economy make
available a new range and quality of experience. At the same time, the
disappearance of old sources of regional and local identity impoverishes
others, leading to a new pursuit of authenticity and individualization.

Shifts in both production and consumption of cultural values create
new socio-spatial meaning. Aspirations toward cultural power primarily clear the landscape of socially obsolete, and segmented, vernacular.
But this process relies on a shift of perspective that in turn is tied to the
social production of a new group of cultural mediators. They enable
vernacular to be perceived, appreciated, and consumed as landscape—

but then also appropriated, marketed, and exchanged in a more intensive way. This group is a critical infrastructure in two senses. On the one hand, their mediation is *critical* to the social processes of spatial and economic restructuring that are especially visible in modern cities at the center of advanced industrial society. On the other hand, their labor produces *critique* that makes people more aware of consumption and distinguishes reflexive consumers from other social groups.

Members of the critical infrastructure produce the didactic prism through which cultural values are appreciated. They conduct walking tours through seedy neighborhoods, pointing out elements of art and history amid decline. They visit restaurants, writing up reactions to dishes and comparing them with the composite menu of their collective experience. By these activities, the critical infrastructure establish and unify a new perspective for viewing and consuming the values of place—but by so doing they also establish their market values. From this point of view, gentrification—like cuisine—is transformed from a *place-defining* into a *market-defining* process.

Ironically, in either landscape or menu, the key elements are substitutable. The chef's grandmother's stew or Indian spices, red caviar on potato pancakes, tortillas wrapped around foie gras: does it matter, so long as each element is "authentically" part of a culinary landscape? In gentrification, too, appropriation of a homogeneous visual standard of cultural power takes precedence over the social community. "We've reached a point," says the chairman of a local community board on the gentrified Upper West Side of Manhattan, "where the young, middle-class family cannot ever come back here. We are adamant about trying to save *the look of the place* even if we cannot save the population group."[67]

There could be no more devastating indictment of the effects on place of market power.

The "death of downtown" suggests that centrality has its contradictions. For developers, centrality is a geographical space; for gentrifiers, it is a built environment. But for a population that is socially or economically displaced from older cities, centrality is a struggle between their own segmented vernacular and a coherent landscape of power.

EPCOT, Disney World, Florida (1990). Photo by William Simon.

8 Disney World: The Power of Facade / The Facade of Power

For that was the charm—that so preposterously, with the essential notes of the impression so happily struck, the velvet air, the extravagant plants, the palms, the oranges, the cacti, the architectural fountain, the florid local monument, the cheap and easy exoticism, the sense as of people feeding, off in the background, very much *al fresco,* that is on queer things and with flaring lights—one might almost have been in a corner of Naples or of Genoa.

HENRY JAMES, "Florida,"
The American Scene (1907)

The modern city's image of centrality is turned inside out by the landscape of power at the bicoastal extremities of the Sunbelt. Without a traditional center or downtown, cities like Los Angeles and Miami can only be seen in fragments. Intensive real estate development does not produce the usual vertical skyline. Seashore, freeways, and canals erupt, instead, in dense clusters of suburban-style housing like the ranch house, beach house, villa, and bungalow, isolated office buildings, and low-lying industrial parks. There is little difference between "city" and "country" in this clustered diffusion.

Under pressure from investment in the built environment, space both expands and contracts. Collective spatial forms expand to include relatively unstructured cities like Los Angeles and Miami as well as increasingly structured exurban areas (Orange County in southern California and Fort Lauderdale–Palm Beach in Florida). But the same forms are also individualized and collapsed into specific journeys: no one would claim to appropriate the entire experience of L.A. or Miami. The automobility that flows through these cities makes some people excited or uneasy, for there is little connection—according to modernist expectations—between built form and urban identity. In Miami, in the architect Michael Sorkin's view, "the pattern of settlement [is] obviously in total thrall to the landscape. Clearly, this [is] a zone to be grasped not through the familiar repertoire of urban categories but through a far broader sense of territory."[1]

Beginning in the 1920s, and with greater force since the recognition of a "power shift" to the Sunbelt in the 1970s, the material landscape of contemporary cities has indeed demanded a broader set of categories than modernism offers. The dynamic interplay between nature and artifice in the built environment of Los Angeles or Miami has forced us to visualize urban development as a set of multiple, decentered processes, and to acknowledge the strong force of derivation over originality in architecture. Furthermore, the forging of a metropolis out of many private jurisdictions has challenged the primacy of public space as an organizing principle of social life. From the outset, moreover, Los Angeles and Miami have grown from service rather than manufacturing economies, wrenching the landscape of power from its nineteenth-century roots. This must be our image of postmodern urbanity. Yet it has been a long time building. Palm trees, fast cars on freeways, hot flamingo pinks and dazzling white villas: the symbols of post–World War II choice and alienation stretch continuously from *Play It as It Lays* to *Less than Zero*. This is the world of Raymond Chandler colonized by Walt Disney's world, where the fantasies of the powerless are magically projected onto landscape developed by the powerful.

The postmodern synergy between landscape and vernacular is structured by the apparent falsity that Henry James long ago derided as "hotel-civilization." When he saw the expensive resort architecture of Palm Beach in 1907, James called it "a Nile without the least little implication of a Sphinx," a set of the "costliest reproductions . . . as if to put to shame those remembered villas of the Lake of Como, of the Borromean Islands." "Instant Portofino," Michael Sorkin likewise snapped about Miami's affluent villas eighty years later. In Los Angeles, a more benign Reyner Banham found "an instant architecture and an instant townscape" in the 1960s. "Most of its buildings are the first and only structures on their particular parcels of land," he wrote, "they are couched in a dozen different styles, most of them imported, exploited, and ruined in living memory."[2] It is impossible to view this landscape from the perspective of a modern city like New York, Chicago, or San Francisco.

In the built environment today, the stage-prop quality of a landscape of consumption—the "instant Portofino" that Sorkin found in Miami, the extravagant "opera" scenery of cottages and oleander that James noted at Lake Como—takes more ingenious root in the social imagination. This landscape is built up by the electronic image that faithfully transmits, yet also renders more abstract, the architectural facade that both mirrors and recedes, the Disneyland that re-creates a built environment for mass leisure consumption, the whole communicating what James in America called "the jealous cultivation of the common mean, . . . the reduction of everything to an average of decent suitability." This is a landscape that asks more imagination of its viewers than it offers.[3]

The entire landscape of cities like Miami and Los Angeles visually projects the liminality between *market* and *place*. The usual forms of social control—by police, employers, corporate elites—are embedded in an amusing architecture and individualized means of consumption like automobiles. Although L.A. and Miami are real cities, they are built on the power of dreamscape, collective fantasy, and facade. This landscape is explicitly produced for visual consumption. Moreover, it is *self-consciously* produced. As James suspected, the best place to view such a landscape is at the very tips of the Sunbelt, where regional identity is least "southern" and "western" and thus most socially constructed.

Miami was, after all, invented three times in this century. Developed out of swampland as a socially, ethnically, and racially exclusive southern resort in the 1920s, Miami differed little in intention from its more exclusive neighbor, Palm Beach. After World War II, a second Miami, monopolized by Miami Beach, developed as a cheaper vacation land for middle-class northerners, mainly ethnic and eventually Jewish; Miami offered a more exotic and more individualized consumption of leisure than social camps in the Catskills. From 1960, following Castro's revolution, a new wave of Cuban exiles and other Central Americans swelled the racially and ethnically segregated population in the inner city. By 1980, bypassing the native black population in business and political organization, they made the Miami area a Latin metropolis, an adjunct to Caracas and Rio and an alternative to Havana. Ethnic recruits and Latin capital created in the third Miami a microcosm of global exchange. While the city always had a service economy, hotels became less important than foreign investment in banks, weapons traffic, and the illegal drug trade.[4]

Los Angeles has also been invented three times in this century. Visualized by celluloid fantasy, Los Angeles first figured as backdrop and back lot in countless silent Westerns. The prewar dream capital was created as production space for the manufacture of films, which was, like tourism, a mass leisure industry. But Los Angeles was also created by making desert and hills habitable for immigrant labor, both skilled and unskilled, outside the film industry, in oil and gas refineries, car making, and light manufacturing. The first Los Angeles was an amalgam of East European Jews, Asians, Chicanos, African-Americans, Okies, and most of all, midwesterners. Invention of the second Los Angeles, which dates from 1940, reflected the new labor force required for military and industrial activities in the port and airport and large, unionized plants. This is the Los Angeles of middle-class affluence and social mobility, an American dream. As in Miami, however, much of the population that was drawn to the city in this period has been passed over in the growth of the third Los Angeles.

Both decentralized and recentralized, the new Los Angeles has a coherent landscape downtown, built by new Asian immigrants and mainly foreign investment in banking and financial services. But it also has inner suburbs where manufacturing branch plants of U.S. firms have rapidly shut down, displacing and cheapening union labor, and other industrial suburbs where electronics and garment plants have continued to grow even during economic recessions. These suburbs are integrated by clusters of high-tech industries, yet they are segregated at work by race and gender and segregated in residential communities by race and class.[5]

The constant reinvention of landscape furnishes a narrative for "footloose" capital. It provides a social geography for the shifting landscapes of the global economy. Yet while the real history of Los Angeles and Miami illustrates the processes of structural change in the U.S. economy, these cities are more interesting as spatial metaphors. We are fascinated by Los Angeles and Miami because we think they show us the future. Their freeways, their "decentering," their "Mondo Condo" pursuit of private leisure: this is the way the future looks. These cities stun because of their unique ability to abstract an image of desire from the landscape and reflect it back through the vernacular. Just as they show the power of facade to lure the imagination, so they also represent the facade of global corporate power.

No single image symbolizes a postmodern city like Los Angeles or Miami the way the steel mill symbolizes the company town or downtown symbolizes the modern city. "Ain't no skyline," an ironic songwriter says about L.A. We see these landscapes, instead, by modes of visual consumption that play with image and reality. Visual consumption of landscape rests on an interplay of nature and artifice that goes back many years. Toward the end of the eighteenth century, the "Eidophusikon"—a construction of pasteboard cut-outs, lights, and sound—created scenes of London, the countryside, and the seashore. In the nineteenth century, dioramas and panoramas manipulated light to make translucent images—often images of city streets—on a screen. Their twentieth-century descendants, Hollywood films, widened spectators' power over darkness while strengthening the hold of the image over its viewers. After the reign of still photography during the Depression and World War II, electronic media completed the transformation of image into power. Broadcast television broke all existing barriers between public and private, local and global, the living room and the world, until the viewers rather than the image became the product.[6]

The domestication of fantasy in visual consumption is inseparable from centralized structures of economic power. Just as the earlier power of the state illuminated public space—the streets—by artificial lamplight, so the economic power of CBS, Sony, and the Disney Company illuminates private space at home by electronic images. With the means of production so concentrated and the means of consumption so diffused, communication of these images becomes a way of controlling both knowledge and imagination, a form of corporate social control over technology and symbolic expressions of power.

FANTASY AS A LANDSCAPE OF POWER

While Walt Disney won fame as a founder of Hollywood's animation industry, his real genius was to transform an old form of collective entertainment—the amusement park—into a landscape of power. All his life Disney wanted to create his own amusement park. But to construct this playground, he wanted no mere thrill rides or country fair: he wanted to project the vernacular of the American small town as an image of social harmony. "The idea of Disneyland is a simple one. It will be a place for people to find happiness and knowledge," Disney said. But "in fact," a recent essay on Disney points out, "it was the appearance of Disneyland, not the idea, that was simple."[7]

Appearance nonetheless caused the great animator some concern when he began to plan Disneyland, the archetypal theme park, which was finally built in Orange County, California, in 1955. Disney hired two architects whose plans didn't quite capture what he had in mind, and giving up on them, used an animator from his studio to draw up architectural designs to his own specifications. Disney's peculiar vision was based on a highly selective consumption of the American landscape. Anchored by a castle and a railroad station, Disneyland evoked the fantasies of domesticity and illicit mobility that were found in the vernacular architecture of southern California. The castle and station were joined on an axis by "Main Street USA," an ensemble of archaic commercial facades. This mock-up in fact idealized the vernacular architecture Disney remembered from his childhood in Marceline, Missouri, before World War I. But Disney had not had a happy childhood. The son of a disappointed utopian who drifted between factory jobs and small business ventures that always failed, Disney designed Disneyland by abstracting a promise of security from the vernacular.

Disney's fantasy both restored and invented collective memory. "This is what the real Main Street should have been like," one of Disneyland's planners or "imagineers" says. "What we create," according to another, "is a 'Disney realism,' sort of Utopian in nature, where we carefully program out all the negative, unwanted elements and program in the positive elements."[8] And Disneyland succeeded on the basis of this totalitarian image-making, projecting the collective desires of the powerless into a corporate landscape of power. In this way it paralleled the creation of a mass consumption society. Disney's designs also included an element of play that was pure Hollywood construction, for Disneyland featured five different stage-set amusement parks, organized around separate themes: Adventureland, Lilliputian Land, Fantasyland, Frontier Land, and Holiday Land. The unique combination borrowed motifs from carnivals, children's literature, and U.S. history.

That Disneyland significantly departed from the dominant fantasy landscape of the time was dramatized when Disney failed to arouse enthusiasm in a convention of amusement park owners that previewed plans for the park in 1953. They criticized the small number of rides, the large amount of open space that wouldn't generate revenue, and the need for constant, expensive maintenance in the theme parks.[9] In their view, Disneyland would never succeed as a business venture. They objected—had they used the now-fashionable word *concept* in those days— that Disneyland was too self-conscious and unrealistic a concept to be an amusement park. But from our point of view, they failed to understand that Disneyland was an ideal object for visual consumption, a landscape of social power. Despite their criticism, Disneyland was commercially successful from the day it opened.

Disneyland offered a multidimensional collage of the American landscape. The playgrounds organized around a theme provided consumers with their first opportunity to view several different landscapes—some imaginative historical recreations and others purely imaginary—simultaneously. With this variety for individual visitors to choose from, Disneyland differed from historical dioramas and reconstructions like Greenfield Village and Colonial Williamsburg, where costumed actors re-created the routines of daily life in an earlier age. Disneyland, moreover, had no educational veneer. It merely told a story, offering the selective consumption of space and time as entertainment. This was the "wienie," as Walt Disney and amusement park owners alike called the lure that attracted customers to a paying event.

Visitors to Disneyland paid for a variety of entertainment experiences linked by the narrative of the different themes. These in turn provided a narrative for different program segments on the Disney Studio's weekly television series. Combining narrative with serial expectations, each visual product of the Disney Company fed into the others. Although commercial spin-offs were not a new creation, this commercialization was the most extensive to take place under a single corporate sponsor. Disney's business growth also related to important processes of change in the larger society: notably, the demographic growth of the baby boom, the spread of television, and the increase in domestic consumption. Moreover, it contributed to the development of both Orange County and the tourist industry. Disney's success coincided with the expansion of the suburbs and a population shift to the Southwest, the growth of the service sector, and a boom in leisure-time activities, including sales of recreational land and travel. Just as the real landscape reflected the intensive, unplanned development of the country by subdivision and mass construction, so the imaginary landscape of Disneyland reflected the growth of mass communications built on visual consumption.

While this kind of entertainment invited escape from the modern world, it also relied upon the centralization of economic power typical of modern society. Consumption at Disneyland was part of a service-sector complex relating automobiles and airplanes, highways, standardized hotels, movies, and television. Furthermore, the social production of Disneyland related a major corporate presence—the Disney Company—to entertainment "creation," real estate development and construction, and product franchising. In all these senses, Disneyland suggested the social and economic potential of liminality in the modern American marketplace.

Disney's second amusement park, Disney World, near Orlando, Florida, was conceived on a somewhat different model. Here the centerpiece was a "wienie" that would lure people to a new utopian vernacular, an imaginary landscape of the future. "EPCOT [the Experimental Prototype Community of Tomorrow] will be like the city of tomorrow ought to be," Walt Disney said.

> It will be a city that caters to the people as a service function. It will be a planned, controlled community, a showcase for American industry and research, schools, cultural and educational opportunities. In EPCOT there will be no landowners and therefore no voting control. No slum areas because we will not let them develop. People will rent houses instead of buying them, and at modest rentals. There will be no retirees. Everyone must be employed.[10]

This vision in part reflected Disney's childhood experiences, as the son of a man with several unsuccessful careers and business failures. It also responded to the lasting significance of social upheaval during the Great Depression. A conservative utopia, EPCOT from the outset joined entertainment values to motifs of social control.

Yet EPCOT was not built exactly to Disney's original specifications. For one thing, the company decided in 1966 that building a residential community involved too much legal responsibility. It decided instead to make its ideal community a temporary haven—that is, a resort colony. Another problem was the lack of available technology to build EPCOT as envisioned by Disney and his imagineers. Although the biggest U.S. corporations signed on as exhibit sponsors to enhance their corporate images, the automated technology to build the attractions in Disney's own pavilions was too expensive for the Disney Company. Disney's Hall of Presidents, for example, was designed in the late 1950s as an automated historical diorama in which the presidents are "played" by robots, but it wasn't feasible for the company to build it until twenty years later. EPCOT itself didn't open as part of Florida's Disney World until 1982.[11]

Disney World's imaginary landscape made dramatic improvements on its closest multimedia precedents, the 1893 World's Columbian Exposition in Chicago and the 1939 World's Fair in Flushing Meadows, New York. Both world's fairs featured the four kinds of attractions that Disney World would later integrate to perfection: amusement parks and rides, stage-set representations of vernacular architecture, state-of-the-art technology, and a special construction of an idea! urban community.

The amusements at the two world's fairs were traditional fairground attractions updated by modern technology. The Ferris Wheel was invented for the 1893 World's Columbian Exposition (the United States's answer to the engineering triumph of France's Eiffel Tower), and visitors to the 1939 World's Fair rode through one of the pavilions in moving chairs. The amusements on the Midway in Chicago were more prominent than any other feature of the 1893 exposition, and the most popular part of the 1939 event also featured carnival attractions.

Both fairs demonstrated their global focus by mounting theatrical performances of foreign "folk" cultures on stage sets representing appropriate vernacular architecture. In 1893, this took the form of a series of "villages," such as "Streets of Cairo," featuring the scandalous female performer Little Egypt. The 1939 fair had a similar World Showcase, before retreating from internationalism in 1940 and concentrating on America's own folk (i.e., ethnic) cultures.

Both world's fairs also featured exhibits of state-of-the-art technology. In 1893, new machinery was displayed as individual material products; by 1939, however, an image of technological progress was abstracted from industrial production and incorporated into the landscape of the fair. On the one hand, technological progress was incorporated as a narrative, the World of Tomorrow, that gave coherence to the various exhibits. On the other hand, technology was applied to the mechanization of the exhibits themselves to ease visual consumption.

Technology dramatized the exhibits' effect and provided visitors with a means of moving around them.

The fourth feature of both world's fairs was an ideal urban community that mapped the social control of landscape design on an unplanned society. The 1893 exposition commissioned prominent architects to design a mammoth "White City" of more than two hundred neoclassical, mainly public, buildings that was meant to contrast a Beaux Arts professional architectural coherence with the disorderly growth of expanding U.S. cities. The 1939 fair shifted this concept from monumental to private architecture, by building an ideal residential community, the Town of Tomorrow, that contrasted with Depression-era conditions in real housing markets. These houses were intended to show how technology could produce attractive housing for the average American.[12]

The World of Tomorrow at the 1939 World's Fair already included the basic components on which the special landscape of EPCOT would rely. Futuristic visions of science and technology were scaled down for domestic consumption and organized as separate paying events. These were sponsored by such large corporate producers as General Motors, General Electric, Eastman Kodak, and AT&T. While their pavilions presented state-of-the-art products as the 1893 Chicago exposition and earlier international exhibitions had done, the 1939 innovation was a focus on process rather than production. The exhibits at the 1939 World's Fair were interactive, involving viewers as participants in the consumption process. Not only did they view the exhibits, they also touched them, asked demonstrators questions about them, and, most important, moved among them. Although mechanization of production was a major cause of unemployment at the time, mechanization in this landscape mediated the process of visual consumption. Significantly, a review of the fair in *Business Week* judged the exhibits of companies that produced consumer goods more effective than those of industrial goods producers.[13] IBM made its business machines more attractive to fairgoers by deliberate choices in visual display. While highlighting its latest electric accounting, payroll, and sorting machines in the center of a circular gallery, IBM surrounded the automated equipment with an extensive international exhibit of paintings that mainly ignored industrial themes. These paintings had been purchased especially for the IBM Gallery of Science and Art at the World's Fair on the suggestion of the company's president, Thomas J. Watson.[14]

The 1939 World's Fair shared three general motifs with Disney World: the high price of admission to separate exhibitions or theme parks, the blend of progress and consumerism in selling corporate image, and the landscape of "a new fantasy world that could be enjoyed because it could be controlled." Not surprisingly, these motifs were related. Mapping the social control of a market economy on vernacular images required the resources of large corporations. The 1939 fair was in fact planned as a commercial venture by corporate sponsors and a steering committee recruited from the business world. But in contrast to Disney World's eventual success, the 1939 World's Fair was a commercial disaster.[15]

Disney World is also bigger and more expensive. It occupies 28,000 acres of south Florida swamp and attracts more than 150,000 visitors a day, who park in 20,000 surface parking spaces. Until 1989, the three-day admission "passport" cost $85, quite a bit more than the $7 a family was likely to spend at the 1939 World's Fair—and that amount, although steep for many families during the Depression, included meals.

The fantasy theme parks in Orlando (Captain Nemo, Pirates of the Caribbean, Space Mountain) are joined by facades of touristic architecture (the Eiffel Tower for France, Italy's St. Mark's Square) where food and souvenirs are sold. Thus Paul Bocuse's restaurant at Disney World expands on the international cultural villages of the 1893 World's Columbian Exposition. Many of the technology exhibits, moreover, represent the same corporate sponsors who built pavilions in 1939. Their exhibits include Spaceship Earth (sponsored by Bell Telephone), The Universe of Energy (Exxon), The World of Motion (GM), Journey into the Imagination (Eastman Kodak) and The Land around Us (Kraft Food Products). The futuristic research offered serves again as a showcase for corporate strategy. As in 1939, progress is identified as a corporate product (as Ronald Reagan used to say in the 1950s, when he was the television host of General Electric Theater, "Progress is our most important product"). Social problems such as the Great Depression and the energy crisis are not ignored. But they are depicted as best resolved by corporate research and development decisions, decisions that benefit consumers.[16]

People-movers at Disney World use sophisticated technology in a strategy of social control over consumption. In 1939, planners and exhibitors could not control the traffic flow of visitors to the fair. At Disney World, however, the solar-powered "traveling theater cars" that propel blocks of sixty visitors through the sights, sounds, and smells of the exhibits literally hold the public captive to the image. The sensation of consuming has become more intense, but also more ambiguous, so that visitors to Disney World feel that while they can control technology, they are also being controlled. Mobility in Disney World is a movement from one enveloping theatrical environment into another, where information blends into an implicit call to consume: Feel! Marvel! Buy!

The stage sets of the theme parks, however, are dwarfed by the entertainment architecture of Disney World's hotels. The Magic Kingdom at Disney World includes ten resort hotels with 5,700 rooms, 1,190 camp sites, 580 vacation villas sold on time shares, and three convention centers. Lake Buena Vista and Walt Disney World Village provide an additional seven hotels, with 3,500 rooms. Although the Orlando complex was completed in the 1960s, new hotels are added continuously. From 1988 to 1990, three super-hotels were built within the grounds: the Grand Floridian, a "Victorian" theme hotel, with 900 rooms; and the Dolphin and Swan hotels, which together hold 2,300 rooms and a 200,000 square foot convention center. The Dolphin and Swan form a temporary residential community for 10,000 people, making the Disney Company the largest hotel and convention center developer in the southeastern United States.

Disney World's newest hotels are theme parks in themselves. Designed by the postmodern architect Michael Graves, the Dolphin and Swan look like the rest of Graves's work—a strong terra cotta facade, pastel colors, and playful decoration—and also resonate with the production values of Disney's animated cartoons. "There's no other commercial project you can compare with Graves's design," says John Tishman, the developer of the hotel complex (in partnership with Metropolitan Life Insurance and the Aoki Corporation, a Japanese construction and real estate development firm). "It is a Disney building, fun and frivolous like a stage set." This stage set is organized around distinctive animal motifs. One hotel is surmounted on the roof by a five-story-tall dolphin; the other, by a giant swan. Although Graves chose these animals, he says, as classical symbols of nature (i.e., Florida's waterfront vernacular), they also symbolize the trademark landscape of the Disney Studios' artifice (e.g., Mickey and Minnie, Pluto, Donald Duck). "They have the kind of warmth that the whole Disney experience gives," Graves says. They show, in other words, the friendly face of power.[17]

The water motif also claims to appropriate the south Florida vernacular. So the Dolphin Hotel features a cascading waterfall that runs down the facade into a series of huge clamshells and ends in a shell-shaped pool supported by four large, sculpted dolphins. The hotels' exterior walls are covered with a pattern of waves and banana leaves, colors are "tropical" blue-green and coral (which are also Graves's signature colors). "We want to create a sense of place that is unique," says Michael Eisner, the chairman of the board of Walt Disney Company.

Yet this sense of place is not unique to Disney—nor to Louis XIV, a source suggested by another architect associated with the project. The Dolphin and the Swan uncannily recall what Henry James saw in Palm Beach long ago "on a strip of land between the sea and the jungle." James describes a landscape where "the clustered hotels, the superior Pair in especial, stand and exhale their genius. One of them, the larger, the more portentously brave, of the Pair," which could be the 26-story Dolphin, "is a marvel indeed, proclaiming itself of course, with all the eloquence of an interminable towered and pinnacled and gabled and bannered skyline, the biggest thing of its sort in the world." This is truly an imaginary landscape for visual consumption: "no world but a hotel-world could flourish in such a shadow."[18]

Hotel civilization is significant to structural transformation in the market economy because it furnishes an imaginary landscape, a prototype design for a collective life based on domestic consumption. It camouflages behind a friendly facade the global, yet centralized, economic power that makes this consumption possible. The replicas of Borromean villas that James derided are now the Dolphin and the Swan; our common culture consists of Mickey Mouse and pink flamingos. "Obviously, there are political implications," E. L. Doctorow observes about the social control implicit in this derivative market culture.

> What Disneyland proposes is a technique of abbreviated shorthand culture for the masses, a mindless thrill, like an electric shock, that insists at the same time on the recipient's rich psychic relation to his country's history and language and literature. In a forthcoming time of highly governed masses in an overpopulated world, this technique may be extremely useful both as a substitute for education and, eventually, as a substitute for experience. Disney symbols, in other words, determine the limits of consumers' imagination.[19]

In the present, however, Disney's imaginary landscape uses the symbols of a common culture to significant economic effect. The opening of EPCOT in 1982 put the Disney Company back in the spotlight on Wall Street, reversing the declining stock prices of previous years. With the company's diversification, moreover, into new entertainment areas (e.g., the production of adult movies and a cooperative venture with MGM at Disney World that includes both movie production facilities and a Hollywood theme park), Disney received glowing reviews in the business press. Licensing arrangements proliferated, for the nature of Mickey and Minnie ensure that "Disney is expandable to anything in the consumer realm."[20]

Yet it is primarily as a creator of landscape that Disney has been praised. Walt's original ability to abstract the desires of the powerless from the vernacular of Main Street and the Midway, and project them as a landscape for mass visual consumption, mapped a new vernacular image of a postmodern society. This has influenced both the real landscape and the perspective from which we view it. On the one hand, Disneyland and Disney World present an imaginary landscape based on a manipulated collective memory and consumption that we also find in downtown shopping malls like Faneuil Hall, Inner Harbor, and South Street Seaport. As early as 1963, James Rouse, the developer of these malls, praised Disney as an urban planner at a conference at Harvard University. On the other hand, Disneyland and Disney World have stimulated a whole regional complex of service-sector activities around tourism and real estate development. No wonder Walt Disney was named by *Los Angeles* magazine in April 1986 as one of "25 people who changed Los Angeles." By the same token, Disneyland and Disney World have shaped the perspective from which the real landscape is viewed. "If heaven ain't a lot like Disney" was the headline *Time* used for an annual "American Best" article on theme parks on June 16, 1986. And Disney World was named one of "50 ideas that changed the American baby" in the May 1988 issue of *American Baby*.

Reyner Banham relates the underlying structure of Disney's landscape to the movie studio lots of Los Angeles. Fantasy presented as public architecture, movie studios were eventually "elevated to the status of cultural monuments, which now form the basis for tourist excursions." Banham suggests that the economic robustness of visual consumption also influenced companies to offer guided tours of their plants, and build theme parks for visitors around their main consumer products. The circle is completed by the Disney–MGM movie studio lot at Disney World, presenting "a Hollywood that never was, and will always be."[21]

The stage-set landscape is a liminal space between nature and artifice, and market and place. It mediates between producer and consumer, a cultural object with real economic effect. The Disney landscape has in fact become a model for establishing both the economic value of cultural goods and the cultural value of consumer products. Just as the "World of Coca Cola" museum at the corporate headquarters in Atlanta places an established consumer product in a narrative framework that renews its cultural legitimacy, so art museums have replaced their encyclopedic manner of display, which induces "museum fatigue," with story-telling strategies. The Disney World narrative is ubiquitous. Ironically, Disney's market-oriented landscape evokes a strong sense of place.[22]

Feeding the synergy between consumer markets, a self-conscious sense of place is also highly desired. Ski resorts combine the perennial alpine resort architecture with entertainment facilities borrowed from Disney fantasy: "Vail (the town, not the mountain) always reminded me of a cross between a fancy hotel and Disneyland," someone writes in a letter to the editor of the *New York Times Magazine*, "no cars, people in funny costumes, entertainment based on ostentation and make-believe." Upscale housing developments, moreover, borrow Disney's abstraction of the Main Street vernacular: "The newest idea in planning is the nineteenth-century town," says the Miami architect Andres Duany, who has become successful as a town planner of historically derived reconstructions. "That's what is really selling."[23]

With conflict designed out, and comfort designed in, the image of a service-sector society is a utopian dream. It is self-consciously produced not to be disturbed by such problems as homelessness, low wages in service-sector jobs (although there have been strikes by Disney World employees), and racial competition. This projection of desire taunts the image of reality. "If you come down here [to Miami after the riots in black neighborhoods that preceded the Super Bowl in 1989] and think this is Disneyland, that's not real," a prominent football player says. But for many consumers, the self-conscious production of the imaginary landscape is what they perceive as real. And it is becoming real, for even though Walt Disney never built the residential community of his dreams at EPCOT, the Disney Development Company, which started up in the mid 1980s, plans to build real residential communities near Disney World. Where does the theme park end?[24]

It has taken forty years to perfect this imaginary landscape. From the two world's fairs of 1893 and 1939, fantasy architecture for mass entertainment moved steadily toward a utopian visual consumption, with strong motifs of mobility, populism, and social control. But it was Disney World that abstracted the desire for security from the vernacular and projected it into a coherent landscape of corporate power. Not surprisingly, most visitors to Disney World are from the upper middle class, bosses rather than workers, and white. Consumers from this social base are most likely to believe they can control history and technology if only they submit to the control of the guiding corporate hand.[25]

Fredric Jameson is wrong about the postmodern landscape of visual consumption. Disney World suggests that architecture is important, not because it is a symbol of capitalism, but because it is the capital of symbolism.

FANTASY IN VERNACULAR ARCHITECTURE

In a scathing short novel he published about Hollywood in 1939, Nathanael West previewed what would happen if a landscape like Disney World ran amok. The centerpiece in *The Day of the Locust* is a stage set painted by the protagonist, Tod Hackett, to represent the burning of Los Angeles, a fiery, apocalyptic vision. Yet Hackett's vision is more Technicolor than tragic: "He wanted the city to have quite a gala air as it burned, to appear almost gay. And the people who set it on fire would be a holiday crowd." The stage set is a metaphor for the real city of Los Angeles, where people dressed, in West's view, as if they were playing roles in a movie, and even supermarkets were bathed in complex colored lights. But here the interplay between nature and culture reflects both the artificial nature of Los Angeles's lush, mountainous Mediterranean milieu, and the natural-seeming artifice of the movie industry. Walking among the stage sets on a studio's back lot, Tod rapidly passes from "an ocean liner made of painted canvas with real life boats hanging from its davits," to "a great forty-foot papier mache sphinx," from a "desert" to "a Western street with a plank sidewalk." "Throwing away his cigarette, he went through the swinging doors of the saloon. There was no back to the building and he found himself in a Paris

street."[26] This fantastic image suggests the visual liminality of landscape in Los Angeles and Miami. While Disney World represents a macro-level landscape of social control, however, vernacular architecture
scales it down to the micro-level of individualized domestic consumption.

"Classic" vernacular architecture in Los Angeles and Miami has
traditionally taken the form of single-family houses. Individualized
mansions on hillside or ocean front differ only in degree from the standardized bungalows of the interior. Just as each house represents a module
of the good life in a contemporary market economy, so built forms raise
individual consumption to a form of civilization. Reyner Banham described this vernacular at the very moment the third Los Angeles began
its rise to global power. He found it in the endless residential enclaves
of the valleys that surround the city, the beach houses, the fantasy architecture of the foothills, and the minimalist glass-and-steel houses off
the freeways. For Banham, as for Henry James before and Fredric Jameson after him, the collective form of this vernacular combines the oldest
fantasy of the good life in the resort hotel with the newest fantasy in
the form of the pedestrian mall. In our time, freeways and homeownership provide democratic access to both collective and individual forms
of consumption, so that Los Angeles appears to Banham as today's ideal
city. It "cradles and embodies the most potent current version of the
great bourgeois vision of the good life in a tamed countryside."[27]

And tamed it has been: by suburban homeowners moving out of
the city and from other regions of the country, by diversified shopping
and business developments that become new civic centers, by the creation of many small firms that perform the specialized operations of high-
tech manufacturing, mainly as subcontractors to a few large corporations who sell to the U.S. military. Much of this development began
with the growth of Los Angeles suburbs at the expense of downtown in
the 1920s, and continued with the expansion of the suburbs from World
War II. To this extent, the growth of Los Angeles represents a long-
term trend of suburban sprawl. But it also represents a new and more
intensive process of development that helps us to visualize the current
period of structural transformation.[28]

Banham wrote *Los Angeles: The Architecture of Four Ecologies*
before industrial and financial power had consolidated on the Pacific
rim. From his perspective, Los Angeles was destined to continue building in a decentralized and diverse manner. Thus in 1971, Banham con-

cluded that the long-term effort by local business people and philan-
thropists to create a downtown civic center had been a failure. Ten
years later, however, the entry of global capital, the expansion of business services, and competition with San Francisco over which city would
manage Pacific-based financial investment forced a spatial reorganization of Los Angeles that strengthened both the center and the suburbs.[29]
On the one hand, there was a massing of control functions in the downtown area. Old government buildings, including the city hall, court-
house, and jail, were surrounded by new skyscrapers, an art museum
and its extensions, a new concert hall, expensive apartments. This development represented an expansion of downtown without gentrification—a pure assertion of financial power at the city's center. At the
same time, however, single-family and apartment houses and shopping
centers continued to be built in the surrounding counties, especially Orange County, which attracted a more diversified commercial base (and
employment) in business and financial services.

In this period, moreover, because of rising land values or nostalgia
for regional cultural forms, the distinctive vernacular of the city's "daydream houses" enjoyed a resurgence through both extensive modernization and a burst of new construction. A postmodern landscape in
which the "ungrammatical" combinations of architectural elements in
these houses "commented" on each other, the built environment in Los
Angeles provided a hedonistic facade for new economic power. New
foreign investment downtown, industrial investment in the suburbs, and
consumer investment in daydream houses coexisted with increasing
geographical segregation of the low-income and minority populations
and police surveillance of communities already terrorized by teenage
gangs.[30] Vernacular architecture attempts to resolve this tension between comfort and power. The houses of movie stars, for example,
combine "power, as signified in a massive and conventionally bland
front (like a provincial city hall) and a rambling, spread out informality
(like a relaxed Texan [with his feet on the coffee table])." Another relatively friendly face of power.[31]

From a broader historical perspective, Reyner Banham distinguishes four different versions of the vernacular in L.A.'s single-family
houses. In "Surfurbia" along the ocean beaches, Banham sees the least
formal and most elegant compromise between nature and artifice. These
are beach houses with simple, strong forms and flat surfaces, whose
spaces flow indoors and outside, linking the modern architecture of post–

World War I and post–World War II Los Angeles. In the foothills, Banham sees culture or artifice triumph over nature, with the fantasy architecture that for many people epitomizes an Angeleno tendency to exaggerate dominant motifs in American culture. While some people find this form of the vernacular in private houses, however, Banham finds the archetypal form of fantasy architecture in public spaces. These are the fast-food shops built in the shape of a hamburger, the Polynesian restaurants in the form of a giant hut, the progenitors of roadside postmodernism in search of cultural roots. Banham describes the eclectic way they exaggerate features of traditional buildings, especially the roof, the wood structure, and the hearth, as part of "the convulsions in building style that follow when traditional cultural and social restraints have been overthrown and replaced by the preferences of a mobile, affluent, consumer-oriented society."[32] Banham's third vernacular is represented by minimalist modern cubes built of stucco and cement on the plains around the city. This is the architecture that accommodated the rising expectations of a growing population. By building a minimalist vernacular in cheap materials on relatively small lots, architects offered Los Angeles consumers the landscape of a villa. Banham's fourth vernacular consists of glass and steel modern houses, which have an antiheroic, improvisatory air. Built to individual designs, often by architects for their own use, they combine unassuming construction techniques with expensive materials.

Comfort and power in any version of this vernacular are inseparable from the massive development and individual appropriation of technology. The reconciliation of human and machine provides "democratic" access, in Banham's view, to the social roles that emerged with mass consumption. Shopping, commuting, touring, and "cruising" all enhance the "illicit pleasures of mobility" that make Angeleno culture so optimistic, in contrast to the "official pessimism" of Western (i.e., modern) culture.[33] If this vernacular defines the sense of place in Los Angeles—in a fuzzy regional way—it is a *place* that derives in large part from *markets* for individual consumption. This point is best illustrated not so much by the corporate architects who design so much of the construction in the region as by the idiosyncratic career of Frank Gehry.

Since he began working as an architect in 1954, Gehry's work has exemplified all four architectures that Banham describes. He has designed simple beach houses in which spaces flow indoors and out, and planes intersect at odd angles to represent the orbital relations of functional areas. He has built adobe cubes for artists' studios and housing. He has exposed the timber of both renovated and new housing structures—to make the finished architecture look more like a process—and used conventional building materials, like glass, steel, plywood, and even chain-link fence, in decidedly nonmonumental ways. Gehry has even designed a small number of fantasy structures in the shape of a fish (lamps, a restaurant, a prison that was exhibited in an art gallery show of "follies"). While for the architect the fish is a personal symbol, for viewers it exemplifies the fantasy vernacular in public spaces.[34]

Although he has many friends in the Los Angeles art world, Gehry didn't break through to the first rank of commissions and architectural recognition until the late 1980s. Many of his houses were in fact designed for artists and upper-middle-class clients rather than rich patrons. Nor did he get requests to design public buildings for corporate clients except the Rouse Corporation, which dropped him when its executives saw the experimental planes and exposed structure in the renovation of his own house in Santa Monica. Gehry also designed a number of museum installations in Los Angeles, and the temporary exhibition hall of the Los Angeles Museum of Contemporary Art, but was passed over in favor of Arata Isozaki for the commission to design the permanent museum.

Gehry's works and career constitute the quintessential Los Angeles vernacular. An absence of high-class commissions compelled him to work the forms of domestic consumption with industrial technology. The major ensemble he designed for the Rouse Corporation (and eventually completed in collaboration with Victor Gruen Associates) is Santa Monica Place, a shopping center that Gehry bound in stucco and chain-link fence. Only after a career in the Los Angeles vernacular did Gehry get the prestigious rewards of his profession: retrospective shows devoted to his work at the Walker Art Gallery and Whitney Museum, an invitation to submit a design in closed competition for a new skyscraper in New York City (later rescinded when Gulf and Western, the developer, decided not to proceed), participation in planning the Massachusetts Museum of Contemporary Art, and the commission to build the Walt Disney Concert Hall, new home of the Los Angeles Philharmonic and centerpiece of L.A.'s downtown civic center. Gehry applies the intimacy of domestic architecture to the concert hall. Besides a 2,500-seat symphony hall and a 1,000-seat chamber-music performance area, Gehry designed a glassed-in foyer—"described by the architect as a 'living-room for the city' "—as well as shops, gardens, and relaxation areas for the musicians.[35]

Gehry's work as a whole describes the liminal juxtapositions that define the modern Los Angeles vernacular. The self-conscious production of Gehry's houses calls attention to itself by "extruded" timber structures. The presence of such a house on a suburban street calls attention to domestic consumption. While a window in Gehry's home provides passers-by with a view into the owners' garden, the standard boxy houses that surround it feature more traditional, enclosed and private, domestic space. Even among shopping centers that compete for drivers' visual attention, Santa Monica Place is a dramatic example of self-conscious production. It announces itself by its tall chain-link fencing and predominant signage as both demarcated and emerging from the freeway, juxtaposing the intimacy of imagining the hidden with open aggressiveness in the name of security.

Gehry's designs have been compared to the city itself, a "planned osmosis" of entrances and exits, fragmented and disconnected through intersecting planes that appear "seduced by the urban eroticism of Los Angeles."[36] In this city, building single-family houses for a competitive market becomes a place-defining process. And building public spaces for individualized consumption also marks a place. Considered in the context of property markets, even a vernacular can become a landscape of power.

Miami has a somewhat different historical vernacular. Like Los Angeles, however, Miami's vernacular also represents the privatization of consumption in public space. Here, too, place is defined by the self-conscious production of single-family houses.

The historical references given exaggerated form in oceanfront and island villas—Miami's archetypal daydream houses—came from an imagined Spanish past, mostly imported from contemporary Latin America. As in California, few buildings remained in Florida from the period of Spanish colonialism. So the "Mediterranean"-style villas and hotels built in Miami and Palm Beach after World War I created a historical vernacular for contemporary housing consumers.[37]

The resort architecture that Addison Mizner was commissioned to build after World War I was a stage set for the very rich who came to southern Florida to spend the winter. He both reproduced the hotel scenery James had observed a decade earlier in Palm Beach—the soft Mediterranean colors in a vague *palazzo* style—and individualized it in family residences or compounds. Each showplace villa gave to the south Florida vernacular an air of self-conscious production. Mizner's work in Florida did not differ substantially from the Gothic Revival or Tudor houses of the rich in the North, some of which were built to his designs. But the spatial concentration of Mizner's houses and country clubs in resort colonies—the abstraction of leisure in a landscape where there was no other vernacular—called attention to domestic consumption. To realize this vernacular, Mizner had to devise solutions to technical problems and problems of supply. He developed new techniques for working with wood and stone that would withstand the tropical climate, and he formed a company to make copies of the antique furniture that went so well with the villas' historical style. During the land boom of the 1920s, Mizner became a real estate developer as well. In 1925 he formed a company to build Boca Raton, "the world's most architecturally beautiful playground." Had the company not run out of funds when the land boom burst, Mizner would have created an entire small city in Mediterranean style.[38]*

During the great period of resort colony construction, the Miami–Palm Beach area developed vernacular styles like those in Los Angeles. Miami had beach houses, oceanfront fantasy architecture in villas and Art Deco hotels, and minimalist modern houses in the shape of stucco-covered cubes in the city's interior. Although the Florida keys were more difficult to tame than the plains of Orange County, nature was steadily pushed back, until the Everglades were colonized as a tourist attraction. Despite nearly continuous construction, however, until the 1980s Miami generated fewer famous architects than Los Angeles (except perhaps for the flamboyant designer of the Fountainebleau Hotel). When the television police series "Miami Vice" went on the air in 1984, the scenery highlighted behind the opening credits each week included a building designed by the young Miami firm Arquitectonica. This was a sensible choice, for the Atlantis apartment tower on Brickell Avenue represents both the vernacular architecture and the landscape of power of the third Miami.

---

* By 1989, "Mizner Village" at Boca Raton had been resurrected as a condominium resort community, with apartments selling for $275,000 and up—as much as it might have cost to build an entire villa in Miami or Los Angeles in Mizner's day.

Built near the old downtown, yet also on the bay, the Atlantis reflects the internationalization of Miami as a Latin center and the recentralization in Miami of Latin American financial capital. The Atlantis is late modern in construction technology and architectural style. Yet it has playful touches of decoration that radically depart from modernism and offer a friendly facade for Miami's economic power. Unlike Frank Gehry's work, the Atlantis does not extrude its structure. Instead, its structure presents an empty center: a square cut-out between the tenth and fourteenth floors reveals the ocean, and at the bottom of the empty space, a single palm tree. This hole in effect conceals the structure, making the building seem to recede before nature. It is a triumph of artifice, a visual illusion. From this view, the Atlantis symbolizes Miami at play, a city whose pleasure is allotted in individual condominium units of beach and sky. The Atlantis mediates between resort and urban architecture, between the Palm Beach hotels that Henry James saw—"on a strip of land between the sea and the jungle, between the sea and the Lake"—and the new metropolis.

Arquitectonica's self-conscious production also makes a fitting symbol for the city of Miami's tourist brochures. Just as "the new high rises contribute substantially to the image Miami has of itself as a city of the future, in which the Caribbean and the North American are being synthesized into something new,"[39] so the new vernacular suggests the liminality between modern and postmodern styles. Arquitectonica's success parallels the representational quality of Frank Gehry's vernacular architecture, and creates a similar aesthetic problem trying to characterize its style.

Arquitectonica's founders, the North American Laurinda Spear and the Peruvian Bernardo Fort-Brescia, call themselves modernists. They use conventional modern building technology to construct tall, white, modern boxes. But this modernism is eclectic, sensual, international. Their forte is the distinctive gesture of decor that evokes the illicit pleasures of consumption: the cut-out and bands of color at the Atlantis; an eighth-floor "drive-through lobby" and undulating penthouse wall at the Imperial. Both the elegance and surface flatness could be postmodern. So could the figurative decor—like that of Michael Graves's hotels at Disney World—embellishing a shopping center called Rio that they designed in Atlanta with golden fish and waterfalls.[40]

Significantly, the vernacular Arquitectonica created in Miami works well with other institutions of global power, especially in Latin America. The architecture critic Joseph Rykwert describes the Banco de Credito building in Lima designed by the firm as alienating to a "disturbing, perhaps poetic" degree, as though alienation has been "sought as an effect." The bank is located on the very edge of the city—a modern structure rising at the foot of the mountains, where it appears as a monument to artifice surrounded by nature. Rykwert finds this isolation typical of the search for security by every financial institution, whose environment—especially in Latin America—is always perceived as hostile. Yet this alienation is also like that of the waterway landscape of Miami or the daydream houses of Los Angeles. It represents comfort and power but requires a security system of guard dogs, burglar alarms, and identity cards. It requires a distance from the urban barrios of the poor. If this vernacular evokes alienation, that is only because it is projected by a landscape of economic power. Like Frank Gehry's work, however, even Arquitectonica's large projects are not monumental. The Banco de Credito combines the electronic images of computers and security system with an office designed for domestic consumption in Miami genre colors: "Incan," as Fort-Brescia says, or Art Deco, neon, soft Mediterranean pastels.

This ability to define a sense of place for market consumption appeals to real estate developers. In Houston, a small developer who hired Arquitectonica to design two townhouse projects likes the firm's style because it attracts "a market segment he refers to as 'innovators, typical yuppies.' " These consumers are drawn to the self-conscious production of Arquitectonica's designs: bands of primary colors (in Houston), varying angles at the roof, which ends in a tower, a gradation of window sizes in portholes, niches, and squares. Although all the parameters of the program were dictated by cost, and the materials are inexpensive stucco and wood, the houses call attention to themselves by a nonstandardized design. "It defines the target market so distinctly," the developer says. "We felt that it was going to be our competitive edge in the [soft] market . . . and . . . we like to get a little attention."[41]

Vernacular architecture has indeed called attention to Los Angeles and Miami. Searching for an image oriented to visual consumption, real estate developers and local elites turn to architects, as they have historically done in periods of economic growth. But the vision of architecture is increasingly expanded and reproduced by means of mass communication, from Disney television programs to "Miami Vice" and glossy lifestyle magazines. In this context, the appeal of visual consumption determines market power: what forms get built and by whom. To a great extent postmodern architecture—like the late modern work of Frank Gehry and Arquitectonica—found its place in the market economy because of its visual image, its facade, which shows an accessible face of power.

A movement in architecture cannot be compared with a stage of economic development. Yet the late modern architecture of Frank Gehry and Arquitectonica define the postmodern landscape: dissonant and discontinuous, playful and humane. It is built in a time of socio-spatial reorganization, when the third Los Angeles and the third Miami become centers of global economic power. The built environment mediates between nature and artifice, between resort and city, between local and global investment. Yet it conveys a sense of place.

The postmodern city is developed with the same factors as before: land, labor, capital, their deployment in space and time. But the city is now designed as an imaginary landscape, for this is where architects self-consciously envision the last creative frontier of a highly industrialized society.

> If in fact post-industrial society is formed by a hyper-industrialized system, having no exterior and no empty spaces, the only virgin territories in which projects and production manage to develop are those of the imaginary, in other words those consisting of spatial narration and stage-sets, of new islands of sense. . . . These are the imaginary territories produced by design.[42]

Henry James glimpsed the abstraction of a similar image of society in the imaginary territory of Florida's hotel civilization. As James foresaw, the vernacular constitutes a powerful control over sociability when it is mapped upon a landscape of consumption.

Like Disney World, Los Angeles and Miami suggest that a new landscape of power requires neither centrality nor monumentality. Instead, it visually reconciles the tension between public and private consumption, global and local capital, market and place. These images, however, are far from settled. The landscape holds both the security and even innocence of Disney World and the pervasive guilt of "Miami Vice."

When "Miami Vice" appeared on American television in 1984, it communicated a postmodern landscape to a mass audience with startling cogency. At least since regional disparities strongly reemerged in the mid 1970s, mass culture had sought an image for the Sunbelt's economic power. Most new television serials just took a Sunbelt location as a narrative "hook," and cloaked local power in regional lore. Power in Texas ("Dallas"), Denver ("Dynasty"), or Sonoma ("Falcon Crest") was depicted by the mock-heroic pseudorealism of a soap opera that could take place anywhere. By contrast, "Miami Vice" aimed to look both self-conscious and unreal. Its production values mirrored a uniquely real, yet curiously unfamiliar, landscape. Visually striking, elaborately staged, with a deliberate absence of "earth tones" despite the versimilitude of location shooting, the program captured the brittle, synthetic quality of a postmodern city. It also resonated with images derived from other mass culture forms. This was the real city artistically considered; yet it was unmistakably an abstract landscape of economic power.

"Miami Vice" had the theatrical look of a music video and used electronic synthesizer themes instead of dialogue. Like a music video, it relied on dreams as both motif and structure. But it distilled the image of a set-piece music video into a one-hour cops-and-robbers framework. Within this framework, sometimes denigrated for not permitting "a writers' show," many scripts were remarkably political. Those that explicitly focused on political subjects often anticipated or closely followed newspaper headlines, usually about covert U.S. support for counterrevolutionary guerrilla warfare in Central America.

The show was also indebted to fashion. Just as the main characters' "designer" dress styles differentiated them from standard detective shows, so the brand names sprinkled through the plots showed a consumer's perspective on market culture. "Tubbs [one of the main characters] wears $800 Verri Uomo double-breasted suits and dark silk shirts with narrow Italian ties. Sonny [another major character] has a gold Rolex and carries a Bren 10-mm semiautomatic pistol, a gun so new it is considered experimental by most special-weapons teams." Similarly, a shipment of stolen televisions contains new Protons rather than the more common Sonys or Zeniths.[43]

The liberation of form from narrative suggests why "Miami Vice" initially won distinction. During its first season, the series got admiring reviews from serious television critics, as well as fifteen Emmy nominations. The look of the show—deliberately abstracted from a Miami vernacular—was projected back on the landscape across America in a range of consumer products, making the show's producer afraid to walk into a chain store. "The first year we were trying to find the cutting edge of something different—a hot, sunbaked world," he says, "which is why I picked Miami. Now, . . . you go into Montgomery Ward, you see pastels. *Vibrating* pastels."[44]

From our point of view, however, "Miami Vice" was distinctive because it mapped quintessentially visual motifs on a society organized by global corporate power. It united the built environment of the city, the manufactured environment of domestic consumption, and the imaginary environment of broadcast television. Yet in the crime genre, "Miami Vice" was hardly original. Since the nineteenth century, detective stories have appealed to both intellectuals and lower classes. Like "Miami Vice," the best U.S. detective novels since the 1920s are stories of cities where crime is pervasive. And since the 1920s, such authors as Raymond Chandler have sprinkled the names of specific products and manufacturers throughout their work, substituting brand names for generic terms (e.g., using "Ronson" for a cigarette lighter and "Ford" for a car), to show that their detectives know their way around the culture. Moreover, broadcast television since the 1950s provided "Miami Vice" with roots. "Take *Dragnet*'s straight-laced duo, mix in *The Mod Squad*'s hip anti-crime attitude and the pacing and style of MTV, and you've got the *Miami Vice* formula down, pal," a reviewer wrote in a parody of the character Sonny's speaking style.[45]

Overrated, morose, spacey: by the second season, the shock of production values paled beside the series' lack of dramatic structure, and by the third season, "Miami Vice" was criticized for parodying itself. Critics "read" consumer products, or read each other, to find new ways to fault it. *Rolling Stone*'s reporter said that in the mix of "adolescent existentialism and street-corner mysticism" there wasn't even anything left to parody; "it'd be like trying to make Xerox copies of Saran Wrap." In *Esquire*, James Wolcott quoted John Leonard, who said the show "has gone beyond postmodern into postliterate." Wolcott added that "Miami Vice" was "unfocused, unfixed, an empty improvisation against a postcard backdrop."[46]

But this was the postmodern landscape that critics and audience initially found so exciting. The facadelike quality that critics began to despise as a lack of reality in "Miami Vice" reflects the interplay of nature and artifice—neon, high tech, Art Deco, empty space—in Miami's built environment, Las Vegas, or the new downtown Atlanta. To some degree the program represents the hybrid of sea and jungle, beach and plastic, of southern Florida. Yet the show's style also represents a new urban reality: "Edward Hopper in Miami," a *Rolling Stone* reporter had gushed during its first season on TV. Like the apparent falsity that made Manet's *Olympia* "modern," it is the falseness of "postcard" Miami that makes it postmodern. And like the Paris painted by Manet, the glittering yet grittier city of Haussmann's time, the Miami shown in "Miami Vice" is both familiar and new.[47]

As an Impressionism for our age, the electronic image is taken for a guide to the real Miami. When Michael Sorkin gets off the plane, he admits to a sensation of living "Miami Vice," renting a flashy Thunderbird and hearing the show's theme music on the radio. When the monologuist Spalding Gray makes a winter pilgrimage to Miami for a vision of something new, he delights in the combination of culturally familiar things—eating bagels in a drugstore, reading "Miami Vice" crime stories in the local papers. Sorkin and Gray look to the electronic image to provide a coherence the real landscape doesn't offer.[48] Even for critics, the electronic image is both a record of, and preparation for, experience. In this universe, it is hard to trace which form of cultural production is derivative, the landscape or its image. The image is refracted, moreover, through different cultural media. Each acts as a facade, reflecting and receding from the landscape. On the one hand, "Miami Vice" derives from music video, but on the other, it provides material for other television shows and articles in magazines. The show becomes a hot item, its stars are interviewed, its production site is the subject of travelogues, and recordings of its sound track are sold. As each visual product migrates across cultural fields, it becomes a source of economic value. This goes beyond the modern age, when art became a commodity. Commodities are now derived from other commodities. In this sense, "Miami Vice" is emblematic of all self-conscious cultural production.

Of course, "Miami Vice" is also emblematic of the city. But this is a city in which no one works at productive tasks, a city where industry is relegated to slimy backwater piers along the Miami River. There it is less visible than the apartment and office towers that shimmer by the Atlantic Ocean and Biscayne Bay. "I just love it," Sonny says to Tubbs, wrinkling his nose in exasperation in a darkened scene, "the smell of industry and stagnant water!" "Miami Vice" is service-sector Miami, where money is made by "deals," not work, and products take the form of contraband arms, illegal drugs, or counterfeit currency. This is a city where cops are the only honest citizens, but many of them are crazy or corrupted, and Sonny and Tubbs find it harder each year to offer a convincing explanation for policing the moral order. Logically, they simply threw down their badges when the series ended in 1989.*

Sonny is simply an American hero, a would-be savior whose role is thrust upon him. Asked why he decided to be a cop, he says, "I want to make the world safe . . . for children." Tubbs, by contrast, comes from a police family; his older brother was killed by a cocaine dealer in New York, so he chooses police work to avenge the family's honor. Faced with a case of official corruption, his only explanation for their exceptionalism is, "We're cool." Since real news events constantly highlight Miami police officers' venality, the motivation of the good civil servant continues to be the major mystery on the show.[49]

Sonny and Tubbs do not really differ from the murderers, gangsters, and sadists they hunt. Because they are undercover agents, they mingle with criminals. Sonny's Rolex and Ferrari, Tubbs's Italian suits and vintage Cadillac convertible are their disguises. What others view as indulgence is work for them, and yet . . . they know they share the criminals' point of view. More important to them than explaining why they're good is fearing that they, too, are evil. "The truth is, I'm a junkie myself," Sonny confesses to a shrink. "I'm hooked on the action." This knowledge makes them "morose." Evil penetrates them as it does the rest of the culture; it is not accidental that the series' title fails to differentiate the police from society (as in the more usual "Mod Squad," "FBI," or "Hawaii Five-O"). Instead, as in "Naked City," the very title equates urban form and sin: "Miami" = "Vice."

This moral ambiguity is not only urban but also part of post-Watergate and post-Vietnam society. Unlike television shows in which a character has "served in 'Nam" as a rite of passage, "Miami Vice" is steeped in doubt about moral values. Patriotism is defined by Oliver

---

* Like the city of Miami, "Miami Vice" also has a problem with urban representation. While the dominant main character Sonny (a white man) is a native Floridian, the subordinate Tubbs (a black man) has recently migrated from New York; although Tubbs's theme music, later released as a popular record, is "You Belong to the City," that city is New York. When the producers provided a special script for the second season premiere, moreover, they shot it in New York. Interviewed about this on another television program, the stars defended the site because "Miami Vice" was "an urban show."

North, the Contras, and Panama's General Noriega. Loyalty is never recognized by federal agents of drug enforcement. Drugs and corruption are not merely among the urban problems with which cops must deal; they are *the* urban problem. The law that should deal with them has rotted from inside, weakened by the very people responsible for enforcing order. These basic assumptions permeate "Miami Vice" and give it both the hardnosed cynicism inherent in the urban crime story and a sensibility to innocence.

Although a critic of the series dislikes the "defeatism" he sees in the tendency to kill off innocent victims, who often expire in Sonny's arms for the final freeze-frame, the post-Vietnam ubiquity of crime must lead to an inalterable pessimism about its elimination. Since no one in "Miami Vice" holds absolute values except the Zen-like Lieutenant Castillo, closure in the form of a definitive ending is impossible. The criminal in fact often gets away. This created periodic problems for the producers, especially during the first two seasons. Crime may be seamy, but the endless seam of crime in "Miami Vice" contradicts police series permeated by older notions either of punishment ("Dragnet") or of redemption ("The FBI").[50]

The moral graying of black-and-white distinctions between crime and the rest of society is as old as the landscape of L.A. and Miami. In American detective novels of the 1920s, especially those of Dashiell Hammett, the detective was no longer a model of rational thought as Conan Doyle's and Poe's had been, and the truth—the solution to a crime—was no longer clear. In detective novels that appeared in the United States after World War II, the detective was not more moral than the criminal he pursued, often using the same methods. The criminal's identity was, moreover, often known in advance, diminishing the expectation of a final resolution. Because this indeterminacy was transferred to detective shows on radio, and then to television, producers saw their task as mediating between titillation (violence) and moral judgment (closure). By 1973, however, the climate surrounding Watergate and Vietnam deepened the dilemmas of crime show production. "Cynicism, the failure of authority, the corruption of society, the rewards of crime; how are these to be presented to a mass audience through a medium which is delicately sensitive to public opinion, official as well as private?"[51]

Having ventured farther outside the norms of closure than most other series, however, "Miami Vice" was especially sensitive to public disapproval. Polls that showed many viewers identified the series with the seductiveness of high-level crime caused the show's producers and the NBC network to deny they glorified criminals. Yet the publication of these survey results resulted in more punishment being written into future episodes. After the surveys, crime still paid, but so did the criminals.[52]

As a 1980s crime show, "Miami Vice" focused on corruption as a normal part of business and government. Policing the moral order reversed the old division between public and private space as undercover surveillance became more important. Undercover agents in the nineteenth century had worked in public space—streets, political assemblies, riots—where crimes were likely to be committed. Since the 1970s, however, major crimes were likely to occur in private space—inside the president's Oval Office, in conversations "inside" a stock trading firm, at a party aboard a yacht. This is the milieu of "Miami Vice."

Sonny and Tubbs also demonstrate that unethical acts in one area of business or government often imply illegal behavior in another. On one show, a young widow financed a drug deal in order to mount a leveraged buyout of her late husband's company, prompting a character to mutter "Blond Ambition," in homage to John Dean's memoir of complicity in Watergate. G. Gordon Liddy, one of President Nixon's team who burglarized the Democratic National Committee office in the Watergate apartment complex in 1972, appeared in two episodes of "Miami Vice" as a Contra leader supported by rich Latin businessmen in Miami. No one in the script—not even a black judge or a football coach—is above corruption. "Selling out," Sonny muses to Tubbs, "it's the American dream."

This attitude illustrates the paradigm shift from series like "Kojak," which represented urban realism in the 1970s. In literature, a similar shift occurred in the 1920s, when the nineteenth-century model dominated by Sherlock Holmes was subverted by the emergence of the "postmodern detective." The new paradigm has two features. On the one hand, the narrator's madness and self-contradictions are now general in society. The awareness of crime as pervasive and undercover is a metaphysical awareness of *self*. On the other hand, the detective's job is no longer to solve an inexplicable death. "In the new metaphysical detective story it is *life* which must be solved."[53]

Significantly, the criticism that has been aimed at "Miami Vice" also fits the crime genre as a whole. "The trouble with the detective novel is not that it is moral but that it is moralistic; not that it is popular but that it is stylized; not that it lacks realism but that it picks up the latest realism and exploits it."[54] "Miami Vice" is no less real, no less violent, no less "flat" than the city of Miami. Nor is it less ambiguous than the postmodern detective who has no crime to solve but knows that there is something rotten in society, or the Arquitectonica facade that both reflects and recedes, hiding the architectural structure.

We don't really know what underlying structure the landscape of Miami represents. How people live in a service economy or an international banking center is still not completely understood. The scope of an economy that runs on "deals" rather than products is made more problematic by the scale of global transactions. Gang wars over the drug trade in Miami or L.A., in which Cuban exiles play the role of middlemen between Colombian suppliers and retailers from black, Latin, and Asian street gangs, appear as part of the international divison of labor. They are somewhat more dangerous than the garment business, but equally vulnerable to noneconomic threats and ethnic solidarity.[55]

In "Miami Vice," the boundaries of illegitimate economic activity cross and merge. Weapons and drug deals are inseparable from white-collar crime and government cover-up, and if everyone is working under cover, there is no way to tell the good from the bad guys. The undercover agents from "Miami Vice" identify themselves in a street fight with teenage thugs—only to find they are facing undercover colleagues from "Metro Gangs."

During its five years in production, the show faced real economic problems. Filming an episode cost up to $1 million, a half million dollars over budget. This was not only double the cost of a standard hour-long network show, but also twice as much as could be recouped by a sale of world syndication rights. To cut costs, the producers discussed moving the filming to L.A., where most television production facilities, including those that process "Miami Vice," are located. Yet the look of the show—the visual distinctiveness that helps it compete for market share—demanded meticulous and elaborate attention to the real detail of place. The producers' dilemma pitted "manufacturing" against "financial" criteria—again, a typical representation of the whole society.[56]

Economic ambiguities about the real "Miami Vice" are echoed in political questions about the real Miami. Decisions that affect all of Central America are made in Washington, D.C., and often coordinated in Miami. This situation gives the city's Latin elite a certain distance from the locality. The veiled, but functional, networks that make these deals work give special meaning to the urban theorists' ideas about the links between a city's economic specialization and its niche in the hierarchy of the global political economy. Since the late 1940s, Miami has played a key role in integrating the Pacific rim economy with that of the Caribbean. But this economy is financed by the illegal drug industry and the CIA, administered by banks legally set up in Miami to deal exclusively in overseas transactions, and protected by local elected officials in the Cuban exile community. Establishing an "enterprise zone" for international banks in the city of Miami has included lowering the initial capitalization required to charter a bank, overlooking the oddity of bank customers depositing shopping bags full of cash, and failing to investigate banks that do not report cash transactions running into billions of dollars. Not surprisingly, terrorism—death threats against citizens and public officials—"just happens to be part of political life," according to former Mayor Maurice Ferre.[57]

Despite its violence, moral ambiguity, and impressionistic structure, "Miami Vice" is viewed as urban realism for a postmodern society. The series has actually encouraged new tourists to come to Miami. "Miami has become a fabled city," Ferre says. "People come to think of it precisely the way they think of the Casbah, or Casablanca, or old Beirut. There is mystery and danger." These tourists, a Chamber of Commerce member says, think that in Miami "every restaurant is a bistro, every women is slim and beautiful, and every man is virile."[58] The image of the city reflects the electronic image created to reflect it. Yet even the real image is peculiarly unsubstantial. Henry James might have been a viewer of "Miami Vice" when he wrote of Florida:

> You may live there serenely, no doubt—as in a void furnished at the most with velvet air; you may in fact live there with an idea, if you are content that your idea shall consist of grapefruit and oranges. Oranges, grapefruit and velvet air constitute, in a manner, I admit, a feast; but press upon the board with any greater weight and it quite gives way—its three or four props treacherously forsake it.[59]

"Miami Vice" illustrates how, by our time, landscape contextualizes both weakness and power. On the one hand, L.A. and Miami abstract the desires of the powerless and institutionalize them in a landscape of power. On the other hand, Disney World both represents and molds these desires.

Like "Miami Vice," Disney World has also suffered from financial problems. When prices of Disney Company shares fell in the early 1980s, the company attracted several hostile takeover offers. Walt Disney's brother Roy lost control of the business, and disputed its future with other relatives. Saul Steinberg, a New York financier who specializes in takeovers, bought a block of shares and engaged Michael Milken, the junk bond innovator and inside trader of Drexel Burnham Lambert, to devise a financial package for complete acquisition. The hostility Steinberg aroused, and the uncertainty surrounding the stock's value, brought in other financial capital. Steinberg was replaced as suitor by Irwin L. Jacobs of Minneapolis and the Bass brothers from Fort Worth. Disney management tried to cut costs by controlling wages and instituted pay cuts of 16 percent over the next three years; employees, including those at Disney World, went out on strike. Under these conditions the Bass brothers bought out Jacobs. Controlling nearly a quarter of equity, the Basses named Michael Eisner the new chairman of the Disney Company, and Eisner embarked upon a corporate strategy of diversification and automation. Eisner succeeded almost immediately. In 1985, it was widely reported, he drew a salary, with bonuses, of $2 million. The company's profits in 1988–89 were more than $700 million, and Disney was banking on expanding its theme parks to both Europe and Japan.[60]

The other side of a fantasy landscape may be sordid or overtly dependent on global corporate power. Yet it continues to appeal. "Florida still had the secret of pleasing," Henry James writes. "The vagueness was warm, the vagueness was bright, the vagueness was sweet, being scented and flowered and fruited; above all, the vagueness was somehow consciously and confessedly weak."[61]

The power of fantasy to attract suggests that the market economy, at bottom, suffers from a cultural problem: how to resolve the tension between weakness and power.

Conclusion

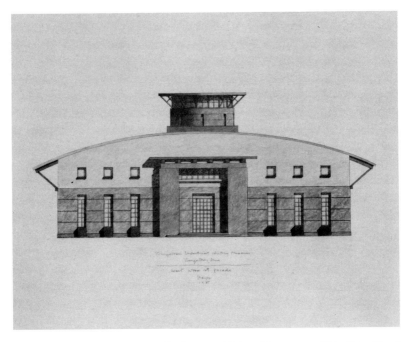

Michael Graves, Historical Center of Industry and Labor, Youngstown, Ohio. West Wood Street Elevation (drawn 1986; built 1990).

9   Moral Landscapes

Preserving Youngstown and Akron and everyone's standard of living there would halt economic growth for the benefit of a few people.

RICHARD D. UTT,
associate chief economist,
U.S. Chamber of Commerce (1981)

We Made VCRs Affordable.

Samsung Advertisement (1987)

Neither deindustrialization nor postindustrial society captures the extent and variety of changes in the contemporary market economy. Advanced industrial societies like the United States are a "quasi-continuum" of places, more or less integrated into the global economy,[1] that face different degrees of gain and loss. The basic asymmetry of power between industry and finance, management and labor, remains unchanged. But chances for economic revival now depend on a more immediate relation with financial power. Although exceptional individuals and committed institutions can reverse a movement toward business failure, their actions are limited by the overwhelming importance of borrowed capital, the lack of a directing role for government and labor, and a tendency to view the economy in abstract terms. Tragically for any attempt to modernize the industrial economy, the will to produce, the direction of investment, and the socialization of desire have been incorporated into the organization of consumption.

It is not easy to see either the short-term results or the long-term advantages of this creative destruction. Those who peer into the distant future foresee either an information society of free consumers or one of dependent importers. Depending on their point of view, they project a population either of computer programmers like those in Silicon Valley or of hamburger cooks à la McDonald's. On the other hand, those who look at the current situation tend to see social polarization based on cheaper wages (a "K-marting of the labor force") and financial speculation that has gone out of control ("casino capitalism"). We would do well to recognize what Charles Dickens depicted in cities of the nineteenth century, and economists like Schumpeter and Polanyi built into their analyses: an industrial landscape is also a moral order. Building a viable economy requires coherent moral values.

The transformation of mature industrial economies also requires reconciling change in economic and cultural values. The visibility of economic restructuring by means of robotics, VCRs, and the travel and leisure industry focuses attention on the question of how new *economic* values are devised for *new* goods and services. But if this were the only change of values that restructuring implied, it would not sow confusion. In a period of widespread change, three other processes are equally important: how we find new cultural values for new goods and services, how we change the old economic values that we ascribe to old goods and services, and how we negotiate new cultural values for the patterns of production and consumption with which old goods and services are entwined. Since the 1940s, the basic cultural meanings and social relations of an industrial economy—the position of blue-collar and many white-collar workers in a firm, the web of labor union, household, and community, and the quality of such basic commodities as "steel," "television," and even "computer"—have been transformed from durables into disposables. This is what "flexibility," at its harshest, implies.

We do not find coherent values in the landscapes of consumption growing around us. Institutions like the shopping mall, the department store, and the museum foster a liminality that removes the distinctions between mercantile display and public exhibition. The surrounding environment—the city, the corporate suburb, and the fantasy center—supports a liminality between nature and culture, market and pleasure, work and leisure, which hides the key role of centralized economic power. People like to consume; they seek their social identity in shopping, comparing goods, and talking about consumption. They find drama, history, and variety in new spaces of consumption. However, as their lives grow more distant from the activities of material production, they lose interest in values that developed during the industrial age: economic equity, labor organization, social justice. At the same time, the decision to cheapen labor and cut back on industrial capacity in the United States makes it harder for men and women to increase their market-based consumption. The socialization of desire toward an unattainable standard of consumption leads to a broader question, that of the "depleting moral legacy" of the economic system.

Between the uprisings against old cultural categories that took dramatic form in universities and urban ghettos in 1968, and the retrenchments that began at the gas pumps in 1973, several writers began a moral examination of dominant economic values. In the United States, Daniel Bell echoed Schumpeter in lamenting the loss of capitalism's "transcendent ethos." For Bell, once the Protestant Ethic had ceased to legitimize and temper financial gain by asceticism and moral restraint, the floodgates of social norms were burst asunder. The rational expectations of modernity enshrined hedonism as the ultimate criterion of the moment, with all the anarchy this loss of restraint implies.[2]

In Britain, Fred Hirsch also noted a widening chasm between the economic system of capitalism and the social construction of needs. In contrast to the decline of self-control in Bell's moral abscess, Hirsch emphasized a scissors-like movement between social appetites and social scarcity. He faulted the economic system's decreasing ability, despite the expansion of material production and the spread of markets for goods, to satisfy the social expansion of desire. On the one hand, the "positional goods" that used to confer social status (e.g., the big house on a lake) are no longer available in infinite supply. On the other hand, when such goods are commercialized—that is, freely available for sale in a market—they lose much of their ability to "position" people in the social structure. Social status is immanent not in the economic value of goods but in the cultural value of getting them or the cultural value of the social group that has already got them. This recalls Edith Wharton's description of "in" restaurants on the Riviera: they are desirable not because they serve good food, but because they attract an upper-class clientele. For Hirsch the gap between material fulfillment and socialized desire, rather than desire itself, depletes capitalism's moral legacy.[3]

Many of the questions that were set out in the preceding chapters—

Why do steel plants close down? Why is labor weak? What is the meaning of industrial obsolescence?—could be answered in fairly straightforward institutional terms. If the financial sector were, for example, obligated to finance domestic industry, the industrial economy would be stronger. If landed elites opposed the corporate move into their localities, industries would be discouraged from choosing new locations. If labor unions outgrew the political culture inspired by industrial organization, the work force would be more open to economic restructuring. Yet the questions I am posing here, after surveying a range of local conditions, are deeper questions about the social and cultural context of economic change. They suggest that long-term processes of abstraction, internationalization, and the shift in social meaning from production to consumption are responsible for America's industrial decline.

Abstraction is not a twentieth-century creation. Jean Agnew suggests that the "historical shift in the market's meaning" in the sixteenth and seventeenth centuries refers to "a gradual displacement of concreteness in the governing concept of commodity exchange." This displacement transformed market forces from the product of concrete, individual transactions of place into the result of the abstract processes, and finally abstract powers, of a market economy.[4] The landscape of Detroit and Weirton relates abstraction to several specific twentieth-century processes. These include the abstraction of the power of heavy industry from material production and the abstraction of the labor process from material products. The case studies of Weirton and McLouth suggest that these processes parallel structural shifts in the economy from manufacturing to services, and from industrial to financial capital.

By looking at Charles Sheeler's, Elsie Driggs's, and Margaret Bourke-White's paintings and photographs of steel plants and other industrial sites, we can trace a changing perspective on heavy industry back to the first third of the twentieth century, the period when this type of industrial production was at its very height in the United States. The emphasis on visual forms, rather than material production, in their work certainly did not *cause* the eventual abandonment of steel investments or incorrect choices of production technology. But the shift of perspective that transformed heavy industry into an object of visual consumption *anticipated* the structural shift in the U.S. economy from producers' to consumers' goods production that began in the late 1920s.

In this context, the shift of cultural perspective prepared the way for a shift of economic perspective. While most people were still working in heavy industry, and were enthralled by the obvious demonstrations of its power, the image of industry grew more visual than visceral, more immediately perceived than historically embedded, and, correspondingly, less material and more abstract. This process of abstraction led to the declining moral legacy of real producers. Except for Diego Rivera's and other Depression-era murals, the image of labor in American society became almost nonexistent. By the same token, the power of labor unions was also dissociated from the labor process. It was abstracted from the shopfloor and the plant to the more distant arenas of national collective bargaining and electoral politics.

Since at least the late nineteenth century, the industrial economy has been a world economy. The "annihilation of space by time" refers to outsourcing at that time on a global scale. Similarly, the mid-twentieth-century system of U.S. industrial production was always integrated with a global system, whether that globalization led to or warded off economic crisis.[5] But beginning in the shifts of economic power of the 1970s, there was a great change in the global culture dominated since the 1920s by exports of ideas and symbols, including management strategies, from the United States. We see this cultural shift in the dramatic contrast between two landscapes of what I have called postmodern power. While international flows of investment capital have restructured the material landscapes of Los Angeles and Miami, Orange County and Orlando, the symbolic landscapes of Disney World and "Miami Vice" indicate an inversion of historical patterns of cultural dependence. Mickey Mouse and Donald Duck, exported as cultural symbols around the world, show the old hegemony of First World capitalism, the smiling face that hid the imperial relations of the former, U.S.-dominated global system. The drug culture of "Miami Vice," however, shows a crumbling hegemony that has been eroded by Third World exports. This is the grimacing face that barely hides core countries' dependence on the capital accumulation of the Pacific Rim and the coca plantations of Latin America.

The shift in the dominant source of social meaning from production to consumption begins at least as early as the widespread circulation of both domestic and imported consumer goods in seventeenth- and eighteenth-century Britain. While this system of consumption was shaped by upward social mobility, social emulation between the classes, and national affluence, the production system was enhanced by government spending, hands-on entrepreneurial investment, easy credit for business investors, available labor to produce new specialized goods and services, and international trade.[6]

Consumption took a more marked, though still rarified, form in the American society that Henry James described around 1905. James equally decried the speculative building booms that displaced old landmarks in New York City and the hotels that presented a self-enclosed project of civilization for transforming a stable world based on *noblesse oblige* and aristocratic culture into an unstable, consumer society. A generation later, the mass production of Model T's and the enhancement of purchasing power by means of higher wages and installment buying plans created the basis for a system of mass consumption. With the post–World War II economic shift from manufacturing to the services, and the simultaneous explosion of standardized consumer goods production, the United States finally had a mass consumption society.

From the 1960s on, the differentiation of consumers' markets by price and social status was paralleled by different strategies of cultural appropriation. Moving corporate headquarters to suburbia followed the upper class's residential patterns in appropriating nature. The biggest corporations were self-confident enough to leave the city's center of power. Over time, their suburban location developed a subjective legitimacy that, in turn, confirmed the rightness of their strategy. By contrast, gentrification revived the upper-middle class's identification with cities by appropriating culture rather than nature. Displaced from old neighborhoods by race or class, urban professionals appealed to a past that wasn't really theirs. Their new central location differentiated them from the rest of the city's population and from the suburban middle class. Their investment in the center supported new cultural institutions that eventually confirmed their choice. In twentieth-century cities, real estate developers appropriated both nature and culture to create a middle-class dream. Home and automobile ownership integrated leisure and work, validating a democratic bourgeois utopia.

Today the mediation of culture is in the hands of a critical infrastructure. More didactic in modern cities, more entertaining in postmodern cities, critique relates the quality of experience to cost and novelty and links production and consumption. Those who produce critique make up a symbolically significant labor market for the service economy. Knowing which artists, clubs, and galleries are "in" and putting into practice the architecturally correct forms of home construction demand a fairly large infrastructure of writers, reviewers, and specialized, though often temporary, service personnel. Creating a tourist economy requires a permanent labor force of waiters, cleaners, cooks, and guides. Disney World's success and the transfer of its labor training and sales techniques to other fields suggest the importance of its ideology to the service economy.

An increasingly reflexive mode of consumption demands a more self-conscious mode of production. Because investors need to get a competitive edge by means of product differentiation, they enhance the social status of design. Similarly, designers, artists, and architects emphasize individualism and ingenuity to get an edge on the competition for both patronage and museum-conferred posterity. This double ring of competition often leads designers to seek "artistic" solutions—like postmodernism—rather than devise new solutions to technical problems. Self-conscious production hides the social control made possible by a concentration of economic power. The appeal of imaginary landscapes, from the hotels in Palm Beach to Michael Graves's hotels at Disney World, is that they offer a retreat from the real world of power. They appeal to the child who delights in visual consumption.

These observations are not meant to argue that consumption, rather than production, is driving the economy. Yet they emphasize that in a contemporary market economy, the *organization of consumption* has just as important an effect on economic and social structure as the organization of production. This is underlined, ironically, by the importance of the organization of illegal drug consumption, especially as it articulates with subsistence production in the Third World and the ethnic division of labor in L.A., Miami, and New York. The organization of consumption is a powerful means of carrying out creative destruction in the economy.

REAL CULTURAL CAPITAL

Cultural strategies of visual consumption permit the selective consumption of space and time. While gentrification and Disney World are fine examples, we can also look at the "new" tourism that juxtaposes nature and culture in the form of home-style inns with French cuisine in rustic surroundings. From our perspective, the most interesting point about these flourishing strategies of cultural consumption is how they articulate with the service economy.[7] Although they certainly manipulate and capitalize on symbols—hence their association with "symbolic capital"—they also produce real economic value. Continuing to analyze cultural capital in only symbolic terms misses its relevance to structural transformation. For this reason I have turned around Fredric Jameson's assertion that "architecture is the symbol of capitalism" and suggested that in an advanced service economy, architecture is the capital of symbolism.

Strategies of cultural consumption rely on effective demand among new demographic and social actors. But just as they are embedded in reflexive—or highly mediated and intellectualized—consumption, so they reinforce self-conscious production. On the supply side, cultural consumption creates employment for a self-conscious critical infrastructure (and lower-level service personnel), and is in turn created by its labor. Cultural consumption contributes to capital accumulation, moreover, by enhancing profits on entrepreneurial investment in production and distribution (e.g., gourmet cheese stores, Cuisinart plants). And as we have seen at both Faneuil Hall and Disneyland, cultural consumption has a positive effect on capital accumulation in real estate development. Cultural goods and services truly constitute real capital—so long as they are integrated as commodities in the market-based circulation of capital.

We can see the economic significance of cultural goods and services by sketching their role in *interacting circuits of economic and cultural capital*. Drawing on David Harvey's illustrative use of Marx's circuits of capital, it is clear that the continuous circulation of capital in a capitalist economy increases the value of commodities produced.[8] These increases in turn expand the value of capital. As it circulates, moreover, capital periodically crosses sectoral and institutional boundaries. Depending on rates of return, investment capital may in the aggregate swing from manufacturing to finance or services, from domestic ventures to offshore projects, from property in the inner city to suburban real estate development. As values fluctuate, capital shifts back, or circulates elsewhere.

It is interesting to speculate, as Harvey has recently done, on the conditions under which changing cultural values reflect change in economic values. But it is even more interesting to ask whether the continuous production of cultural commodities, moving between "economic" and "cultural" circuits, continually increases the economic value of investment capital. "Circuits of cultural capital" may offer us a key to understanding the structural linkage between cultural and economic values today.[9]

As the discussion of urban form suggests, architects' designs become more useful economic tools to speculative real estate developers when they are published, theorized about, and disseminated within the architectural profession. Plenty of magazines and reviews have been founded in the last few years for this sort of intra-professional publicity, and some architects have also published picture books featuring their projects. These are more than just coffee-table books. Publicity expands the cultural value of designers' ideas, and in the process enhances the market value of both the architects and their buildings.* Similarly, downtown property values rise with the development of new cultural practices like nouvelle cuisine. In this context, nouvelle cuisine is not only the product or social practice of some expensive restaurants, but also a published, theorized, and professionally disseminated culinary discipline. The interacting circuits of economic and cultural capital that underlie gentrification can be charted in a fairly simple way (see fig. 2).

In a physical infrastructure of old townhouses and lofts in the heart of the city, architectural restorations provide a new element in market culture that both comments on existing modes of new construction and initiates a new mode of its own. At the same time, in the service economy, a set of interrelated amenities caters to the local market of townhouse and loft residents. The concentration of these markets, and the relative autonomy of cultural producers, creates a downtown "scene."

This scene in turn attracts more investment in local real estate. As more people move into the area, adopting the cultural values of the innovators, they create more demand for replicas of old crafts products.† The increase in demand provides more of a mass market for Victoriana and chintz, which eventually encourages the establishment of new magazines and more publicity for this kind of cultural strategy. When the proponents of this strategy succeed in appropriating central spaces, they seek to protect their claims (in terms of both economic and cultural values) by establishing a historic landmark district. Once the local government designates such a district, changes that do not

---

*This circuit of cultural capital reflects historical and cultural differences. In Italy, for example, architects or designers who want to solidify their professional reputation have traditionally made a claim as theorists by publishing, especially in their own journals. In the United States, however, where one group of modern architects have even published their taped conversations, this means of enhancing value is rather new.
†In chapter 7 I pointed out that this cultural strategy combined demand for both authenticity and good new design. Indeed, the regulation of replicas in an age of all-too-mechanical reproduction poses problems, and constitutes a market/place in itself for certification of artisanal authenticity by mainstream cultural institutions.

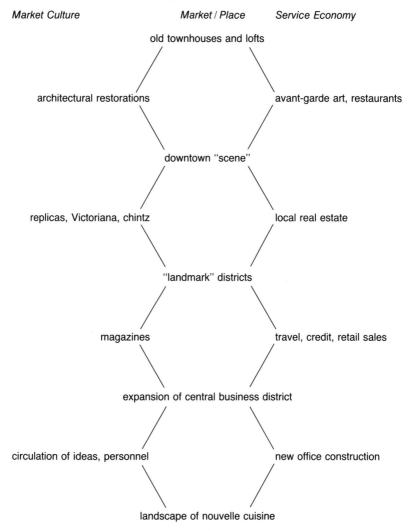

Market Culture   *Market / Place*   *Service Economy*

old townhouses and lofts

architectural restorations   avant-garde art, restaurants

downtown "scene"

replicas, Victoriana, chintz   local real estate

"landmark" districts

magazines   travel, credit, retail sales

expansion of central business district

circulation of ideas, personnel   new office construction

landscape of nouvelle cuisine

Figure 2. Circuits of cultural capital: gentrification.

conform to these cultural values are declared "out of character" and
not allowed.

Landmarking has great economic value, for it spurs more publications about historic preservation and architectural restoration, and also
attracts tourists and shoppers. These new economic values now encourage large-scale developers to undertake the expansion of the central
business district by means of new office and apartment construction.

The central district is transformed into a new marketplace for relatively upscale shopping and residence as well as business services. The new buildings and the international circulation of ideas and creative, professional, and financial personnel who work in them expand the marketplace, and the landscape of nouvelle cuisine. This in turn enhances the economic value of the built environment downtown, increasing investment pressure on old townhouses and lofts.

Disney World, moreover, is a complex of service-sector and entertainment functions that enhance both economic and cultural values. Mickey and Minnie are mass products in all their guises, and the numbers of people who stay in Disney World hotels, or buy houses or timeshares in Orlando or near mixed-use developments inspired by the Disney World model, are far greater than the numbers of people involved in gentrification. From the point of view of circuits of capital, however, Disney World is a set of cultural goods and services that articulate with the mass production system in a service economy (see fig. 3).

These circuits of economic and cultural capital begin with the actual stage sets and movie studios that had moved to Hollywood from New York—to decrease production costs—by 1920. This double fantasy land of dream products in a dream climate inspired its own sort of vernacular architecture in and around Los Angeles. The vernacular grew into a market culture, both commenting on and reproducing the norms of fantasy production in films. Just as Hollywood films became an important U.S. export, so the film industry located in Hollywood generated real estate development.

As one of Hollywood's products, animated cartoons, developed bigger markets, it inspired the postwar construction of a new sort of amusement park in the orange groves of Anaheim. Disneyland created a marketplace in Orange County for new service occupations, new housing, and other kinds of development. At the same time, it generated still more products in the image of Mickey, Donald et al. These developments inspired new architectural designs, which were incorporated into the fantasy ecology of Los Angeles. Publicized in magazines and seen in television series, this in turn encouraged tourism and retail sales. By the same token, when the buildings of Arquitectonica were shown on "Miami Vice," and the firm's principals appeared on "The Today Show," as they did in 1989, they enhanced the value of Miami as a marketplace for the work of creative personnel.

The imagineers and others created television shows featuring

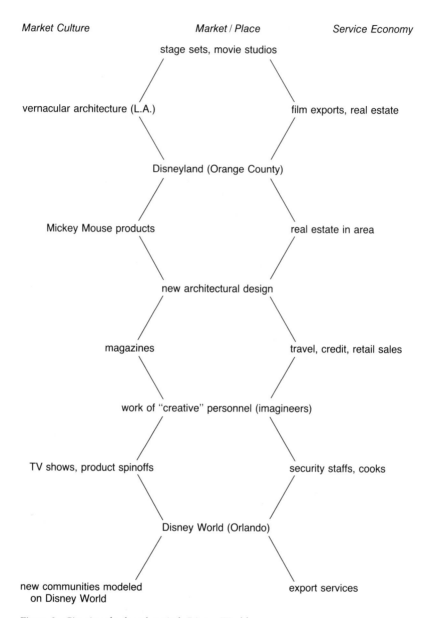

Figure 3. Circuits of cultural capital: Disney World.

Disney characters and more product spin-offs. These fruits of their labor constituted a market culture that both commented on Disney creations and responded to demand for Mickey and Minnie facsimiles. At the same time, the flow of visitors who sought a more immediate experience in Disneyland generated more jobs in the service economy for security guards, hotel staff, and cooks.

These markets in turn inspired the development of an even bigger, more complex Disney World in an underutilized area near Orlando, Florida. As a multi-use exurban complex of new construction, Disney World represented a considerable marketplace. But it had even greater potential. On the one hand, its socially harmonious elaboration of Main Street created a market culture that commented on the fragmentation of American (and by extension, modern) society, while it quickly became a model for the development of new residential communities from Seaside, Florida, to Mashpee Commons on Cape Cod, both of which were designed by the historicist postmodern architects Andres Duany and Elizabeth Plater-Zyberk. On the other hand, Disney World's tremendous commercial success created demand for more export services, notably by "franchising" Disney theme parks in France and Japan. (Tokyo Disneyland is operated under license from Walt Disney Company; Euro Disneyland is 49 percent owned by Disney.) These have in turn initiated their own regional circuits of economic and cultural capital: developing land, training a service labor force, supporting film, video, and television production.

In the United States, the creation of place by means of Disney markets was confirmed by Disney World's addition of an MGM movie set and Hollywood theme park in 1989. In 1990, Universal Studios opened a competing theme park nearby. These reproduced the initial circuit of cultural capital.

From our viewpoint, it is irrelevant whether cultural capital constitutes a primary, secondary, or tertiary circuit of capital, in line with the ideas of Harvey, Henri Lefebvre, and other urban political economists. But it seems only logical that in the contemporary market economy, investment in cultural capital would offset cyclical devaluation in other parts of the same circuit—for example, in local industries and the built environment. Downriver near McLouth, for example, has drawn investment in leisure and entertainment facilities, although not to an extent that would compensate for structural disinvestment in autos and steel. Countercyclical investment also reflects relative rates of return. In this sense, investment in the mass production or distribution of cultural commodities grows out of the entertainment industry. Finally, investment in cultural capital becomes more profitable because of the inelasticity of demand for certain cultural goods and services that are now deemed essential, at least by that richest stratum of the population with an increasing share of income. While the demand for socially accepted cultural symbols like Mickey and Minnie Mouse remains relatively high, their supply is expanded by licensing agreements, product replicas, and reproduction through different cultural forms (TV, films, toys, advertisements). Yet the economic efficacy of cultural capital may also be a matter of image-creation. Cultural investment "screens" investment in the services. As cultural capital, Disney World suggests both the power of facade and a facade of power.

Because circuits of cultural capital are formed in real spaces, they suggest how space in an advanced service economy is really formed. Neither solely "productionist" nor merely "local," space is structured by, and structures, circuits of capital that incorporate real estate development, amenities and services, and visual consumption. On the one hand, the linkage between cultural capital and real estate development enables new economic structures (e.g., the service economy, global financial markets) to be *localized*. On the other hand, the choice of specific sites as landscapes of cultural consumption (e.g., downtown, Orange County) represents the geographical *location* of these economic structures. Moreover, building theme parks, theme towns, and other artificial complexes (such as an Amazon rain forest) is now a favored strategy of economic renewal. Unable to attract front or back offices, some cities use abandoned manufacturing sites as their doorway to a service economy.

Although magazines may seem a trivial part of this scenario, they play an increasingly important role, along with other means of mass communication, in developing new circuits of capital based on cultural consumption. The American Express Company, for example, during the last years of the 1980s bought a number of "lifestyle" magazines produced for specific local markets, including *L.A. Style* and *New York Woman*, as well as the more panoramic *Food and Wine*. American Express based its publishing strategy on the fact that 70 percent of its twenty million credit card holders live in the top twenty cities of the country. "We want magazines in cities where they live," the president of American Express Publishing says. "And the advertising side can build its relationships with our customers." By the same token, a small number of rich real estate developers in New York City have recently bought or founded newspapers in the city. As individuals they are expressing a whim, a desire, eccentricity. But they are also active agents in a circuit of cultural capital, linking mass communications, the local service economy, and real estate development.[10]

The spatial mediation of cultural consumption affects the redistribution of benefits among social classes. We have seen that with the actions of landed, political, and corporate elites, a suburb's visual homogeneity is a useful base for encouraging social homogeneity among the upper middle class. Gentrifiers' and developers' ability to appropriate central spaces by means of visual consumption has the real effect of displacing lower-income residents. Building the Disney-like complex of Opryland outside Nashville, rather than renewing and expanding it on the Grand Ol' Opry's original site in the center of the city, prolongs the economic crisis of the downtown area.[11] While such an expansion might well create the same sort of displacement as gentrification and publicly sponsored urban renewal, it nonetheless deprives the inner city of a significant redevelopment project linked to the new service economy. But this suggests an important constraint imposed on cultural capital by political economy. Strategies of cultural consumption may only complement, rather than contradict, strategies of capital accumulation.

SPACE AND MARKETS

Despite its importance to economic and cultural organization, space is a conceptual orphan. Although geographers claim it, they traditionally tend to describe space and leave theorizing aside. Because it is not so well conceputalized, moreover, writing about space that goes beyond traditional geographical description of where things are tends to sound "spacey." Especially among sociologists of culture, writing about space is mainly word play, for they fail to integrate the influence of Foucault and Baudrillard with the material interests of Braudel. Recently, however, working across academic disciplines, several writers have tried to transform space from a fairly vague or static category into a dynamic set of historically and economically contingent relations. Thus David Harvey speaks of creating a materialist historical geography, Charles Tilly wants to write a spatially informed history, and Edward Soja refers by means of the "postmodernization of geography" to socially determined spatial structures. Speaking for sociology, Anthony Giddens insists on the *structuring* qualities of space and time, which reflect and also influence the values and behavior of individuals and social institutions.[12]

In earlier writing, I called the city—as a densely concentrated, economically specialized, and socially differentiated space—a "matrix of capital accumulation."[13] Because a city or any other space reflects these macro-level economic forces, it is more *structured* than *structuring*. A city in this sense exhibits two different kinds of spatial structure. On the one hand, it is a localization of global economic and social forces. On the other, it is a nodal point, or a location, in a world capitalist order. But space also structures people's perceptions, interactions, and sense of well-being or despair, belonging or alienation. This structuring quality is most clearly felt (and most visible) in the built environment, where people can erect homes, react to architectural forms, and create—or destroy—landmarks of individual and collective meaning. Space's structuring ability is also shown in geographical location, which determines proximity and convenience, land values, and typical cultural patterns (e.g., south versus north, urban versus rural, hill versus valley). Space makes material form for the differentiation of a market economy.

Space also structures metaphorically. Because they are easily visualized, spatial changes can represent and structure orientations to society. Space stimulates both memory and desire; it indicates categories and relations between them. These considerations suggest that space is a major *structuring medium*. The key structural shifts in the twentieth-century political economy are located in a symbolic geography of space (e.g., Sunbelt versus Frostbelt, L.A. and Miami), and localized in spatial metaphors that explore the relation between economic power and cultural representation: the autonomy of the steel industry, the power of productive labor, the social homogeneity of residential communities, the centralization of economic and cultural power, and ability to hide centralized power in sensual "weakness." Because landscape is the most important product of both power and imagination, it is the major cultural product of our time.

Space as a Structuring Medium

Political-economic forms	*Cultural forms*
Location	Symbolic geography
Localization	Spatial metaphor

Deindustrialization and gentrification are two sides of the same process of landscape formation: a distancing from basic production spaces and a movement toward spaces of consumption. We usually see this process in partial—that is, local—terms. Red Baker's neighborhood in Baltimore is submerged in the development of Inner Harbor, localizing a structural shift from manufacturing to services. Downtown Manhattan, L.A., Miami, and Westchester County are rebuilt or redeveloped as corporate centers, localizing different forms of global financial power. As individual landscapes are re-formed, however, the localization of power they represent has a cumulative effect. On the one hand, the concentration of investment by multinational corporations, banks and other financial institutions, and cultural producers who cater to and comment on their presence remakes the world hierarchy of cities and places. Westchester becomes a favored corporate headquarters location, while Weirton and Detroit weaken. On the other hand, shifts between landscapes of production and consumption have a dramatic effect on socio-spatial structure. Weirton, Detroit, and Yonkers recede into an archaic vernacular; downtown Manhattan and nearby inner city areas are incorporated into a landscape of power. Main Street at Disney World telescopes this process. It abstracts the image of an archaic vernacular and incorporates it into an imaginary, more subtle landscape of economic power.

The rapid inversion of spatial categories—from landscape of power to vernacular, or vernacular to landscape of power—gives our time a peculiar instability. It is important to emphasize that this inversion of spatial categories is not the result of individual or even group mobility so much as it is the result of both structural changes in the economy and cultural strategies for social and spatial differentiation.

I have used "liminality" to describe the cultural mediation of these socio-spatial shifts. Liminality in our sense depicts a "no-man's-land" open to everyone's experience yet not easily understood without a guide. Defining the symbolic geography of a city or region, liminal spaces cross and combine the influence of major institutions: public and private, culture and economy, market and place. As the social meaning of such spaces is renegotiated by structural change and individual action, liminal space becomes a metaphor for the extensive reordering by which markets, in our time, encroach upon place. On the micro-level, liminality is best reflected in the process by which a landscape of power gradually displaces the vernacular.

A striking pair of illustrations in W. G. Hoskins's book *The Making of the English Landscape* shows how the landscape of the English country house gradually displaced the rural vernacular during the period from about 1650 to 1750. By 1709, the aristocratic country house Wimpole, in Cambridgeshire, was separated and differentiated from the vernacular countryside of peasants' dwellings and fields by an elaborate set of landscaped gardens, paths, outbuildings, and a formal avenue by which visitors approached the house. As on other aristocratic domains, the house was originally built next to a village that had traditional claim to the site. But during the eighteenth century, like other aristocratic landowners, the family that owned Wimpole decided to improve the look of the place. Since the site of the old village interfered with new landscaping arrangements, the village was torn down and rebuilt outside the gates of the park. During the same period, by contrast, another country house, Easington, was only partly differentiated from the surrounding rural vernacular. It lacked both a park and formal gardens; no walls or avenue separated it from the cottages of the village and a sheep dip. The family had nonetheless begun to put in place the aristocratic cultural strategy of appropriating space from the vernacular, constructing the typical landscape of power of their own social class. As Hoskins says, "Only lawns separate the house on three sides from the peasant landscape; but the beginnings of order are apparent in the relationships of the parish church to the big house and in the rows of young trees newly planted."[14]

Our twentieth-century landscapes show no less dramatic patterns of spatial appropriation. From 1950 to 1980, the industrial vernacular of Westchester County was landscaped into a relatively homogeneous corporate headquarters location that conforms to local landscapes of power, consisting of semirural residential communities of the upper and upper-middle classes. During the 1970s and 1980s, gentrification took downtown areas that were recognized as coherent places and transformed them from industrial "wastelands" and "inaccessible" ghettos into markets for affluent and educated segments of the middle class, including the critical infrastructure. During the 1980s, the exurban area of Orlando / Disney World, developed as a fictive theme park to cater to a transient market for entertainment, became the nucleus of a real, permanent place.

This study of landscapes of economic power is a cultural artifact of its time and place. If I had written it when I began research, in 1980, it would have been part of the heated debate over deindustrialization. In the middle of the 1980s, it might have been a critique of the cultural capital wielded by yuppies. Writing after 1985, however, I was able to recognize the extraordinary influence of a service economy, and also to lay a dispassionate emphasis on the organization of consumption.

But the researcher's social and geographical position does not lack contradictions. Imagine that at the end of the workday you are leaving the investment banking offices on the eighteenth floor of the American Express Tower, a new and distinguished postmodern office building in the World Financial Center in Lower Manhattan. Softly you tread the beige carpets past the interior reception area, whose walls are lined with prints of New York harbor in the eighteenth century. The elevators whisk you down past digitally marked floors, and when you get to the lobby, you pass the advanced electronic security system at two reception desks. These desks are continuously staffed by a team of courteous, but persistent, personnel.

You leave the building through a turnstile and a glass door along with other employees: young white men in pin stripes, even younger black men and women in casual clothes, all chatting about the day's events. You join a slightly larger stream of people coming from the Oppenheimer and Dow Jones Towers, crossing over West Street in an enclosed skywalk, and together you walk through the purple-carpeted lobby of #1 World Trade Center. The stream of people builds up to a marching throng as you enter the main concourse of the World Trade Center, with its shops and banks and passages to subway lines. A major work force is dispersing on its nightly journey home. Private conversations at this point rise to a roar; it is like the roar of the city, but more muted because of the indoor mall.

You walk through the concourse to get to your subway line. You go down a flight of stairs, cross a landing where four homeless men are sleeping on flaps torn from cardboard cartons, and look forward to the short trip home.

Reader, I have walked through this landscape of economic power.

An emphasis on the culture of the economy indicates that the landscape is broader, has deeper roots, and relies on more interconnections than government alone can control. Neither a national industrial policy nor local control over the economy commands broad political support. Even under these conditions, gentrification and Disney World are prominent, but not inevitable, models of the future. The landscapes we have looked at indicate three factors that could remake the moral legacy of industrial capitalism: public institutions on the state level that are committed to maintaining a skilled work force, financial institutions that dedicate both funds and expertise to domestic economic needs, and a more fluid sense of enterprise that links technical innovation, financial expertise, and material production.

The history of Weirton, West Virginia, shows both the strength and weakness of local autonomy. No firm in a traditional industry can survive without ties to global markets. Because the Weirton buyout was done without significant government intervention, these ties had to pass through bankers who could tap new sources of investment capital. Significantly, the local support that nourished Weirton came from a residential or consumption community rather than a community based only on work. This underlines how we need to recognize new forms of mobilization going beyond industrial production. "Saving" a local community, moreover, is not feasible without connecting local and global capital.

McLouth Steel indicates the paradoxical power of productive labor in conditions of industrial disinvestment. A graphic case of abandonment by its major customer, the auto industry, McLouth demonstrates that neither cities nor firms can survive without productive work. Yet a lack of investment capital from financial institutions twice threatened McLouth's survival. A political decision on the creditors' part, rather than such "economic" factors as the cost of capital or comparative advantage, seems to be at fault. This situation can only be countered by alternative political pressures—in McLouth's case, from the labor union and the state. But other ideas that are already in the air—for example, tapping pension funds for industrial investment, or developing new forms of nonvoting equity that would curb investors' financial aggressiveness—should be seriously examined. While potential investments that are not targeted on short-term gain are often criticized as "social" investments, the collaboration among McLouth's secured creditors should remind us that *all* investment takes place in a social context. A preference for takeover deals, or investing in debt, property, and high-status consumption, indicates a specific socialization of desire. It does not indicate a lack of investment capital. Intervening, moreover, in a positive way at McLouth were members of local political, financial, and labor union elites, who were ineffective in redirecting investment toward other potential shutdowns. In this case, a will to produce determined the direction of investment capital.

Westchester County shows how local elites can complement elite decisions in the international economy. Corporate headquarter relocation gave new strength to the local desire to keep property values high, which demanded the suppression of industrial production. The elite cohesion that supported this goal excluded nonwhites, unionized workers, and local elected officials in the industrial towns. In contrast to McLouth and Weirton, the abstract image of social homogeneity that directed change in Westchester excludes the economically weakest part of the existing population.

Gentrification and Disney World suggest alternative scenarios for reorganizing space in terms of consumption. They rely on explicit ties between culture and economy and between middle-class consumers and global corporations. Yet these local landscapes also run into limits posed by investment capital, elite support, and resistance by existing populations. Whether gentrification and Disney World are viable scenarios for economic growth under any conditions requires further examination. They imply a continuing interaction of financial investment and cultural production that could lead in two directions: deeper social roots for the service economy and more pervasive corporate control over the visual imagination.

A primary focus of the future agenda should be the notion of *public value,* which until now has referred to the reorganization of space for environmental quality. Used by planners and groups of community residents since the mid 1970s, public value suggests that there is an irreducible minimum balance that should be maintained between natural and social forces in the landscape—between built and unbuilt spaces, or new and old construction. Preserving public value by limiting development is also democratic to the extent that it permits growth but regulates it by local control. Thus public value is not incompatible with self-interest. While it responds to market forces, unlike private value it also reflects the culture of place.[15]

A sense of public value implicitly shaped the thinking of Weirton's investment bankers, the people from the Michigan Commerce Department who supported McLouth, and the Port Authority program of industrial redevelopment that converted the Otis Elevator plant to other manufacturing uses. In these cases, public value preserved a balance between production and consumption and found a working landscape to be the best basis of moral order. For their own individual reasons, the actors who were involved resolved the dilemma Polanyi described: the dilemma of destroying habitation to foster improvement. More often, public value is held captive to private value. Downtown and in most of Westchester County, elites have joined forces with affluent men and women to exclude those who cannot keep up with the improvement brought by market forces. At Disney World, and in new residential communities based on a similar vernacular image, improvement explicitly rejects the social variety of habitation. In these cases, public value seeks security by exclusion, so that the culture of place conforms to market values. This seems to be a greater danger in a landscape of consumption than in a landscape of production.

Whether a more productive and equitable economy requires new forms of ownership or restrictions on luxury consumption is still as debatable as in Schumpeter's time. But it does demand a notion of public value that compels men and women to use investment for intelligent long-term ends, such as ensuring an economic basis for mass consumption. The cases of landscape we have examined make it obvious that no sudden solution will appear to resolve these issues. Landscapes grow by accretion; they are historically and culturally bound. They always show asymmetries of power. We are bound by these cultural representations even when power relations seem most autonomous (as in history of the steel industry), most contradictory (in simultaneous impoverishment and gentrification of the central city), or most fantastic (at Disney World).

Certainly the inscription of capital in space maps new forms of social control. But these forms are not predetermined. "Market forces" include social and cultural as well as economic factors. The concept of markets itself is dynamic. Only as a marketplace of direct exchange does its meaning seem absolutely clear, uncontested, bounded by space and time. Like this original marketplace, however, markets are socially constructed by conscious actors who form allegiances and shift direction. They can redefine the basis of market culture from ownership to public value.

Such a change does not address the issue of *whose* perspective should determine public value. The landscapes we have looked at show incorporation of critical actors at best, exclusion and displacement of the unprivileged at worst. The basic problem of asymmetry shapes how local institutions can resist the demands of global market culture. Not only production spaces such as auto plants but also consumption spaces such as fast food chains, shopping malls, and Disney World impose their own rules on the vernacular. When the landscape shifts entirely to a service economy oriented toward consumption, even the social imagination—the ability to envision alternatives—is corrupted. Nonetheless, the terms of debate have shifted. Critics can no longer call upon the working class to save society. That class is too differentiated and too involved in consumption to respond to the old industrial vision of reform. Nor can artists and architects be counted on to oppose economic power. They are too involved in market production to draw up alternatives. Calling upon local communities to generate change is also a romantic notion. Local actors are far from autonomous (if they ever were). Although they aim to preserve vernacular forms, they usually end up tying them to a landscape of power.

The problems with forming an agenda in terms of public value are that it is vague, it doesn't resolve issues on the national level, and it doesn't address inequalities of power. By making choices explicit, however—like the discredited idea of industrial policy—public value calls attention to the crucial question of how elites disengage themselves from one form of capital investment and move to another. Moreover, depending on how it is implemented, public value mandates a discussion of development goals on the basis of citizenship rather than ownership. While this resembles an economic democracy, it carries no guarantees.

For the past hundred years, market culture has emphasized consumership over citizenship. Yet the innate populism of the United States is receptive to a politics that emphasizes local continuity, a social return on investment to citizens rather than shareholders' financial returns, and obligations on businesses to put down roots. Men and women still want to live in specific places. This could mark the beginning of an alternative market culture.

Notes

CHAPTER 1. MARKET, PLACE, AND LANDSCAPE

1. Joseph Schumpeter, *Capitalism, Socialism and Democracy* [1942] (New York: Harper & Row, 1962), p. 83; emphasis in original.

2. Joseph Schumpeter, *The Theory of Economic Development* [1934] (New York: Oxford University Press, 1961), p. 156; Henry James, *The American Scene* [1907] (Bloomington: Indiana University Press, 1968) pp. 102ff.

3. See Karl Polanyi, *The Great Transformation* (Boston: Beacon Press, 1957).

4. Interpreting recent responses to an American public opinion survey on these themes, "one might say," Robert E. Lane suggests, "that facilitating *earning* is best, *giving* to the truly needy is acceptable, but *taking,* even from the rich, is bad" ("Market Justice, Political Justice," *American Political Science Review* 80 [1986]: 392).

5. Polanyi, *Great Transformation,* p. 34.

6. Jean-Christophe Agnew, *Worlds Apart: The Market and the Theater in Anglo-American Thought, 1550–1750* (New York: Cambridge University Press, 1986), pp. 22–23.

7. Ibid., p. 39. In *The Origins of English Individualism* (New York: Cambridge University Press, 1978), Alan Macfarlane argues that the change to a market society, with land and labor markets and extensive geographical and social mobility, occurred much earlier—in the thirteenth century.

8. Fernand Braudel, *The Structures of Everyday Life* [1979], vol. 1 (New York: Harper & Row, 1981), pp. 501–2, citing Sebastien Mercier's contemporary account.

9. On the slow development of "market culture" in France during

this period, see William M. Reddy, *The Rise of Market Culture: The Textile Trade and French Society, 1750–1900* (Cambridge: Cambridge University Press, 1984).

10. Lion Murard and Patrick Zylberman, *Le Petit Travailleur infatigable: Villes-usines, habitat et intimités au XIXe siècle*, 2d ed. (Paris: Recherches, 1976), p. 38. Casting a somewhat different light on this description, the labor historian Herbert Gutman has observed that the small size of an industrial town like Paterson, New Jersey—relative to a big city like New York or London—and the composition of its population made the employers' exercise of power both more visible and more vulnerable to organized labor (*Work, Culture, and Society in Industrializing America* [New York: Knopf, 1976], pp. 257–58).

11. In recent years these processes have generated a number of significant scholarly studies linking social class, local community, and local and national political organization. Among the most interesting of these—and my formative reading—were John Foster, *Class Struggle and the Industrial Revolution: Early Industrial Capitalism in Three English Towns* (London: Weidenfeld & Nicolson, 1974), and Alan Dawley, *Class and Community: The Industrial Revolution in Lynn* (Cambridge, Mass.: Harvard University Press, 1976).

12. Mark Granovetter, "Labor Mobility, Internal Markets and Job-Matching: A Comparison of the Sociological and the Economic Approaches," *Research in Social Stratification and Mobility* 5 (1986): 3–39.

13. "Changes in Labor Law Studied by Both Parties," *New York Times*, December 4, 1986; "U.S. Panel Divided on Aiding Displaced Workers," *New York Times*, January 12, 1987.

14. Product cycle from the work of Raymond Vernon, "International Investment and International Trade in the Product Cycle," *Quarterly Journal of Economics* 80 (1966): 190–207; profit cycle from Ann Markusen, *Profit Cycles, Oligopoly, and Regional Development* (Cambridge, Mass.: MIT Press, 1985).

15. On local government's increased activism for economic development, see Richard Child Hill and Cynthia Negrey, "The Politics of Industrial Policy in Michigan," in *Industrial Policy: Business and Politics in the United States and France*, ed. Sharon Zukin (New York: Praeger, 1985), pp. 119–38; on these programs, see "Funds and Jobs Pledged to Boston Students," *New York Times*, September 10, 1986; "Boston Businesses Give a Future to the Young," *New York Times*, September 14, 1986; "7 Cities Picked in Plan to Foster School Attendance," *New York Times*, April 18, 1987.

16. On the "costly asset," see Matthew Edel, Elliot D. Sclar, and Daniel Luria, *Shaky Palaces: Homeownership and Social Mobility in Boston's Suburbanization* (New York: Columbia University Press, 1984). For conceptual statement of some of the controversies over elevating consumption to the generator of "real divisions of material interest," see Peter Saunders, "Beyond Housing Classes: The Sociological Significance of Private Property Rights and Means of Consumption," *International Journal of Urban and Regional Research* 8 (1984): 202–27, and also David Thorns, "Industrial Restructuring and Change in the Labour and Property Markets in Britain," *Environment and Planning A* 14 (1982): 745–63.

17. Similarly, modern philosophy and social theory deemphasize space (or geography) and favor time (history). See E. J. Soja, *Postmodern Geographies* (London: Verso, 1989); J. A. Agnew, "Devaluing Place: 'People Prosperity versus Place Prosperity' and Regional Planning," *Environment and Planning D: Society and Space* 2 (1984): 35–46.

18. Wolfgang Schievelbusch, *The Railway Journey,* trans. Anselm Hollo (New York: Urizen, 1979), pp. 57–72; John R. Stilgoe, *Common Landscape of America, 1580 to 1845* (New Haven: Yale University Press, 1982), pp. 28–29; and Joshua Meyerowitz, *No Sense of Place: The Impact of Electronic Media on Social Behavior* (New York: Oxford University Press, 1985).

19. See A. J. Scott and M. Storper, "Industrial Change and Territorial Organization: A Summing Up," in *Production, Work, Territory: The Geographical Anatomy of Industrial Capitalism,* ed. Allen J. Scott and Michael Storper (Boston: Allen & Unwin, 1986), pp. 301–11; Allan Pred, *Place, Practice and Structure: Social and Spatial Transformation in Southern Sweden; 1750–1850* (Cambridge: Polity Press, 1986); Doreen Massey, *Spatial Divisions of Labor: Social Structures and the Geography of Production* (New York: Methuen, 1984); and Michael Peter Smith and Joe R. Feagin, eds., *The Capitalist City* (New York: Blackwell, 1987).

20. See Neil Smith, *Uneven Development* (Oxford: Blackwell, 1984) and "Deindustrialization and Regionalization: Class Alliance and Class Struggle," *Thirtieth North American Meetings of the Regional Science Association* 54 (1984): 113–28; Massey, *Spatial Divisions of Labor.*

21. Most of the literature emphasizes "equalization" among regions, but on increasing heterogeneity within regions, cf. William W. Falk and Thomas A. Lyson, *High Tech, Low Tech, No Tech: Recent Industrial and Occupational Change in the South* (Albany: State University of New York Press, 1988), and on West Germany, Josef Esser

and Joachim Hirsch, "The Crisis of Fordism and the Dimensions of a 'Postfordist' Regional and Urban Structure," *International Journal of Urban and Regional Research* 13 (1989): 417–37.

22. Massey, *Spatial Divisions of Labor*, pp. 194–234.

23. Ann Markusen, Peter Hall, and Amy Glasmeir, *High Tech America* (Boston: Allen & Unwin, 1986), pp. 144–69.

24. Edward J. Malecki, "Technological Imperatives and Modern Corporate Strategy," in *Production, Work, Territory*, ed. Scott and Storper, pp. 67–79; Barry Bluestone and Bennett Harrison, *The Great American Job Machine: The Proliferation of Low Wage Employment in the U.S. Economy* (study prepared for the Joint Economic Committee, U.S. Congress, 1986); U.S. Department of Commerce, Bureau of Economic Analysis, *Regional Differences in Per Capita Personal Income Widen in the 1980s* (August 20, 1987).

25. After 1987, however, housing prices and state tax revenues, including personal income tax revenues, dramatically declined in the bicoastal states, although unemployment rates were still lower than in the rest of the country. Democratic Staff, Joint Economic Committee, U.S. Congress, *The Bi-Coastal Economy: Regional Patterns of Economic Growth during the Reagan Administration* (July 9, 1986); Robert Kuttner, "Dukakis, Cuomo, and Other Egg-Spattered Faces," *Business Week*, December 4, 1989.

26. Capital versus community: Barry Bluestone and Bennett Harrison, *The Deindustrialization of America* (New York: Basic Books, 1982); restructuring for labor or capital: Mark Goodwin and Simon Duncan, "The Local State and Local Economic Policy," *Capital & Class* 27 (Winter 1986): 14–36; life space versus economic space: John Friedmann, "Life Space and Economic Space: Contradictions in Regional Development," in *The Crisis of the European Regions*, ed. Dudley Seers and Kjell Ostrom (London: Macmillan, 1983), pp. 148–62; people versus place prosperity: Agnew, "Devaluing Place."

27. The avatar of the deindustrialization thesis has been Bluestone and Harrison's *Deindustrialization of America;* for the other side, see Robert Z. Lawrence, "The Myth of U.S. Deindustrialization," *Challenge* (November–December 1983), and "Is Trade Deindustrializing America? A Medium-Term Perspective," in *Brookings Papers on Economic Activity* (Washington, D.C.: Brookings Institution, 1983); Richard B. McKenzie, *The Economics and Politics of Plant Closings* (San Diego: Pacific Institute, 1983); and, in the continuing debate over "industrial policy" and "industrial competitiveness," see Zukin, ed., *Industrial Policy*, and cf. the minimization of deindustrialization in William J. Baumol, "America's Productivity 'Crisis': A Modest Decline Isn't

All That Bad," *New York Times,* February 15, 1987. On the exports of U.S.-based multinationals—from their overseas operations—see Robert E. Lipsey and Irving B. Kravis, "Sorting Out the Trade Problem: Business Holds Its Own as America Slips," *New York Times,* January 18, 1987. And for an argument that capital investment has *not* declined, see Paul Craig Roberts, "Investment Is Fine—It's the Critics Who Are Wrong," *Business Week,* August 21, 1989.

28. This framework parallels the definition of place as a historically contingent social and material construction in Allan Pred, "The Social Becomes the Spatial, the Spatial Becomes the Social: Enclosures, Social Change and the Becoming of Places in Skane," in *Social Relations and Spatial Structures,* ed. Derek Gregory and John Urry (New York: St. Martin's Press, 1985), pp. 337–65.

29. While these uses of landscape and vernacular are mine, see John Brinckerhoff Jackson, *Discovering the Vernacular Landscape* (New Haven: Yale University Press, 1984) and "Urban Circumstances," *Design Quarterly* 128 (1985); D. W. Meinig, ed., *The Interpretation of Ordinary Landscapes* (New York: Oxford University Press, 1979); Stilgoe, *Common Landscape of America;* Denis E. Cosgrove, *Social Formation and Symbolic Landscape* (London: Croom Helm, 1984); Daniel Miller, *Material Culture and Mass Consumption* (Oxford: Blackwell, 1987); Lester Rowntree, "Cultural/Humanistic Geography," *Progress in Human Geography* 10 (1986): 580–86; Denis Cosgrove and Stephen Daniels, eds., *The Iconography of Landscape* (Cambridge: Cambridge University Press, 1988).

30. See Kenneth Clark, *Landscape into Art* [1949] (Boston: Beacon Press, 1961), pp. 1–15; John Barrell, *The Idea of Landscape and the Sense of Place, 1730–1840: An Approach to the Poetry of John Clare* (Cambridge: Cambridge University Press, 1972), and *The Dark Side of the Landscape: The Rural Poor in English Painting, 1730–1840* (Cambridge: Cambridge University Press, 1980); and Cosgrove and Daniels, eds., *Iconography of Landscape.*

31. "Repetition and singularity" from Rosalind E. Krauss, "The Originality of the Avant-Garde," in *The Originality of the Avant-Garde and Other Modernist Myths* (Cambridge, Mass.: MIT Press, 1985), p. 166.

32. E. P. Thompson, "Time, Work-Discipline, and Industrial Capitalism," *Past and Present* 38 (1967): 90; emphasis added. The approach of Michel Foucault, whose historical study of the architecture of punishment focused on the Benthamite Panopticon and the nineteenth-century penitentiary, would go much farther in suggesting the schema of social control implicit in a landscape's composition. See *Dis-*

cipline and Punish: The Birth of the Prison [1975], trans. Alan Sheridan (New York. Pantheon Books, 1977); cf. M. Christine Boyer, *Dreaming the Rational City: The Myth of American City Planning* (Cambridge, Mass.: MIT Press, 1983).

33. On Vancouver, see David Ley, "Liberal Ideology and the Post-industrial City," *Annals of the Association of American Geographers* 70 (1980): 238–58; on the downside of Silicon Valley, see AnnaLee Saxenian, "The Urban Contradictions of Silicon Valley: Regional Growth and the Restructuring of the Semiconductor Industry," *International Journal of Urban and Regional Research* 7 (1983): 237–62.

34. These ellided changes of landscape have inspired a number of challenging studies, including Marshall Berman, *All That Is Solid Melts into Air* (New York: Simon & Schuster, 1982), T. J. Clark, *The Painting of Modern Life* (New York: Knopf, 1985), Stephen Kern, *The Culture of Time and Space, 1880–1918* (Cambridge, Mass.: Harvard University Press, 1983), and Schievelbusch, *Railway Journey.*

35. Meinig, "Introduction," in *Interpretation of Ordinary Landscapes,* p. 6; Robert Venturi et al., *Learning from Las Vegas,* rev. ed. (Cambridge, Mass.: MIT Press, 1977).

36. J. B. Jackson, "The Order of a Landscape," in *Interpretation of Ordinary Landscapes,* ed. Meinig, pp. 153–63.

37. J. B. Jackson, "Concluding with Landscapes," in *Discovering the Vernacular Landscape,* pp. 145–57.

38. David Harvey, "The Geopolitics of Capitalism," in *Social Relations and Spatial Structures,* ed. Gregory and Urry, pp. 128–63. This reworking of capital through the creative destruction of the built environment is a recurrent theme, perhaps the major theme, in David Harvey's work. See Harvey's *The Urbanization of Capital* and *Consciousness and the Urban Experience* (both Baltimore: Johns Hopkins University Press, 1985).

39. Meinig, "Symbolic Landscapes," p. 183; on metropolitan de-concentration, see M. Gottdiener, *The Social Construction of Urban Space* (Austin: University of Texas Press, 1985); and for criticism of mass production and standardization in the built environment, see Kenneth Frampton, "Towards a Critical Regionalism: Six Points for an Architecture of Resistance," in *The Anti-Aesthetic: Essays on Postmodern Culture,* ed. Hal Foster (Port Townsend, Wash.: Bay Press, 1983), pp. 16–30.

40. In the small, but growing, literature criticizing the mass production and standardization of landscapes, see, for example, E. Relph, *Place and Placelessness* (London: Plon, 1976), and *The Modern Urban Landscape* (Baltimore: Johns Hopkins University Press, 1987). Cf. Christine

Boyer, "The City of Collective Memory" (unpublished essay, 1988). On the techniques required for "saving" the cast-iron facade in Baltimore, consider this endorsement: " 'It is important nationally as an example of how these buildings can be revived by being disassembled and replaced on other sites when they cannot stay on their original sites,' says Margot Gayle, president of Friends of Cast-Iron Architecture in New York, which supported a Baltimore architect, David G. Wright, in his battle to save the facade" ("A City Saves a Cast-Iron Facade," *New York Times*, February 5, 1987).

41. Daniel Bell, *The Coming of Post-Industrial Society* (New York: Basic Books, 1973), p. 37.

42. For an especially rich collection, see Bryan Roberts, Ruth Finnegan, and Duncan Gallie, eds., *New Approaches to Economic Life / Economic Restructuring: Unemployment and the Social Division of Labor* (Manchester: Manchester University Press, 1985). For a somewhat different organization of these materials, see Scott and Storper, eds., *Production, Work, Territory*.

43. Adapted from Scott and Storper, "Industrial Change and Territorial Organization," in *Production, Work, Territory*, ed. Scott and Storper, p. 310.

CHAPTER 2. "CREATIVE DESTRUCTION": THE INNER LANDSCAPE

1. Fredric Jameson, "Postmodernism, or the Cultural Logic of Late Capitalism," *New Left Review*, no. 146 (July–August 1984): 53–93, esp. 89–92. Although this impressive essay has influenced my grasp of postmodern culture, my interpretation differs in three major respects: in denying an immanent cultural logic of advanced capitalism in favor of finding consistent ambiguities and polarities; in emphasizing continuities rather than discontinuity with modernism, especially in consumer culture; and in rejecting Jameson's contention that postmodernism privileges space over time just as modernism privileged time over space.

2. John Rajchman, "Postmodernism in a Nominalist Frame, "*Flash Art* 137 (November–December 1987): 51. Charles Jencks defines postmodern visual forms in terms of both revivalism and "imminent creativity," and counts dissonance, pluralism, urbanism, anthropomorphism, irony, parody, and "multivalence" among postmodern tropes (Jencks, *Post-Modernism: The New Classicism in Art and Architecture* [New York: Rizzoli, 1987]). The term *postmodernism* was narrowly used in the 1930s; it gained currency in the 1960s among New York artists and critics to refer to the exhaustion, or institutionalization, of high modernism.

3. Joseph Giovannini, "Design Notebook," *New York Times,* March 12, 1987. At the same time, however, postmodern architecture's emphasis on ornament, flexibility, and color have reconstituted the use of such construction materials as steel and granite. Thomas Fisher, "P/A Technics: The Uses of Steel," *Progressive Architecture,* July 1987: 100–105; Albert Scardino, "New Look in Skyscrapers Revives Quarries," *New York Times,* August 5, 1987.

4. "Post-Modernism Hits the Road," *Architectural Record,* June 1985, p. 79.

5. See Edward Relph, *Place and Placelessness* (London: Plon, 1976) and *The Modern Urban Landscape* (Baltimore: Johns Hopkins University Press, 1987).

6. "Postmodernism of resistance and . . . reaction" from Hal Foster, "Postmodernism: A Preface," in Foster, ed., *The Anti-Aesthetic: Essays on Postmodern Culture* (Port Townsend, Wash.: Bay Press, 1983), p. xii. I have excluded from this discussion both feminism and antimilitarism.

7. See Marshall Berman, *All That Is Solid Melts into Air* (New York: Simon & Schuster, 1982); Stephen Kern, *The Culture of Time and Space, 1880–1918* (Cambridge, Mass.: Harvard University Press, 1983); Wolfgang Schievelbusch, *The Railway Journey,* trans. Anselm Hollo (New York: Urizen, 1979).

8. T. J. Clark, *The Painting of Modern Life* (New York: Knopf, 1985), p. 49.

9. For differentiation as the key sociological issue in contemporary society, see the different approaches taken by Niklas Luhmann, *The Differentiation of Society,* trans. Stephen Holmes and Charles Larmore (New York: Columbia University Press, 1984), and Pierre Bourdieu, *Distinction: A Social Critique of the Judgement of Taste,* trans. Richard Nice (Cambridge, Mass.: Harvard University Press, 1984).

10. Victor Turner has written about liminality in several different works. See, for example, "Liminal to Liminoid, in Play, Flow Ritual: An Essay in Comparative Symbology," in *From Ritual to Theatre* (New York: Performing Arts Journal Publications, 1982), pp. 20–60. See also chapter 1 above.

11. John Updike, *Rabbit Is Rich* (New York: Knopf, 1981).

12. Don DeLillo, *White Noise* (New York: Viking, 1985); page numbers given parenthetically in the text are from this edition.

13. Robert Ward, *Red Baker* (New York: Dial Press, 1985); page numbers given parenthetically in the text are from this edition.

14. Jay McInerney, *Bright Lights, Big City* (New York: Vintage,

1984); page numbers given parenthetically in the text are from this edition.

15. Tama Janowitz, *Slaves of New York* (New York: Crown, 1986); Adam Gopnik, "The Blue Room," *New Yorker,* February 23, 1987, pp. 34–38.

16. Brett Easton Ellis, *Less than Zero* (New York: Simon & Schuster, 1985); page numbers given parenthetically in the text are from this edition. Nathanael West, *The Day of the Locust* [1939] (New York: Farrar, Straus, 1957).

17. William Sharpe and Leonard Wallock, "From 'Great Town' to 'Nonplace Urban Realm': Reading the Modern City," in *Visions of the Modern City: Essays in History, Art and Literature,* ed. Sharpe and Wallock (Baltimore: Johns Hopkins University Press, 1987).

18. Frederick Barthelme, *Moon Deluxe* (New York: Simon & Schuster, 1983); page numbers given parenthetically in the text are from this edition.

CHAPTER 3. THE URBAN LANDSCAPE

1. See David Harvey, *The Condition of Postmodernity* (Oxford: Blackwell, 1989), pp. 210–307. Harvey's apparent willingness to incorporate culture into Marxist analysis brings to a head the question of *how* to integrate aesthetics and political economy, culture and capital.

2. In Victor Turner's view, liminality does not exist outside of preindustrial, and certainly precapitalist, society, where social categories are stable. Men and women in an advanced market economy may *choose* a sort of political, professional, or artistic liminality, or marginality; this Turner calls a *liminoid* state. On Walter Benjamin, see Susan Buck-Morss, *The Dialectics of Seeing: Walter Benjamin and the Arcades Project* (Cambridge, Mass.: MIT Press, 1989).

3. See T. J. Clark, *The Painting of Modern Life* (New York: Knopf, 1985), ch. 1; David Harvey, *Consciousness and the Urban Experience* (Baltimore: Johns Hopkins University Press, 1985); Mark Gottdiener, *The Social Production of Urban Space* (Austin: University of Texas Press, 1985); John R. Logan and Harvey Molotch, *Urban Fortunes: The Political Economy of Place* (Berkeley and Los Angeles: University of California Press, 1987). On the other hand, Herbert Gans argues strenuously against economic reductionism in attempts to explain socio-spatial structures; see, for example, "American Urban Theory and Urban Areas," in *Cities in Recession,* ed. Ivan Szelenyi (Beverly Hills: Sage, 1984), pp. 278–307.

4. See Fredric Jameson, "Postmodernism, or the Cultural Logic of Late Capitalism," *New Left Review,* no. 146 (July–August 1984): 53–93; these issues are less schematically rendered in Logan and Molotch, *Urban Fortunes.*

5. David Harvey, "Flexible Accumulation through Urbanization: Reflections on 'Post-Modernism' in the American City," in *The Urban Experience* (Oxford: Blackwell, 1989); cf. Logan and Molotch, *Urban Fortunes,* ch. 4, and "Postscript: More Market Forces," in Sharon Zukin, *Loft Living: Culture and Capital in Urban Change,* 2d ed. (New Brunswick, N.J.: Rutgers University Press, 1989).

6. See William Severini Kowinski, *The Malling of America* (New York: William Morrow, 1985). "Only financial institutions were in a position to understand the implications of suburbanization, even partially, and to coordinate and plan, however imperfectly," write Beth Mintz and Michael Schwartz (*The Power Structure of American Business* [Chicago: University of Chicago Press, 1985], p. 43).

7. "According to fashion experts, Italian companies have consolidated their design, textile and production resources in Milan over the past decade, and though each Italian boutique may be relatively small, it is part of a much larger organization operating on a world scale," writes Joseph Giovannini, "The 'New' Madison Avenue: A European Street of Fashion," *New York Times,* June 26, 1986; see also Richard J. Meislin, "Quiche Gets the Boot on Columbus Avenue," *New York Times,* July 25, 1987.

8. Lisa Belkin, "Benetton's Cluster Strategy," *New York Times,* January 16, 1986.

9. Benetton recently expanded by diversifying into financial services, building on its network of outlets—but this basis has turned out to be problematic. On Benetton's history, see Andrea Lee, "Profiles: Being Everywhere (Luciano Benetton)," *New Yorker,* November 10, 1986, and "Why Some Benetton Shopkeepers Are Losing Their Shirts," *Business Week,* March 14, 1988; on McDonald's, see "McWorld?" *Business Week,* October 13, 1986, and Joseph K. Skinner, "Big Mac and the Tropical Forests," *Monthly Review,* 37, no. 7 (December 1985): 25–32.

10. The extreme "populist" statements are Robert Venturi, *Complexity and Contradiction in Architecture,* rev. ed. (New York: Museum of Modern Art, 1977), and Venturi et al., *Learning from Las Vegas,* rev. ed. (Cambridge, Mass., MIT Press, 1977). On the search for corporate distinction by means of architecture, see Stephen Kieran, "The Architecture of Plenty: Theory and Design in the Marketing Age," *Harvard Architecture Review* no. 6 (1987): 103–13.

11. Ron Drucker at seminar in Boston, "Was Postmodernism the Heir to the Preservation Movement? What Will Come Next?" quoted in "Preservation and Postmodernism: A Common Cause?" (editorial), *Architectural Record,* June 1987, p. 9; Ada Louise Huxtable, "Creeping Gigantism in Manhattan," *New York Times,* March 22, 1987. See also Adrian Forty, *Objects of Desire: Design and Society from Wedgwood to IBM* (New York: Pantheon Books, 1987).

12. Besides the Japanese, major foreign investors in trophy buildings include British, Dutch, and West German pension funds. "Real Estate Trophy Hunt," *New York Times,* August 23, 1987. Citicorp in *Business Week,* April 3, 1989; General Foods building in *New York Times,* August 19, 1987.

13. Robert A. M. Stern et al., *New York 1930: Architecture and Urbanism between the Two World Wars* (New York: Rizzoli, 1987), pp. 511–13.

14. Calvin Tomkins, "Forms under Light," *New Yorker,* May 23, 1977, pp. 43–80.

15. See Douglas C. McGill, "Taking a Close Look at the Art of Post-Modernist Architects," *New York Times,* August 31, 1987, and any issue from 1988 of such fashion magazines as *Vogue* and *Elle.* Despite the commercial success of such accounts of architectural history as Witold Rybcynski's *Home: A Short History of an Idea* (New York: Viking, 1986) and Tom Wolfe's *From Bauhaus to Our House* (New York: Farrar, Straus & Giroux, 1981), however, there may still be an apparent abysmal ignorance about architectural facts ("Cultural Blindspot," *Progressive Architecture,* July 1987, p. 7).

16. H. I. Brock, "From Flat Roofs to Towers and Slats," *New York Times Magazine,* April 19, 1931, pp. 6–7, 16, quoted in Stern et al., *New York 1930,* p. 515; also see Kieran, "Architecture of Plenty."

17. "What we hadn't foreseen [in redeveloping downtown San Francisco] was that there would be a tendency to seek out national firms, and not to take any risk with architecture," the city's director of planning says (*New York Times,* December 5, 1987). See also Paul Goldberger, "Architecture View: A Short Skyscraper with a Tall Assignment," *New York Times,* March 26, 1989.

18. The architect continues: "The identity of Boston, Back Bay, and Newbury Street does not reside in the overscaled developer-driven buildings by superstars. We are very guarded (very Yankee) in Boston. We are concerned by what superstars have built here . . . by what is being built . . . and the commitments the all-stars have made for parallel design time for projects in other cities and countries. We are wary of additional watered down, trendy, inflated 'Boston' buildings that will

never really become Bostonian" (George E. Marsh, Jr., "Letters," *Architectural Record,* May 1987, p. 4). In general, however, city planning agencies in Boston (and San Francisco) have reacted more strongly than in other cities against speculative overbuilding.

19. Giorgio Vasari, *Lives of the Artists* [1550, 1568] (London: Penguin Books, 1965), p. 169.

20. "They say that at CBS the most prized assets are the highly celebrated, hard-to-replace television personalities responsible for the network's news coverage" (Alison Leigh Cowan, "Tisch is Holding a Hot Potato," *New York Times,* March 14, 1987); " 'The superstar is the giant bonanza,' said Al Teller, the president of CBS Records. 'The big hit is to develop superstar careers. That is the biggest win you can have' " (Geraldine Fabrikant, "A Long and Winding Road: Band's Quest for Stardom," *New York Times,* July 31, 1987). Conversely, as profits have fallen, many Wall Street financial firms have eliminated their superstars, or highest revenue-producers, and restored power to traditional managers ("The Decline of the Superstar," *Business Week,* August 17, 1987, pp. 90–98).

21. Stern et al., *New York 1930,* pp. 19, 513–14, quotation from builder William A. Starrett (1928), pp. 513–14. Henry James, *The American Scene* [1907] (Bloomington, Indiana: Indiana University Press, 1968), pp. 83–84. Andrew Saint suggests that the constant cycles of rebuilding initiated in Chicago from the 1870s by business cycles and by fire resulted in an aggressive construction industry and a commercially oriented group of architects who, "a French observer said, 'brazenly accepted the conditions imposed by the speculator' " (Saint, *The Image of the Architect* [New Haven: Yale University Press, 1983], p. 84). American-style market competition among architects could be expected to shock a visitor from France, where commissions were mainly sewed up by a civil service–Ecole des Beaux Arts network.

22. Putman quoted in Joseph Giovannini, "Westweek, Star-Studded Los Angeles Design Event," *New York Times,* April 2, 1987. Also see Anne-Marie Schiro, "Lacroix: Meteor or Constant Star?" *New York Times,* April 22, 1988.

23. Catherine W. Zerner, "The New Professionalism in the Renaissance," in *The Architect,* ed. Spiro Kostof (New York: Oxford University Press, 1977), p. 158.

24. Cf. Stuart Ewen, *All Consuming Images: The Politics of Style in Contemporary Culture* (New York: Basic Books, 1988). The posthumous transfer from design sketch or prototype to mass market product reaches ludicrous extremes, as reported in Joseph Giovannini, "Marketing Frank Lloyd Wright," *New York Times,* March 24, 1988.

25. "The Prisoner of Seventh Avenue [Halston]," *New York Times Magazine*, March 15, 1987, pp. 16ff.; Michael Gross, "In Search of the Perfect Angel," *New York Times*, August 30, 1987; Bob Colacello, "The Power of Pierre," *Vanity Fair*, September 1987. At lower levels of the design professions, however, employees may chafe at the limits on their professional autonomy—see Maeve Slavin, "Interiors Business: Jobs Are Not What They Used to Be," *Interiors*, September 1983, pp. 130–31.

26. Debora Silverman, *Selling Culture: Bloomingdale's, Diana Vreeland, and the New Aristocracy of Taste in Reagan's America* (New York: Pantheon Books, 1986), p. 11. See also Fred Ferretti, " 'The L.A. Spirit' Makes a Splash in Brooklyn," *New York Times*, April 19, 1985; Cathleen McGuigan, "The Avant-Garde Courts Corporations," *New York Times Magazine*, November 2, 1986.

27. Money center banks guaranteed $20 million in long-term loans and $10 million in short-term loans for Faneuil Hall before construction began, but the loans were all made contingent on a $3 million participation by Boston financial institutions (*Fortune*, April 10, 1978, pp. 85–91, cited in Mintz and Schwartz, *Power Structure of American Business*, p. 61). For a discussion of historic preservation as both an aesthetic paradigm and a redevelopment strategy, see Zukin, *Loft Living*, pp. 75–78.

28. Stephen Kern, *The Culture of Time and Space, 1880–1918* (Cambridge, Mass.: Harvard University Press, 1983), pp. 187–91; Wolfgang Schievelbusch, *The Railway Journey*, trans. Anselm Hollo (New York: Urizen, 1979), pp. 161–69.

29. Robert Thorne, "Places of Refreshment in the Nineteenth-Century City," in *Buildings and Society*, ed. Anthony D. King (London: Routledge & Kegan Paul, 1980), pp. 228–53; Gunther Barth, *City People: The Rise of Modern Culture in Nineteenth-Century America* (New York: Oxford University Press, 1980); Rosalind H. Williams, *Dream Worlds: Mass Consumption in Late Nineteenth-Century France* (Berkeley and Los Angeles: University of California Press, 1982); Susan Porter Benson, *Counter Culture: Saleswomen, Managers and Customers in American Department Stores, 1890–1940* (Urbana: University of Illinois Press, 1986); James, *American Scene*, pp. 102–6.

30. Jameson, "Postmodernism," pp. 81, 82.

31. James, *American Scene*, pp. 440–41.

32. See Dennis R. Judd, "Electoral Coalitions, Minority Mayors, and the Contradictions in the Municipal Policy Agenda," in *Cities in Stress: A New Look at the Urban Crisis*, ed. M. Gottdiener, *Urban Affairs Annual Reviews* 30 (1986): 145–70; Larry Bennett, "Beyond Urban Renewal: Chicago's North Loop Redevelopment Project," *Ur-*

ban Affairs Quarterly 22 (1986): 242–60; Chester Hartman, *The Transformation of San Francisco* (Totowa, N.J.: Rowman & Allenheld, 1984).

33. Jeffrey R. Henig, "Collective Responses to the Urban Crisis: Ideology and Mobilization," in *Cities in Stress,* ed. Gottdiener, p. 243.

34. Silverman, *Selling Culture,* p. 19.

CHAPTER 4. STEELTOWN: POWER AND AUTONOMY IN WEIRTON, WEST VIRGINIA

1. Edward Greer, *Big Steel: Black Politics and Corporate Power in Gary, Indiana* (New York: Monthly Review Press, 1979), pp. 72–89.

2. Quotation from Francis G. Couvares, *The Remaking of Pittsburgh: Class and Culture in an Industrializing City, 1877–1919* (Albany: State University of New York Press, 1984), p. 86; on craft workers in the steel industry, see David Brody, *Steelworkers in America: The Nonunion Era* (Cambridge, Mass.: Harvard University Press, 1960); David Montgomery, *The Fall of the House of Labor* (Cambridge: Cambridge University Press, 1987), ch. 1.

3. Horace B. Davis, "Company Towns," *Encyclopedia of the Social Sciences* (New York: Macmillan, 1931), 4:119–23.

4. Greer, *Big Steel,* p. 63.

5. On the design and use of River Rouge, whose integrated facilities supplanted the earlier Ford assembly line at Highland Park, see David A. Hounshell, *From the American System to Mass Production, 1800–1932* (Baltimore: Johns Hopkins University Press, 1984), pp. 267–68.

6. See *LIFE: The First Decade* (New York: Time, 1979); *Precisionist Perspectives: Prints and Drawings* (New York: Whitney Museum of American Art at Philip Morris, 1988); *Charles Sheeler* (New York: Whitney Museum of American Art, 1988); Vicki Goldberg, *Bourke-White* (New York: International Center for Photography, 1988).

7. Photographs of Chartres and the Rouge in *Charles Sheeler;* on the *Vanity Fair* submission, see Mary-Jane Jacob, "The Rouge in 1927: Photographs and Paintings by Charles Sheeler," in *The Rouge: The Image of Industry in the Art of Charles Sheeler and Diego Rivera* (Detroit: Detroit Institute of Arts, 1978), pp. 13–14.

8. Linda Downs, "The Rouge in 1932: The *Detroit Industry* Frescoes by Diego Rivera," in *The Rouge: The Image of Industry in the Art of Charles Sheeler and Diego Rivera,* p. 72.

9. Couvares, *Remaking of Pittsburgh,* ch. 7.

10. For a decade-by-decade account of the steel industry's conflicts

with the federal government, see Paul A. Tiffany, *The Decline of American Steel* (New York: Oxford University Press, 1988).

11. Similar questions have been posed about the autonomy of the *local state* and local elites, especially concerning the constraints on states when they try to implement their preferred strategies for economic growth. See, for example, Simon Duncan, Mark Goodwin, and Susan Halford, "Policy Variations in Local States: Uneven Development and Local Social Relations," *International Journal of Urban and Regional Research* 12 (1988): 107–28, or John Logan and Harvey Molotch, *Urban Fortunes* (Berkeley and Los Angeles: University of California Press, 1987).

12. Henry W. Broude, *Steel Decisions and the National Economy* (New Haven: Yale University Press, 1963), p. 21.

13. These numbers, which refer to blast furnace and basic steel product workers, are from Richard Belous, *Employment and Compensation in the U.S. Steel Industry: Problems and Prospects* (Washington, D.C.: Library of Congress, Congressional Research Service, 1984), p. 5. Periodic employment figures from *Business Week* are different.

14. On mini-mills, see Charlotte Breckenridge and David J. Cantor, *Regional Aspects of Shifts in the Steel Industry in the United States* (Washington, D.C.: Library of Congress, Congressional Research Service, 1983); Zoltan J. Acs, *The Changing Structure of the U.S. Economy: Lessons From the Steel Industry* (New York: Praeger, 1984), pp. 98ff.; Jonathan P. Hicks, "Nucor's Ambitious Expansion," *New York Times,* June 30, 1986; "U.S. Minimills Launch a Full-Scale Attack," *Business Week,* June 13, 1988, pp. 100–102.

15. *Business Week,* September 19, 1977. On the British economists and the persistence, against the facts, of perceptions of steel as playing a key structural role in the U.S. economy, see Broude, *Steel Decisions and the National Economy,* esp. pp. 29ff. Broude says, under certain "circumstances . . . there may be times when the economy is unable to get out from under the industry's strategic structural position *in time* or *at costs* that will allow it to ignore what may be taking place in the industry" (p. 3). Also see Rayner Banham's argument that European architects like Le Corbusier tended to mythologize, rather than copy, the forms of industrial structures in the United States, in *A Concrete Atlantis: U.S. Industrial Building and European Modern Architecture* (Cambridge, Mass.: MIT Press, 1986).

16. Robert W. Crandall, *The U.S. Steel Industry in Recurrent Crisis* (Washington, D.C.: Brookings Institution, 1981), p. 125.

17. On pressures on Big Steel by both the Eisenhower and Kennedy administrations, and the Democratic-dominated Congress, see Gardiner C. Means, *Pricing Power and the Public Interest* (New York: Har-

per, 1962); Broude, *Steel Decisions and the National Economy;* and Tiffany, *Decline of American Steel.*

18. The industry's historical desire to reduce capacity and its antipathy to diversification are asserted by Tiffany, *Decline of American Steel.*

19. See Linda Brewster Stearns, "Capital-Market Effects on External Control of Corporations," in *Structures of Capital: The Social Organization of the Economy,* ed. Sharon Zukin and Paul DiMaggio (Cambridge: Cambridge University Press, 1990), pp. 175–201; Crandall, *U.S. Steel Industry in Recurrent Crisis,* pp. 28–30; Tiffany, *Decline of American Steel,* pp. 139ff., quotation from *Iron Age,* p. 180; Acs, *Changing Structure of the U.S. Economy,* pp. 174ff.

20. Tiffany, *Decline of American Steel,* pp. 134, 181; Crandall, *U.S. Steel Industry in Recurrent Crisis,* pp. 81ff.

21. Broude, *Steel Decisions and the National Economy,* pp. 110ff.

22. See *Business Week,* June 23, 1975, September 17, 1979, February 25, 1985.

23. Achs, *Changing Structure of the U.S. Economy,* p. 93; Crandall, *U.S. Steel Industry in Recurrent Crisis,* pp. 34–38, 83.

24. Data on imports, employment, and hourly compensation from Crandall, *U.S. Steel Industry in Recurrent Crisis;* see also Belous, *Employment and Compensation in the U.S. Steel Industry.* Data on profit rates from World Steel Dynamics, "Financial Analysis of International Steelmakers," cited in statement of Frank W. Luerssen, chairman, Inland Steel Company, on behalf of the American Iron and Steel Institute, in U.S. Congress, Senate Committee on Labor and Human Resources, Subcommittee on Employment and Productivity, *Employment and Productivity Trends in the Steel Industry,* 98th Congress, 2d sess., March 22, 1984, p. 91.

25. On steel regions' problems in Japan, see, for example, Steve Lohr, "Critical Shift for Japan's Steel," *New York Times,* March 20, 1984; on France, see Sharon Zukin, "Markets and Politics in France's Declining Regions," *Journal of Policy Analysis and Management* 5, no. 1 (Fall 1985): 40–57, or Alan David Stoleroff, "Deindustrialization in Nord–Pas-de-Calais: The Restructuring of Capital and the Disorganization of Traditional Working-Class Community" (Ph.D. diss., Rutgers University, 1983).

26. Trigger pricing is based on the attempt to establish a "fair" price based on efficient Japanese producers' costs at near-full capacity. It seeks to avoid the endless controversy associated with accusations that foreign producers "dump" steel in the U.S. market at less than producers' prices, and also aims to minimize impact on consumers' prices. For a full explanation of the strategy behind trigger prices, devised by a

group working with Treasury Secretary Anthony Solomon in the Carter administration, see Crandall, *U.S. Steel Industry in Recurrent Crisis.* On distinctions between officials of Commerce, HUD, and White House advisers, see the case studies of shutdowns in David Bensman and Roberta Lynch, *Rusted Dreams: Hard Times in a Steel Community* (New York: McGraw-Hill, 1987) and Staughton Lynd, *The Fight against Shutdowns: Youngstown's Steel Mill Closings* (San Pedro: Singlejack Books, 1982).

27. Again, the litany of blame and responsibility sounded the same in every country. See Ira Magaziner and Robert B. Reich, *Minding America's Business* (New York: Harcourt Brace Jovanovich, 1982); Tony Manwaring, "Labour Productivity and the Crisis at BSC: Behind the Rhetoric," *Capital and Class* 14 (Summer 1981): 61–97; Michael Schwartz and Sharon Zukin, "Deindustrialization in the United States and France: Structural Convergence, Institutional Contrast," *Political Power and Social Theory* 7 (1988): 293–320.

28. *Business Week,* June 23, 1975. Even "rational" critics disagree about the degree of steelmakers' commitment to diversification prior to the 1970s. Peter Brantly and Michael Schwartz, "Intercorporate Power and the Decline of the Steel Industry" (paper delivered at American Sociological Association annual meetings, Atlanta, 1988), take this criticism of the industry from Achs, *Changing Structure of the U.S. Economy,* but their paper also emphasizes the pressure steelmakers faced from the financial community.

29. *Wall Street Journal,* July 22, 1980, p. 1. On Love's background, also see "National Intergroup: How Pete Love Went Wrong," *Business Week,* March 6, 1989.

30. See discussion and references to the business press in Schwartz and Zukin, "Deindustrialization in the United States and France."

31. National Steel Corporation, *Annual Report, 1981* (Pittsburgh); *Moody's Industrial Manual* (New York: Moody's, 1982).

32. *New York Times,* January 31, May 20, May 21, May 25, May 28, June 12, August 6, August 2, September 12, and October 23, 1985; *Wall Street Journal,* June 6 and August 12, 1985.

33. Despite periodic crisis reports on steel through the 1970s, including "Steel's Sea of Troubles" (September 19, 1977), the first *Business Week* article that described a *structural* crisis, "Big Steel's Liquidation," appeared in the issue of September 17, 1979.

34. On the more favorable prognosis for steel in the Great Lakes region, see Crandall, *U.S. Steel Industry in Recurrent Crisis,* pp. 140–46.

35. See Terry F. Buss and F. Stevens Redburn, *Shutdown at*

Youngstown (Albany: State University of New York Press, 1983), and references cited in Schwartz and Zukin, "Deindustrialization in the United States and France."

36. For an interesting comparison, see David C. Perry, "The Politics of Dependency in Deindustrializing America: The Case of Buffalo, New York," in *The Capitalist City*, ed. Michael Peter Smith and Joe R. Feagin (New York: Blackwell, 1987), pp. 113–37.

37. See Robert B. Reich and John D. Donahue, *New Deals: The Chrysler Revival and the American System* (New York: Times Books, 1985) and Davita Silfen Glasberg, "Chrysler Corporation's Struggle for Bailout: The Role of the State in Finance Capitalist Society," *Research in Political Sociology* 3 (1987): 87–110.

38. This is my reading, especially in light of Weirton, of the account in Lynd, *Fight against Shutdowns*.

39. Bensman and Lynch, *Rusted Dreams*. Greer, *Big Steel*, contrasts new black elected officials in Gary with the old political machine based in the white ethnic community, which failed for decades to confront the air and water pollution caused by U.S. Steel.

40. Lynd, *Fight against Shutdowns*, p. 164.

41. In addition to the published sources listed in the following notes, my information and interpretation of the Weirton buyout reflect interviews I conducted with participants between July 1983 and October 1984: interviews with an investment banker from Lazard Frères, a management consultant from McKinsey and Company, and an attorney from Willkie, Farr, and Gallagher in New York; with the president of the labor union local and the union's attorney in Weirton; with a leader of the dissident rank-and-file workers in Steubenville, Ohio; and with a commercial banker who participated in the ESOP loan in Detroit. All respondents were promised that they would not be quoted by name.

42. "Weirton Scabs" from Terry Dodsworth, "Weirton Steel: A Cooperative Effort at Resurrection," *Financial Times*, September 11, 1985; also see Jonathan Prude, "ESOP's Fable: How Workers Bought the Steel Mill in Weirton, West Virginia, and What Good It Did Them," *Socialist Review* 78 (November–December 1984): 27–60; Mary Williams, "The Weirton Steel That Was and May Yet Be," *Progressive*, November 1982, pp. 30–36; *New York Times*, March 14, 1983; Jeffrey Leites, "Continuity and Change in the Legitimation of Authority in Southern Mill Towns," *Social Problems* 29 (1982): 540–50.

43. Calculated by David Radick from the U.S. Census, Weirton-Steubenville SMSA, 1960, 1970, 1980.

44. *New York Times*, June 8 and July 4, 1982, and interviews.

45. See Prude, "ESOP's Fable"; Peter Pitegoff and Staughton Lynd,

"Workers Can Be Choosers," op-ed page, *New York Times,* October 27, 1982; Joyce Rothschild-Whitt, "Worker Ownership: Collective Response to an Elite-Generated Crisis," *Research in Social Movements, Conflict and Change* 6 (1984): 167–94; Raymond Russell, "Using Ownership to Control: Making Workers Owners in the Contemporary United States," *Politics and Society* 13 (1984): 253–94; "A Coming Surge in ESOPs," *New York Times,* January 6, 1985.

46. See Felix Rohatyn, *The Twenty-Year Century: Essays on Economics and Public Finance* (New York: Random House, 1984).

47. Sources on market conditions, in addition to interviews, include Weirton Joint Study Committee, Inc., Weirton Steel Corporation, *Disclosure Document Regarding the Acquisition of the Assets of the Weirton Steel Division from National Steel Corporation and the Establishment of the Weirton Steel Corporation Employment Stock Ownership Plan (ESOP)* (Weirton, West Virginia, August 19, 1983), pp. 27–29, and Williams, "The Weirton Steel That Was and May Yet Be."

48. Joint Study Committee, *Disclosure Document,* p. 17.

49. "Making Money—and History—at Weirton," *Business Week,* November 12, 1984, pp. 136–40; Dodsworth, "Weirton Steel," *Financial Times,* September 11, 1985; "Has Weirton's ESOP Worked Too Well?" *Business Week,* January 23, 1989; *New York Times,* January 26, 1989.

50. "At National Intergroup, the Choice May Be Love or Money," *Business Week,* July 11, 1988; *New York Times,* November 11, 1988; "National Intergroup: How Pete Love Went Wrong," *Business Week,* March 6, 1989; "Japan's NKK Buys More of National Steel," *New York Times,* April 26, 1990.

51. In 1976, *Business Week* reported that residents of Steubenville reluctantly opposed Weirton's air pollution, which they related to a rising incidence of heart disease and bronchitis, because the steel industry kept the unemployment rate in the area down to 6 *percent* (February 2, 1976).

52. *Wall Street Journal,* October 18, 1984; *New York Times,* March 31, 1985.

CHAPTER 5. MOTOWN'S STEELTOWN: THE POWER OF PRODUCTIVE
LABOR IN DETROIT

1. Unemployment data from the Metropolitan Affairs Corporation, reported in the *Detroit Free Press,* June 30, 1988, and from the U.S. Department of Labor, in the *New York Times,* August 3, 1988.

2. Historical background on Detroit's political economy from

Richard Child Hill, "Uneven Development in Metropolitan Detroit," ch. 2 in Joe T. Darden et al., *Detroit: Race and Uneven Development* (Philadelphia: Temple University Press, 1987), and Sheldon Friedman and Leon Potok, "Detroit and the Auto Industry: An Historical Overview" (paper delivered at a Conference on Economic Crisis and Political Response in the Auto City: Detroit and Turin, Harvard University, Center for European Studies, 1981).

3. Jeffrey A. Leib, "Steelmakers Listen to Detroit," *New York Times,* August 8, 1985; "The Steelworkers Are Getting Desperate," *Business Week,* December 30, 1985; "Steelmakers Are Running Out of Options," *Business Week,* June 23, 1986; *McLouth Steel Corporation* (New York: Lazard Frères, 1982).

4. In addition to some scarce published sources, information on McLouth is drawn from two waves of interviews I conducted. From 1982 to 1984, following the bankruptcy reorganization, I did interviews in Detroit, New York City, and Washington, D.C., with McLouth's CEO, corporate attorneys, and investment banker (Lazard Frères); the lead representative of one of the firm's secured creditors and two of the secured creditors' attorneys; the director of District 29 of the United Steel Workers' Union and the president of USW Local 2659; a member of Congressman John Dingell's Washington staff; the director of the Economic Development Agency in the U.S. Department of Commerce; and a business reporter from the *Detroit News* who covered the bankruptcy proceedings. In 1988, following the ESOP restructuring, I conducted interviews in Detroit and New York City with McLouth's financial vice-president, the director of USW District 29 (again), the director of the State of Michigan Department of Commerce, the director of the Auto and Steel Division of the Michigan Commerce Department, and McLouth's investment banker (this time, Shearson Lehman Hutton). As in the Weirton interviews, I promised the respondents they would not be quoted by name.

5. "Tale of Woe," *Forbes,* May 15, 1977, p. 54.

6. David Halberstam, *The Reckoning* (New York: Morrow, 1986), p. 604; on McLouth, see *Forbes,* May 15, 1977; *Wall Street Journal,* August 18, 1980, and June 18, December 8, and December 9, 1981; *New York Times,* December 17, 1981, December 29, 1982, December 17, 1985; *Iron Age,* January 4, 1982. This discussion of McLouth's business history also relies on my interviews and materials collected by District 29 of the USW.

7. In addition to interviews, this history of the McLouth bankruptcy relies on records from U.S. Bankruptcy Court, Eastern District of Michigan, Southern Division, December 8, 1981, through September

21, 1982, collected by Robert Luke, and a chronology prepared by USW Local 2659.

8. In addition to my interviews, useful (if sometimes contradictory) information was derived from the *New York Times*, March 3 and May 2, 1982. Since McLouth has been a privately held firm since its sale to Cyrus Tang, not all data are released publicly.

9. On Tang, see "The Gambler Who Salvaged McLouth Steel," *Fortune*, May 2, 1983, pp. 113–14; *Wall Street Journal*, September 13, 1982; *New York Times*, December 29, 1982.

10. *New York Times*, January 6, February 5, July 30, and October 28, 1987; "Cancel the Funeral—Steel Is on the Mend," *Business Week*, October 5, 1987; "Big Steel Is Humming Again—It Just Needed Some Oil," *Business Week*, August 8, 1988.

11. See the wave of favorable articles on ESOPs in *Business Week*, April 24 and May 8, 1989, and cover story, May 15, 1989.

12. See Robert N. Stern and Tove Helland Hammer, "Buying Your Job: Factors Affecting the Success or Failure of Employee Acquisition Attempts," *Human Relations* 31 (1978): 1101–17.

13. For a brief overview, see George Sternlieb and Carole W. Baker, "Placing Deindustrialization in Perspective," in *Women, Households, and the Economy*, ed. Lourdes Beneria and Catharine R. Stimpson (New Brunswick, N.J.: Rutgers University Press, 1987), pp. 85–107.

14. See Richard Child Hill and Cynthia Negrey, "Deindustrialization and Racial Minorities in the Great Lakes Region, USA," in *The Reshaping of America*, ed. D. Stanley Eitzen and Maxine Baca Zinn (Englewood Cliffs, N.J.: Prentice Hall, 1989), pp. 166–78, and James Jacobs, "Black Workers and the New Technology: The Need for a New Urban Training Policy" (unpublished paper, Industrial Technology Institute / Michigan Community College, Ann Arbor, 1987).

CHAPTER 6. THE MILL AND THE MALL: POWER AND HOMOGENEITY IN WESTCHESTER COUNTY

1. George A. Lundberg, Mirra Komarovsky, and Mary Alice McInerny, *Leisure: A Suburban Study* (New York: Columbia University Press, 1934), pp. 27–37; Alex Shoumatoff, *Westchester: Portrait of a County* (New York: Coward, McCann & Geoghegan, 1979).

2. Nineteenth-century motifs of suburban exclusion and consumption are described in a slightly less instrumental manner by Robert Fishman, in *Bourgeois Utopias: The Rise and Fall of Suburbia* (New York: Basic Books, 1987).

3. For a general view, see Jean Gottman, *Megalopolis: The Urban-*

ized Northeastern Seaboard of the United States (Cambridge, Mass.: MIT Press, 1961), ch. 4, and Kenneth Jackson, *Crabgrass Frontier: The Suburbanization of the United States* (New York: Oxford University Press, 1981), pp. 183ff.; cf. John R. Stilgoe, *Borderland: Origins of the American Suburb, 1820–1939* (New Haven: Yale University Press, 1988).

4. See Ann R. Markusen, "Class and Urban Social Expenditure: A Marxist Theory of Metropolitan Government," in *Marxism and the Metropolis,* ed. William R. Tabb and Larry Sawers (New York: Oxford University Press, 1978), pp. 90–111, and John R. Logan and Harvey Molotch, *Urban Fortunes* (Berkeley and Los Angeles: University of California Press, 1987).

5. For convenience, see the summary in Jackson, *Crabgrass Frontier,* pp. 190ff.

6. David Harvey, *The Urbanization of Capital* (Baltimore: Johns Hopkins University Press, 1985); Gwendolyn Wright, *Building the Dream* (Cambridge, Mass.: MIT Press, 1981), pp. 248–58; Richard L. Florida and Marshall M. A. Feldman, "Housing in U.S. Fordism," *International Journal of Urban and Regional Research* 12 (1988): 187–210. For an alternative emphasis on life cycle and social class, see the essay by Herbert F. Gans, "Urbanism and Suburbanism as Ways of Life: A Re-evaluation of Definitions," in *People and Plans* (New York: Basic Books, 1968), pp. 34–52.

7. See William H. Whyte, Jr., *The Organization Man* (New York: Simon & Schuster, 1956), esp. pp. 295–434. Of course, the main concern of the many books written about this symbolic landscape at the time (e.g., the novel *The Man in the Gray Flannel Suit,* the humorous essays in *Please Don't Eat the Daisies,* John Cheever's short story "The Swimmer," and David Riesman's sociological treatise *The Lonely Crowd*) was *conformity,* shown by a paradoxical combination of lack of individual initiative and hyperorganization. All in all, in the years following the political purges of McCarthyism, this image of conformity was not incorrect.

8. See E. Relph, *The Modern Urban Landscape* (Baltimore: Johns Hopkins University Press, 1987); Mark Gottdiener, "Recapturing the Center: A Semiotic Analysis of Shopping Malls," pp. 288–302 in *The City and the Sign: An Introduction to Urban Semiotics,* ed. M. Gottdiener and Alexandros Ph. Lagopoulos (New York: Columbia University Press, 1986); William Severini Kowinski, *The Malling of America* (New York: Morrow, 1985).

9. Lundberg et al., *Leisure.*

10. "The Coming Crisis in Slobovia" is the final chapter in the generally positive local history by Richard F. Crandell, *This Is Westchester:*

A Study of Suburban Living (New York: Sterling Publishing, 1954). In the 1961 edition, this chapter was replaced by the much more positive "A New Look for an Old County," which implied that a pro-development attitude had prevailed. See also Marilyn E. Weigold, ed., *Westchester County: The Past Hundred Years, 1883–1983* (Valhalla, N.Y.: Westchester County Historical Society, 1984), pp. 46, 188ff.

11. Regional Plan Association, *Information Bulletin,* nos. 80, August 1952, and 87, June 1957.

12. Shoumatoff, *Westchester;* Mary Lou Mayo, "Residential Patterns and Their Socio-Economic Correlates: A Study of Blacks in Westchester County, New York" (Ph.D. diss., Fordham University, 1974); on the development "dilemma" of commercial expansion vs. residential satisfaction, see *Changes in Westchester and How People Feel about Them* (White Plains, N.Y.: Westchester County Department of Planning, 1955), a pro-growth study and pamphlet funded by David Rockefeller, who was also a member of the planning commission from North Tarrytown.

13. For a similar view of suburban stratification on the national level, see Logan and Molotch, *Urban Fortunes,* pp. 181ff.

14. All except Baekeland from J. Thomas Scharf, *The History of Westchester County* (Philadelphia: Preston, 1886), pp. 93ff.

15. Scharf, *History of Westchester County;* David Sicilia, "Technological Risk in Manufacturing, 1850–1880, Yonkers, New York: A Case Study" (MS, Brandeis University, Department of the History of American Civilization, 1985).

16. Scharf, *History of Westchester County,* p. 102.

17. Information on elevator automation from Grace Palladino, "A Promise and a Warning: Building Service Workers and Automation in New York City, 1936–1970" (paper delivered at the Sixth Annual North American Labor History Conference, Detroit, October 1984).

18. French data courtesy of Inspection du Travail, Ministry of Labor, 1983.

19. At the end of the 1980s, Otis was still the world's largest elevator firm, with a market share of 60 percent of the elevators in the world's tallest buildings and 22 percent of all new elevator and escalator installations valued at $6 billion or more. See *Moody's Industrial Manual* (New York: Moody's, 1982); Ronald Fernandez, *Excess Profits: The Rise of United Technologies* (Reading, Mass.: Addison-Wesley, 1983), pp. 246–51; Katya Goncharoff, "New Hope for Those Impatient with Elevator Service" (microprocessors), *New York Times,* July 24, 1983; N. R. Kleinfield, "Otis's '29 Stories Full of What-Ifs,' " *New York Times,* July 2, 1989.

20. Lawrence J. Tell, "Plant Shutdowns: The Cities Fight," *New York Times,* May 15, 1983; interview with member of the mayor's Otis Elevator task force, 1983.

21. *New York Times,* April 2, 1985. Though fewer than 3 percent of all taxable properties in Yonkers throughout the 1970s were vacant, this was twice the vacancy rate in White Plains. Similarly, equalized assessed property value per person in Yonkers was half that in White Plains (*Commercial and Public Construction in Westchester County* [White Plains, N.Y.: Westchester County Department of Planning, January 1982], p. 79). For continuation of the trends to concentrate office building in the center of the county, and keep vacancies in White Plains to a minimum, see *Commercial and Public Construction in Westchester County,* May 1986, and "Westchester Market Survey," *Westchester Office Buildings, 1988,* pp. 9–10.

22. Interview with former plant manager, Otis Elevator Company, Yonkers, 1985; *Labor Relations Reference Manual* (Washington, D.C.: Bureau of National Affairs, Inc., 1984), no. 115, p. 1281; and various newspaper articles on UT. According to the Westinghouse Electric Corporation, which started to phase out elevator manufacturing at a New Jersey plant in 1985, low-cost, high-quality elevator parts were easily imported from suppliers in France, Brazil, and South Korea (*New York Times,* April 2, 1985).

23. The Life Savers shutdown was covered in the "Talk of the Town" column in the *New Yorker,* February 18, 1985. Because he ran into unforeseen structural problems at the same time as the 1987 stock market crash, however, the developer was faced with a marketing crisis. He decided to lure tenants by offering below-market-rate mortgages and a combined rental-purchase option. See *New York Times,* August 25, 1989.

24. On GM, see *New York Times,* August 21, 1982; May 10, 1984; June 14, 1985; February 4, 1987.

25. Interview with manager of Port Authority industrial park, Yonkers, 1985.

26. Minutes of New York State, Emergency Financial Control Board, Yonkers, various meetings, 1984; interview with assistant city manager, Yonkers, 1985.

27. Crandell, *This Is Westchester* (1954 ed.), p. 179.

28. "Westchester's 44 Largest Employers," March 1975, courtesy of Westchester County Association. Categories for public-sector employers vary in the association's various surveys.

29. After the federally mandated break-up of AT&T, the newly independent regional company NYNEX was created from New York Telephone. Data courtesy of Westchester County Association. Differ-

ences in data reporting account for some of the discrepancies in listings, and numbers for firms from Metro North through Technicon represent full-time employees in 1986.

30. Yonkers is the *only* area in the county to export rather than import labor. "Import and Export of Labor within Sub-Areas," *Commercial and Public Construction in Westchester County,* January 1982, p. 91.

31. Between 1980 and 1984, 37 percent of all new office space in the New York metropolitan region was built in New York City, 11 percent in Bergen County, 10 percent in Westchester, and 10 percent in Middlesex (*Commercial and Public Construction in Westchester County,* May 1986, p. 31). After 1985, however, more office space was built in the suburbs than in New York City (*New York Times,* July 27, 1985; April 29, 1986).

32. See, for example, Regina Belz Armstrong, *The Office Industry: Patterns of Growth and Location* (Cambridge, Mass.: MIT Press, 1972), pp. 44–53; Christopher B. Leinberger and Charles Lockwood, "How Business Is Reshaping America," *Atlantic,* October 1986, pp. 43–52; Logan and Molotch, *Urban Fortunes.*

33. Sidney M. Robbins and Nestor E. Terleckyj, *Money Metropolis: A Locational Study of Financial Activities in the New York Region* (Cambridge, Mass.: Harvard University Press, 1960), p. 43. This volume was part of the Twentieth Century Fund study of New York City headed by Edgar M. Hoover and Raymond Vernon. Radical economists began to emphasize the pressure to decentralize fifteen to twenty years later, as part of the developing debate about cities and deindustrialization, and usually stressed the labor factor. Cf. David M. Gordon, "Capitalist Development and the History of American Cities," in *Marxism and the Metropolis,* ed. Tabb and Sawers, pp. 25–63.

34. For a highly critical view of IBM's business strategy, see Richard Thomas DeLamarter, *Big Blue: IBM's Use and Abuse of Power* (New York: Dodd, Mead, 1986). Raymond Vernon says with hindsight that the Twentieth Century Fund study of New York City erred by not forecasting the spread of computers and thus underestimating the potential for decentralization of offices (interview, 1985).

35. Interview, General Foods, 1985; Crandell, *This Is Westchester* (both eds.), pp. 182–83, emphasis added.

36. *Changes in Westchester,* pp. 17, 22; Crandell, *This Is Westchester* (1961 ed.), p. 238; Weigold, ed., *Westchester County.*

37. Information on moves from interviews, IBM, General Foods, Regional Plan Association, Westchester County Association, 1985. Cf. William H. Whyte, Jr., who claims in *The City* (New York: Random

House, 1988) that most corporations moved their headquarters to the Westchester-Fairfield area if their chairmen already lived there.

38. *New York Times,* February 21, 1989.

39. Quoted in Thomas J. Lueck, "An Office Boom Transforms Once-Ailing Connecticut City," *New York Times,* March 10, 1985.

40. General Foods executives said they interviewed only three applicants for every job in Westchester compared to eleven in New York City; see Crandell, *This Is Westchester,* p. 51. On Texaco, various interviews, Westchester County, 1985. Cf. K. Nelson, "Labor Demand, Labor Supply and the Suburbanization of Low-Wage Office Work," in *Production, Work, Territory,* ed. Allen J. Scott and Michael Storper (Boston: Allen & Unwin, 1986), pp. 149–71.

41. See *Attitudes of Westchester Business Leaders toward Westchester County as a Business Location* (White Plains, N.Y.: Westchester County Association Inc. and Westchester County Bankers Association), published biennially since 1977; median income and house prices from *New York Times,* September 27, 1987.

42. *Attitudes of Westchester Business Leaders* (1985); for attention to the spatial aspects of corporate interlocks, see Roger Friedland and Don Palmer, "Park Place and Main Street: Business and the Urban Power Structure," *Annual Review of Sociology* 10 (1984): 393–416. Thanks to Roger Friedland for his friendly interest in Westchester; he bears no blame for my interpretation.

43. Nick Ravo, "Fairfield County Losing Its Corporate Midas Touch," *New York Times,* February 21, 1989.

44. *Changes in Westchester,* p. 1.

45. Regional Plan Association, *The Region's Agenda* 13, no. 3 (December 1983): 2–3.

46. See *Planning and Zoning Problems: Papers Presented at the 1931 Conference of the Westchester County Planning Federation* (White Plains, N.Y.: Westchester County Planning Federation, 1931) and *Westchester County and the Regional Plan* (New York: Regional Plan Association, 1932).

47. For an uncritical view, see Weigold, ed., *Westchester County,* pp. 102ff.

48. Robert A. Caro, *The Power Broker: Robert Moses and the Fall of New York* (New York: Knopf, 1974), p. 162; Weigold, ed., *Westchester County;* Fishman, *Bourgeois Utopias.*

49. On the gradual emergence of countywide government, over the objections of towns and villages, see Weigold, ed., *Westchester County,* pp. 152ff.

50. *The Future of Westchester County* (New York: Regional Plan Association, 1971), p. 5.

51. Regional Plan Association, *Information Bulletin*, no. 4 (October 19, 1931), p. 9; *Westchester County and the Regional Plan*, p. 19.

52. *Westchester County and the Regional Plan*, p. 28.

53. Marilyn E. Weigold, *Pioneering in Parks and Parkways, 1895–1945* (Chicago: Public Works Historical Society, 1980), pp. 24–25.

54. See *The Selection of the Headquarters Site of United Nations in New York in 1946, the Participation Therein by a Westchester County Special Committee and the Conclusion of the Matter by the late John D. Rockefeller, Jr., in Purchasing a Site on the East River and Presenting It to the United Nations*, comp. Otto E. Koegel (n.p., 1971). In William Zeckendorf's 1971 autobiography, *Zeckendorf* (New York: Holt, Rinehart & Winston, 1970), the real estate developer claims the East River site was his idea and Rockefeller paid for it (pp. 63–78). Cf. Caro, *The Power Broker*, pp. 772–75. Although my friend Bob Fitch has stressed all along that many of the Rockefellers' strategies were conceived to protect the economic value of Rockefeller Center, Caro emphasizes Robert Moses' role as intermediary. Moses suggested to the Rockefellers, on behalf of the mayor of New York City, that it would be advantageous to have the UN in the city.

55. See Henry Etzkowitz and Roger Mack, "Imperialism in the First World: The Corporation and the Suburb" (paper presented at Pacific Sociological Association meetings, San Jose, March 28–30, 1974).

56. Those who lived farther from development projects tended to like them better than those who lived nearby, especially since they benefited from greater increases in property values (*Changes in Westchester*, p. 8 and passim).

57. *Changes in Westchester*, and "People, Jobs and Land, 1955–1975," *Regional Plan Association Bulletin*, no. 87 (June 1957), p. 46.

58. *Future of Westchester County*, pp. 17–18.

59. See *Future of Westchester County*, esp. p. 7; Weigold, ed., *Westchester County*, p. 244.

60. Weigold, ed., *Westchester County*, pp. 244ff.

61. Weigold, ed., *Westchester County*, p. 247; interview with staff member, White Plains Department of Planning, 1985.

62. Interview, director, Mount Vernon Business Attraction and Retention Program, 1985.

63. See *Westchester 2000: Ecology, Economy, Demography Task Force*, Final Report, April 1, 1985.

64. See *Westchester County as a Business Location* (1985), pp. 33–34.

65. *Westchester 2000*, pp. 34–36; *Characteristics of Job Openings, Mid-Hudson Metropolitan Areas* (Albany: New York State Department of Labor, January–December 1987), pp. 73–92.

CHAPTER 7. GENTRIFICATION, CUISINE, AND THE CRITICAL INFRASTRUCTURE: POWER AND CENTRALITY DOWNTOWN

1. See Robert E. L. Faris, *Chicago Sociology, 1920–1932* (Chicago: University of Chicago Press, 1970); Martin Bulmer, *The Chicago School of Sociology* (Chicago: University of Chicago Press, 1984); David Ward, *Poverty, Ethnicity, and the American City, 1840–1925* (Cambridge: Cambridge University Press, 1989). For criticism of the Chicago School sociologists' heritage and parallels with central place theory, see Mark Gottdiener, *The Social Production of Urban Space* (Austin: University of Texas Press, 1985), ch. 2.

2. Lewis Mumford, *The City in History* (New York: Harcourt, Brace & World, 1961), pp. 544, 552. For an interesting critique of the migration of Simmel's imagery not only through the Chicago School but also into painting and art history by means of urban expressionism, see Rosalyn Deutsche, "Representing Berlin: Urban Ideology and Aesthetic Practice," in *The Divided Heritage: Theories and Problems in German Modernism*, ed. Irit Rogoff and MaryAnne Stevens (Cambridge University Press, forthcoming).

3. Until the 1960s, Western European cities retained a different model of the center from that of the United States. Two elements of the traditional, even preindustrial, center were most important: the persistence of both an upper-class and a working-class presence. Usually people ascribe this continuity in European downtowns to cultural values. I would say, however, that it reflects institutional factors, such as property and tenure rights, zoning laws, and small business conditions, as well as the financial demands of post–World War II reconstruction. The net result was to delay the massive programs of urban renewal and new suburban construction that were mounted in the United States after 1949. During the 1970s, with the movement out of the center of many indigenous middle-class and working-class families, the decay and demolition of old buildings, and the arrival of new immigrants (mainly temporary or "guest" workers) looking for cheap accommodations, European downtowns began to show the same strains between centrality and power as U.S. cities.

4. See Manuel Castells, *Luttes urbaines* (Paris: Maspero, 1973);

Sharon Zukin, "A Decade of the New Urban Sociology," *Theory and Society* 9 (1980): 575–601; Gottdiener, *Social Production of Urban Space;* Michael Peter Smith and Joe R. Feagin, *The Capitalist City* (New York: Blackwell, 1987); and on the crafting of central positions by means of zoning and urban redevelopment, see Robert Fitch, "Planning New York," in *The Fiscal Crisis of American Cities,* ed. Roger E. Alcaly and David Mermelstein (New York: Vintage, 1977), pp. 246–84, and Roger Friedland, *Power and Crisis in the City* (London: Macmillan, 1982).

5. Henri Lefebvre, *La Production de l'espace* (Paris: Editions Anthropos, 1974), pp. 65, 121; emphasis in the original.

6. Ibid., pp. 357–58.

7. David Harvey, *Social Justice and the City* (Baltimore: Johns Hopkins University Press, 1973), ch. 5. Harvey's subsequent work, including a historical account of the mid-nineteenth-century reconstruction of Paris under Baron Haussmann's leadership, and the impetus of major real estate interests and investment banking houses, attempts a more full-blooded presentation of "creative destruction" of urban space and time, when "the created spaces of capitalism, the spaces of its own social reproduction . . . have to be annihilated" (*Consciousness and the Urban Experience* [Baltimore: Johns Hopkins University Press, 1985], p. 28).

8. Neil Smith, *Uneven Development* (New York: Blackwell, 1984), pp. 119–24; Nigel Thrift, "The Fixers: The Urban Geography of International Commercial Capital," in *Global Restructuring and Territorial Development,* ed. Jeffrey Henderson and Manuel Castells (London: Sage, 1987), pp. 203–33.

9. Harvey, *Social Justice and the City,* p. 189. This process is graphically described in Harvey's study of the rebuilding of Paris, 1850–70, in *Consciousness and the Urban Experience,* pp. 63–220.

10. See Thomas Bender and William R. Taylor, "Culture and Architecture: Some Aesthetic Tensions in the Shaping of Modern New York City," in *Visions of the Modern City,* ed. William Sharpe and Leonard Wallock (Baltimore: Johns Hopkins University Press, 1987), pp. 189–219, esp. pp. 212–17.

11. John Berger, "Manhattan," in *The Sense of Sight* (New York: Pantheon Books, 1985), p. 67. Berger's perception of Manhattan "as a moral idea, an abstraction" influenced my thoughts about centrality.

12. Neil Smith, "Gentrification, the Frontier, and the Restructuring of Urban Space," in *Gentrification of the City,* ed. Neil Smith and Peter Williams (Boston: Allen & Unwin, 1986), pp. 15–20. While it may fool the middle class, this ideological smokescreen is transparent to the "indigenous." As a Hispanic attorney for a municipal agency in New York

City describes the co-op conversion of the apartment house where she is living, "Gentrification is contemporary manifest destiny used to move out minorities, and that's why I'm staying. They're so used to Puerto Ricans who can't afford to buy that I'm going to buy" (*New York Times,* March 27, 1988).

13. See Peter D. Sahlins, "The Limits of Gentrification," *New York Affairs* 5, no. 4 (1979): 3–12; Brian J. L. Berry, "Islands of Renewal in Seas of Decay," in *The New Urban Reality,* ed. Peter E. Peterson (Washington, D.C.: Brookings Institution, 1985), pp. 35–55; J. I. Nelson and J. Lorence, "Employment in Service Activities and Inequality in Metropolitan Areas," *Urban Affairs Quarterly* 21, no. 1 (1985): 106–25; Smith, *Uneven Development* and "Of Yuppies and Housing: Gentrification, Social Restructuring, and the Urban Dream," *Society and Space* 5 (1987): 151–72.

14. For a detailed review of economic and cultural approaches to gentrification, see Sharon Zukin, "Gentrification: Culture and Capital in the Urban Core," *Annual Review of Sociology* 13 (1987): 129–47.

15. For general political background, see Jack Newfield and Paul DuBrul, *The Abuses of Power* (New York: Viking, 1977), and Martin Shefter, *Political Crisis / Fiscal Crisis* (New York: Basic Books, 1987).

16. On the rent gap, see Neil Smith, "Toward a Theory of Gentrification: A Back to the City Movement by Capital Not People," *Journal of the American Planners Association* 45 (1979): 538–48; for criticism of the concept, noting that redevelopment by gentrification is only one possible option, see Robert A. Beauregard, "The Chaos and Complexity of Gentrification," in *Gentrification of the City,* ed. Smith and Williams, pp. 35–55; and for defense of the rent gap explanation in terms of opportunity, see Smith, "Of Yuppies and Housing."

17. For an early acknowledgment of these "exceptions" to the ecological model, see Walter Firey, "Sentiment and Symbolism as Ecological Variables," *American Sociological Review* 10, no. 2 (1945): 140–48.

18. See Neil Smith, "Gentrification and Capital: Theory, Practice and Ideology in Society Hill," *Antipode* 11, no. 3 (1979): 24–35; Paul R. Levy and Roman A. Cybriwsky, "The Hidden Dimensions of Culture and Class: Philadelphia," in *Back to the City,* ed. Shirley Bradway Laska and Daphne Spain (New York: Pergamon, 1980), pp. 138–55; Roman A. Cybriwsky, David Ley, and John Western, "The Political and Social Construction of Revitalized Neighborhoods: Society Hill, Philadelphia, and False Creek, Vancouver," in *Gentrification of the City,* ed. Smith and Williams, pp. 92–120; and Conrad Weiler, "The Neigh-

borhood's Role in Optimizing Reinvestment: Philadelphia," in *Back to the City,* ed. Laska and Spain, pp. 220–38.

19. See Sharon Zukin, *Loft Living: Culture and Capital in Urban Change,* 2d ed. (New Brunswick, N.J.: Rutgers University Press, 1989).

20. Nathan Silver, *Lost New York* (New York: Schocken, 1967).

21. Jane Jacobs, *The Death and Life of Great American Cities* (New York: Vintage Books, 1961); Herbert Gans, *The Urban Villagers* (New York: Free Press, 1962); Marc Fried and Peggy Gleicher, "Some Sources of Satisfaction in the Residential Slum," *Journal of the American Institute of Planners* 72, no. 4 (1961): 305–15. Also see Special Committee on Historic Preservation, U.S. Conference of Mayors, *With Heritage So Rich* (New York: Random House, 1966; repr. 1983).

22. On the low cost of living downtown for single women, see Damaris Rose, "Rethinking Gentrification: Beyond the Uneven Development of Marxist Theory," *Society and Space* 1 (1984): 47–74, and on the spatial formation of the gay community in San Francisco, see Manuel Castells, *The City and the Grassroots* (Berkeley and Los Angeles: University of California Press, 1983), ch. 14.

23. For the initial description, see Ruth Glass's introduction to *London: Aspects of Change,* ed. Centre for Urban Studies (London: MacGibbon & Kee, 1964), pp. xiii–xlii. For glowing support of the widespread diffusion of the mode of development that combines gentrification, historic preservation, and downtown reinvestment in the United States, see "Spiffing Up the Urban Heritage" (cover story), *Time,* November 13, 1987, pp. 72ff.

24. The work of Pierre Bourdieu seems basic to this analysis, especially his emphasis on the tastes of people with more cultural than economic capital. See Bourdieu, *Distinction: A Social Critique of the Judgement of Taste,* trans. Richard Nice (Cambridge, Mass.: Harvard University Press, 1984). My argument nonetheless suggests a more complex and historically contingent account of, first, the rising social acceptance of cultural capital, and, second, its association with the current transformation of the urban center, which is as observable in the IVième, Vième, or XVième arrondissements of Paris as in New York.

25. Andree Brooks, "About Real Estate: Brooklyn School Converted to Housing," *New York Times,* March 25, 1988. Of course, the developer exaggerates both the rapidity and feasibility of gentrification in this area.

26. Quotation on the artist from Meyer Schapiro, quoted in Diana Crane, *The Transformation of the Avant-Garde: The New York Art World, 1940–1985* (Chicago: University of Chicago Press, 1987),

p. 83. For the rise of the real estate market in living lofts, and their transformation from artists' to luxury housing, see Zukin, *Loft Living*.

27. John Logan and Harvey Molotch make a start toward recognizing the complexity of the gentrification process by incorporating the Marxist conflict between use values and exchange values: "Whether among rich or poor neighborhoods, in the central city or urban fringe, neighborhood futures are determined by the ways in which entrepreneurial pressures from outside intersect with internal material stakes and sentimental attachments" (*Urban Fortunes*, p. 123).

28. Quotation from Patrick Wright, "The Ghosting of the Inner City," in *On Living in an Old Country: The National Past in Contemporary Britain* (London: Verso, 1985), pp. 228–29. On the contested claims for space around Union Square in downtown Manhattan between discount stores that cater to an immigrant, working-class, and outer-borough clientele, and the cultural values of the early-twentieth-century loft buildings that make up the Ladies' Mile, see Martin Kronauer, "Urban 'Revitalization' and Community Participation" (Ph.D. diss., Free University of Berlin, 1987); cf. Rosalyn Deutsche, "Krzysztof Wodiszko's *Homeless Projection* and the Site of Urban 'Revitalization,'" *October* 38 (Fall 1986): 63–98.

29. Other cities, however, may have stronger pro-neighborhood, antidevelopment orientations. In Chicago, for example, the administration of Mayor Harold Washington countered developers' plans to convert the manufacturing zone of Goose Island while gentrification and new construction expanded the downtown elsewhere.

30. National Endowment for the Arts study of artists and gentrification cited in Dennis E. Gale, *Neighborhood Revitalization and the Postindustrial City: A Multinational Perspective* (Lexington, Mass.: Lexington Books, 1984), p. 155.

31. Obituary notice in *New York Times*, September 5, 1986.

32. An organization called "City Lore, a center for urban folk culture on the Lower East Side, [has] set out to capture some of New York City's neighborhood institutions on film and on tape before they go the way of Steeplechase Park *and the Belmore Cafeteria"* (Elizabeth Kolbert, "Street Life: Keeping 'Beloved Places,' " *New York Times*, March 28, 1988; emphasis added.

33. Michael Musto, "The Death of Downtown," *Village Voice*, April 28, 1987, pp. 15–20.

34. Cf. Rosalyn Deutsche and Cara Gendel Ryan, "The Fine Art of Gentrification," *October* 31 (Winter 1984): 91–111.

35. On the lack of profitability of waterfront shopping centers in Flint, Michigan, and Toledo, Ohio, in contrast to Baltimore and Bos-

ton, see "Jim Rouse May Be Losing His Touch," *Business Week,* April 4, 1988, pp. 33–34. By the same token, the apparent success of South Street Seaport in downtown Manhattan is really questionable. Some stores that aimed at an affluent tourist clientele have failed, giving rise to talk about revamping them as service stores for a local population: a transformation from new urban landscape to new urban vernacular. See Mark McCain, "Commercial Property: A Troubled Urban Mall; Rouse Makes Plans for the South Street Seaport; Among Prospects, Shops to Serve the Community," *New York Times,* March 13, 1988.

36. In subsequent years, partly responding to local and paying users' complaints, city authorities made more stringent rules to bar the homeless from the subways, Penn Station, the bus terminals, and other public spaces, while ignoring private owners' attempts to bar the public—especially the homeless public—from such "public spaces" as plazas and gallerias that enjoyed a zoning bonus. Richard Levine, "Plan Urges New Look at Terminal," *New York Times,* January 11, 1987; Bob Fitch, "Put 'Em Where We Ain't," *Nation,* April 2, 1988, p. 466; *New York Times,* April 11, 1988; October 1 and 25, 1989; Helen Thorpe, "Open to the Public?" *New York Observer,* March 12, 1990. For a contrasting historical survey of downtown Manhattan, cf. Emanuel Tobier, "Gentrification: The Manhattan Story," *New York Affairs* 5, no. 4 (1979): 13–25.

37. William E. Schmidt, "Riding a Boom, Downtowns Are No Longer Downtrodden," *New York Times,* October 11, 1987.

38. Michael Musto, *Downtown* (New York: Vintage Books, 1986), p. 5.

39. *New York,* December 25, 1989–January 1, 1990, p. 3. For acknowledgment of the significance to restructuring of shopping and consumption in general, cf. Beauregard, "Chaos and Complexity," pp. 44–45, and Smith, "Of Yuppies and Housing," pp. 165–70.

40. Schmidt, "Riding a Boom."

41. Musto, "Death of Downtown."

42. Thanks to Stephen Duncombe on waiters and Henri Peretz on clothing salespersons.

43. Cf. William Leiss, "Icons of the Marketplace," *Theory, Culture and Society* 1, no. 3 (1983): 10–21, and Smith, "Of Yuppies and Housing."

44. Russell Baker, "Worse than Gluttony," *New York Times,* January 4, 1986.

45. Wright, "Ghosting of the Inner City," p. 230.

46. Edith Wharton, *The House of Mirth* [1905] (New York: Bantam, 1984), p. 175. Cf. Pierre Bourdieu's version of the same pursuit of

positional goods: "The sense of good investment which dictates a withdrawal from outmoded, or simply devalued, objects, places or practices and a move into ever newer objects in an endless drive for novelty, and which operates in every area, sport and cooking, holiday resorts and restaurants, is guided by countless different indices and indications, from explicit warnings ('Saint-Tropez'—or the Buffet de la gare in Lyon, or anywhere else—'has become impossible') to the barely conscious intuitions, which . . . insidiously arouse horror or disgust for objects or practices that have become common" (*Distinction*, p. 249).

47. Quotation from Francis X. Clines, "The Simple Life, with Lobster, in Wales," *New York Times*, September 20, 1987; on the use of marketed objects to create an awareness of consuming and hence an awareness of life, see "Interview with Ettore Sottsass," *Industrial Design*, January–February 1988, p. 31.

48. Note the difference between considering "taste" as cultural *capital* and cultural *product*. While the former interpretation emphasizes the autonomy of cultural producers (though seeing them as a dominated part of the dominating class), the latter indicates once again their dependence—as a service class—on larger markets. Also note that while I emphasize the *labor* of the critical infrastructure, most writers tend to emphasize their *preferences*. Cf. Bourdieu, *Distinction*, and Scott Lash and John Urry, *The End of Organized Capitalism* (London: Polity Press, 1987), ch. 9.

49. Quotation from John Urry, "Cultural Change and Contemporary Holiday-Making," *Theory, Culture and Society* 5 (1988): 35–55. On tourism as a modern pilgrimage in search of authentic experience, see Dean McCannell, *The Tourist* (New York: Schocken, 1976).

50. Barbara Novak, *Nature and Culture: American Landscape and Painting, 1825–1875* (New York: Oxford University Press, 1980); emphasis hers.

51. Saskia Sassen-Koob, "Growth and Informalization at the Core: A Preliminary Report on New York City," in *The Capitalist City*, ed. Michael Peter Smith and Joe R. Feagin (New York: Blackwell, 1987), p. 141.

52. Reviewing cultural goods and services provides both entrepreneurial business opportunities and various kinds of employment. The publication of amateur restaurant reviews that began in the late 1970s, for example, has grown into a small industry, with "founders" sharing the same cultural values as their readers. Publishers of amateur restaurant reviews are well educated, by training often corporate attorneys or bankers, have traveled in Europe, and love good food. See Richard W. Stevenson, "Restaurant Guides: Personalized Views of New York Scene,"

New York Times, August 14, 1985, and Trish Hall, "Zagat Restaurant Guides: Whose Voice Is Being Heard?" *New York Times*, February 8, 1989.

53. John Nielsen, "Even Those Who Serve Must Audition for the Part," *New York Times*, March 2, 1988; cf. Tom Wolfe's observation in *The Bonfire of the Vanities* (New York: Farrar, Straus & Giroux, 1987)—reflecting both new service class patterns and an older ethnic division of labor—that there are no black waiters in restaurants in Manhattan.

54. Trish Hall, "A New Spectator Sport: Looking, Not Cooking," *New York Times*, January 4, 1989. On earlier shifts in the food press that to some degree prepared the way for new gourmets, see Stephen Mennell, *All Manners of Food* (Oxford: Blackwell, 1985), ch. 9–10.

55. Eric Schmitt, "Discount Stores for Fledgling Gourmets," *New York Times*, February 3, 1988.

56. Waverley Root, "A Simple Lunch with Paul Bocuse," *New York Times Magazine*, December 17, 1972.

57. Bryan Miller, "With a Gallic Touch: Three French Chefs at Epcot," *New York Times*, January 6, 1988.

58. Waverley Root, *The Food of France* [1958] (New York: Knopf, 1972), pp. 3–12.

59. See Jack Goody, *Cooking, Cuisine and Class* (Cambridge: Cambridge University Press, 1982), and Mennell, *All Manners of Food*.

60. A. J. Liebling, *Between Meals* (San Francisco: North Point Press, 1986), p. 9.

61. Unfortunately, the resurgence we are describing occurred just after Waverley Root passed from the scene. See Waverley Root and Richard de Rochemont, *Eating in America: A History* (New York: Ecco Press, 1976), esp. the last chapter, "Where Do We Go from Here?" Earlier the authors state, "The second half of the nineteenth century was characterized by the painstaking efforts of many men to put new edibles before the public; the second half of the twentieth century was characterized by the diligent efforts of many others to reduce the number of edibles that would be put before the public. A mass-market economy did not want to be bothered with a superfluity of products; it was more profitable to concentrate on handling a minimum number of foods than a maximum number" (pp. 233–34).

62. Marian Burros, "A Tribute to American Cooking," *New York Times Magazine*, June 2, 1985, p. 69, and "New American Eating Pattern: Dine Out, Carry In," *New York Times*, October 30, 1985.

63. "Chefs' Debate: Innovation vs. Classic French Food," *New York Times*, May 13, 1987. Cf. Liebling, *Between Meals*, who asserts that

312 Notes to Pages 213–220

the tradition of great restaurants in France began to decline around 1914, partly because new industrial work drew potential apprentices into other occupations.

64. *New York Times*, August 9, 1985.

65. Craig Mishler, "The Texas Chili Cook-Off: An Emergent Foodway Festival," *Journal of Popular Culture* 17, no. 3 (1983): 22–31. By the same token, compare the restaurant described in Peter H. Lewis, "The Open-Pit Barbecue: A Texas Tradition in Good Hands," *New York Times*, January 13, 1988: "The owner is a 74-year-old Hawaiian-born woman of Japanese descent, the manager is a classically trained British chef, the cooks are originally from Mexico and the waitress is a hillbilly from souther Missouri." By the same token, in interwar France, when commercial tourism and a rise in disposable income increased the flow of visitors to the countryside, a mass pursuit of affordable wine led to the discovery, or in some cases the invention, of little *rosés* (Liebling, *Between Meals*, pp. 75–76).

66. John Bryce, "Le Grand Restaurant," *House and Garden*, March 1988, pp. 72–76.

67. David W. Dunlap, "West Side Sites to Be Weighed as Landmarks," *New York Times*, November 17, 1986; emphasis added.

CHAPTER 8. DISNEY WORLD: THE POWER OF FACADE / THE FACADE OF POWER

1. Michael Sorkin, "Travel: Miami Virtues: Sun, Sea and Dazzling Urban Design," *Vogue*, January 1986, p. 140; lack of correlation between urban form and social form from Reyner Banham, *Los Angeles: The Architecture of Four Ecologies* (London: Allen Lane, Penguin Press, 1971), p. 237. Also see E. W. Soja, "Taking Los Angeles Apart: Some Fragments of a Critical Human Geography," *Environment and Planning D: Society and Space* 4 (1986): 255–72 and James J. Flink, *The Automobile Age* (Cambridge, Mass.: MIT Press, 1988), pp. 140–48.

2. Henry James, *The American Scene* [1907] (Bloomington: Indiana University Press, 1968), pp. 447, 462; Sorkin, "Travel," p. 142; Banham, *Los Angeles*, p. 21.

3. James, *American Scene*, p. 442; cf. David Rieff, *Going to Miami: Exiles, Tourists, and Refugees in the New America* (Boston: Little, Brown, 1987), pp. 11, 24–27. James on Lake Como from *Italian Hours* (Boston: Houghton Mifflin, 1909), pp. 131–32.

4. See Raymond A. Mohl, "Miami: The Ethnic Cauldron," in *Sunbelt Cities: Politics and Growth since World War II*, ed. Richard M. Bernard and Bradley R. Rice (Austin: University of Texas Press, 1983),

pp. 58–99; Penny Lernoux, "The Miami Connection," *Nation,* February 18, 1984, pp. 186–98; Joan Didion, *Miami* (New York: Simon & Schuster, 1987); Rieff, *Going to Miami.*

5. See Edward W. Soja, "Economic Restructuring and the Internationalization of the Los Angeles Region," in *The Capitalist City,* ed. Michael Peter Smith and Joe R. Feagin (New York: Blackwell, 1987), pp. 178–98; Allen J. Scott, *Metropolis: From the Division of Labor to Urban Form* (Berkeley and Los Angeles: University of California Press, 1988), pp. 91–202; Mike Davis, *City of Quartz: Excavating the Future in Los Angeles* (London: Verso, 1990).

6. Eidophusikon, dioramas, and panoramas described in Wolfgang Schievelbusch, *Disenchanted Night: The Industrialization of Light in the Nineteenth Century,* trans. Angela Davies (Berkeley and Los Angeles: University of California Press, 1988); also see Francis D. Klingender, *Art and the Industrial Revolution* (London: Paladin, 1972), pp. 86–87; Joshua Meyerowitz, *No Sense of Place: The Impact of Electronic Media on Social Behavior* (New York: Oxford University Press, 1985), p. 73.

7. Martin Pawley, "Tourism: The Last Resort," *Blueprint,* October 1988, p. 38.

8. Cleaning the past of its contradictions is developed in Mike Wallace, "Mickey Mouse History: Portraying the Past at Disney World," *Radical History Review* 32 (1985): 33–57; imagineers quoted on pp. 35–36.

9. Pawley, "Tourism: The Last Resort," p. 39.

10. Quoted in ibid., p. 39.

11. Wallace, "Mickey Mouse History," pp. 38, 42.

12. Fair descriptions from Steve Nelson, "Walt Disney's EPCOT and the World's Fair Performance Tradition," *Drama Review* 30 (Winter 1986): 106–46; Warren I. Susman, "The People's Fair: Cultural Contradictions of a Consumer Society," in *Culture as History* (New York: Pantheon Books, 1984), pp. 211–29; and M. Christine Boyer, *Dreaming the Rational City* (Cambridge, Mass.: MIT Press, 1983), pp. 46–50.

13. Susman, "People's Fair," p. 224.

14. 50 Years of Collecting: Art at IBM, exhibit at IBM Gallery of Science and Art, New York City, 1989.

15. Susman, "People's Fair"; quotation at p. 228.

16. Emphasized in Wallace, "Mickey Mouse History," pp. 42ff.

17. Pawley, "Tourism: The Last Resort"; quotations from Joseph Giovannini, "At Disney, Playful Architecture Is Very Serious Business," *New York Times,* January 28, 1988. These motifs are congruent with

Walt Disney's intentions from the very beginning. The circular plan, "deliberate sensory overload," and lack of differentiation between real and surreal surroundings were meant to make people forget their everyday lives. See Patricia Leigh Brown, "In Fairy Dust, Disney Finds New Realism," *New York Times,* July 20, 1989.

18. James, *American Scene,* p. 443.

19. E. L. Doctorow, *The Book of Daniel* (New York: Random House, 1971), p. 289. Product tie-ins have convinced some critics that the colonization of fantasy foreseen by Doctorow has already arrived. Janet Maslin, "Like the Toy? See the Movie," *New York Times,* December 17, 1989.

20. Entertainment industry analyst quoted in Douglas C. McGill, "Mickey Sells; Is He Now Oversold?" *New York Times,* May 20, 1989. On connections between new products, licensing, profits, and stock values, also see *New York Times,* August 29 and November 6, 1989.

21. Banham, *Los Angeles,* pp. 127ff.; quotation on Hollywood theme park from Michael Eisner's introduction to "Magical World of Disney" television program celebrating opening of the Disney–MGM Studios, April 29, 1989.

22. Trish Hall, "Making Memories Go Better: Coke Plans Museum in Atlanta," *New York Times,* November 23, 1988; Allon Schoener, "Can Museums Learn from Mickey and Friends?" *New York Times,* October 30, 1988.

23. Quotation on Vail from *New York Times Magazine,* December 25, 1988; Duany quoted in Philip Langdon, "A Good Place to Live," *Atlantic,* March 1988, p. 45. Duany's team come into a development site for a day, consult with local architects and the appropriate developers, feed on-site data into their computer model, and generate a town plan based on elements of vernacular architecture and local desires (*Progressive Architecture,* May 1989, pp. 84–88).

24. Football player quoted in George Vecsey, "Amid Uneasiness, Super Bowl Visitors Stream In," *New York Times,* January 19, 1989; see also "Report: Disney in Florida," *Progressive Architecture,* March 1990, p. 80.

25. In the mid 1980s, after EPCOT opened, more than 90 percent of visitors were white, their median income was $35,700, 48 percent held professional and technical jobs, and 26 percent were managers and administrators (Wallace, "Mickey Mouse History," p. 53).

26. Nathanael West, *The Day of the Locust* [1939] (New York: Farrar, Straus, 1957), pp. 334, 351.

27. Banham, *Los Angeles,* pp. 156–57, 238.

28. See Banham, *Los Angeles;* Scott, *Metropolis;* E. W. Soja, R.

Morales, and G. Wolff, "Urban Restructuring: An Analysis of Social and Spatial Change in Los Angeles," *Economic Geography* 59 (1983): 195–230.

29. Banham, *Los Angeles*, pp. 201ff; Soja, "Economic Restructuring and the Internationalization of the Los Angeles Region."

30. Charles Jencks, *Daydream Houses of Los Angeles* (New York: Rizzoli, 1978); on concentration of poor and minorities, see Soja et. al., "Urban Restructuring"; on gangs and police, see Davis, *City of Quartz*.

31. Jencks, *Daydream Houses*, p. 10.

32. Banham, *Los Angeles*, p. 124.

33. Banham writes: "The private car and the public freeway together provide an ideal—not to say idealized—version of democratic urban transportation: door-to-door movement on demand at high average speeds over a very large area" (*Los Angeles*, p. 217; see also pp. 127, 242). Cf. Scott L. Bottles, *Los Angeles and the Automobile* (Berkeley and Los Angeles: University of California Press, 1987).

34. *Frank Gehry: Buildings and Projects*, comp. and ed. Peter Arnell and Ted Bickford (New York: Rizzoli, 1985).

35. Michael Kimmelman, "Disney Concert Hall Design Selected," *New York Times*, December 13, 1988.

36. Germano Celant, "Reflections on Frank Gehry," in *Frank Gehry: Buildings and Projects*, p. 5. Cf. Davis, *City of Quartz*, pp. 236–40.

37. See Donald W. Curl, *Mizner's Florida: American Resort Architecture* (Cambridge, Mass.: MIT Press and the Architectural History Foundation, 1984) and Rieff, *Going to Miami*, pp. 8ff. Cf. Karen J. Weitze, *California's Mission Revival*, vol. 3 of *California Architecture and Architects* (Los Angeles: Hennessey & Ingalls, 1984).

38. Curl, *Mizner's Florida*.

39. David Rieff, "A Reporter at Large: The Second Havana," *New Yorker*, May 18, 1987, p. 65.

40. On the Imperial, see "Once Again, Primary Colors," *Architectural Record*, July 1983, pp. 92–95; on Haddon Town Houses in Houston, see "Introductory Passage," *Architectural Record*, August 1984, pp. 88–91; on Banco de Credito in Lima, see Joseph Rykwert, "Arquitectonica: Sede del Banco de Credito, Lima," *Domus*, November 1988, pp. 30–32, and Karen D. Stein, "Bankers' Trust," *Architectural Record*, February 1989, pp. 90–99.

41. Most important, Arquitectonica charged a low fee for all this quality. Developer interviewed in Charles K. Gandee, "Those New Kids in Town," *Architectural Record*, June 1985, p. 119.

42. Andrea Branzi, "Cose e Case," *Domus*, November 1988, p. 18.

43. Emily Benedek, "Inside Miami Vice," *Rolling Stone*, March 28, 1985, p. 56; see also Pat Aufderheide, "Music Videos: The Look of the Sound," in *Watching Television*, ed. Todd Gitlin (New York: Pantheon, 1986), pp. 120–21. By the late 1980s, when violence from the crack epidemic decimated many urban populations, "Miami Vice" was denounced as a showcase for automatic weapons.

44. Elvis Mitchell, " 'Miami Vice' Is Losing Its Virtue," *Rolling Stone*, March 27, 1986, p. 137.

45. Geoffrey H. Hartman, "Literature High and Low: The Case of the Mystery Story," in *The Poetics of Murder*, ed. Glenn W. Most and William W. Stowe (San Diego: Harcourt Brace Jovanovich, 1983), pp. 210–29; F. R. Jameson, "On Raymond Chandler," in ibid., pp. 136–39; James Wolcott, "Mixed Media: Mann at His Best," *Vanity Fair*, February 1987, p. 20.

46. Tom Shales, "The Re Decade," *Esquire*, March 1986, p. 69, and also see p. 17; Wolcott, "Mixed Media," p. 20; Mitchell, " 'Miami Vice' Is Losing Its Virtue," p. 45.

47. On Manet, see T. J. Clark, *The Painting of Modern Life* (New York: Viking, 1985), esp. p. 111.

48. Sorkin, "Travel," p. 140; Spalding Gray, "Christmas in Miami," *Fame*, December 1988, pp. 160–61. Films, of course, provide a precedent for the setting of expectations by visual consumption.

49. On venality, see Lernoux, "The Miami Connection," and Pete Hamill, "White Line Fever: How Cocaine Corrupted a City," *Village Voice*, August 26, 1986, pp. 21–27. For a more negative, though still undetermined, view of the characters' "coolness," see Todd Gitlin, "Car Commercials and *Miami Vice*: 'We Build Excitement,' " in *Watching Television*, pp. 156–60.

50. Wolcott, "Mixed Media," p. 20; cf. Dennis E. Baron, "Against Interpretation: The Linguistic Structure of Television Drama," *Journal of Popular Culture* 7 (1974): 950: "The punisher, represented by Inspector Erskine [on "The FBI"], becomes an Old Testament vindictive god for those who scorn the law, a New Testament merciful one for those wishing to come back to its protection."

51. Horace Newcomb, "The Mystery: Order and Authority," *Journal of Popular Culture* 7 (1974): 970; also see Stefano Tani, *The Doomed Detective: The Contribution of the Detective Novel to Postmodern American and Italian Fiction* (Carbondale: Southern Illinois University Press, 1984).

52. Thomas Morgan, "NBC Rebuts Poll Results on Drugs," *New York Times*, September 3, 1986.

53. Michael Holquist, "Whodunit and Other Questions: Meta-

physical Detective Stories in Postwar Fiction," in *Poetics of Murder,* ed. Most and Stowe, p. 173; also Tani, *Doomed Detective,* p. 51.

54. Hartman, "Literature High and Low," in *Poetics of Murder,* ed. Most and Stowe, p. 225.

55. Mike Davis with Sue Ruddick, "Los Angeles: Civil Liberties between the Hammer and the Rock," *New Left Review* 170 (July–August 1988): 53.

56. Los Angeles, of course, is not only competing with New York for television production, but has lost processing work through both automation and offshore production, especially in animated cartoons. Scott, *Metropolis;* Mitchell, " 'Miami Vice' Is Losing Its Virtue," p. 136; Aljean Harmetz, "Universal Television at Top in Prime Time," *New York Times,* October 24, 1985; Peter J. Boyer, "Production Cost Dispute Perils Hour TV Dramas," *New York Times,* March 6, 1986; Richard W. Stevenson, "A Financial Battle to Make TV Series," *New York Times,* April 27, 1987.

57. Lernoux, "The Miami Connection"; quotation from p. 192; cf. Didion, *Miami.*

58. "The Civic Virtues of 'Miami Vice,' " *Economist,* September 13, 1985, p. 26.

59. James, *American Scene,* p. 411.

60. For an anecdotal account of the takeover attempts, see John Taylor, *Storming the Magic Kingdom* (New York: Knopf, 1987). For a recent prognosis on the company's European and Japanese theme parks, see "An American in Paris," *Business Week,* March 12, 1990, pp. 60–64.

61. James, *American Scene,* p. 461.

CHAPTER 9. MORAL LANDSCAPES

1. "In reality, the field presents itself as a quasi-continuum of situations, that is, of local regimes and modes of insertion within the global economy," writes Alain Lipietz ("New Tendencies in the International Division of Labor: Regimes of Accumulation and Modes of Regulation," in *Production, Work, Territory,* ed. Allen J. Scott and Michael Storper [Boston: Allen & Unwin, 1986], p. 24).

2. Daniel Bell, *The Cultural Contradictions of Capitalism* (New York: Basic Books, 1976). Despite different subjects and points of view, the "decline and fall" by hedonism argument occurs repeatedly now in sociological, cultural, and organizational analyses of American society. In *The Reckoning* (New York: William Morrow, 1986), David Halber-

stam looks back to an auto industry that lived for production rather than stock values. Robert N. Bellah et al. prefer the civil society of eighteenth-century town meetings to the twentieth-century psychotherapy that promises self-help and self-gratification (*Habits of the Heart: Individualism and Commitment in American Life* [Berkeley and Los Angeles: University of California Press, 1985]). James Fallows criticizes the contemporary tendency to lock in social status by tastes in consumption (and grades on exams) (*More Like Us: Making America Great Again* [Boston: Houghton Mifflin, 1989]).

3. Fred Hirsch, *Social Limits to Growth* (London: Routledge & Kegan Paul, 1977); see also Adrian Ellis and Krishan Kumar, eds., *Dilemmas of Liberal Democracies: Studies in Fred Hirsch's Social Limits to Growth* (London and New York: Tavistock, 1983). "Depleting moral legacy" is Hirsch's term.

4. Jean-Christophe Agnew, *Worlds Apart: The Market and the Theater in Anglo-American Thought, 1550–1750* (Cambridge: Cambridge University Press, 1986), p. 56.

5. See Erica Shoenberger, "From Fordism to Flexible Accumulation: Technology, Competitive Strategies, and International Location," *Environment and Planning D: Society and Space* 6 (1988): 248–49.

6. Neil McKendrick, John Brewer, and J. H. Plumb, *The Birth of a Consumer Society: The Commercialization of Eighteenth-Century England* (London: Europa Publications, 1982); others date the structural importance of mass consumption in economic development somewhat earlier: Chandra Mukerji, *From Graven Images* (New York: Columbia University Press, 1983), ch. 5, and Joan Thirsk, *Economic Policy and Projects* (Oxford: Clarendon Press, 1978).

7. John Urry has done a preliminary analysis of "Some Social and Spatial Aspects of Services," *Society and Space* 5 (1987): 5–26, but he is concerned with production rather than consumption, which leads him to focus on labor force, labor process, and spatial relocation and scale.

8. David Harvey, *The Limits to Capital* (Oxford: Blackwell, 1982) and *The Urbanization of Capital* (Baltimore: Johns Hopkins University Press, 1985).

9. In recent work David Harvey tries to link nontraditional, large-scale investment in culture in a broad sense ("flexible accumulation") with new strategies for the organization of production ("flexible technology"). As this discussion suggests, however, I think all of the existing analyses that try to understand "postmodernism" in terms of a "post-Fordism" that is fundamentally determined in the sphere of production are doomed to miss the major innovation of the shift from production to consumption.

10. Geraldine Fabrikant, "The Media Business: An Odd Couple Fills a Gap in Los Angeles," *New York Times,* March 20, 1989; Edwin Diamond, "The New (Land)lords of the Press," *New York,* February 27, 1989, pp. 44–50.

11. Paul Goldberger, "Grand Old Athens in the Land of Grand Old Opry," *New York Times,* March 5, 1989.

12. For a good sample of this work, see the pieces in Derek Gregory and John Urry, eds., *Social Relations and Spatial Structures* (New York: St. Martin's Press, 1985), cited in chapter 1.

13. See, for example, "A Decade of the New Urban Sociology," *Theory and Society* 9 (1980): 575–601, and "Postscript: More Market Forces," in *Loft Living: Culture and Capital in Urban Change,* 2d ed. (New Brunswick, N.J.: Rutgers University Press, 1989).

14. W. G. Hoskins, *The Making of the English Landscape* [1955] (London: Penguin Books, 1985), pp. 170–74. Here again, however, culture and politics shape economic behavior. During the seventeenth century, a period of similar national affluence in the Netherlands, Dutch landscape was far less concerned with mapping seigneurial differentiation from the rural vernacular. See Svetlana Alpers, *The Art of Describing: Dutch Art in the Seventeenth Century* (Chicago: University of Chicago Press, 1983), pp. 148–49.

15. See Tony Hiss, *The Experience of Place* (New York: Knopf, 1990).

Index

Compositor: Maple-Vail Book Manufacturing Group
Text: 10/13 Sabon
Display: Sabon
Printer and Binder: Maple-Vail Book Manufacturing Group

3761